Transforming Secondary
Middle and High School Dual Language Programs

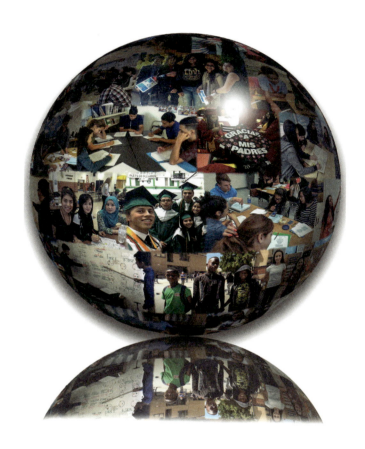

Virginia P. Collier and Wayne P. Thomas

Dual Language Education of New Mexico

Albuquerque, NM

Fuente Press

DUAL LANGUAGE EDUCATION OF NEW MEXICO
FUENTE PRESS

1309 Fourth St. SW, Suite E

Albuquerque, New Mexico 87102

www.dlenm.org

©2018 by Virginia P. Collier and Wayne P. Thomas

All rights reserved. No part of this book may be reproduced in any form or by any electronic or mechanical means, including information storage and retrieval systems, without permission in writing from the publisher, except by a reviewer, who may quote brief passages in a review, with the exception of reproducible figures, which are identified by the Thomas and Collier copyright line and can be photocopied for educational use only.

Library of Congress Control Number: 2018952739

ISBN 978-0-9843169-9-1

DEDICATION

***To all dual language graduates everywhere:**

High school graduation is typically a time
when graduates feel elation, but also uncertainty about their futures.
As we approach the end of our own careers
and you approach the beginning of yours,
we remind you that you have received
a dual language education,
the most powerful and best possible preparation for you
to meet the needs and requirements of your personal future.

Please accept our sincere hopes and dreams for your success
as you make the future your own by inventing it,
by applying your own values to it,
and by creating a more enlightened and transformed world for all of us to live in.
As parents and grandparents ourselves, we are so very proud of you!

ACKNOWLEDGMENTS

As always, we are tremendously grateful to the staff of Dual Language Education of New Mexico (DLeNM), and especially to its executive director David Rogers, for his sustained support of our professional efforts in dual language education. For this book, Ruth Kriteman has served as our lead editor, with some assistance from Dee McMann, the editor of our previous books. Ruth has cheerfully offered us the advantages of her deep professional background as she worked with us to clarify and elucidate our points and positions in this book. DLeNM is not only our publisher, but DLeNM staff are our professional collaborators, and we count on their expertise and experience to make our books the best and most pragmatically useful to our readers that they can be. However, any remaining errors of commission or omission (and we hope there are none) are our own.

We are also grateful to our hundreds of professional friends in many U.S. states whom we have met over our 36 years of professional travel. You have labored long and hard to bring successful and well-implemented dual language programs to your school districts and to your states. We have always looked forward to visiting you, to admiring your professional work, and to contributing to your success from a national research perspective in any way you deemed valuable. Nineteen of you have been willing to go further by contributing your experience in secondary dual language education to the chapters of this book, and we have greatly enjoyed our more intensive interactions with you as we developed your ideas and ours into the final version. We have earnestly tried to bring your individual and collective points of view and your authentic advice to the attention of all those who wish to develop successful secondary dual language programs. Your detailed understanding of how secondary dual language schooling works so well in your local contexts has contributed greatly to our efforts to develop both the regional and national dual language perspectives that we present in this pioneering book. Thanks to the knowledge that you have shared to guide other dual language educators, thousands of dual language graduates will join our multilingual/multicultural future with great confidence and passion for creating a transformed world.

Table of Contents

Dedication iii

Acknowledgments v

Part I—Introduction

Chapter One—Why Secondary Dual Language Schooling 1
    Dr. Virginia Collier and Dr. Wayne Thomas

    Topics Addressed in This Book 2
    Differences Between Elementary and Secondary Dual 2
        Language Schooling
        Cognitive demand
        Teenagers
        Basic program design
    Who Participates in Secondary Dual Language Programs 4
        English learners
        Heritage speakers
        Native English speakers
    Scheduling Issues 6
    Hiring Dual Language Faculty 6
    Instructional Strategies 7
        DL teaching innovations
        Separation of the two languages
    Curricular Materials 9
    Dual Language Administrative Practices 9
    Professional Development 9
    Collaboration Across Secondary Departments 10
    Institutional Impediments 11
    Dual Language Student Leadership 12
    Program Evaluation 13
    Equity Issues 14
    Whole-School Dual Language Education 14
    Organization of the Chapters 16

Chapter Two—Designing Sustainable Secondary Dual Language Programs... 19
Cindy Sizemore

What Is Dual Language at the Secondary Level? 20
Who Participates in Secondary Dual Language Programs? 22
    Students continuing from elementary DL
    Recently arriving immigrants
    Transitional bilingual education students
    World language students
    How does this mix of student populations work?
What Are the Logistical Considerations for a Successful Secondary Dual Language Program? 24
    DL courses are taught in the partner language.
    DL core courses required for graduation
    Balancing DL courses for each grade level and subject
    Electives
    DL summer opportunities
    DL career and technology courses
    Master scheduling
    Marketing your secondary DL program
    DL secondary program leadership
What Is the Role of Student Leadership in Secondary Dual Language Programs?..28
    Student advocacy
    Student advisory board

Chapter Three—The Rationale for Secondary Dual Language Schooling 31
Jeremy Aldrich

Distinctives of Secondary Dual Language Programs 33
Dual Language Program Outcomes 34
    Cognitive benefits of bilingualism
    Partner-language proficiency
    Cultural competence
    Positive sense of identity
    School satisfaction and completion
Models in the U.S. and Around the World 39
    Articulating a cohesive program
    Transitioning between levels
    Translanguaging
Meeting the Needs of Stakeholders 42

　　　　Students
　　　　Teachers
　　　　Administrators
　　　　Parents
　　Future Directions for Research 47

Part II—Implementation Experience and Advice

Chapter Four—Nebraska: Omaha Public Schools' Secondary Dual Language Program 51
Katy Cattlett and Dr. Rony Ortega

　　OPS Dual Language Program History 53

　　OPS Dual Language Program: Middle School Models 55
　　　　R.M. Marrs Magnet Center (Grades 5-8)
　　　　Beveridge Magnet Middle School (Grades 7-8)
　　　　Norris Middle School (Grades 6-8)
　　OPS Dual Language Program: High School Model 57
　　　　High school DL courses
　　　　Parent, student, and school DL contracts
　　　　College & Scholarship Saturday Program
　　Staffing a High-Quality Dual Language Program 60
　　　　Grow-your-own bilingual teachers
　　　　Bilingual Career Ladder Program
　　　　High School Education Academy
　　English Learners in Secondary Dual Language 62
　　Plans for the Future 62

Chapter Five—Texas: The Story of the Pharr-San Juan-Alamo Independent School District Secondary Dual Language Program .. 63
Dr. Mario Ferrón and Mario Ferrón, Jr.

　　The Context...64
　　The Beginning 64
　　Choosing the Campus 65
　　Selecting the Teachers..65
　　Getting Ready for DL Instruction—A Personal Story...........................66
　　The DL Students 67
　　The Outcomes..69
　　Moving into High School..70
　　DL Success in Science..72
　　Lessons Learned: Expanding the Secondary DL Program Districtwide.73
　　More Challenges 75

Chapter Six—Illinois: A Systemic Approach to Building a Secondary Dual Language Program: The Story of Highland Park High School . 77
Dr. Tom Koulentes

    Highland Park High School Dual Language Program 79
    Awakening 79
    Dual Language Fridays: Allocating Time for Systemic Planning and
    Program Implementation 80
    Developing a Mission and Focus 81
    Identifying and Hiring High-Quality Dual Language Instructors........... 83
    Coordinating Staff Development.. 84
    Actively Educating our Superintendent, Board of Education, and
    Community about Dual Language 88
    Seal of Dual Language... 91
    Initial Achievement Data and Results... 92
    Moving Forward 97

Chapter Seven—Oregon: Woodburn School District—Two Secondary Schools with Dual Language Programs 99
Dr. Victor Vergara

    Woodburn School District Strategic Plan, Goal #3........................... 100
    Valor Middle School.. 101
    Valor History 101
    Valor Middle School Dual Language Program Structure................... 101
        Multilingual development goal
        Biliteracy pathway
        Curriculum and instruction
        Materials
        Assessments
        Professional development
        English language development
        Multicultural families and community involvement
    Dual Language High School: Academy of International Studies (AIS) 107
        AIS History
    AIS High School Dual Language Program Structure 108
        Multilingual development goal
        Biliteracy pathway
        Curriculum and instruction
        Curriculum requirements
        Materials
        Assessments
        Professional development
        English language development

    Multicultural family and community involvement
Seal of Biliteracy..114
Dual Language Courses for Newcomers to Secondary Schools.........114
Staff Recruitment at the Secondary Level 116
Summary..116

Chapter Eight—Texas: Houston Independent School District—Dual Language Expansion to Secondary Schools: Challenges and Successes in a Large Urban School District.. 117
Dr. Virginia Elizondo

Dual Language for All: Programming...119
Site-Based Management 119
Master Schedule: Common Planning 120
    Materials 121
    Feeder Pattern and Recruitment 121
    Status of the Spanish Language in the Southwest U.S.....................122
    Student Admission to the Secondary DL Program 122
    Transportation 123
    Newcomers 123
    Leadership Changes 124
    DL Staffing and Professional Development 124
    Teacher Cohesiveness and Compatibility 124
    Culture 125
    Where We Are Today..125

Chapter Nine—California: Norton Science and Language Academy—Adventures in Dual Immersion: Growing a Middle School Within a Whole-School TK-8 Dual Language Program 127
Erin Bostick Mason

A Fairy Tale Begins...128
Many Roles, One Theme 128
Impact on Staff 129
Impact on Students...129
Appealing to Students...130
Balancing Commitment and Flexibility, While Maintaining Stamina 130
Adapting Plans, While Staying on Course 131
The School Community 132
Staffing 132
Reflecting and Restructuring Middle School 132
Transitioning from Elementary to Middle School...135

The First Iteration 135
Credentialing 135
Reflecting After Years One and Two 137
    Strengths in our middle school
    Challenges with the six-period schedule
    Homework and grading
    Time in the school schedule for teacher collaboration
    Single subject and multiple subject credentials for teachers
Reinventing our Middle School Structure 139
    Essentials for our middle school
    New middle school schedule
    Scheduling teacher collaboration time
    Staffing the electives
Summary 141

Chapter Ten—New Mexico: Albuquerque Public Schools— La historia de dos escuelas bilingües: Bilingual Seal Development 143
Mishelle Jurado, Lisa Harmon-Martínez, and Dr. Gabriel Antonio Gonzales

Los principios—The Beginnings 144
El sello bilingüe—The Bilingual Seal at Albuquerque High School 145
    Expanding Spanish language arts requirements
    The portfolio process
    Assessing the two languages
El sello del estado de Nuevo México—The New Mexico State Seal of
Bilingualism-Biliteracy 150
El sello bilingüe de las Escuelas Públicas de Albuquerque—The APS Bilingual
Seal 151
The Albuquerque High School Dual Language Program 157
    Visibility
    Combined language arts department
    Official state AP content courses taught in Spanish
    Equity and empowerment
Atrisco Heritage Academy High School, Continuing the Work 158
Recomendaciones para el futuro—Recommendations for the Future 161

Chapter Eleven—Florida: The School District of Palm Beach County—Show Me the Way: One Practitioner's Path to Success in Secondary Dual Language Immersion 163
Dr. David Samore

Okeeheelee Middle School 166
Is There a Place for Secondary Dual Language Schools? 167
How Does Dual Language Compare to Other Strategies to Raise Student Achievement? 167
Which Students Gain Most from Dual Language Education? 168
What Are the Root Causes of Unsuccessful Dual Language Schools? 168
    Lack of strong elementary DL feeder schools
    Other curricular choices at the secondary level make 6-12 DL harder to sustain.
    The lack of understanding of school administrators who control support of DL programs
How Do I Know What a Successful Dual Language Program Looks Like? . 170
Is There a Secondary Dual Language Template that Can Be Replicated Successfully? 171
Principle #1: The Identification of the DL Leader Is a Deciding Factor 171
Principle #2: Be Prepared to Hunt for High-Quality Dual Language Teachers 172
Principle #3: Be Patient 173
Principle #4: Remaining in the Language 173
Principle #5: Language Assessment for a Dual Language Secondary School 174

Chapter Twelve—New York: South Bronx Community Charter High School—Dual Language, Science, Technology, Engineering, and Mathematics (STEM) Classes, and Visionary Education 175
Mario Benabe

Utilizing Indigenous & Afrocentric Rituals in Dual Language Settings 177
From Project-Based Learning (PBL) to Pro Black/Brown Learning (PBL) 179
Designing Programming to Support Culturally and Linguistically Diverse Students with Disabilities 182
Conclusion 185
Appendix A: Identifying Community Social Issues and Representing Them Using Quipus 187
Appendix B: Student Exhibit of Bronx Community District 3 192

Chapter Thirteen—California: Tearing Down Walls, Building Bridges, Lessons Learned! 197
Dr. Michele Anberg-Espinosa

Lessons Learned from Secondary Dual Language Implementation in Urban Multilingual Contexts 198
Dual Language Leadership 198
Informing Stakeholders 199
Strengthening Vision and Purpose 200
    Student motivation
    Encouraging high expectations
Building Bridges between Elementary and Secondary Teachers:
It's a PK-12 Conversation 201
Curriculum Development and New Secondary DL Teachers 202
Moving Beyond Strictly Language Goals Toward Equity 204
    Needs of students
    Is dual language for ALL?
    A case study about African American student longevity
    Beyond language into changed communities
    Getting race on the table
    Racial identity development
Concluding Thoughts 209

Part III—Graduates Speak, Teacher Preparation, and a National View

Chapter Fourteen—Secondary Dual Language Graduates Speak Up: Experiences, Impact, and Advice 213
Elizet Moret and Irán Tovar

1. Thinking about your secondary experience (middle & high school), as a participant in a dual language education program, what was most enjoyable? 214
2. What core curricular courses did you take in the partner language in middle and high school? 215
3. Did the dual language program at your district provide other activities (after-school, extracurricular, clubs, etc.) that promoted the dual language program and exposed students to the cultural aspects of the program? 216
4. What advice would you give students who are considering continuing their dual language program participation at middle and high school? 216
    Trust the program.
    Reasons for continuing in DL

5. What advice would you give to administrators of dual language programs when considering the development of such programs at middle and high school?.. 217
    Stay true to the program and be flexible.
    Hire native-speaking DL teachers.
    Respect regional varieties of the partner language.
    Offer rigorous DL content courses in a wide range of subjects.

6. Were there any classes/courses you had to give up in middle and/or high school to continue in the dual language program?............................ 218
    Flexibility for electives and core DL classes

7. What courses would you like for an administrator/school district to consider for dual language program participants?.. 218

8. What do you think administrators can do to further assist dual language teachers in supporting the academic success of dual language students? ..218
    Professional development in DL for all administrators
    Professional development in DL for all secondary teachers

9. What specific experiences during your participation in the dual language program at the secondary level made the biggest impact on your life?...... 219
    Bonds with speakers of the partner language and with family
    International travel, scholarships, and employment opportunities

10. How has your participation in the dual language program impacted your professional career?... 219
    Using their bilingualism in professional contexts

11. In reflecting upon your overall experience, how has your participation in the dual language program made an impact on your life?..................... 220

Closing.. 221

Chapter Fifteen—Transforming Secondary Dual Language Teacher Preparation 223
Dr. Joan R. Lachance

The National Dual Language Teacher Shortage 224
The Unique Nature of Dual Language Academic Development in Secondary School.. 224
Recommendations from Dual Language Educators in North Carolina and New Mexico.. 225
Core Theme One: Preparing Teachers to Transform DL Classrooms 226
    Dual language pedagogy
    Biliteracy development
    Multilingualism and rigor
    Authentic dual language materials
    Authentic assessment
Core Theme Two: Transforming Dual Language Teacher Preparation 229

    Teachers as ongoing learners
    Dual language program structures
    Program evaluation and learner assessment
    Historical/community factors
    Educators' sociocultural influences
    Parents: Demystifying dual language
    "Home-grown" teachers
    Institutions of higher education (IHEs) and school district collaboration: Clinical partnerships
Proposed Coursework: A Thematic Crosswalk 231
    Biliteracy and Second Language Acquisition in Dual Language Teaching
    Authentic Assessment for Dual Language Learners
    Dual Language Methods and Advanced Pedagogies
    Dual Language Clinicals and Internship
Teacher Preparation and Accreditation:
A Call for National Dual Language Teacher Preparation Standards 233
Appendix: Overview of Study Participants, Interviews, Classroom Observation, and Data Analyses 234

Chapter Sixteen—Secondary Dual Language Education: A National View 235
Dr. Wayne Thomas and Dr. Virginia Collier

The Past 20 Years 236
    Gap closure research
    Cognitive benefits
    Dramatic expansion of dual language
The Bilingual Seal and Statewide Dual Language Movements 236
    Major state initiatives
    Lack of federal funding
Education for a Transformed World 237
Building on the Successes of PK-5 Dual Language Education 238
    Research rationale for secondary dual language
    Opportunity costs for not providing secondary dual language
    Improving NAEP test scores, state by state, with PK-12 dual language programs
The New Future: Transforming U.S. Education 239

References 241

Index 254

Contributing Authors 259

PART I

Introduction

Chapter One
Why Secondary Dual Language Schooling

Dr. Virginia Collier and Dr. Wayne Thomas

In our book Why Dual Language Schooling (2017), we boldly stated that dual language education is the mainstream, the standard curriculum taught through two languages. It is not a separate, segregated program. Dual language classes are for all students. Furthermore, we have asserted in all our books that it is a non-negotiable that dual language programs should continue throughout all grades, PK-12. Even now, secondary dual language programs are beginning to influence some university curricula, so we expect that in the future dual language courses will exist on some campuses all the way through PK-16.

Today we estimate that there may be 2,500 or more two-way (two language groups being schooled together through their two languages) dual language elementary programs (Grades K-5 or PK-5) in public schools in the U.S. and many more being developed each year (Thomas & Collier, 2017, p. 17). We don't yet have an accurate count of how many of these programs have expanded into the secondary years, but several hundred are listed in the Dual Language Schools Directory *(http://www.duallanguageschools.org)*. Dual language middle and high school programs are definitely on the rise as parents and educators recognize the importance of this relatively new and growing trend.

So what do we mean when we explore the possibility of dual language classes for young adults in middle and high school? That's what this book is all about! We have brought together the voices of experienced and knowledgeable secondary dual language educators from 10 states. The contributors to this book have been secondary dual language teachers, principals, coordinators of dual language programs, central office administrators, teacher trainers, researchers, and state leaders of dual language programs. They have a great deal of rich information to share with you regarding what works well in secondary dual language education, as well as many of the challenges that can occur when the dual language program expands to Grades 6-12. We encouraged each one of these veteran educators to present their school district's experiences as guidance for planners of secondary dual language programs. The experiences presented here are from school districts of all sizes, including very large urban contexts, small cities, border towns, rural contexts, and a few stories of individual schools.

Some of you as readers of this book may have been only recently introduced to the idea of dual language schooling, or may be dual language educators preparing to expand your program to the secondary level in your school district. We also expect that some of you reading this book may be very experienced secondary dual language implementers, trying to solve some program challenges and are looking for new ways to approach your decision making. We hope that all the contributors to this book will inspire you, whether you are new to dual language, just starting to expand to secondary, or very experienced secondary dual language educators.

Topics Addressed in This Book

In this introductory chapter, we are going to guide you through the themes that the authors have in common across all their diverse contexts. These themes have emerged as important issues to be addressed very early in the planning process for secondary dual language programs. The following themes are topics that will be addressed throughout this book.

• How secondary dual language (DL) schooling is different from elementary DL schooling

• Who participates in secondary DL programs

    - English learners, including newcomers

    - Heritage speakers of the partner language

    - Native English speakers

• Scheduling of middle and high school DL courses

• Finding academically proficient, subject-certified secondary bilingual teachers

• Instructional strategies/separation of languages in secondary DL classes

• Secondary DL curricular materials

• Innovative secondary DL administrative practices

• Professional development for secondary DL and all staff

• Collaboration across secondary departments for successful DL implementation

• Institutional impediments to DL and how to address them

• DL student leadership and input for program improvement

• DL program evaluation and measures of success

• Equity issues

• The advantages of whole-school dual language for all Grades K-12

Differences Between Elementary and Secondary Dual Language Schooling

As dual language classes expand into the middle and high school years, many issues emerge that require different decisions from those made for the elementary school DL program. Figure 1.1 illustrates some of the contrasts between elementary and secondary instructional contexts, including particular concerns that English learners face.

> Figure 1.1
> **The Secondary School Context as Compared to the Elementary School Context**
>
> **Instruction:**
>
> - cognitive demand is greater—more emphasis on analyzing, making connections, determining strategies, and drawing evaluative conclusions (rather than stating facts, memorizing, and following predetermined instructions)
> - tests are more difficult
> - curriculum is more comprehensive, more difficult, and more advanced
> - language is more complex and more difficult
> - subjects are isolated (harder for students to make connections between subjects and real world)
>
> **Students:**
>
> - are more self-determining regarding their learning
> - are more subject to external influences (outside of school)
> - are more subject to peer pressure
> - are more emotionally volatile
>
> **English Learners:**
>
> - experience a larger achievement gap if not in DL courses
> - have less time remaining in school for gap closure
> - typically overestimate their true skill levels (in English and in curricular mastery)
> - require sensitive and nuanced instruction
>
> Copyright © 2008-2018, W.P. Thomas & V.P. Collier. All rights reserved.

Cognitive demand. The cognitive demand of academic work is dramatically increased with each grade level. In addition, the average difficulty of test items and the cognitive capabilities required to score well on tests increase each year. Subjects at the secondary level tend to be taught in silos, with teachers who are specialists in their subject areas and less willing to develop interdisciplinary thematic units that connect to real-world problem solving.

Teenagers. Then there are the age differences. More than elementary students, teenagers are sometimes moody, or exuberant, or withdrawn, or caring, expressing all the extremes of emotions and may not understand themselves yet as they experience all their emotional and corporeal changes. In addition, their brains are "re-organizing." They may have many more responsibilities outside of school, and as young adults they may respond to peer pressure to do things that have consequences they didn't intend. At middle school and especially high school age, they are starting to view their world from an adult perspective, examining choices that they have in school and reflecting on how these choices will prepare them for adult life. For bilingual learners, this includes their perceptions of how they will use their two languages and cross-cultural experiences as adults. DL planners must keep the needs of teenagers at the center of their program decisions, because these students have choices (athletics, music, drama, AP courses, etc.) that didn't exist at the elementary school level.

Basic program design. Categories used for initial program design, such as 90:10, 80:20, or 50:50 for defining instructional time in each language at the elementary level **do not apply to secondary schools.** Secondary DL programs are first defined by the amount of and type of coursework offered in the partner (non-English) language, starting with a language arts course (e.g., Spanish language arts). Next, a fundamental decision is which core content courses required for graduation—and often tested in English at the end of the year with high-stakes state assessments—will be taught in the partner language. Some English-only staff may challenge this decision, but fully proficient DL students will learn content knowledge and take tests equally well in both English and the partner language. All of the authors in this book highly recommend offering partner language coursework in the challenging core courses as an important step to ensure that DL will eventually be perceived as the mainstream curriculum, taught through two languages.

Furthermore, it is important to offer core content AP courses in the partner language as soon as feasible. This is because **students who have been through DL in Grades K-5 are already experiencing the cognitive benefits of bilingualism, which means that they are typically among the highest scoring students in the school.** They are ready for AP courses, and if these are not offered in the DL program, they will enroll in English-only AP courses. They want to accelerate their path into college courses, the DL program should encourage and facilitate this. This is true for low-income students, former English learners, and native English speakers. Bilingually schooled students are high achievers, and this reality is fully visible at the high school level, so DL secondary educators need to be prepared for students with greater capabilities and more advanced needs than non-DL students!

DL coursework in English is a different story. Students who received K-5 DL classes will enroll in the general education courses in English that already exist, including AP courses. For English learners who are recently arrived newcomers will receive the ongoing curriculum that the English as a second language (ESL) staff has developed as a part of the DL program, including ESL/sheltered content courses. In the next section, we will address other issues for these new arrivals.

Who Participates in Secondary Dual Language Programs

English learners. At the secondary level, English learners are increasingly diverse as categorized by how much formal schooling they received in their primary language (L1), the amount of schooling received in L2, literacy development in L1 and L2, the number of students at one school who speak the same L1, and many other issues. Thus, in the secondary years, it becomes much more complicated to appropriately provide for the needs of this diverse group. Yet if these students speak the partner language of the DL program, they belong in the DL courses. For these students, it is important to receive schooling in their mother tongue, keeping them on grade level in the development of subject knowledge while they work on fully mastering English. This opportunity will accelerate their academic growth faster than any other strategy. Yes, they should also receive excellent ESL content courses for half of their academic work, but more English is not better. In fact, more English tends to lessen their long-term achievement.

This phenomenon can be seen in our research findings presented in Figure 1.2, which shows that high school English learners in an excellent ESL content program (but no DL) who received 6 or more years of English schooling and 4 years or less of L1 schooling did not do as well as those who received at least half of their schooling in L1 in their home country before arriving in the U.S. For the secondary DL coursework, part of English learners' academic day (ideally half) should be spent in courses taught in their L1. (Also see Thomas & Collier, 2012, p. 60, Figure 4.9, and p. 116, Figure 7.2.) A consistent theme of this book is that newcomers, along with heritage speakers of the partner language, belong in the DL program. We all strongly recommend this.

Figure 1.2

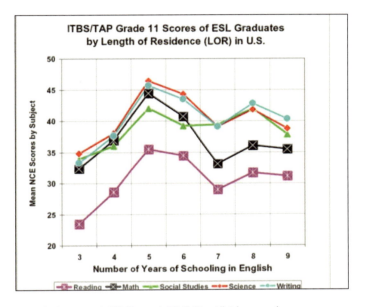

Copyright © 2002-2018, W.P. Thomas & V.P. Collier. All rights reserved.

Heritage speakers. This group of students is also very diverse. Heritage speakers of the partner language definitely belong in the DL program. They can be identified as English learners, bilinguals, and those who have lost their heritage language, but let's focus first on those who are fluent in English. For example, when Latinos join the Spanish-English DL program in Grades K-5, they develop literacy in their heritage language as well as English, and they benefit from the cognitive acceleration that bilingualism brings. They then should continue DL into the secondary years. In contexts where language minority groups are low achievers, those who join the DL program become the high achievers. By middle and high school level, DL heritage speakers are among the highest achievers in the school, scoring higher than non-DL heritage speakers (Thomas & Collier, 2014; see Chapters 5, 7, and 10 of this book).

Native English speakers. To participate in secondary DL classes, native English speakers must be academically proficient in the partner language. The academic rigor is so high in the DL middle and high school courses that students just beginning acquisition of the partner language cannot be included. That means that native-English-speaking parents must be encouraged to enroll their children at age 5 in the K-5 DL program, so that they will be academically bilingual/biliterate and ready for secondary DL courses. In fact, it is the DL native-English-speaking parents who often demand continuation of the program into the secondary years, so they can be DL program advocates to help persuade other families to continue in the program. The presence of the native English speakers helps resolve issues of equal status of the two languages and affirms the importance of developing adult levels of bilingualism and cross-cultural understanding.

Scheduling Issues

The persons who develop the DL master schedule of classes for middle and high school must have extensive experience with scheduling and remain flexible as the needs of the DL program change with the influx of DL students from feeder elementary schools and newcomer immigrants who arrive throughout the year. Flexibility is also required to accommodate the schedules of the DL teachers to include a common planning time. Providing students with access to electives also requires attention and flexibility. All of the authors in this book recommend that DL secondary programs offer a minimum of two year-long classes each year in the partner language (one language arts class plus one content area class), and more when the program has a sufficient number of DL students and qualified staff. For high schools, as the program grows, schedulers will need to increase the number of sections of each DL course. ESL faculty are responsible for developing the ESL content coursework and coordinating the scheduling of these courses with the DL courses taught in the partner language that the newly arriving English learners need. In this book, if you want to dig deeper into scheduling issues, start by reading Chapter 2, authored by Cindy Sizemore. Also read Chapter 9 where Erin Mason describes scheduling as the key program-planning issue to address at the middle school level for the DL program to be successful throughout Grades K-12.

Hiring Dual Language Faculty

All of the authors in this book state that high-quality DL faculty are essential to secondary DL program success. All DL teachers must be academically proficient in the language of instruction AND certified to teach their content area at the secondary level. Furthermore, the teachers need to be sensitive to the diverse needs of their DL students and willing to address them. The population of classes taught in the partner language may include the DL students who have been in the program since the early elementary grades, along with recent arrivals who received schooling in their home country and are on or close to grade-level achievement. These classes might even include students who have developed significant proficiency in the partner language through world language classes and who have been granted permission to enroll in the class through an assessment measure in the partner language. All of these students have to learn to work together, and the teacher must use instructional strategies that take advantage of this mix, while teaching a rigorous, academically challenging course. If the DL course is Advanced Placement (AP) level, students will be taking the course for college credit. These are teaching challenges that demand highly qualified bilingual faculty.

Some regions of the U.S. have a significant number of bilingual Spanish/English teachers, but this is not common. Finding bilingually certified teachers for partner languages other than Spanish is even more challenging. This means recruiting from other states and sometimes hiring faculty from other countries. Several authors have provided a number of suggestions for seeking qualified bilingual teachers. This is an important first step to planning a successful DL program, and it is wise to start hiring secondary bilingual personnel before the elementary DL program reaches fifth grade. Chapters 3 and 4 have some good guidance for hiring bilingual faculty. In Chapter 6 you will read about a five-step planning process (including DL teacher hiring) that a high school developed that took 5 years of careful strategizing. The first public whole-school DL program in southern California described in Chapter 9 involved a number of years of careful planning and strategic hiring of DL staff before it was actually implemented. It's never too early to start visualizing and preparing for your middle and high school DL program!

Instructional Strategies

DL teaching innovations. Secondary teachers usually focus on teaching the subject in which they have been certified. They are preparing their students for the high-stakes tests in their specialty subject and concerned about how they will be evaluated. DL teachers are additionally responsible for teaching their subject matter through the partner language, which is the second language of some of their students; therefore, they must integrate second-language teaching strategies into their lessons at all times. The same is true for the ESL DL teachers, who must teach academic content using English as a second language techniques. Instructional strategies taught by trainers of Guided Language Acquisition Design (OCDE Project GLAD®, www.ocde.us/projectglad) and Sheltered Instructional Observation Protocol (SIOP®, Echevaría, Vogt, & Short, 2016) provide a wide variety of strategies to creatively build students' use of academic vocabulary and subject-specific language. Second-language innovative teaching strategies include developing thematic units that help students see the connections to real-world problem solving (see Figure 1.3), and using cooperative learning to facilitate student-to-student peer teaching and language practice (Thomas & Collier, 2017, pp. 74-75). Some examples of possible teaching strategies are illustrated in Chapter 12, and the process of designing coursework for certification of secondary DL teachers is provided in Chapter 15.

Figure 1.3

In this thematic unit, how will you ...

- enjoy yourself (you, the teacher)?
- integrate many content areas?
- experience multiple intelligences?
- tackle local community issues that need solving?
- use the knowledge and resources of your school community (including parents)?
- use technology?
- stimulate collaborative learning?
- integrate authentic assessment?
- help students read, read, read and write, write, write?
- help students understand power relations (critical pedagogy)?
- use students' primary language?
- help students grow emotionally?

(in the long run, there is nothing to fear ... how can we get to a better place?)

Copyright © 1996-2018, V.P. Collier & W.P. Thomas. All rights reserved.

Separation of the two languages. One of the major issues that secondary DL staff must resolve is to decide when the two languages should be instructionally separated and when they can be used together in meaningful ways. Most DL programs at the secondary level choose to offer academic courses that are taught in either the partner language or in English, with no use of the other language allowed in that course. But there are many exceptions to this "rule," depending on the geographical/sociological context and patterns of use of the two languages in the community.

As you read each chapter in this book, you will find that authors vary greatly in their advice on this issue. For example, in the DL high school program in Omaha, Nebraska (Chapter 4), courses are taught using both languages as needed, because they are serving both DL students from elementary schools and many newly arrived, older Spanish-speaking immigrants. Some of these older students need L1 coursework to make up for schooling lost as they left their country of origin, and have fewer years to acquire English (in comparison to their younger siblings). Their DL high school program is a unique college preparatory program, very popular in the Omaha Latino community. The support systems provided by the DL staff in both Spanish and English assist many students to successfully graduate and continue into university studies.

A contrasting perspective is presented in Chapter 11, in which Dr. David Samore is adamant that "immersion" in the second language is essential to students' complete proficiency in L2. His perspective comes from that of world language educators who have developed world language classes and international exchange programs that "immerse" older students in the target language, with no English allowed. As principal of a DL immersion school, he requires that all of his teachers stay strictly with the language of instruction (some classes taught only in English, others only in Spanish), with no translation, no code-switching, no "translanguaging" (García, Johnson & Seltzer, 2017). In general, research shows that separation of the languages is especially important in the beginning stages of L2 acquisition, so that students pay attention to and absorb their new language without relying on their L1 for quick translation (Thomas & Collier, 2012).

The term "immersion" is itself a controversial and confusing term. World language educators in the U.S. often use this term to refer to one-way (one language group being schooled through two languages) DL programs for native English speakers, because that is the term that Canadians use for their one-way DL programs. However, most bilingual/ESL educators in the U.S. do not like the term "immersion" because it was misused during the 1980s and 1990s by the English-only movement to imply that English learners should be "immersed" in only English, incorrectly citing the Canadian research on "immersion" which teaches the curriculum through two languages, not one. In spite of this history, some states such as California use the term "dual immersion" for their two-way DL programs (see Chapter 9). In this book when the term "immersion" is used, the authors mean that the school curriculum is taught using two languages, with some courses in English, some courses in the partner language, and sometimes both of the languages are used together.

There are good reasons for using both languages together in some secondary DL classes, based on local context. Some of the authors are located in communities that are very bilingual, such as New York City and school districts along the Mexico-U.S. border, as well as many communities of the southwest U.S. In these regions, Spanish and English are used interchangeably by bilinguals as they code-switch back and forth. Separation of the two languages can be very artificial, especially for bilinguals who have grown up with the two languages from birth. Thus DL teachers in bilingual communities find a variety of ways to honor the use of the two languages for bilingual contexts. See Chapter 10 for more discussion of this issue, especially regarding the assessment process for the awarding of the bilingual seal upon high school graduation.

Within classroom lessons, explicit units can be developed in language arts classes that examine the use of code-switching in the community, or study bilingual literature of the southwest U.S., or compare and contrast the two languages to support cross-linguistic transfer. For biliteracy development in the early grades of elementary school, it is important to connect the two languages by "bridging" (Beeman & Urow, 2013), and the same concept can be applied to secondary DL classes across the content areas. The term "translanguaging" is used to refer to many aspects of use of the two languages in one class (García, Johnson, & Seltzer, 2017). Chapter 3 presents more detail on translanguaging. In the planning stage for the secondary DL program, the DL staff must make careful decisions about when the two languages should remain separate and when it is appropriate to use both languages together in instructional settings.

Curricular Materials

All of the authors agree that finding high-quality curricular materials in the partner language is one of the biggest challenges when developing secondary DL coursework for the content areas. Even though many U.S. publishing companies are expanding their choices for textbooks in Spanish, and the market is growing as secondary DL Spanish/English programs increase in number, choosing the appropriate materials can be very difficult (see Chapter 8). It is an even harder to find curricular materials in partner languages other than Spanish. Teachers in the Russian/English DL program in Woodburn, Oregon (Chapter 7), found it necessary to translate curricular materials from English to Russian for some subjects.

More multiple-language materials are available for language arts classes because of the existing demand for world language courses at the middle and high school level. However, these materials may only be easily accessible for the world languages that are commonly taught in the U.S.—e.g., Spanish, French, German, Portuguese, and Russian. Finding the language arts textbooks for Vietnamese, Korean, Mandarin Chinese, Japanese, Arabic (fourth largest world language), Hindi (fifth largest world language), and other languages can be more challenging (Thomas & Collier, 2017, p. 15).

Then there's the high level of instruction that DL students require. As the elementary DL students move into the secondary years, they are often ready for very demanding and advanced language arts classes, such as Spanish 5 and 6, as well as AP language arts classes. These levels of study are equivalent to college courses, but university textbooks may not meet the high school students' needs. Authentic literature (written by well-known authors, not translations) is an essential element of these upper-level language arts classes.

Dual Language Administrative Practices

All of the authors stress the importance of having administrators who understand and fully support the DL program. This includes the superintendent, central office administrators, principals, counselors, and other administrative support staff. In large urban school districts, the biggest challenge is frequent turnover in leadership positions; this caused ups and downs in the successful implementation and support for DL (see Chapters 8, 11, and 13). All staff must understand why DL is superior to English-only approaches for English learners and let their professional practice be guided by this understanding. In particular, each principal should study the research that supports DL effectiveness, both in general as well as specific research-based strategies and procedures used in DL programs. Also, each DL principal should be directly involved with the DL program, understanding each component and supporting each DL teacher. Since principals are responsible for evaluating the teachers in their building, they participate in monitoring the levels and degree of DL program implementation and compliance with the planned program (see Chapter 6). As the DL program grows, DL teachers, together with administrators, can discuss and negotiate changes to the original plan, making sure that what they decide meets the needs of all the DL students, and has a research-based rationale.

Some superintendents have become passionate advocates of DL programs, providing additional funding and support for DL classes. When this occurs, many schools have been able to improve the quality of their DL courses. This usually jump-starts the expansion of the program into more schools within the district, including growing the program into more middle and high schools (see Chapters 5, 7, 8, and 10). Sometimes DL grows to be districtwide, as in the Woodburn School District in Oregon, where DL (Spanish/English or Russian/English) classes are provided in all elementary and middle schools as well as in the high school Academy of International Studies (Chapter 7). An English-plus track (with world language classes in either Spanish or Russian) is provided for the few families whose children choose not to enroll in DL. Superintendent Walt Wolfram began this initiative towards DL districtwide; Superintendent David Bautista expanded the DL program to all schools, and Superintendent Chuck Ransom continues leading this exemplary DL school district (serving mostly low-income families), that graduates over 90% of its English learners.

Professional Development

Ongoing professional development focusing on DL instructional strategies is an important key to successful secondary implementation, providing needed support for the DL teachers who should have a voice in choosing what they need to learn in staff development opportunities. These professional development sessions should include all staff who work with English learners, so that those who are not part of the DL program understand and facilitate the essential role that L1 schooling plays in educating newly arriving immigrants as they acquire English. In addition, these staff development sessions can assist all teachers who teach in English in learning the innovative L2 strategies that significantly help their English learners as they attend classes taught in English. In Chapter 15, Dr. Joan Lachance provides a comprehensive overview of coursework needed for secondary DL teachers.

Chapter 6 includes an interesting perspective on the different staff development needs of DL teachers, depending on whether they are monolingual English speakers, bilingual from birth, proficient in English first and later acquired the partner language, or the opposite. In Chapter 7, several innovative ideas for professional development are proposed. One of these is regular "learning walks" in which DL teachers and administrators have the opportunity to visit DL classes in other schools or even other districts, with a shared focus as they observe each classroom. The DL staff end these "learning walks" with a non-evaluative interactive discussion of the teaching strategies that they observed, including planning next steps to refine their own teaching practices.

Collaboration Across Secondary Departments

As a DL secondary program grows, it is important for collegial collaboration to occur across different subject areas. Both the DL bilingual teachers teaching in the partner language and the DL ESL teachers belong to at least two departments, their subject-area specialty and the DL program. ESL teachers need to coordinate closely with the English language arts faculty and the content areas that the ESL staff have chosen to teach. A powerful combination occurs when secondary teachers choose to team teach, such as an ESL teacher teaming with one of the biology faculty. Another form of team teaching is for two subject-area specialists to develop a thematic unit, so that students attending their separate subject areas see the connections across the two disciplines and focus on real-world problem-solving that evolves out of the thematic unit chosen (see Chapter 12). Another subject area that calls for DL collaboration involves the language arts and world languages staff. Chapter 10 illustrates how, establishing co-coordinators of the Spanish language arts and English language arts departments can lead to curricular alignment across two languages and better serving the needs of the DL students as the program grows.

Institutional Impediments

The greatest challenges that secondary DL programs have to face occur in the initial stages of planning and program development. Chapter 5 illustrates well the step-by-step process that bilingual teachers and staff may go through when DL is begun in a borderland school district that had been implementing only transitional bilingual education and ESL. This historical sociolinguistic context of the region has long devalued Spanish. At the beginning stages of development of the DL program, the historical pattern prevailed in attitudes among staff that the newly arrived English learners should be "immersed" in English. It took several years before some monolingual staff attitudes began to change. Once the DL students in the secondary program started to outperform all other students in the school district, more and more staff began to believe in the program. Long-term research results confirmed the continued high achievement of the DL students. This school district in south Texas, Pharr-San Juan-Alamo, has graduated an impressive number of DL students, many of whom were former English learners of mostly low-income background, who are now pursuing their undergraduate, master's, and doctoral studies.

However, institutional and staff resistance to teaching students, especially English learners, in both English and the partner language is much more pervasive than just in borderland school districts. Several contributors to this book have described working with well-meaning and otherwise well-informed professional educators in their district who sincerely believe that "more English is the answer" to meeting the needs of English learners. Yet dual language research shows conclusively that students' mastery of the curriculum increases with more cognitive development and student engagement through courses in both the partner language and English. More English is NOT better (Thomas & Collier, 2012).

In addition, the opinion that "if we test in English, then we should teach more in English" is also common and equally unsupported by research findings. Testing should occur in the language that will yield the most valid, reliable, and accurate test score at the time of testing (see Figure 1.4). Instruction, especially with cognitively demanding material, is most effective in the language that the student knows best at the time of instruction. In both testing and instructional contexts, the appropriate language may well be the mother tongue of English learners, at least for a minimum of half of the available instructional time while they are moving toward full proficiency in English. However, when they have fully mastered both English and the partner language, then both teaching and testing can occur with equal success in either language (see Figure 1.5). Attitudes that are based on "common sense" and that are unsupported by data-based research represent institutional impediments to the operation and success of DL programs that should not be ignored by DL planners. Those who implement DL programs in the secondary years must be prepared to demonstrate that commonly believed myths are indeed false by making the relevant large-scale and long-term research available to district educators. All educators should be encouraged to base their practice on the available, compelling, data-analytic research, and not on "common sense."

Figure 1.4

> **A Commonly Heard Myth ...**
>
> "If we are going to test English learners in English,
> Then we should teach them more in English."
>
> **Translation:**
> (from cognitive psychology)
> If we test them in the language (L2)
> that produces a less valid,
> less reliable, less accurate,
> and systematically lower test score,
>
> Then we should teach them in the language (L2)
> in which they are
> less-efficient learners
> and will master less content.
>
> Copyright © W.P. Thomas & V.P. Collier, 2012-2018. All rights reserved.

Dual Language Student Leadership

In Chapter 2 you will encounter author Cindy Sizemore's passion for listening to DL students. The high school DL program in Ysleta Independent School District initiated the first DL student advisory board for DL students to recruit and mentor younger students to continue in the program and to provide input to the DL staff regarding potential changes to the program. A unique feature of this DL program was student service to the community. During their high school years, the DL students were asked to volunteer their services to a professional or service context of great interest to them in which they had to use their bilingualism to carry out the job. This reinforced their reasons for developing their bilingualism to high-proficiency levels and helped them see the importance of their continuation of DL throughout all grades of school. It also led to a preview of how they might expand their interests and uses of their bilingualism in their professional lives. Chapter 14 chronicles DL graduates' experiences as adults and their recommendations to DL educators.

Another example of student connections to a future profession is the Education Academy at Omaha South High Magnet School (see Chapter 4). DL high school students can explore their interest in becoming bilingual teachers by taking a 2-year sequence of courses that provides dual enrollment with

Figure 1.5

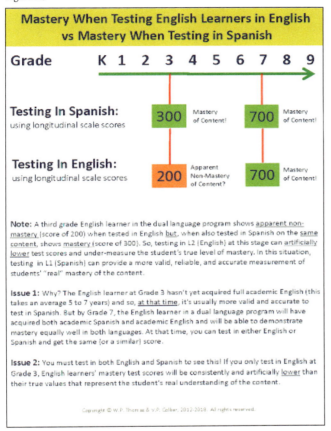

the local community college. With the shortage of bilingual teachers, this is a great way for school districts to grow their own DL teachers. Omaha Public Schools has already succeeded in hiring three of their DL graduates who took advantage of this opportunity.

Program Evaluation

What best measures the success of the secondary DL program? For those students who have attended the DL program from Grades K-8, certainly student attainment on the eighth grade state tests is one clear longitudinal measure. In our North Carolina research, we found that by Grade 8, DL students were outperforming those in monolingual English classes by as much as 1 or 2 years of higher achievement on the state tests in reading and math (Thomas & Collier, 2014). Furthermore, we were able to break this down by student groups and every DL student group did significantly better than their comparison group not in DL—English learners, Latinos, African Americans, Caucasians, students of low-income background, and students with special needs. In all of the chapters of this book, authors report much higher test scores for secondary DL students in comparison to non-DL students.

High school graduation rates are another important indicator of DL program success, especially for English learners attending the DL program. The graduation rates reported from school districts described in Chapters 4, 5, 6, 7, 8, and 10 are phenomenal for DL students. For example, before the DL program started in the Woodburn School District the graduation rate for English learners was 41%, and now it is over 90%, year after year. Chapter 14 summarizes some fascinating interviews with DL graduates from K-12 DL programs in three states. These graduates all report that the DL program strongly influenced their lives as adults in very positive and profound ways. In summary, DL students in their secondary years reap the long-term benefits of cumulative cognitive development that come with adult bilingualism and biliteracy, applied to all fields of knowledge. Also, DL students develop deeper proficiency levels of English than non-DL students because of the powerful impact of schooling through two languages.

Equity Issues

Three authors passionately delve into equity issues in Chapters 6, 12, and 13. DL must be built on the foundation of "a deep, unwavering commitment to educational equity for all students," Dr. Tom Koulentes asserts, in essence, "changing an English-dominant system and creating space and status for non-English languages in a public school environment is equity work." Dr. Michele Anberg-Espinosa calls this the "hidden curriculum" of DL programs. She proposes that secondary DL teachers include explicit lessons about race, culture, and language to assist with identity development for all students.

Equity work also includes ensuring that historically underserved groups in public schools have equal access to the DL program, including English learners, students of low-income background, students with special needs, and students of all ethnic backgrounds. Our North Carolina research findings (Thomas & Collier, 2014) revealed that African American students in both rural and urban contexts who enrolled in DL classes for Grades K-8 achieved at dramatically higher levels than their African American peers not in DL. This was also true for low-income students of all ethnic backgrounds and students with special needs. In fact, the DL African American students' gains, as measured by Grade 6-8 weighted average effect sizes, were substantially larger than those of English learners in DL, who also made dramatic gains.

In Chapter 12, author Mario Benabe makes the case for culturally responsive education, in which "… all students and staff feel safe, supported, empowered, and important." Furthermore, he and his high school students challenge DL educators to work towards an inclusive model in the DL classroom that supports not only students of all different ethnic backgrounds, but also students with disabilities, so that all groups can work together and assist each other in the learning process.

Whole-School Dual Language Education

Erin Bostick Mason, in Chapter 9, writes about the many advantages of having a whole-school dual language campus. Her school has added one grade each year, from transitional kindergarten (TK, for children who turn 5 years old between September 1 and December 31) and kindergarten through Grade 8, with plans to complete all high school grades, making it eventually a TK-12 campus, with all classes and all grades participating in dual language schooling. Most secondary schools operate the DL program as only one of several options; a whole-school model solves many of the problems that challenge DL strands within each school (see Figure 1.6).

Figure 1.6

DL Strands and DL Schoolwide: Some Issues and Considerations	
Strands	**Schoolwide**
Non-DL staff may feel that DL classes are "favored" and may increase their efforts to compete with DL teachers for resources, smaller classes, and administrative attention. (John Henry effect)	All staff are "on the same page" – no complaints about perceived differences in resource allocation, class-size, etc.
Parents who prefer English-only can choose ESL-only or all-English classes for their students in their local school.	Students whose parents prefer English-only must be provided for at neighboring schools or by other means.
Higher achievement of DL students can lead to perceptions of "gifted" (DL) vs "not gifted" (non-DL) classes.	All of school's students feel and are perceived as "gifted."
Non-DL staff or parents may work to undermine the DL program.	Staff and parents strongly support the DL program.
Higher achieving students may choose DL; or low-achieving students may be placed in non-DL classes. (Selection effect)	All student groups participate in the DL program - no selection.
Existing segregated student groups may remain segregated.	Students of diverse backgrounds in socioeconomic status and ethnicity are integrated into all classes.
DL magnet schools usually have DL schoolwide.	In a districtwide DL magnet school, district resources and capabilities are used efficiently. However, student transportation to local DL school from other attendance areas may be necessary.

Copyright © 2013-2018, W.P. Thomas & V.P. Collier. All rights reserved.

When dual language occupies every classroom in a school, there are no competing agendas and no questioning of the multilingual/multicultural goals of the school. Because all student groups participate in the DL program, the mix of students across ethnicities and social classes leads to a collaborative understanding of collegial problem-solving that students carry into their adult lives. The DL administrators and teachers are facilitators of everyone's developing bilingualism and cross-cultural perspectives, with no one attempting to undermine the program. The whole school can celebrate diversity and academic excellence in a welcoming multilingual context.

Organization of the Chapters

Part I: Introduction. This book is divided into three parts. Part I provides three important introductory chapters that guide the reader through an overview of the planning process, implementation strategies needed, and the research rationale for secondary DL programs to be developed and sustained.

• Chapter 1 (by Drs. Collier & Thomas). In this first chapter we have presented some of the main topics that are discussed in depth throughout the book.

• Chapter 2 by Cindy Sizemore leaps into an overview of decision making for secondary DL programs—how they're developed, who they're for, what purposes they serve, and the role of DL student leadership.

• Chapter 3 by Jeremy Aldrich delves into the research findings and publications that inform the field of secondary DL education. This excellent overview identifies variations in secondary DL programs, DL program outcomes, promising practices from secondary DL around the world, and ways to meet the needs of DL students, teachers, administrators, and parents.

Part II: Implementation Experience and Advice. Part II consists of 10 chapters that describe the specifics of DL implementation at middle and high school level. All of these writers have extensive experience over many years as implementers of secondary DL programs, and the stories they share are deeply felt and passionately expressed. The states where these public school DL programs are located are California, Florida, Illinois, Nebraska, New Mexico, New York, Oregon, and Texas. These accounts come from large and small urban contexts, borderlands, and rural areas, serving diverse students of middle and low socioeconomic backgrounds.

• Chapter 4 by Katy Cattlett and Dr. Rony Ortega chronicles the amazing success of the Omaha Public Schools, Nebraska, secondary DL program.

• Chapter 5 by Dr. Mario Ferrón and Mario Ferrón, Jr., shares the "ups and downs" at the beginning stages of DL program implementation and some of the astounding achievements of DL students in Pharr-San Juan-Alamo Independent School District on the Texas border with Mexico.

• Chapter 6 by Dr. Tom Koulentes details the planning process and first years of implementation of DL at Highland Park High School in the northern suburbs of Chicago, Illinois.

• Chapter 7 by Dr. Victor Vergara chronicles the incredible expansion into districtwide K-12 DL in Woodburn School District, Oregon, with both a Spanish/English and Russian/English program.

• Chapter 8 by Dr. Virginia Elizondo presents the successes and challenges with the expansion of secondary DL in Houston Independent School District, the seventh largest school district in the U.S.

• Chapter 9 by Erin Bostick Mason illustrates the advantages of a whole-school model of DL TK-8, with plans to grow grade by grade into a comprehensive TK-12 DL public school, in her account of Norton Science and Language Academy, located in San Bernardino, California.

• Chapter 10 by Mishelle Jurado, Lisa Harmon-Martínez, and Dr. Antonio Gonzales chronicles the development of the Bilingual Seal along with the DL program in two high schools in Albuquerque Public Schools, New Mexico.

• Chapter 11 by Dr. David Samore tells the story of Okeeheelee School located in the School District of Palm Beach County, Florida.

• Chapter 12 by Mario Benabe provides details of teacher decision making and lesson planning in a DL high school in the Bronx, New York City.

• Chapter 13 by Dr. Michele Anberg-Espinosa wraps-up this section with an overview of challenging DL decision making in large urban contexts, and the importance of addressing equity issues.

Part III: Graduates Speak, Teacher Preparation, and Conclusion. Part III of this book celebrates the promise of the future that is evolving through DL education.

• Chapter 14 authors Elizet Moret and Irán Tovar share their insightful interviews with graduates of secondary DL programs. They asked some DL high school graduates to provide advice for DL educators to guide decision making for development and expansion of DL programs at the secondary level.

• Chapter 15 by Dr. Joan Lachance delves into the complexities of coursework needed to prepare secondary DL teachers.

• Our concluding Chapter 16 (by Drs. Thomas & Collier) discusses the transformation now occurring in U.S. schools with secondary DL expansion, some of the major research findings that inform secondary DL education, the nationwide bilingual seal movement, statewide DL developments, and the amazing promises that secondary DL schooling provides for all our students.

Enjoy ride! Dual language education, when well-implemented, has conclusively demonstrated its power to transform U.S. education. We hope that you will use the strong foundation from dual language research in your own secondary program development. We also hope that you will "go to school" on the advice and experiences of all of these deeply passionate and knowledgeable middle and high school dual language educators who have contributed to this book, so that dual language education can become the general education model for secondary students everywhere!

Chapter Two
Designing Sustainable Secondary Dual Language Programs

Cindy Sizemore—Ysleta Independent School District, El Paso, Texas

Introduction by Collier & Thomas: *This overview chapter is a revealing, deep, and comprehensive journey into the important considerations necessary for secondary dual language implementation. Cindy Sizemore was one of the first dual language leaders in the U.S. to design a comprehensive dual language high school program. She passionately presents important decisions that must be made throughout the planning and maturing stages of a secondary dual language program: what courses should be provided in the partner language, who should be encouraged to enroll in the dual language classes, how to effectively schedule core courses and electives, how to market the program, and the important role that dual language student leadership plays in helping shape the program. We highly recommend reading this chapter carefully for the many rich insights and examples of creative innovations proposed for secondary DL coursework.*

A dual language secondary program, at its most simplistic, is a program at the middle and high school level that uses two languages. But it is so much more complex than that! Dual language education programs are organic, complex entities that form and re-form in a primordial sea of culture, identity, social justice, coming-of-age, language, politics, education, history, adolescence, leadership, advocacy, and multiculturalism. Students and adults enter these waters with different motivations, different perspectives, and different needs. They emerge bilingual, biliterate, and knowing more about themselves and about the world than they did when they entered. Dual language education is a transformative process for all who choose to participate.

In any one chapter, it is impossible to address the many complexities of secondary dual language (DL) education. Here, I will pose questions that focus primarily on grade-level academic achievement and biliteracy development as constructs for developing and implementing successful, viable secondary DL programs. This is not intended to diminish or dismiss the many other equally important components of secondary DL programs. The questions are:

What is dual language at the secondary level?

Who participates in secondary dual language programs?

What are the logistical considerations for a successful secondary DL program?

What is the role of student leadership in secondary DL education?

Full Stop –

Let's address the elephant in the room—Why do we need a different definition and conversation for secondary DL when elementary DL programs have long shown positive outcomes? The simple answer is that secondary school structures are much more complex than those in elementary school, making it necessary to develop a program that not only functions within its complexity, but thrives. While elementary schools tend to be much smaller than secondary schools and are typically organized by homerooms and grade levels, secondary campuses are like a Las Vegas mega buffet; the choices are endless, but in the end, you need to develop a well-balanced plate that meets all of your needs and wants. From the great menu of classes, programs, and activities available in the master schedule, every student needs to develop a personal schedule in which they meet their state-mandated graduation requirements and follow an elective pathway that reflects their individual interests. Students must also determine what level of coursework they want/need, from remedial to advanced, including any courses required for college credit or industry certification. And, they are also expected to join organizations, play sports, participate in fine arts, and explore a variety of opportunities.

Given these complexities, it is necessary to re-think how we organize, define, and manage a secondary DL program so that it meets many diverse student needs and develops near-equal literacy skills in two languages at or above grade level. Programs that limit choices, hinder participation in other groups, teams, or organizations, or that do not provide academic support as well as academic advancement are difficult to maintain. Student choice and student voice must be reflected and heard within the dynamic, complex structure of the DL secondary program.

What Is Dual Language at the Secondary Level?

For the purpose of this chapter and for developing a framework for designing sustainable DL secondary programs, I will work with language outcomes-based definitions, while recognizing that students live, work, learn, and play for many reasons and motivations. A DL program is a program in which two languages are developed across a broad range of academic and social contexts to near-equal abilities in both, across all language domains. My students clarified this definition by saying that, in DL programs, students develop proficiency in both languages so that they are prepared for the educational, career, and life paths of their choice, in both languages, anywhere the language is spoken. Further, DL programs intentionally develop leadership, cultural competence, and advocacy skills.

A DL program is not a transitional bilingual program in which students' native language is developed and used to access academic content until they can access that content in English at a later time, when the native language is minimized or dropped altogether. DL is also not a Spanish for native speakers' program (or any other partner language), housed in the world languages

Figure 2.1

> **Dual Language Secondary Goals (Ysleta ISD)**
>
> - Attain high academic abilities in both the partner language and English at or above grade level,
> - Become fully bilingual and biliterate,
> - Develop multicultural competency,
> - Develop student leadership, and
> - Prepare students for global careers and global citizenship.

department or in collaboration between world languages and bilingual/English as a second language (ESL) departments. Programs organized by world languages or bilingual/ESL departments tend to develop partner-language skills in a narrow academic band, pulling from a language arts and world languages curriculum with performance and literacy goals typically lower than the literacy expectations in English. In summary, the DL program goals for biliteracy are the defining consideration. DL programs have the goal to develop near-equal abilities in both languages throughout all aspects of the school curriculum.

While elementary DL programs are defined by the percentage of time spent in each language, this definition becomes increasingly difficult to maintain in the secondary world that is governed by bell schedules, class changes, electives, and specific course requirements. In secondary DL programs, percentages are replaced with numbers of core, literacy, and elective classes provided at each grade level or grade cluster. In middle school, which can be Grades 6 or 7 through Grade 8 or 9 depending on each school system's structures, the minimum expectation is that students have at least one class each year focused on grade-level language and literacy development in each program language, and a minimum of one, preferably two core content classes in the non-English language annually. More robust programs also provide elective courses in the non-English language. By the end of middle school, the vast majority of core DL students who have attended DL classes since kindergarten should have attained grade-level academic abilities and literacy in both the partner language and English. Students who have not attained grade-level literacy abilities in the non-English language struggle in high school core classes as content-specific academic literacy demands are extremely high.

The minimum expectation at the high school level is that core DL students complete eight yearlong classes (two per year) taught entirely in the non-English language with at least four of these classes coming from the core academic subjects of math, science, social studies and grade-level language arts. Robust electives, internships, and other opportunities are highly recommended. It may seem overly prescriptive to say that at least four courses, preferably more, must come from the core content areas, but this is because there is an expectation of high biliteracy development and at or above grade-level achievement.

This expectation of high biliteracy development and above grade-level achievement was reinforced by my early DL high school students so much that it was incorporated into the requirements for the DL graduation honor seal. A group of my students came to talk to me because they were concerned that a few of the students had acquired their eight classes in the partner language entirely through elective courses in business and art. These students, they pointed out, had a much more limited level of literacy in the partner language that did not meet the expectation of near-equal abilities in both languages. After much conversation about biliteracy and proficiency levels, as well as leadership and program design, the students agreed that there indeed was a difference in proficiency outcomes and that the requirement should be changed for future students. Those who had completed the requirements as stated when they began their high school DL adventure were not affected.

Who Participates in Secondary Dual Language Programs?

Quite simply, DL participants fall into three overly simplified groups: non-English-dominant speakers, speakers of both program languages, and English-dominant students (see Figure 2.2). At the elementary level, these groupings vary from equal distribution of each group to a predominance of one group or another. The distinguishing factor that makes it a DL program is the program goal—the development of high levels of grade-level academic achievement and literacy in both program languages. If there is no expectation to continue developing both languages throughout the educational experience (i.e., the non-English language is dropped at some point), it is more of a transitional bilingual program when viewed from a kindergarten through graduation, systemwide, or district perspective. When this is the case, it is important that both the elementary and secondary campuses have a plan for continuing to support English language development for all student groups. Campus leadership should also take into account students who are entering with high proficiency in the non-English language and find ways to address native-language academic development and refinement through the heritage speaker or world language programs. Most importantly, this group benefits greatly from secondary dual language programs.

Figure 2.2

Intentional Program Intersections

Recent Arrivals	Core Dual Language	Advanced World Languages
*Develop and refine native language abilities across all content areas	*Develop near-equal abilities in both languages across all content areas	*Develop and refine partner language abilities in narrow areas of the curriculum
*Develop English language abilities across all content areas	*Develop near-equal abilities in both languages across all content areas	*Develop English language abilities across all content areas
*ESL and sheltered courses in English *Participate in native-language core classes with core dual language students	*Courses available in core contents and electives in both languages as well as advanced world language classes such as AP/IB	*Participate in advanced world language classes and elective classes in the partner language
	*Goal for transitional bilingual students is to join dual language core with appropriate native-language supports	

terms of program goals, individual student needs, student past-program participation, and student language abilities. It is also important to remember that students do not stay together in the same groupings all day. They change classes and classmates several times during the day, which allows students to participate in DL classes based on their needs while still receiving supports and advancement through other programs and/or classes. The student categories I will speak to are core K-12 DL students, recent arrivals who are speakers of the non-English language, advanced world language students, and students who have participated in transitional bilingual or similar programs at an earlier level. Of course, added to this list, are those serendipitous few who discover the program, demand entry, and succeed. Also, all language learners and speakers live, work, play, and learn in the areas between definitions; individual consideration for DL program participation must always remain an integral part of secondary DL programs.

Students continuing from elementary DL. Core DL students are those students who began the DL program at the elementary level and are continuing to the secondary level. These students are well on their way to becoming balanced bilinguals and are capable of successfully taking classes, core and elective, in either language. Some core DL students may continue to need support or remediation in one or both of the program languages, particularly in the early middle school grades. This is consistent with native English speakers who continue to need support or remediation to gain grade-level English literacy or academic concept mastery and should not be treated as a student or program failure. Research has consistently shown that it takes at least 5 to 7 years to develop academic parity in a second language in a well-implemented DL program (Thomas & Collier, 2017). I must strongly question programs that exit or remove students because they have not become fully grade-level proficient in either of the program languages by a given grade level. This seems to be a decision based on poor understanding of research in language acquisition, pressure for English academic performance, or possibly even political considerations. Students need opportunities at each grade level to develop literacy in both languages, to take core content in both languages, and to explore electives in both languages to the greatest extent possible. DL programs should not be, and were never intended to be, elite programs designed exclusively for high-performing students. On the contrary, DL programs were born of the pains of social justice and a demand for equity in education for English learners.

Recently arrived immigrants. Recent arrivals comprise the next group of students who **should absolutely participate in DL programs because they need literacy development and core-class instruction in their native language, the DL program's non-English language, while they also participate in English as a second language coursework.** With careful master-schedule planning, recent arrivals can and should have access to DL classes as well as ESL/sheltered classes to build a schedule that meets their unique needs. DL participation allows recent arrivals to continue academic development in their native language while learning English. This is essential to their ultimate success in English and to keep up or catch up to grade-level mastery of subjects in their native language. DL classes also give these students access to a bilingual peer group who can quickly help them become an integral part of the school.

Transitional bilingual education students. Students from late-exit transitional or similar bilingual programs are another group of students who should be encouraged to participate in DL programs to the greatest extent possible. These students may be stronger in one language than the other, but have literacy systems developed in both languages at varying levels. Depending on their level of literacy in the program's non-English language, these students may be able to jump right in to core classes and literacy classes in the non-English language, may require additional support, or may be more comfortable participating in non-English electives while building their academic language and literacy skills.

World language students. Advanced world language students are another group to consider for DL program participation. While the stereotypical world language curriculum begins with basic communicative tasks, culture, geography, travel, and familiar topics, advanced students develop high levels of literacy in a language arts curriculum in which they study authors from another country where the partner language is spoken, read authentic texts in the partner language, and engage with partner language speakers at home, through virtual connections, and in-country travel. The trend in world languages is to broaden the curriculum by developing language for specific purposes in courses such as medical terminology, business, technology, theater, and other areas. Some of these courses may lead to industry certifications or even bilingual internships. These electives are appropriate and desirable for a variety of language speakers from all of the groups mentioned – core DL students, recent arrivals, advanced world language students, former bilingual-program students, and serendipitous finds.

How does this mix of student populations work? All of the above begs the question: if DL is defined by outcomes, how can these students with different abilities, needs, and performance trajectories all participate in a DL program? Before I begin to answer that, think about a time when you were in the same place as other people, but you might have had different reasons for being there, differing levels of knowledge about the topic, and different expectations for using the information. For example, imagine you were taking a defensive driving course. You were there to get a discount on your insurance, as were several others in the course. Some, possibly sitting in the back of the room, were there to get a traffic ticket dismissed. Others, who tended to ask complex or unusual questions, were taking the course as one in a series to become a professional driver, and the last group was preparing for their first driver's license. All four groups came to the class with differing abilities, needs, and performance trajectories, yet they were all able to successfully complete the course. The diversity in the classroom provided a richness to the learning that can only be found when differences are embraced, heard, and reflected upon. The opportunity to serve the needs of diverse student groups with differing abilities, goals, and perspectives is best accomplished when the secondary master schedule is built around student needs and intentional program intersections.

What Are the Logistical Considerations for a Successful Secondary Dual Language Program?

Building a successful secondary DL program boils down to logistical considerations as campuses get larger and graduation plans become more constrained. Before beginning to develop your school's course options, you must review what is required and what is optional for students on your campus. What courses are required for graduation? Are there a variety of graduation plans and endorsements? As you learn the graduation plan, think about logical classes to be taught in the program's partner language. Keep in mind that the goal is to develop depth and breadth of language abilities across the spectrum of academic subjects and electives. Plan so that partner language literacy options are available at every level and that a few courses in each subject area are offered in the program languages across the middle school years and the 4 years of high school. **Try to avoid concentrating several years of a core subject in the same language; give students the opportunity to develop discipline-specific academic language and confidence in both languages.** You don't want students to have content-specific language and literacy in one language and have to use circumlocution or lower level vocabulary to get through the subject in the other language. As students have repeatedly reminded me, the goal is to develop near-equal abilities in both languages so they can choose their own path and be equally successful in either language anywhere it is spoken.

DL courses are taught in the partner language. It is important to remember that all the courses currently offered on your campus in English are available to all your DL students. The classes that you need to develop are those courses taught in the non-English language. This may be a paradigm shift in thinking for some; however, it is important to understand. The DL program coordinator is not responsible and certainly not in control of the curriculum delivered in English, except possibly with the exception of English as a second language and sheltered-content classes. The DL students can choose from everything that interests them (each program, magnet strand, sport, fine art, business class, etc.) that their hearts desire and their developing brains need. The "DL classes" are those classes that are taught in the non-English language and available to DL core students as well as other students for whom these classes are beneficial, especially newly arriving immigrants. The DL designation of the course is meant to indicate that the course is taught in the partner language.

DL core courses required for graduation. This means that when selecting coursework to teach in the partner language, consider first the classes that are within the graduation plan that many students will need to take. Do not offer a significant number of courses outside the graduation plan; students don't have room in their schedule for this and will be forced to choose. When selecting core classes to offer in the partner language, look at how many credits/courses are required in that subject, whether the classes are offered at the regular and honors/AP/IB level, and at what grade levels the students are tested for state accountability. If a particular course requires a 4-year sequence, could you offer two of those four courses in the non-English language?

If your administration, central office, or community are concerned (unnecessarily) that if the course is not taught in English test scores will fall, then look at the courses and years that the subject is not tested to offer in the partner language. Consider the language of the discipline. Is it possible to offer the course in the partner language and then have students read primary sources in the original language? For example, many states require four courses in social studies and have some sort of state exam that covers American history. Consider offering that class in English and reading the primary source documents in English. What if another course requirement is world history or Latin American history? Could Chicano studies fulfill a social studies requirement? Offer that course in Spanish and have the students read primary-source documents in Spanish. Would one of these classes be a good companion class or prerequisite for Spanish literature?

Meet with your world languages department and see how you can work together to support one another. What does the state require in science and in math? What makes the most sense programmatically and pragmatically to offer in the non-English language? How do you register enough students to offer a class and meet student needs along with graduation plans?

Balancing DL courses for each grade level and subject. When answering these questions, think also about the grade level at which these courses are offered and spread them out so that the DL student has the opportunity to take some core classes in the partner language and some in English every year. Learn what courses are prescribed and which allow some choice. For example, one district required 4 years of science courses. Three of the science courses were prescribed; the fourth allowed for some choice. One of the choices was a course entitled Scientific Research and Design within which students learned how to develop high-level year-long scientific research projects following their interests. The district chose to offer this course in the partner language because students who were interested in different aspects of science could come together in this section and study their chosen topic and be in the same class as students with other interests. This course and the resulting research also fulfilled the requirement for a capstone project and entry into various science competitions with scholarship money as prizes. The demand for this class was high and appealed to many students, which in turn resulted in strong enrollment and excellent language development, with the class becoming a consistent DL offering and a highlight of the high school's advanced curriculum.

Electives. It is highly unlikely that your core DL students will travel together throughout the day. They have their own interests and these will necessarily separate them throughout much of the school day. DL students come together in partner-language classes that meet their needs. When developing electives, follow graduation plans and student interests. Many states require that students take an elective in fine arts, technology, or speech. These courses are typically without prerequisites and are open to students at all grade levels, allowing you to pull from a larger pool of students. At the secondary level, class offerings are all about derrières in chairs—a certain number of students is required for a class to make; below that number, a class may be closed. When offering theater, computer information systems, or professional communication in the partner language, students are getting double benefit for their efforts; the class satisfies a graduation requirement and a DL course option. The program is also getting more bang for the buck by being able to offer elective opportunities that attract students from more grade levels. More student groups ensure higher enrollment while providing more choice for students to follow their interests.

DL summer opportunities. Another possibility is to offer specialized courses in the summer and open them up to more than one school so that students have unique opportunities. Thus, programs that are not yet large enough to support electives have new options for their students. Summer programs also lend themselves to community partnerships, performance classes, service learning, and other types of more innovative learning opportunities. Students can partner with a local theater company and produce a play in the partner language; work with a local non-profit to create marketing materials in the partner language to help reach non-English-speaking customers; serve as bilingual docents at the zoo, children's history, or art museum, learning about a feature at the zoo or museum, improving communicative abilities, and providing a service to non-English-speaking visitors; partner with a community-based organization, learning about the impact of poverty on the elderly and designing a project to provide a service—home repair, meal delivery, or other service.

The only limitation is the imagination of your students and DL program guides. Make it real; make it have an impact; make it bilingual. It is all about student choice and student voice—bilingual voices that reach twice as far and cannot be ignored. When bilingual and DL education was under fire in my district, a mentor told me, "Be so good that they simply cannot ignore your students and the positive, transformative impact of DL education." Our students' actions and accomplishments continue to resonate much louder than our words.

DL career and technology courses. When a student has attained near-equal abilities in both the program language and English, we must carefully consider how bilingual abilities become a true asset for the student. In the real world, one great value of bilingualism is the ability to interpret and/or translate languages to facilitate comprehension between people with different language backgrounds. How can we bring this skill into the classroom in an authentic way? The logical answer is in courses where there is an authentic need to move between languages to complete a real-world task. Career and technology programs are recommended for bilingual and biliterate students, including language development for specific purposes such as medical terminology or languages for educators/law enforcement/business, etc. These classes are excellent opportunities for DL students, alongside advanced world language and ESL students, to develop career-specific language, increase employability skills, and possibly attain bilingual industry certifications or college credits. Additionally, internships in student-interest areas can be used to refine language skills and develop real-world skills. Many schools already have half-day internships in place that can be developed into bilingual internships and mentorships where students learn how to use both languages effectively in the workplace, following their own career interests.

Master scheduling. All the planning and innovative course development in the world is worthless if you cannot get students into the classes. Scheduling conflicts can kill a program quickly. Who is teaching what, where, and at the same time as what other courses? The magic is in the master. How is the master schedule developed? What classes get priority; how many students requested a particular class? Will there be one, two, or three sections? Are there enough students at varying levels to offer both regular and advanced sections? How many teachers are available to teach that particular class? What other classes do they also teach? To all DL advocates: make yourself knowledgeable about master scheduling! You must know which classes and programs are the greatest competitors with DL classes. Can you develop a partnership? Change the scheduling options? How can students get the best of both worlds, their dream activity, class, or program, and at the same time continue DL participation? Develop a relationship with the administrators, counselors, and the person in charge of master scheduling; become an indispensable part of the scheduling team. These positions can facilitate program growth or contribute to program death, depending on the degree to which DL students' interests and goals can be met in the master schedule.

Marketing your secondary DL program. A unique characteristic of the DL program is that it does not have a predictable course plan beyond the classes that are taken in the non-English language. Unlike a magnet program or career pathway where students are grouped together and take the same or similar classes by grade level, a DL student can follow any graduation plan and take coursework taught in the non-English language. The reason for this is that DL is not a career interest, an academic focus, or a fine-arts strand. Many students entered the DL program at the elementary level and have continued through to middle and high school. As they have grown and matured, they have developed their own unique interests, talents, and needs, and deserve the opportunity to pursue them without giving up the DL program. Biliteracy and multiculturalism are the medium through which instruction is received in any and every area in which a student has an interest. Students are chasing their futures, developing their interests in two or more languages and preparing to take their place in the world in the area of their choice; they are not just "learning a language." DL is so much more than just language learning. It is life, heritage, culture, opportunity, access, justice, empowerment, voice and, and, and ...

When planning or revamping your program, it is important to think about the developmental stages of the students entering the program. They are early adolescents who are getting their first opportunity to select classes and exert their independence from adults. They aren't in elementary school anymore and many of them don't want to continue a program that they may see as a connection to elementary school. How do you make your program attractive to adolescents ... to their parents? Some parents may move their children to an all-English program believing that it's time to buckle down and get focused on English. Some don't want to fight the battle for biliteracy or understand its value. What is the perceived payoff for the students if they continue in the DL program? Is it AP classes and college credits?

DL students must have a strong DL program that includes literacy intervention for those students who need it in either language, as well as advancement for those who are performing above grade-level expectations. Students cannot and should not be forced to choose between participation in a coveted magnet program and the DL program; between their musical passion and the DL program; between an international baccalaureate and the DL program; between anything and the DL program. The DL student is unique, even more so than the monolingual student, and should not have his/her options limited because of program participation. An effective master schedule based on students' needs and requests is an elusive, tedious, difficult, work-intensive masterpiece, but it is a challenge worth accepting. Our students are worth it!

DL secondary program leadership. There is great complexity developing DL programs in secondary schools where core DL and other students can and should have access are in virtually every program and strand on campus. Therefore, it is critical that there is a person or team who can unite the students and the DL faculty and help them to develop an identity and a presence on campus within student activities and within the leadership structures of the school. That person or team needs to be passionate about educating students in more than one language; be adept at uniting teachers from different departments and viewpoints; understand graduation plans, special programs, and master scheduling; be able to develop relationships with diverse student populations; and market and recruit students to continue in the DL program. Obviously, this person will need help in accomplishing all of these tasks, and the best place to look is to the students themselves.

What Is the Role of Student Leadership in Secondary Dual Language Programs?

Leadership skills multiply with language skills

> As we globalize and work across more countries, more significant than knowing a second or third language, there is a rising need for people skilled in understanding context that stems from how people speak or interact. This goes beyond issues of inclusiveness and having a culturally diverse workforce. It is much more an issue of leadership in being about to comprehend and hold different perspectives readily and why people may think in different ways. (Shah, 2014)

Student advocacy. Advocacy is a critical part of DL programs. Those involved in the program must often fight to get it established, to gain adequate funding, to find teachers, to continue it to the next grade level, and to demand that it continue to the next grade cluster or that it continue at all. These advocates are typically adults—those with children in the program and those who work in the programs alongside educational and political groups that support bilingual education. While adult advocacy is crucial to DL success, students must also assume this role as they move into secondary school and "opt-in" to DL programs. Students who began the program in early elementary have never known a monolingual education and may not fully understand the unique opportunity that they have through their bilingualism. As DL advocates, parents, and educators, it is crucial that we help our young students understand that education is an opt-in process and that there is choice at every level—in coursework, focus, and interests. Students who understand this can voice their choice and demand the educational setting and opportunity that they want. Those who don't choose get the leftovers, the classes with open seats, the less-requested pathways, the more generic options.

One way to help students see the opportunities in DL is to have older DL students recruit, mentor, and guide younger students to continue in the program. Adolescents often are more receptive to their peers than they are to adults. This is also an initial step to developing student leadership. In deciding how they are going to approach students to enroll in the next level, students need to reflect and learn about the program they are in. Why are they in DL and what is it that keeps them there? Students can create promotional materials, interview other students and staff, present at pre-registration meetings, to the faculty, or even a conference. What is DL and why should it continue?

Student advisory board. As students learn about the program and why they are there, the next natural question is, "How can it be better?" This is an excellent place for the development of a student advisory board, a student-leadership class or club, and an opportunity for the DL coordinator or teacher to work with students on moving from program planning to implementation of their suggested improvements. As my own DL advisory board took shape, it was student voice that led us in directions that we had not imagined. Some of the early conversation centered around complaints and concerns. As the sounding board and adult guide, I helped my students move from complaining to advocating to proposing solutions. Students' main concern was about availability of classes and classes that were initially scheduled and then got cancelled due to low student requests—the infamous derrières in chairs requirement. When students understood that a class had to have a certain number of students in order to make, they challenged the principal—if they could get the required enrollment, would he re-open the class? They recruited students and he honored the agreement. This is student advocacy and responsibility at its finest. As they prioritized their issues and determined how they wanted to proceed, we had meetings with administrators and counselors and came to agreements that met the needs of both the campus and the DL students. As other students saw what was happening, many who had dropped out of the DL program came back, others appeared and asked to join, more students signed up from the middle school to continue, and we, as a student-faculty team, found ways to open DL classes to students we hadn't thought of before, including former late-exit bilingual students, advanced world language students, recent arrivals, and others. Faculty agreed to join the DL program and offer their class in Spanish; students were recruited and enrolled with the agreement that the DL advisory board would tutor and support those whose language was a little rusty so that they could be successful in the new classes. The program expanded from primarily core-class offerings to the addition of electives in art, technology, and business based on student requests and faculty availability. The DL student advisory board was born and the students grew by leaps and bounds in their understanding of advocacy, of the power and beauty of DL, and in their confidence in themselves individually and as a team.

In conclusion, it is important to keep in mind that a DL program is organic and changes as it grows, as the number of participants expands and as the program develops its niche on a campus, within a feeder pattern, in a district, a state, and in our country. At its most simplistic, DL secondary programs continuously develop and monitor literacy and oracy in both languages; intentionally develop language and literacy during all classes; cultivate students' perception of biliteracy as an asset; and foster student leadership skills. As we work with dual language programs, we must be open to change, to student needs, and be unabashedly unafraid of rocking the educational status quo in order to provide our students and our communities the educational opportunities that they deserve.

Chapter Three
The Rationale for Secondary Dual Language Schooling

Jeremy Aldrich—Harrisonburg City Public Schools, Virginia

Introduction by Collier & Thomas: *This overview chapter provides a rich and detailed review of research findings and publications that focus on secondary dual language education. While these programs are relatively new within the U.S., the issues that secondary educators face have solutions when looking at worldwide patterns for schooling in multilingual contexts. Jeremy Aldrich takes us on a wide-ranging tour through some of the major questions that recent research is beginning to address: differences between elementary and secondary dual language, as well as established language programs in secondary; secondary dual language program outcomes; promising practices from dual language programs around the world; and meeting the needs of all stakeholders participating in dual language education—students, teachers, administrators, and parents.*

The Dual Language Schools Directory lists hundreds of middle and high schools in the United States with dual language programs, and the number is growing every year *(http://www.duallanguageschools.org)*. School leaders need solid information to design effective programs and avoid some of the most common pitfalls. This chapter examines what research literature has to say about dual language programs at the middle and high school levels, and how research in related fields might enrich the future direction of these programs.

In dual language (DL) programs, students receive a significant percentage of their core academic instruction in a language other than English, which is often referred to as the "partner" language (Thomas & Collier, 2012). The first DL school in modern U.S. history was Coral Way Elementary in Miami, where in 1963 a group of Cuban-American parents found a way for their children to maintain their home language (Spanish) while learning English (Freeman, Freeman, & Mercuri,

2005). The early success of Coral Way and other pioneering schools paved the way for the 1968 Bilingual Education Act, federal legislation which provided support for a variety of bilingual approaches to educate English learners (Baker & Wright, 2017; England, 2009). Some bilingual programs were more effective than others; in general, programs which emphasized subtractive bilingualism (that is, those programs which aimed to transition to English-only education as quickly as possible while subtracting the other language) were less successful than programs which emphasized additive bilingualism (maintaining both languages and valuing bilingualism as an asset; de Jong & Howard, 2009).

Today, there are a number of flavors of DL programs in the United States and Canada, including two-way dual language (mixing heritage speakers of English and the partner language), one-way immersion or world language immersion (for heritage speakers of English to learn the partner language), developmental bilingual or one-way dual language (for linguistically and culturally diverse learners to preserve and reach high levels of proficiency in their mother tongue and English), and Indigenous programs focused on native language revitalization for Native American groups (Fortune & Tedick, 2008; Thomas & Collier, 2012). Each of these flavors of DL has specific associated practices and the field of DL research in the United States has coalesced around three main camps.

One camp, centered around Dual Language Education of New Mexico (DLeNM) and its annual La Cosecha conference, focuses primarily on two-way and one-way DL, as well as native language revitalization for Native American groups. DLeNM prefaces its mission by noting that "Four decades of research provide a road map for developing a multilingual, multicultural citizenry" *(dlenm.org)*. A second camp, centered around the Center for Advanced Research on Language Acquisition (CARLA) at the University of Minnesota and its biennial Conference on Immersion and Dual Language Education, tends to focus on one-way immersion for native English speakers. This focus emerges from CARLA's role as a federally funded National Language Resource Center, "whose role is to improve the nation's capacity to teach and learn foreign languages effectively" (CARLA, *carla@umn.edu)*. And the third camp, centered around the National Association for Bilingual Education (NABE, *nabe.org)* and its annual conference, has a special focus on transitional and developmental bilingual programs for English learners, as well as one-way and two-way DL. The lines between these camps are not totally rigid; some conference presentations and journal articles within each camp address other flavors of DL. Each camp stands to gain from the knowledge and research presented elsewhere, but special attention should be given to how each camp uses terminology like "bilingual education," "immersion," and even "dual language;" what is seen as a positive or neutral word in one camp may carry negative overtones in another. For the purposes of this chapter, research dealing with any of the flavors of DL, as well as research dealing with related themes, is included.

Typically, DL programs in the United States continue only until the end of the elementary grades (de Jong & Bearse, 2011). However, a small but growing number of DL programs are choosing to extend into the middle and high school years. The non-negotiables stated in DLeNM guidelines include the expectation that a school district will commit to developing the DL program for Grades PK-12 (Thomas & Collier, 2012, p. 32). It is striking that although many states encourage the continuation of DL programs beyond the elementary level, only a few offer logistical support or professional development for actually doing so (U.S. Department of Education, 2015). This chapter looks at existing research, much of which has emerged in the last decade, and addresses some of the prevalent questions about extended DL programs.

- How are DL programs at the secondary level different from traditional world language classes and programs for heritage speakers? How are they different from elementary DL programs?

- What academic, social-emotional, and other outcomes can be expected from DL programs that extend beyond the elementary level?

- What are some promising practices emerging from programs around the world?

- How can school leaders plan to meet the needs of all stakeholders and navigate common challenges for secondary DL programs?

Distinctives of Secondary Dual Language Programs

In the United States, a typical student's school experience with a language other than English, if it happens at all, begins in middle or high school. Students complete two to four levels of courses in a target language (formerly called a "foreign language") like Spanish, French, German, or Latin which might culminate in an Advanced Placement course for possible college credit, but generally language education takes a back seat to other "core" subjects and graduation requirements (Brecht et al., 2013; O'Rourke, Zhou, & Rottman, 2016). Traditionally, the focus in world language programs is learning about the target language and associated cultures. In DL programs, on the other hand, students learn through the partner language with courses designed to combine content and language acquisition as students study typical school subjects like math, science, social studies, fine arts, and so on. Students who have been part of DL programs since elementary school will likely have a high level of skill in the partner language that makes traditional world language course offerings inappropriate for them (U.S. Department of Education, 2015). For example, some DL secondary programs offer Advanced Placement (AP) college-level Spanish language in the eighth or ninth grade rather than viewing it as a culminating course at the end of high school, but continue to offer other language and content courses in the partner language during the high school years (González Ornelas & Ornelas, 2014; U.S. Department of Education, 2015).

For educators familiar with DL programs at the elementary level, some of the typical practices in middle and high school DL programs might be surprising. Some of these practices are based on the changing academic and social needs of adolescents, while other changes are the result of necessary concessions to the patterns of middle and high school staffing and scheduling. As C. Sizemore (2014) points out, secondary school structures are inherently different from elementary school structures, and those elementary structures cannot simply be imposed or transferred to the secondary level. Unlike elementary programs which are designed for 50-90% of the day to be in the partner language, secondary DL programs usually offer students the chance to continue taking around 25% of their overall course load in the partner language (de Jong & Bearse, 2011). Implications of this diminished role for the partner language are discussed later in this chapter. Program designs vary greatly but typically include at least one core content course (math, science, or social studies) taught in the partner language each year as well as a course focused on language or literature in the partner language (U.S. Department of Education, 2015). It should be emphasized here that the two courses each semester in the partner language requirement is a bare minimum for whether a secondary program can really be considered a DL program; schools can and should strive to offer more options for students in the partner language (see Chapter 2).

An emerging trend within world language programs is to offer a special track for "heritage speakers," who are typically defined as linguistically and culturally diverse students exposed to a non-English language through their home or community, and who may have some limited receptive or productive abilities but who have not received prior formal education in the language. Heritage speaker programs, like other world language programs in the United States, most commonly begin at the secondary level (Leeman, 2015). Often, the focus is on developing literacy skills and exploring issues of identity. However, heritage speaker programs often struggle with a lack of materials and teacher preparation which diminish their potential positive impact on linguistically and culturally diverse students (Faltis & Ramírez-Marín, 2015). DL students in high school who have been a part of elementary and middle school DL classes typically have already developed advanced literacy skills in both languages, and they need core content classes taught in the partner language, so school leaders should thoughtfully plan how to address the needs of both the DL and heritage speaker students.

Dual Language Program Outcomes

Previous research focused on the long-term academic impacts of DL programs that stop at the end of elementary school, examining outcomes such as performance on English reading and math assessments and reclassification out of English learner status (Thomas & Collier, 2012). If there are additional benefits to be gained from extending DL programs into middle and high school, what might those benefits be? Current research literature suggests several positive outcomes from giving students more years of DL education.

- Cognitive benefits related to high levels of bilingualism
- Increased proficiency in the partner language
- Higher levels of cultural competence and related social/emotional skills
- Stronger sense of positive ethnic identity for linguistically and culturally diverse students
- Augmented sense of school satisfaction
- Lower dropout rate and higher graduation rate

Before digging into each of these areas, let us pause for a moment to consider what happens when DL programs stop at the end of elementary school. Opportunities to use the partner language for academic purposes dwindle in an English-dominant secondary school environment. Consequently, functional language skills in the partner language stagnate at an elementary school level or, worse, disappear entirely. As the saying goes, "If you don't use it, you lose it." English learners who have made great progress in English to reach the mainstream of academic achievement lose their daily contact with high-achieving English-speaking peers and consequently lose access to a great network of cultural capital. The language and culture of the linguistically and culturally diverse students goes from the status of celebrated (in DL programs) to marginalized (in mainstream English-dominant programs), resulting in disengagement from school. Although there are many logistical challenges to continuing DL into middle and high school years, the alternative is grim, particularly for linguistically and culturally diverse students who benefit so much from well-implemented DL programs. Indeed, de Jong (2011) argues that program evaluations which consider only a narrow set of positive outcomes (such as judging the value of a DL program solely based on the impact it has on English reading and math scores) miss the point. While these measures are considered policy-relevant, they are not advocacy-based. There needs to be a shift towards a focus on the features of programs that actually help or hurt students.

Cognitive benefits of bilingualism. In their landmark longitudinal studies, Thomas and Collier (2012) have demonstrated that English learners in two-way DL programs completely close the achievement gap in English reading, averaging at the 62nd normal curve equivalent (71st percentile) on standardized English reading tests by the end of sixth grade. In another recent study involving more than 1,100 students attending two-way and one-way DL programs in Portland (Oregon) Public Schools, Steele et al. (2017) found significant academic gains for students in DL. The reading performance of eighth grade students in DL was 7 to 9 months higher than a control group, and the English learner reclassification rate was also higher among students in DL. There was no observable difference in math or science performance, but even that finding is significant since students had received some or all of their instruction in math and science in the partner language, and yet student achievement on English-language tests of those areas was not negatively impacted (Steele et al., 2017).

Thomas and Collier (2012) have hypothesized that these kinds of academic gains are largely due to cognitive benefits of bilingualism and biliteracy, as well as receiving cognitively demanding instruction for a large part of the day. Some of the specific cognitive benefits of bilingualism include:

- Increased ability to filter out distracting information (Marian & Shook, 2012)

- Faster switching between different kinds of mental tasks (Bialystok & Craik, 2010)

- Quickly noticing and responding to new information (Nicolay & Poncelet, 2015)

- Greater creativity when solving problems (Leikin, 2013)

- Delaying age-related cognitive decline and dementia (Perani & Abutalebi, 2015)

Of course, cognitive development is affected by many factors and thus it would be overly simplistic to say that bilingualism is some kind of magic pill that makes a brain function maximally. Rather, it seems that bilingualism is more like a piece of workout equipment. If it is used, it can make the brain stronger and healthier than it would be otherwise. This analogy helps explain the answer to an obvious question: wouldn't students in DL have already developed enough bilingualism during their elementary years to reap the cognitive benefits? Evidence like the Thomas and Collier (2012, 2014) studies suggest that yes, there are ongoing cognitive benefits in adolescence from having "worked out" the brain in prior schooling. How much greater might those benefits be if rather than putting bilingual skills in the corner like a forgotten stationary bike, adolescents continued to work out their brains by using their bilingual skills throughout their schooling?

Indeed, a number of studies that show cognitive benefits for bilingualism relate longer term use of both languages to higher levels of cognitive benefit (Perani & Abutalebi, 2015; Zied et al., 2004). Further, the benefits of bilingualism are almost certainly subject to sustaining a minimal level of proficiency; this concept is referred to as the "threshold hypothesis" (Cummins, 1979; De Cat, Gusnanto, & Serratrice, 2017; de Jong, 2011). As an extreme example, simply knowing how to say hello and count to 10 in another language would not be a sufficient level of bilingualism to accrue its cognitive benefits. A high school student or adult who had a long-forgotten DL education as a young child but who had not had meaningful opportunities to use their bilingualism could be in danger of slipping below the necessary threshold of proficiency to accrue cognitive benefits. In summary, the mental workout of bilingualism leads to a number of positive benefits for brain health and function. DL programs which continue into the secondary level offer an opportunity for students to keep developing into deeper cognitive levels throughout adolescence and into adulthood.

Partner-language proficiency. Logically, one expected benefit from extending DL programs through high school would be a higher level of proficiency in the partner (non-English) language, since the students would be using that language more frequently and at a higher cognitive level than in a typical monolingual school environment. Secondary DL programs are preparing students to use their bilingualism as adults in the workplace, ultimately requiring a very high proficiency level in both languages.

Some research conducted in one-way immersion programs for native English speakers suggests a possible "plateau effect" on language proficiency, without the benefits of being schooled with partner-language peers in a two-way DL program. It seems that native English speakers in one-way programs can get stuck at a particular proficiency level at the end of elementary school and may stay there until the end of middle school. Fortune and Tedick (2015) examined teacher perceptions of student language proficiency for 248 students in four Spanish one-way immersion programs. They found that although teachers reported the students' Spanish proficiency grew between kindergarten and Grade 2, as well as between Grades 2 and 5, growth was stagnant between Grades 5 and 8 in the areas of oral fluency, grammar, vocabulary, and listening comprehension (Fortune & Tedick, 2015). However, the study's reliance on teacher perceptions may have led to a significant lack of interrater reliability; the middle school teachers may well have been scoring students more harshly than the elementary school teachers even though the students' skills had actually grown. Additionally, there were only a small number of students (24) in the oldest cohort in Grade 8.

Another recent study using an external assessment of partner language proficiency (the Standards-based Measurement of Proficiency [STAMP] test) with a larger number of students found continued growth in the partner language throughout middle and high school immersion programs (including a variety of different program models). The research only considered the scores of students who did not speak the partner language at home, and found that additional time in an immersion program had a positive correlation with the percentage of students scoring level 5 or higher in reading, writing, and speaking, although reading performance lagged behind other skills (Center for Applied Second Language Studies, 2013). The study also compared immersion students to students in the fourth year of a traditional high school program, and found that immersion students outperformed high school world language students in reading by Grade 8, and in speaking by Grade 6. This further illustrates why simply placing DL students into the upper levels of traditional world language courses would not meet the needs of those students.

In another recent study, also using the STAMP test as a measurement instrument, students in Portland's DL programs were tested between Grades 3-8 (for Spanish, between Grades 4-8). The year-by-year change rates varied by language skill, and listening skills seemed to show little movement for each of the groups. Overall, students in Spanish DL programs on average scored in the intermediate mid to high range by eighth grade, while students in Japanese programs scored intermediate low to mid, and students in Chinese programs remained novice high in reading while achieving intermediate mid to high scores on listening, speaking, and writing (Burkhauser et al., 2016).

Taken together, these findings suggest that periodic assessment in the partner language should be included in the program design of middle and high school DL programs, and the assessments used should be reliable and valid. Regular assessment of the partner language communicates that growth in language proficiency is an important goal of the program (Fortune & Tedick, 2015). However, these kinds of tests should not become yet another high-stakes stressor for teachers and students. As García, Johnson, and Seltzer (2017, p. 26) point out, "All bilinguals are emergent bilinguals in some aspect or another, in certain situations and with different interlocutors. Students' linguistic performances shift ... and cannot simply be captured by a one-time proficiency score."

Cultural competence. Cultural competence is often cited as the third goal of DL programs (alongside bilingualism/biliteracy and grade-level academic performance), but Feinauer and Howard (2014) point out that there is a lack of consensus on what this goal means, and even what it is called (other terms used include: positive cross-cultural attitudes and behaviors, biculturalism, cross-cultural awareness, and cross-cultural understanding). At a basic level, to develop cultural competence students must have the opportunity to experience multiple viewpoints and practices and must also reflect on their own cultural identity against contrasting backdrops. As Allport (1979, p. 486) wrote, "No person knows his own culture who knows only his own culture." DL programs, through their topics of study, student composition, and program design, can foster a rich sense of linguistic and cultural pluralism that is often lacking in monolingual school settings. In a qualitative study of 48 high school DL students' attitudes and perceptions, de Jong and Bearse (2011) found that students believed they were both bilingual and bicultural, although Anglo students were more likely to describe themselves as "culturally aware" than bicultural.

Paris (2012, p. 95) has suggested that schools develop "culturally sustaining pedagogies [which] support young people in sustaining the cultural and linguistic competence of their communities while simultaneously offering access to dominant cultural competence." Through lived experiences in bilingual communities in and out of school, DL programs that extend into middle and high school offer the possibility of expanding students' cultural horizons in ways that monolingual school environments cannot (Pilotti, Gutiérrez, Klein, & Mahamame, 2015). But this will not happen automatically. Program leaders must design intentional opportunities for promoting cross-cultural contact followed up by critical reflection (Feinauer & Howard, 2014; Walton, Paradies, Priest, Wertheim, & Freeman, 2015).

Positive sense of identity. One of the defining characteristics of adolescence (the age of most middle and high school students) is developing a sense of one's own identity as a person (Feinauer & Howard, 2014). The normal trajectory for heritage speakers of minority languages in the United States, unfortunately, is to lose contact with their family's language and culture over time (Geerlings, Verkuyten, & Thijs, 2015). At the same time, adolescents in a society with social stigma attached to ethnic identities struggle to figure out just what their ethnic identity is and what it implies for their range of possibilities in life. DL programs at the secondary level can contribute to a positive self-identity, both culturally and academically, particularly for language minority students.

The negative impact of "stereotype threat" has been well documented for many types of identities and many types of tasks (Spencer, Logel, & Davies, 2016). Essentially, the idea of stereotype threat is that when you feel you are part of a group that is not expected to do well on a particular kind of task, your performance on that task is disrupted (Steele & Aronson, 1995). In school, the cultural habits of students from the dominant culture and the English language itself are privileged in many subtle and not-so-subtle ways (Tedick & Wesely, 2015). Short-term interventions, like self-affirmation writing activities, which are designed to counter the negative impact of stereotype threat are appealing, but may not have much effect (Dee, 2015). DL programs at the middle and high school level, on the other hand, can intentionally foster a positive sense of identity and fight against harmful stereotypes (Feinauer & Howard, 2014; Tedick & Wesely, 2015).

Zarate, Bhimji, and Reese (2005) posit that a strong bicultural identity leads to higher academic achievement among language minority students. They conducted individual interviews with a large group of Latino students (who had not been in DL programs) in the Los Angeles metropolitan area and asked them to choose which identities they felt best described themselves from a long list of possibilities. Then they interviewed students about why they selected or rejected each label. The adolescents on average selected three different ethnic labels. Although 75% of the participants were born in the United States, only 35% chose the label "American." Students often described their choices based on their parents' nationality or their own place of birth. The label "Latino" was more associated with speaking Spanish, while "Chicano" was described as implying limited Spanish skills. Half of the students rejected the label "Hispanic" as an imposed term. The labels which indicated a sense of bicultural identity that included the dominant culture (such as Mexican American, Chicano, and American) had a moderate correlation with academic achievement, as measured by future college plans and prior middle school scores and teacher ratings (Zarate, Bhimji, & Reese, 2005). In another study, a strong sense of positive ethnic identity appeared to be a buffer against the negative effects of low school connectedness when looking at reading test results (Santos & Collins, 2016). DL programs at the middle and high school may wish to explicitly explore ethnic labels and bicultural identities, both for Latino students and others. There are many possible content areas with relation to the theme of identity, particularly literature, social studies, and fine arts, although even math (census sampling) and science (genetics) may have overlap with this important theme.

In discussions about a positive sense of ethnic self-identity, an adolescent's proficiency in their heritage language also plays a role. A synthesis of available studies across many different ethnic groups indicates that there is a small to medium positive correlation between ethnic identity and heritage-language proficiency (Mu, 2015). But the natural trend in an English-dominant school setting is for adolescents to grow to prefer English over their heritage language (Geerlings, Verkuyten, & Thijs, 2015). This contributes to a decline in a sense of positive ethnic self-identity, as language barriers harm family connections and make it more difficult for parents and other family members to transmit their ethnic values (Mu, 2015).

In summary, the development of positive ethnic self-identity is an ongoing and complicated process (Zarate, Bhimji, & Reese, 2005). DL programs seeking to cultivate a positive sense of ethnic identity must attend to more than just language proficiency. At the same time, the increased language proficiency afforded by long-term DL programs could be reasonably expected to contribute to ethnic identity in ways that elementary-exit programs cannot. Additionally, through affirming the value of ethnic identities, providing positive role models in the curriculum, opening new opportunities for family engagement, and cultivating a sense of school connectedness (feeling safe, included, and cared for), DL programs at the middle and high school level can make significant contributions to students' positive sense of identity.

School satisfaction and completion. Why do students drop out of high school? Research has identified three major categories of causes: students are "pushed out" by consequences for their academic and non-academic behaviors (such as poor grades, attendance, and discipline issues), they are "pulled out" by life circumstances such as needing to work or to support a family, or they "fall out" because of apathy and general dissatisfaction with school (Doll, Eslami, & Walters, 2013). Secondary DL programs can have an impact on each of these areas.

A promising model for avoiding the "push out" factors is found in Nebraska, where the Omaha South High Magnet School's DL program offers a challenging and supportive college preparatory environment (Omaha Public Schools, 2016; see Chapter 4). Each student is required to participate in a formal meeting annually to discuss his/her progress and goals. DL students also take part in a same-grade advisory period weekly. Staff monitor student academic progress through teacher team meetings and regular progress reports that are reviewed biweekly. Students who are falling behind are required to participate in tutoring during their lunch time, which is one of the expectations laid out in a dual language contract that students and parents must sign to join the program. Other stipulations include a commitment to avoid illegal behavior, that parents participate twice a year in conferences and provide a working phone number to the school for ongoing communications, and that each student fill out at least three scholarship applications and at least three college applications during their time in the program. In addition to in-school help for completing those applications, a Saturday program is offered with the support of community volunteers. The introduction of this scholarship help in 2011 resulted in a dramatic increase in college scholarships offered to students in the DL program. Starting in their junior year, DL students may also participate in an Education Academy which includes two college-credit courses in the field of education. The Education Academy is part of the division's effort to recruit more bilingual teachers for the future (Ortega, 2014). Taken together, this network of supports and high expectations pulls students toward graduation and postsecondary success rather than pushing them out of high school early.

Many of the life circumstances that lead to students feeling "pulled out" of high school because of pregnancy/parenting or the perceived need to work are not within the direct control of school leaders. However, schools can have an influence. Research suggests that a positive ethnic identity (as discussed earlier) correlates with a reduction in risky sexual behaviors, although mixed results have been reported for Latino youth (Rivas-Drake et al., 2014). Latino youth and parents report that some of the protective factors against risky sexual behaviors include academic achievement, having life goals, and having access to information that students and parents can understand (Bosma, Orozco, Barriga, Rosas-Lee, & Sieving, 2017). For students who feel pulled out of school by the need to earn money, DL programs can offer increased job prospects and career-advancement opportunities by students attaining a high level of bilingualism (de Jong & Bearse, 2014; Harmon-Martínez & Jurado, 2014).

Some dropout factors relate to "falling out" due to apathy and lack of connection to school. In a number of qualitative studies, secondary students report liking and valuing their previous or current experiences in DL programs (Bearse & de Jong, 2008; Cortina, Makar, & Mount-Cors, 2015; Lindholm-Leary & Borsato, 2001). Particularly when students feel they are highly proficient bilinguals, they perceive positive cognitive and social benefits from their bilingualism and have higher satisfaction with their school experiences (Lindholm-Leary, 2016). There is a saying that "perception is reality." When DL students perceive that they are part of a special school opportunity and that they are developing skills they are proud of, they feel more connected and committed to their school experience.

Models in the U.S. and Around the World

Articulating a cohesive program. Internationally, many education systems that have DL-like programs favor developmental bilingualism; students learn in their home language first and then add other languages as time goes on (Alidou, Glanz, & Nikiema, 2011). In some countries like Papua New Guinea and South Africa, education eventually shifts to English-only in higher grades (England, 2009; Malone & Paraide, 2011). In other countries, like Singapore and most European countries, even when education shifts primarily to one dominant international language such as English there is still a stringent requirement for continued development in the students' home language (England, 2009; Freeman, Freeman, & Mercuri, 2005). At the secondary level there are three basic models for dividing languages during the school day: a time-based model (the same teacher uses both languages at specified times), a person/subject-based model (teachers share students and each teacher uses one language exclusively), or a combination model (for example, Teacher A teaches in language 1 during the first week, while Teacher B teaches in language 2; the following week, the teachers switch which language they are using). The model used to decide how to divide the time has implications for the status of each language and the number and kind of bilingual role models available to students (Purkarhofer & Mossakowski, 2011).

Within the United States, a few states have created clear expectations for extended DL programs from kindergarten through the end of high school. In Utah, students in Grades 7-9 take upper-level honors coursework in the partner language and an optional "Culture and Media" course. In ninth or tenth grades, they take AP Language and Culture, and for the remainder of their high school years they take one "bridge" course in the partner language annually which confers both high school credit and college credit, through a collaboration with seven universities in the state (Landes-Lee, 2015). Similarly, Delaware outlines an expectation for DL students to take honors-level partner language classes in Grades 6-8, an AP Language and Culture course in ninth grade, and university-level courses in the partner language for Grades 10-12. Georgia's plan mirrors Delaware's, with the addition of an expected content course in the partner language during each year of middle school (U.S. Department of Education, 2015).

Where state-level departments of education have not created clear expectations, school districts and individual schools have stepped in to fill the void. In Portland, Oregon, middle school students take a language arts class and a social studies class in the partner language each year. In high school, they typically only take one advanced language class per year in the partner language (Steele et al., 2017). In San Diego's Nestor Language Academy, middle school students learn for half of the day in Spanish through the end of eighth grade, taking social studies, math, and Spanish language arts in the partner language. In high school, students have the option of continuing with Advanced Placement (AP) college-level courses in Spanish (U.S. Department of Education, 2015). Some of these efforts fall below the expected minimum availability of two classes annually in the partner language, including at least one core content course, which have been described as "non-negotiable" components of high school DL programs (de Jong & Bearse, 2011; Sandy-Sánchez, 2008; U.S. Department of Education, 2015). Some schools are able to meet and exceed that minimum requirement, such as Omaha South High Magnet School's DL program. During their high school years, out of 31 options, students must take at least 12 academic courses (three per year) taught in the partner language as well as a course in Spanish language or literature each year (Omaha Public Schools, 2016; see Chapter 4). (Also see Chapters 5-13 for other secondary DL models that include more courses in the partner language.)

Transitioning between levels. Transitions from elementary to middle school or from middle to high school present good opportunities for students and their families to celebrate their success and re-commit to active participation in the DL program. In Summit County, Colorado, students moving from the middle to high school DL program take part in a "freshman fiesta" event to reflect on their growth as bilinguals, demonstrate a schoolwide commitment to the strand program, and set challenging Spanish proficiency targets for their high school years (Westerberg & Davison, 2016). At Omaha South High Magnet, students and their families sign a contract asking them to step up to challenging academic and behavioral expectations when they move into the high school program from middle school (Ortega, 2014).

Continuing progress towards a long-term goal can also be part of the transition process between schools. As an example, some DL programs offer a special diploma seal such as the "Seal of Biliteracy" for demonstrating high levels of proficiency in two languages. Numerous states have adopted policies to award a seal of biliteracy for meeting specific proficiency targets in English and another language *(http://www.duallanguageschools.org;* U.S. Department of Education, 2015; see Chapter 16). However, individual school districts can add additional criteria to raise the bar even further for students in DL programs. In Summit County, Colorado, criteria for earning a "Dual Language Diploma" include not just language proficiency but also travel, community service, and developing a portfolio (Westerberg & Davison, 2016). In New Mexico, the Albuquerque Public Schools offered a Seal of Biliteracy for graduates even before their state government did (see Chapter 10). Criteria include completing course requirements and passing a portfolio presentation. Requirements for the seal are shared annually in Spanish language arts classes, and a periodic review of each DL student's grades and course schedules helps keep students on track to achieving the seal. The seal is valued as a sign of academic performance and denotes cultural connections and career opportunities (Harmon-Marínez & Jurado, 2014).

Transitions between school levels can also be a good time to extend the multilingual/multicultural identities of students by adding a third or additional language to their formal schoolwork. While studying three or more languages during secondary school is a rarity in the United States, the mantra of multilingual education in Europe for many years has been "mother tongue plus two." The Common European Framework of References for Languages provides a list of proficiency descriptors and the European Language Portfolio is widely used to record language growth in multiple languages. European efforts at multilingualism often incorporate Content and Language Integrated Learning (CLIL) which, similar to DL approaches, teach language through curricular content rather than simply about language (Cenoz & Gorter, 2015). Within the small but influential network of schools known as European Schools, a compulsory third language is introduced around Grade 8 and continued until graduation. Additionally, students with different first languages are intentionally integrated in classes called "European Hours" aimed at fostering cross-cultural understandings and experiences (de Jong, 2011; Freeman, Freeman, & Mercuri, 2005).

Translanguaging. An area of emerging debate within the field of DL research is related to the traditional strongly held idea of "strict separation of languages." This philosophy, which has sometimes been expressed as a core tenet or non-negotiable of DL instruction, says that during partner language instructional time only the partner language should be used by teacher and students, and only resources in the partner language should be part of instruction (Thomas & Collier, 2012; see pp. 33-38 for discussion of exceptions to this position; see also Chapters 1 and 10). However, bilingual people in the real world typically do not maintain such a rigid separation of languages in their daily lives. For example, a person might read an interesting news article in Spanish, discuss it in English with a coworker and then in Spanish with a friend, and finally write a post on social media with their thoughts about the topic that includes segments in both Spanish and English.

One term used to describe this natural flow that bilinguals use to draw on all their language assets in daily life is "translanguaging," and some educators in bilingual contexts are beginning to create space for translanguaging practices (Creese & Blackledge, 2010). In the classroom, translanguaging practices can be included in advanced phases of instruction and might include students talking about what they are learning in the language they prefer, using resources in multiple languages to provide multiple perspectives on a topic being studied, or sharing their projects or writing in different formats, in different languages, for different audiences (García, Johnson, & Seltzer, 2017). These kinds of practices have the potential to push students to higher levels of academic output than they would have in a strictly monolingual class environment, and also recognize that in DL programs students do not always fit neatly into boxes such as "native English speaker" or "native Spanish speaker" (de Jong, 2016; García, Johnson, & Seltzer, 2017).

A concern about the use of translanguaging practices in DL classrooms is that permitting or inviting students to use whichever language they choose for a particular task might lead to students using only the language that they feel most comfortable with and never fully developing their skills in the other language (Martin-Beltrán, 2014). This is especially a concern in the early stages of second language acquisition. Indeed, no research to date has examined how the use of translanguaging in the classroom impacts students' language proficiency. Instead, the focus of translanguaging research so far has been on how translanguaging enables students to use their full linguistic repertoires to produce their best possible academic products (Rubinstein-Ávila, Sox, Kaplan, & McGraw, 2015). Students use translanguaging practices to invite co-construction with other students, to defend or explore word choice, and to "meet halfway" to negotiate meaning (Martin-Beltrán, 2014). Translanguaging practices employed in previously English-monolingual classrooms may also help students bring the partner language into a larger part of their day, countering the trend for students to view the DL program as merely "the sum of the classes offered in the non-English language only" (Montone & Loeb, 2000, p. 4). Since translanguaging is a natural phenomenon for bilingual people, secondary-level DL programs need to develop and articulate a stance towards translanguaging. Adolescents are either embracing or rejecting aspects of their identity, including their bilingual identity, and a thoughtful approach to translanguaging in school helps students in that process (de Jong, 2016).

Meeting the Needs of Stakeholders

Many groups in both the school and community contexts play a part in the success (or failure) of secondary DL programs. Students, teachers, administrators, and parents have their own needs, goals, and concerns which should be carefully balanced. While DL programs at middle and high school may differ in format and course offerings, they share a number of common challenges in meeting the needs of their stakeholder groups.

Students. As discussed previously, high school students who have been part of DL programs since elementary school report valuing their experiences, but there is more to the story. Students from different backgrounds seem to perceive different benefits from their participation in DL programs. Latino students who had been in a Spanish/English two-way DL program said they felt bicultural and that "being able to speak Spanish was important because it allowed them to stay true to their roots and remain connected to their families" (Bearse & de Jong, 2008, p. 331). Non-Latino students from English-dominant homes who had been part of the same program reported that they did not feel bicultural but instead felt "culturally aware," and perceived that the main benefits of learning Spanish were college preparation and additional career opportunities. Both groups of students expressed a diminished sense of overall program identity in high school and noted that having less time in their school day devoted to Spanish instruction seemed to be harming their Spanish oral proficiency. Students also noticed a shift in Spanish language arts from a focus on function to a focus on form (Bearse & de Jong, 2008; de Jong & Bearse, 2011). These converging and divergent perspectives from students in the same program present a case for differentiated goals for different types of students, and for ensuring that the partner language receives sufficient instructional time during or beyond the school day to develop full bilingualism and biliteracy. It also reinforces the notion that "biculturalism" needs to be cultivated as intentionally as the other program goals. (See Chapter 14 for more findings from interviews with DL graduates.)

A major challenge for middle and high school programs is student attrition. When the number of students in a cohort declines, it is hard to continue offering a variety of courses to meet the needs and interests of secondary students. DL programs do not usually accept new students in middle and high school unless the student has had a significant amount of formal education in the partner language, such as a recent arrival from a country that speaks the partner language or a heritage speaker who is bilingual (see Chapter 2), so attrition in DL programs can be very difficult to mitigate (Freeman, Freeman, & Mercuri, 2005). While a trickle of students join it may feel as though a flood of students is exiting. The causes for attrition are many: students drop out of the program to pursue other appealing course offerings when there are schedule conflicts; students need high-level coursework or specialized courses not available in the partner language; or students feel their proficiency in the partner language is not adequate to continue in challenging upper-level coursework (González Ornelas & Ornelas, 2014; C. Sizemore, 2014).

When clarified, the causes of attrition each suggest a possible solution. Schools can employ student participation to select which courses, including compelling electives, will be offered within their programs such as medical Spanish, Spanish theatre, or engineering (S. Sizemore, 2014). Content areas that usually have a large number of levels such as math might be taught in English to avoid the inability to offer the appropriate range of coursework in the partner language (González Ornelas & Ornelas, 2014). And students (and their teachers) should have clear and research-based language proficiency goals to avoid disappointment over their perceived inadequacy in the partner language (Fortune & Tedick, 2015; C. Sizemore, 2014).

The flip side of stemming the negative effects of attrition is intentionally building student motivation and excitement for the DL program. Students often enter DL classes as young elementary school students, with little voice or choice in their parents' decision to enroll them. As they get older, students need to feel a sense of personal interest and commitment to sustain their motivation to stay in DL. For example, students might be asked to sign a commitment letter to continue in the middle or high school DL program (González Ornelas & Ornelas, 2014). Faltis and Ramírez-Marín (2015) identified six practices that promote student enthusiasm and success for secondary students in bilingual programs.

- *Assigning teachers responsive to the needs of bilingual students.* How do their middle and high school teachers, even in English-dominant courses, acknowledge students' bilingual skills and anticipate their challenges? It is important to position students as competent bilingual language learners and to reaffirm that identity frequently (de Jong, 2016).

- *Providing students access to rigorous DL academic classes including AP coursework.* AP coursework in the partner language need not be restricted to language and literature classes; schools like Omaha South High Magnet offer AP Calculus, World History, and Government in Spanish (Omaha Public Schools, 2016).

- *Offering continuous contact with bilingual counselors who serve as resources and advocates.*

- *Planning for multiple opportunities to build school-wide relationships with adults and peers.* For example, in one middle school program students build a shared identity with a group of peers by participating in a "house" (cohort) with its own name, chants, banners, and special field trips (Grant, 2014).

- *Providing access to extracurricular activities and community-based programs.*

- *Offering course schedules that consider students' prior academic experiences and their future goals.*

DL programs may also wish to celebrate and extend the skills of students by creating opportunities for learning beyond the school walls. On a smaller scale, students might take part in parent-information sessions or be invited to present at DL professional conferences (Grant, 2014). Or individual courses might require community-service learning projects such as tutoring younger students, staging a performance for area nursing homes, or creating a community conservation project. Using the partner language in meaningful contexts outside of the classroom can boost students' confidence in speaking and suggest possible career paths where bilingualism/biculturalism are valued (Pascual y Cabo, Prada, & Lowther Pereira, 2017). School programs might also develop a tradition of participating in international trips on an annual basis (Grant, 2014). One interesting model for school trips designed to develop linguistic and cultural competence is in Australia, where students learning Indonesian visit a sister school in an Indonesian-speaking country and participate in shared group projects with students from their host families (Walton, Paradies, Priest, Wertheim, & Freeman, 2015). The projects are designed on the basis of Intergroup Contact Theory, which emphasizes equal status of all participants as they engage in cooperative activities in a social environment that encourages reflection and prejudice reduction (Allport, 1979).

Teachers. A frequently expressed concern for DL programs is finding qualified staff who can teach in the partner language and who also meet state licensure requirements. Many districts have turned to hiring international teachers on short-term cultural exchange visas; these educators may be excellent language models but often struggle to adjust to the American educational system (U.S. Department of Education, 2015). Hiring practices that focus solely on teacher endorsements or language proficiency may miss essential skills that are not always readily tested, such as the ability to explain things clearly, to anticipate student mistakes, to engage student interest, and to understand how to plan and carry out instruction (Kissau & Algozzine, 2017). Regardless of how they're hired, though, what do teachers in DL programs need to flourish, particularly in middle and high schools?

Research suggests that one key challenge for DL teachers is balancing their roles as language teachers and content teachers. Because of teacher licensure and school accountability measures, secondary teachers often see themselves as primarily teachers of their content area (math, social studies, art, computers, etc.) and may mistakenly feel that language is an optional instructional component that "will surface naturally as an outcome of content instruction" (Cammarata & Tedick, 2012, p. 262). Such an approach is unlikely to produce satisfactory language outcomes for students. As teachers become aware of the need for intentionally focusing on language alongside content, they report needing specific professional development in using available resources, deciding which aspects of language to focus on in their instruction, and receiving ongoing support for their identity transformation as a teacher (Cammarata & Tedick, 2012). These concerns are similar to those of teachers in Europe who are charged with implementing a Content and Language Integrated Learning (CLIL) approach in their bilingual classrooms but report that they have limited understanding of the theory, methodology, or available instructional materials (Pérez Cañado, 2016). If teachers are to successfully teach both language and content, they need training to do so (Tedick & Wesely, 2015).

DL teachers also need support to integrate with the larger community of teachers in their school, particularly in schools where DL teachers make up only a small percentage of the overall teaching staff. Particular attention should be paid to teacher status (for example, are Spanish language arts teachers "core" teachers like English language arts teachers, or "elective" teachers like Spanish as a world language teachers?) and with whom the DL teachers share common planning time (de Jong, 2011; de Jong & Bearse, 2014). Teachers who are not part of the DL program may worry about their own job security and whether new DL courses will crowd out other existing offerings, and may want to understand and participate in how decisions are made within the DL program

(Forman, 2016). These kinds of tensions, if they remain unaddressed, could harm teacher morale and performance.

Another frequent challenge for secondary DL teachers, in almost any program model, is finding or creating curriculum in the partner language which is up-to-date and reflective of state content standards (Montone & Loeb, 2000). Teachers in new programs will need to create or adapt curriculum with limited materials, and would benefit from a planning year before the program launches, to attend conferences, visit other DL schools in their region, and participate in professional development to help them in their curriculum development (González Ornelas & Ornelas, 2014; C. Sizemore, 2014). Teachers need to be prepared for the different acquisition patterns their students will have experienced; former English learners are likely to shift towards English dominance over time, while native English speakers continue to be English dominant. Therefore, DL teachers who teach in the partner language are likely to see a wide range of skill levels among their students which complicates the development of curriculum that is both grade-appropriate and differentiated to student needs (de Jong, 2011).

In short, DL teachers need to be strong language models, sensitive to the needs of many different student profiles, creative and flexible masters of their content areas, good team players, and resourceful curriculum developers. On top of all that, they need to have a sizeable toolkit of effective classroom instructional practices. In a math class, this might include using math journals, hanging a math word of the day on a string around the teacher's neck, using engaging review strategies like a ball toss, and building mathematical discourse using "Chalk Talks" (Rubinstein-Ávila, Sox, Kaplan, & McGraw, 2015). In a humanities class, this might mean helping students create critical autobiographies to provide an authentic context to connect their fiction and non-fiction reading (de Jong, 2011). In all classes, it requires an attention to the ongoing language development of students, prompting them to use longer utterances in speaking and writing and artfully developing an appropriate stance towards translanguaging (de Jong, 2011; Li, Steele, Slater, Bacon, & Miller, 2016). Although this list of desired skills and classroom practices may seem daunting, the good news is that willing teachers can develop any and all of these traits through professional development and ongoing collaboration.

Administrators. Building-level administrators in DL programs, like their teacher colleagues, need a range of skills to be successful because they perform a variety of roles. These roles include being a guru (of DL research and professional connections), a proponent (particularly with internal audiences not directly involved in the dual program), an overseer (recruiting, hiring, and documenting learning), a cultural unifier (between staff members and families), and a change agent (leading the necessary changes to build and sustain the program); (Rocque, Ferrin, Hite, & Randall, 2016). Building administrators, even if they find themselves inheriting an existing program from their feeder schools, need to be deeply engaged in their school's DL program and play an especially important role in listening to and reassuring parents that their children will receive the supports they need to be successful (González Ornelas & Ornelas, 2014). For new middle and high school programs it is especially helpful to take a planning year to build a committee of staff who are invested in the success of the program, visit other schools, and identify needed resources while keeping the larger school community (and the families of their future students) up to date (Grant, 2014; Montone & Loeb, 2000).

District-level administrators can play a role in the success of DL programs as well (Collier & Thomas, 2014). Teachers and building-level administrators will likely have numerous and perhaps even conflicting expectations for the appropriate role of district-level leaders: some may wish district leaders to be primarily resource providers, while others might look for more direct coordination of the DL staff. Some might want district-level staff to provide ready-made curriculum, while others may wish them to step back and simply provide accountability and support for building-level creativity (Forman, 2016). Clearly, one of the most important roles for district-level leaders is to make sure that their colleagues in schools have the professional development, time, and financial resources they need to implement a successful program (Grant, 2014). They can also encourage vertical articulation between schools to help each level—elementary, middle, and high—see its role in the formation of students over time (Collier & Thomas, 2014; Montone & Loeb, 2000).

Parents. Often, parents are less visible in middle and high schools than in elementary schools. Nonetheless, they remain as key partners in the education of their children. Parents who had once been ardent supporters of DL when their children were in elementary school may find their commitment wavering, particularly if their child is resistant to remaining in DL and they feel they may have other more important parent/child battles to fight (C. Sizemore, 2014). To help parents maintain enthusiasm about their child's DL education, it may be especially helpful to create lots of artifacts—such as websites, newsletters, and videos—that highlight their children's bilingual skills and ongoing growth (Westerberg & Davison, 2016). Some of those same tools to maintain student enthusiasm, such as international trips reserved for DL students and specialized elective offerings, may also result in greater parent buy-in if schools make a little extra effort to keep parents informed (Montone & Loeb, 2000; C. Sizemore, 2014). When communicating with parents, it is also worth remembering and nurturing some of the goals that caused parents to sign up their child for DL in the first place, such as a competitive edge in future careers, a greater sense of connection with a heritage culture, and more exposure to diversity (de Jong & Bearse, 2014).

Parent engagement can and should go beyond communication. Parents have frequently been some of the most vocal and successful advocates in sustaining DL programs (Cortina, Makar, & Mount-Cors, 2015). They can speak from personal experience about what it means to their child, their family, and their community for DL programs to have the needed resources to continue to thrive through the end of high school. And, of course, parent engagement can have a profound impact on the success of individual children. Arias (2015) contrasts traditional and nontraditional models of parent involvement. In traditional models, beliefs about what constitutes effective parent involvement are based on one culture's view. In the traditional model, communication focuses on the needs of the school. Non-traditional models, on the other hand, focus on what the school can do to support parents and families (Bivins, 2014). They seek a reciprocal understanding between schools and homes. Common barriers for families, especially those from marginalized backgrounds, include an inability to understand English, cultural concern about interfering with the work of the school, unfamiliarity with the system, lack of education, too many responsibilities, negative past school experiences, negative or condescending attitudes of school personnel, and lack of transportation or childcare (Arias, 2015). Despite their best efforts, schools may feel like unwelcoming or even hostile environments for many parents, so community-based organizations can serve as a neutral space for schools and parents to connect. Two models for community-based organizations serving in this role are the Padres Comprometidos effort from National Council of La Raza (which includes components specifically for parents of secondary school students) and the Parent Institute for Quality Education which provides a variety of programs aimed at parents and at educators to help bridge the home/school divide (Arias, 2015).

Future Directions for Research

There are still many gaps in the existing research about secondary DL programs. There have not been any studies to date comparing the trajectories of students who exit DL programs at the end of elementary schools with those who continue through middle and high school. Existing data-collection instruments for academic outcomes rely heavily on test scores in English reading and math, which tell only part of the story about what students stand to gain from a multilingual, multicultural education (Valentino & Reardon, 2015). It would be helpful, too, for future research to develop more nuanced views about student diversity than the typical binary heritage English/heritage Spanish lens (Geerlings, Verkuyten, & Thijs, 2015; Tedick & Wesely, 2015). And research has only begun to scratch the surface of what types of teacher professional development have the greatest impact on secondary DL programs (Cammarata & Tedick, 2012; Tedick & Wesely, 2015). The field of research is ripe for harvest as middle and high school dual language programs continue to grow around the United States and around the world.

The author wishes to thank Dr. Rebecca Fox for her invaluable suggestions in improving this manuscript, and to the many experts who generously provided their insights and time throughout the development of this literature review: Virginia Collier, Ester de Jong, Virginia Doherty, Tara Fortune, Kathryn Lindholm-Leary, Rita Oleksak, David Rogers, Jennifer Steele, and Diane Tedick.

PART II

Implementation Experience and Advice

Chapter Four
Nebraska: Omaha Public Schools' Secondary Dual Language Program

Katy Cattlett and Dr. Rony Ortega—Omaha Public Schools

Introduction by Collier & Thomas: *Part II of our book focuses on the specifics of DL implementation. This lead chapter tells the remarkable story of the secondary DL program in the Omaha Public Schools where the largely first-generation Mexican American community enjoys high graduation rates, substantial scholarship awards, and continued study at the university level among their high school population. This large and growing DL college-preparatory program has become a turning point for the community and a phenomenal success. English learners who participate in the DL program achieve significantly higher than non-DL students on the state tests in reading, writing, and math. They also experience a significantly lower number of behavioral referrals. Bonds grow between the DL teachers and students, who work together to ensure that everyone enrolled in the DL program will graduate from high school. Some of their bilingual graduates are already coming back to teach in their school district, adding to the richness of their shared community bilingual resources. Omaha South High Magnet School was named 2018 International Spanish Academy of the year by the Ministry of Education of Spain.*

The Omaha Public Schools (OPS) continues to serve more English learners than any other school district in Nebraska (see Figure 4.1). The educational outcomes of these more linguistically, culturally, and academically diverse groups of students are impacted by how school districts choose to respond to this demographic shift. Seventeen years ago, OPS responded to the needs of native Spanish-speaking students with a two-way 50:50 K-12 dual language program. While providing a means to improve the English proficiency and educational outcomes of English learners, the initiative has most importantly offered both native Spanish and native English speakers the enrichment opportunity to become bilingual, biliterate, and bicultural.

Figure 4.1

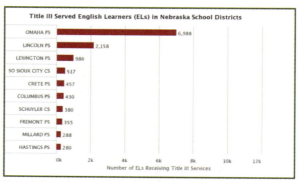

National Clearinghouse for English Language Acquisition - https://ncela.ed.gov/t3sis/nebraska.php

Today the OPS K-12 dual language (DL) program is one of a growing number of K-12 DL programs nationally and serves about 3200 students at six elementary schools, three middle schools, and one high school. The three middle schools are spread throughout the city of Omaha. Marrs Middle School is located in south Omaha and is the school where DL started 17 years ago in OPS. Norris Middle School, in the center of Omaha, is the school that most recently added a DL program. Beveridge Middle School is located in the western part of the city and is the magnet for DL. These three middle school DL programs feed into one high school, Omaha South High Magnet School (OSHMS). OSHMS is a large urban magnet school for information technology, visual arts, performing arts, and dual language. While OSHMS draws students from throughout the city, the school largely reflects its surrounding community with 78.6% Hispanic students out of 2,457 total.

It is to no one's surprise that student demographics have shifted to a more linguistically, culturally, and academically diverse group of students. The concern, however, is that these English learners (ELs), on average, achieve at rates below their native English-speaking peers, particularly in the secondary years (Fry, 2007, 2008). This means schools must better prepare themselves to address the particular linguistic, cultural, and learning needs of these students. Research shows that DL programs are an effective way to meet the needs of English learners and close the achievement gap (Lindholm-Leary, 2001; Thomas & Collier, 2002, 2012). Recent data from the Omaha Public Schools Research Department (2016) showed that overall:

• OPS DL students had significantly higher average state test scores on the Nebraska State Accountability Assessment (NeSA) than non-DL students in reading, math, and writing.

• Both ELs and non-ELs who participated in the DL program tended to have higher NeSA scores than those who did not participate.

- Both free/reduced lunch and non-free/reduced lunch students who participated in the DL program tended to have higher NeSA scores than those who did not participate.

- DL program participation appears to have had the largest impact on NeSA math scores.

- Teachers report that DL students were considerably more affectively engaged than non-DL students.

- DL students had a significantly lower number of behavioral referrals than non-DL students.

Building on the strong data coming from the program, OPS has continued its commitment to provide students with a K-12 DL pathway. The secondary programs continue to grow to meet the needs of students coming from elementary DL programs as well as the new immigrant arrivals. There is no assessment or requirement for students to move to the next level of the program. Additionally, any student who is a fluent speaker of Spanish can join the program any time that there is space available. The DL program is considered the optimal program model for English learners in the Omaha Public Schools.

OPS Dual Language Program History

When many in the country first hear about the DL program in the Omaha Public Schools, the first question that comes to mind is, "where?" Many envision Nebraska as a rural state with small pockets of denser population. While that may be true for much of the state, Omaha is anything but rural. In fact, it is one of the top 50 school districts in the nation in terms of size. Also, the Omaha Public School district serves a very diverse student population in a state not known for its diversity.

Figure 4.2

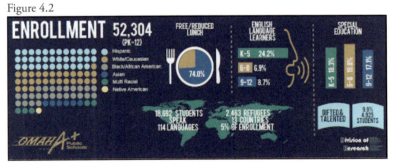

Omaha Public Schools - *https://district.ops.org/*

As seen in the infographic above, OPS is a large urban district. The student population tops 52,000 with over 18,000 (35.7%) students coming from homes where a language other than English is spoken. Of those 18,000 students, approximately 80% speak Spanish. The school district is approximately one third Hispanic, one third Caucasian and one third African American. As of the 2014-15 school year, there are more Hispanic students than any other ethnic group. As seen in Figure 4.3, the percentage of Hispanic students served in OPS continues to grow each year.

Figure 4.3

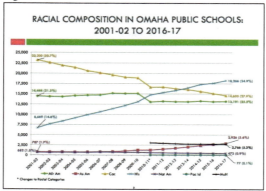

In the late 1990s, the shift to a more linguistically, culturally, and academically diverse student population that was beginning to take place caused OPS leaders to look for better ways to serve English learners in the district. Additionally, a new leader in the English as a second language (ESL) program brought with her some experience with bilingual education. After visiting several programs and researching program model types, OPS made the decision to offer a two-way 50:50 dual language program in the fall of 2000. Along with beginning an elementary DL program, a commitment was made to continue the program K-12.

In the fall of 2000, R.M. Marrs Elementary opened the first DL program in the state of Nebraska. Sixty students and their families in kindergarten and first grade were recruited to be the pioneers in what would eventually become a large, well-respected educational opportunity for Omaha families. At the time of implementation, there was virtually no bilingual education in the state. The only ESL programs in the state provided no first language support. There were several times during the early years of the program when people questioned the use of taxpayer dollars to teach Hispanic students Spanish. This did not dissuade OPS leaders and the program continued.

In the fall of 2004, what was then Marrs Elementary became R.M. Marrs Magnet Center, a middle school serving students in Grades 5-8. The elementary students from Marrs moved to a nearby newly constructed school, Gómez-Heritage Elementary School, and the DL program was moved there as well. It was at this transition in the fall of 2004 that the first group of DL students was ready for fifth grade in middle school, and Marrs Magnet Center began a new DL model where the language of instruction was determined by course, rather than by percentage of instructional minutes (which is the 50:50 elementary model). It was decided at that time that secondary DL in OPS would require that students take Spanish language arts and at least one content area in Spanish, more if possible.

Meanwhile, in the fall of 2001, South High School first offered DL classes to its students. From the fall of 2001 until the first group of students from the elementary/middle school program arrived in the fall of 2009, the DL program at South High School primarily served high-performing heritage speakers of Spanish and highly motivated English speakers. Students were offered bilingual courses in the core content areas of math, science, and social studies. In those early years, these courses were conducted 50% in English and 50% in Spanish, alternating the language of instruction by day. DL students were also encouraged to take a Spanish course, with most students enrolling in the Spanish for Spanish Speakers Program.

Once the first group of Marrs Magnet Center K-8 DL students were preparing to enter South High School, DL leaders began to have conversations about whether the high school design of switching the language of instruction daily would serve these K-8 students well. The students' original elementary DL program had alternated the language of instruction by day. But the DL students coming from Marrs were used to studying one core content course in Spanish, as well as Spanish language arts, and not switching the language of instruction each day. The DL leaders found that with one day in each language, the students were not putting forth effort to learn through their second language. They would, in effect, turn off during instruction in their non-dominant language. DL leaders wondered if this would be the same for the older students at South. At that time a new DL coordinator was selected to lead South's program. Over the next few years he led the transformation to the current model described below.

OPS Dual Language Program: Middle School Models

In the planning stages of the program, it was decided that a 50:50 program, with approximately half of students' classes provided in Spanish, would best meet the needs of students in the Omaha Public Schools. As the program transitioned to middle school the commitment was to require Spanish language arts and one content area in Spanish each year. This continues to be the standard, but the goal is to offer a 50:50 program, K-12, when staffing and student demographics permit.

R.M. Marrs Magnet Center (Grades 5-8). The first middle school program at Marrs Magnet began by offering language arts, math, and science in Spanish for incoming fifth graders. (Science is no longer offered in Spanish.) The following year the program expanded to sixth grade offering language arts and social studies in Spanish. As the program has expanded at the middle level, the content offered in Spanish is largely dependent upon staffing availability. Marrs is the largest DL program at the middle school level in OPS. Currently students have access to language arts and one content area in Spanish at each grade level (See Figure 4.4).

Figure 4.4
R.M. Marrs Magnet Center Course Offerings by Grade Level

Grade	Courses in Spanish
5	Spanish Language Arts
	Dual Language Math 5
	Advanced Dual Language Math 5
6	Spanish Language Arts
	Dual Language Social Studies 6
7	Spanish Language Arts
	Dual Language Science 7
8	Spanish Language Arts
	Dual Language Science 8
	Honors Dual Language Physical Science

Beveridge Magnet Middle School (Grades 7-8). This school was added as a second option for middle school DL students via a Foreign Language Assistance Program (FLAP) grant awarded to OPS in 2007. In addition to language arts and content area instruction, Beveridge worked to integrate its other magnet themes, global studies and the arts, with its new DL offerings. The result was that students could choose to take DL Art or DL Showcase as an elective. In the DL Showcase course, students study and perform dances from Spanish-speaking countries. With the core offerings of language arts, science, and math in Spanish, students were able to continue the 50:50 model program through high school (See Figure 4.5).

Figure 4.5
Beveridge Magnet Middle School Course Offerings by Grade Level

Grade	Courses in Spanish
7	Spanish Language Arts Dual Language Math 7 Honors Dual Language Pre-Algebra Honors Dual Language Algebra Dual Language Science 7
8	Spanish Language Arts Dual Language Pre-Algebra Honors Dual Language Pre-Algebra Honors Dual Language Algebra Dual Language Science 8
All	Dual Language Art Dual Language Showcase

Norris Middle School (Grades 6-8). In the fall of 2012 a third middle school, Norris, began implementing the DL program in sixth grade. This was primarily due to overcrowding at one of the DL feeder elementary schools. Norris was a campus with a significant Spanish-speaking English-learner population, which added an incentive to expand to Norris rather than other school options. Through teacher recruitment and commitment from the Norris leadership team, students there are able to benefit from a 50:50 instructional model as well (See Figure 4.6).

Figure 4.6
Norris Middle School Course Offerings by Grade Level

Grade	Courses in Spanish
6	Spanish Language Arts Dual Language Math 6 Dual Language Social Studies 6
7	Spanish Language Arts Dual Language Math 7 Dual Language Social Studies 7
8	Spanish Language Arts Dual Language Pre-Algebra Dual Language Social Studies 8

OPS Dual Language Program: High School Model

At Omaha South High Magnet School (OSHMS), students have the opportunity to "major" in any one of the four magnet areas, including DL. The option to major gives students a focused path of study and also prepares them for the process of selecting and completing a major at a college or university. The high school DL program is set up as a college preparatory program with the expectation that bilingual students will attend college or enroll in other post-secondary career paths after high school. The program in 2017-18 has 674 DL students in Grades 9-12 and is projected to grow due to an increase in the elementary feeder programs.

The DL teachers are content-area endorsed, and some also hold or are working on a district-paid bilingual education and/or ESL endorsements. Most of the DL teachers share a common planning period that they use weekly to discuss student concerns, develop curriculum, and participate in Student Assistance Team meetings. This common planning period, coupled with various other means to monitor students, allows for the DL staff to maintain close relationships with the students while providing a way to quickly address any concerns.

High school DL courses. OSHMS offers its students a traditional nine-period schedule, and DL students take their core content classes in DL—about half of their daily schedule. DL courses are taught 90% in Spanish with the summative assessments typically administered and completed in English. OSHMS offers 31 core content DL courses (see Figure 4.7 below), including honors, AP, and college dual-enrollment options. In addition to the required DL core content courses, students are expected to take Spanish as a subject each year of high school. These Spanish courses are geared for native Spanish speakers who by their senior year take AP Spanish Language and AP Spanish Literature. Due to the limited number of bilingual teachers, several of the DL teachers loop with students and have them in class multiple years. This is actually a benefit to both students and teachers; students enjoy a lasting relationship with the teacher during their 4 years of high school, while teachers get to know the students well and can support them readily and effectively from day one.

Another way that OSHMS has built a community that expects and encourages academic excellence is by placing DL students in a grade-level specific DL advisement class with DL teachers as mentors. This weekly advisement class provides additional time to disseminate grade-level or college information, assist students with state test preparation, and check on the overall progress and engagement of the students.

Figure 4.7
Dual Language Course Offerings at Omaha South High Magnet School

Dual Language Course Offerings OSHMS

Math	Science	Social Studies	Other
•DL Pre-Algebra	•DL Chemistry*	•DL Modern World History	•DL Information Technology Fundamentals*
•DL Algebra I*	•DL Biology*	•AP DL U.S. Government & Politics	•Honors DL Latin American Studies
•DL Algebra II*	•DL Physical Science*		
•DL Geometry*	•DL Physics*	•AP DL Comparative Government & Politics	
•Honors DL Pre-Calc/Trig	•Honors DL Anatomy & Physiology	•DL Human Geography*	
•AP DL Calculus A		•DL U.S. History*	
		•DL Mexican American History	
		•DL Economics*	
		•DL American Government	

* Course is offered in regular academic level and honors level

All DL students who fall behind academically are required to attend school-provided tutoring during their lunch time until their grades and school work are satisfactory. This expectation is laid out in the student, parent, and school DL contract. DL students who repeatedly fall behind are referred to the Student Assistance Team, with a meeting scheduled with the student, parent, and DL school staff.

Figure 4.8 presents the OPS Dual Language Belief Statement. This is an important document that all participating DL families and students study, and that all DL staff agree to honor. It is a statement of shared accountability and commitment to the DL program.

Figure 4.8
Omaha Public Schools' Dual Language Belief Statement

> Administrators, teachers, and staff within the dual language program of the Omaha Public Schools are dedicated to ensuring that each child acquire the skills and knowledge to succeed in a global society by working towards the following goals:
> 1. High-academic achievement
> 2. Bilingualism
> 3. Biliteracy
> 4. Cross-cultural abilities

These goals will be achieved by engaging in the following practices:

- Literacy and content instruction will be provided in two languages (English and Spanish) for all dual language students, Grades K-12. Literacy development follows the simultaneous-literacy model.

- The dual language program will seek out opportunities for the enhancement of cross-cultural competencies and student self-esteem through curriculum, school, and community resources.

- All K-12 students, once admitted into the dual language program, will be encouraged to maintain participation in the program.

- Teachers, administrators, and parents/guardians will work closely together to identify any additional interventions that a student may require to experience success within the program.

- All curriculum will be clearly aligned with district content standards, grade-level expectations, and scheduling guidelines.

- K-6 students will spend at least 50% of the instructional time in Spanish. Secondary (7-12) students will participate in a minimum of language arts and one content area class in Spanish annually.

- Teachers will maintain a specified target language rather than switch from one language to another during instruction. Visitors to the classroom will also be encouraged to maintain that target language. All resources will align to the target language of the classroom.

- Every K-6 teacher will implement a daily take-home book/reading program within his/her classroom setting. Students will, thus, have equal exposure to English and Spanish literature in the home.

- Reading, writing, and oral language assessments are provided in both English and Spanish.

- Student achievement/progress will be clearly documented and tracked in Grades K-12.

- Parental/guardian support is an essential component of the program and, thus, highly encouraged and supported.

- Elementary dual language partner teachers are expected to work as a team, lesson planning together on a weekly basis (at a minimum). Building administrators will ensure that teachers have joint planning time as appropriate.

- Secondary dual language teams work together to ensure that a comprehensive support system is created for students and their families. Building administrators will ensure that teachers have common team time.

- Teachers are encouraged to participate in ongoing professional development activities including best practice in dual language so that they are knowledgeable of proven educational methods/instructional strategies. Teachers are highly encouraged to obtain an ESL and/or bilingual education endorsement(s).

- The dual language program is ever evolving. The program will be continually evaluated and altered in accordance with available research.

Parent, student, and school DL contracts. All incoming ninth grade DL students and parents are required to meet with a DL coordinator, counselor, or administrator, and after they have agreed to the DL contract, they are officially part of the high school program. The contract outlines expectations for the student, the parents, and the DL school personnel. For example, it is an expectation that the DL students agree to additional support when they are struggling academically and that they not be involved with any gang, drug, or other criminal behaviors. It is also an expectation that the parents be involved in their student's education, have a working telephone where they can be reached, and attend parent-teacher conferences twice a school year, at a minimum. Parents and students who are repeatedly unable to meet their end of the contract can be exited from the DL program through our student assistance team process, but this is a very rare occurrence. One of many expectations parents and students hold for the DL school personnel is the facilitation of college/university and scholarship applications for all DL students before graduation. These applications are typically supported through the DL senior-level Wednesday advisement class and the College & Scholarship Saturday program.

College & Scholarship Saturday Program. This program provides additional support to DL students on Saturday mornings. Community volunteers, many from local colleges and universities, offer one-on-one support to students in completing their college essays and applications, as well as scholarship applications. This program, originally designed for DL students only, has expanded to a building-wide opportunity.

Staffing a High-Quality Dual Language Program

Just as in the rest of the country, there is a significant teacher shortage in the state of Nebraska. Additionally, teachers with experience in bilingual education or DL are very rare. OPS DL teachers come from many places to teach in the program. A variety of strategies are employed to develop a high-quality staff for our DL students.

Grow-your-own bilingual teachers. An endorsement in bilingual education was not offered in the state of Nebraska until 2007. Until the fall of 2017 there was only one university in the state that offered the program. For this reason, most teachers in the OPS DL Program were neither familiar with best practices in bilingual education nor endorsed to teach it. Grant funds support teachers in obtaining ESL and bilingual education endorsements through cohort programs. Groups of teachers study together in a series of classes offered through local universities in collaboration with OPS ESL and DL leadership. This ensures that teachers are equipped with the knowledge and skills necessary to be successful in the classroom. To add to the teachers' elementary or secondary teaching certification, the bilingual education endorsement program at the partner institution, the University of Nebraska at Omaha, is a sequence of four graduate-level courses. There are two goals in this program. The most important goal is to allow teachers to learn about best practices in bilingual education and improve their programs and instruction in their buildings. The second is to provide teachers with an opportunity to practice their Spanish at high levels. Some of our secondary teachers are not native speakers or are native speakers but have not had an extensive education in their first language. The quality of the program is greatly enhanced when teachers are given many opportunities to improve their language.

Bilingual Career Ladder Program. The Bilingual Career Ladder Program was established by the ESL office to increase the number of bilingual teachers in the district. This program supports full time, bilingual staff members with financial assistance to take courses leading to teaching certification. Many DL teachers have taken advantage of this program. Some have come from other countries with education degrees but lack specific requirements for Nebraska certification standards. Others had degrees in other fields such as biology or chemistry and needed coursework in education. A few have begun some college coursework with the dreams of completing a degree in education. The funding source is not unlimited so staff must apply for the program. Priority is given to those who are closest to certification and/or are pursuing certification in a high-need area. Eight of the 39 Spanish-speaking secondary DL teachers for the 2017-18 school year have been supported by the Bilingual Career Ladder Program.

High School Education Academy. The Education Academy at South High Magnet was a program that grew out of a need for bilingual teachers. The program allows students to explore the education field by taking a 2-year course sequence that is part of the dual enrollment offerings from a local community college. The courses offer opportunities for students to observe and support classrooms at nearby schools with DL as part of their studies. Since its inception, the school district has supported expansion of the program at other schools in an effort to increase the diversity of the OPS teaching staff. Three former DL students have returned to OPS to begin their teaching careers as DL teachers. Several others are currently studying education and plan to return to OPS upon graduation.

When it is not possible to find enough high-quality teachers to meet the demands of the growing program, OPS partners with the state of Nebraska to contract teachers from Mexico and Spain. The Nebraska Department of Education sponsors J-1 visas for teachers to work throughout the state. Several districts utilize this program to meet their demand for world language teachers. OPS takes advantage of this opportunity for both the world language and DL classes. The teachers typically have more than 5 years of teaching experience in their home countries as well as advanced degrees. The initial visa is for 3 years with the option to extend it for an additional two. Currently the DL program contracts 11 visiting teachers from Spain and Mexico, K-12. Several other former visiting teachers have made Omaha their home

English Learners in Secondary Dual Language

The leaders in the ESL office in OPS believe that the DL program is the optimal model for English learners; thus all Spanish-speaking, newly arrived English learners are offered the opportunity to enter the program in middle school and high school. The OPS ESL office sees acquiring academic English as a long-term process that may extend into the university years and does not want students to be held back in their progress in the content areas such as math, science, and social studies while learning English. Enrollment in the DL program also provides the students with the opportunity to access more rigorous college-preparatory coursework. Many of the more recently arrived English learners have shared that they are able to continue their formal English language studies in local community colleges and universities, demonstrating that they are meeting the academic benchmarks necessary for college entrance. More study is needed on the success of newly arrived English learners in secondary DL programs, but the evidence in Omaha is promising.

Plans for the Future

The Omaha Public Schools' K-12 dual language program has created an opportunity for English learners to retain and build upon their native language and culture, which are seen as resources, not deficits. The middle and high school dual language programs have permitted students to reach high levels of both English and Spanish proficiency and academic achievement.

What's more, this program has helped to increase OPS' graduation rate, scholarship dollars, and college enrollments. With a commitment to high-academic achievement and clear and shared goals, the overall success of the OPS dual language program rests in the fact that students and parents are empowered in a program that plays to their strengths and that validates and affirms their native language and culture. We look forward to continuing the growth and effectiveness of our two-way 50:50 K-12 dual language program in the years ahead.

Chapter Five
Texas: The Story of the Pharr-San Juan-Alamo Independent School District Secondary Dual Language Program

Dr. Mario Ferrón and Mario Ferrón, Jr.—
San Antonio Independent School District

Introduction by Collier and Thomas: *This story is from a pioneering secondary dual language program in a school district located in the Río Grande Valley on the Texas-Mexico border. It illustrates the potential for transformation of English-only attitudes into bilingual collaboration. The authors take us step by step through the implementation process, showing that each hurdle leads to eventual student success, as more secondary schools add DL classes and the DL students show what they can do when given the opportunity to be schooled through their two languages. Several student stories demonstrate the amazing power of dual language schooling for transforming lives. An especially important theme is the advantages of opening the DL program to newly arriving Spanish-speaking immigrants. This chapter again illustrates the high achievement of the DL students compared to non-DL students, even though the majority of the DL students are English learners of low-income background.*

Consider what it would take for a medium-sized Texas school district to provide a successful secondary dual language program. This is our perspective after teaching for more than 15 years in this school district's dual language program. The following narrative details the challenges the dual language program faced, the approaches followed to keep the program successful and sustainable, and the outcomes the program has generated over time.

The Context

Pharr-San Juan-Alamo (PSJA) Independent School District (ISD) is located on the Texas border with Mexico. With more than 32,000 students enrolled, Hispanics represent 99.1% of the student population; with 43.8% identified as English learners (ELs). These indicators are about five times larger than the national average of 21.7% Hispanic students and four times larger than the nationwide average of 10.3% ELs. The level of education in the area is significantly lower than the national average. Only 16.7% of the population 25 years and older hold a bachelor's degree, much lower than the national average of 29.8%. Poverty is also an important factor; the median household income for the area, $34,782, is much lower than the nation's $53,889. More than 31% of the area's families live below the poverty level, almost three times the national average of 12%, and 88% of the students in PSJA are labeled as economically disadvantaged, more than double the national average of 42.9%.

The Beginning

Since 1968, Hispanic English learners in PSJA were traditionally placed in subtractive bilingual programs that provided them with little instructional support in Spanish. Even though 84.7% of the population in the community spoke a language other than English at home, only 41.5% of the students in the district were enrolled in bilingual/ESL education. In 1994, the reauthorization of the federal Bilingual Education Act provided Title VII grants specifically earmarked to support dual language programs. Many school districts in Texas took advantage of this opportunity and PSJA was not an exception.

Thanks to this Title VII grant, in 1995 PSJA phased in dual language (DL) instruction from Pre-K to third grade in three of the 21 elementary schools in the district. In each of these schools, transitional bilingual education (the minimum of L1 support required in Texas) was gradually phased out and replaced by DL instruction (the enrichment model of L1 support). Spanish-speaking students were automatically placed in DL, including recent immigrants at all grade levels available. English-speaking students, including Hispanics being raised bilingually, were also invited to participate in the program, and many of these families enrolled their children in the DL program. The grant included a collaborative program design and professional development with Professor Leo Gómez at the University of Texas-Pan American.

Even though the program was being satisfactorily implemented, by 1999 the political winds changed and the grant funds decreased. As with many other DL programs across the nation, the DL program at PSJA was destined to end. However, thanks to strong advocacy efforts from parents and program leaders, a second federal grant provided 5 more years of funding.

Once the funding challenge was solved, a new challenge arose. The new Title VII grant provided funds to support the vertical or horizontal expansion of the program. Since other elementary schools were not interested in implementing DL, the decision was to expand the program into middle school or forfeit the funding once the program reached fifth grade. The first step was to find a middle school that could ensure a successful and sustainable program.

Choosing the Campus

Liberty Middle School was selected as PSJA's first DL middle school for a variety of reasons—its feeder pattern, which included two of the elementary schools providing DL education, and the campus' new location, which facilitated access from all existing DL campuses. However, the most important attribute that supported the selection of Liberty Middle School was the eagerness of the campus principal, against the advice of many of her middle school peers, to implement one of the first DL middle school programs in South Texas. The principal and teachers received extensive training in DL implementation, attended state and national conferences, and visited Ysleta Independent School District, another Texas district starting a middle school DL program.

An additional challenge was that PSJA's elementary implementation was guided by a highly structured DL model. PSJA did not have a similarly structured model to guide their middle school implementation. The district decided to follow some of the traits of the elementary program and deliver middle school DL instruction through three content areas: fine arts, Spanish language arts, and social studies. Teaching math in Spanish was not considered an option for two main reasons: math had always been taught in English in the PSJA elementary DL schools, and math was state assessed in English every year in the middle school grades. For many key stakeholders, teaching a state-assessed course in Spanish was unthinkable if students were to be assessed in English, a notion we later found to be invalid. DL social studies instruction was approved mainly because this subject is only tested in the eighth grade, and students don't need to pass the test to move on to high school. From the seven periods included in the students' schedules, DL students would take three periods delivered entirely in Spanish every day.

Another important decision was that middle school DL students would not be segregated from the English-speaking population for the entire day. DL students would attend specific sections of Spanish language arts, social studies, and fine arts delivered in Spanish, but during the English-delivered sections they would merge with students in the general education classrooms. One more key decision was that because the DL students would receive advanced instruction in Spanish language arts, the district would grant them high school credit for the seventh grade Pre-Advanced Placement (AP) Spanish course and the eighth grade AP Spanish course and all DL students would take the AP Spanish test at the end of the year.

Selecting the Teachers

As the instructional materials required to support DL instruction were identified and acquired, the next step was to identify the teachers delivering instruction in Spanish. The campus already had three excellent teachers to support sixth grade implementation. The sixth grade Spanish language arts teacher was highly proficient in Spanish. Born and educated in Mexico, her expertise in the Spanish language was an asset for the students. The other two DL teachers were not as proficient in academic Spanish; however, their motivation and commitment to the students and the program exceeded expectations. The DL social studies teacher's lessons were challenging and culturally relevant, and his students were engaged and highly motivated to learn and to continue developing their Spanish. The drama teacher decided to provide his students the opportunity to participate in plays delivered entirely in Spanish. His students became so engaged in theatrical production in Spanish that it eventually generated an extraordinary outcome by the time students reached high school. We will talk about this in the PSJA DL high school section below.

Even though many DL campus practices at Liberty Middle School mirrored the elementary DL schools, many other practices did not. Daily announcements were not delivered in both languages and many members of the staff were not trained in the goals of the program. This unfortunately allowed for many students and staff to maintain a deficit perspective about Spanish speakers, leading to decisions not in the students' best interests. For example, contrary to the DL practices at the elementary level, Spanish-speaking recent immigrants were not placed in the DL program but placed in ESL and mainstream monolingual courses taught in English. This practice led to the development of a subtle student hierarchy—DL students were eventually perceived as "the cream of the crop" at the campus, followed by the mainstream English-speaking monolingual students, and at the bottom of the hierarchy, the Spanish-speaking ESL students. Regardless of the fact that most recent immigrants were at or above level proficient in Spanish, they were not placed in the Spanish-delivered courses because, according to one of the assistant principals, "What these students need is English, not Spanish." Thus, we found that many of the mainstream staff did not understand the theoretical framework that supports DL instruction that leads to superior achievement in both English and Spanish.

As the DL program expanded to seventh grade, two more teachers were incorporated into the program. The Pre-AP Spanish teacher, born in the Río Grande Valley, was highly proficient in both languages and cultures and sensitive to the needs of the local students. He knew how to develop culturally relevant instruction and how to motivate students to continue developing their Spanish proficiency. However, the seventh grade social studies teacher exhibited the opposite attitude towards the program. Although born and raised in Mexico and highly proficient in academic Spanish, he didn't support the development of the students' first language, especially for his recent-immigrant students. Even though hired to deliver his instruction entirely in Spanish, he was delivering instruction mostly in English; his PowerPoints and handouts were in English and he would switch to Spanish only when observed by an administrator. Rather than be guided by a thorough understanding of the goals and research-based strategies of the DL program, he felt pressured to accept the task of teaching in Spanish. Eventually, this teacher mentioned that he felt he was "doing a disservice to the students by teaching in Spanish." Through this experience, the DL directors learned that, while Spanish academic proficiency is a desirable attribute in DL teachers, such proficiency does not guarantee faithful implementation. A thorough understanding of the program and a thoughtful commitment to authentic DL teaching practices are two important attributes to look for when hiring DL teachers.

Dr. Ferrón (one of the authors of this chapter) became the eighth grade DL social studies teacher (and I will now switch to "first person" for this portion of the story). During my hiring interview I was asked a myriad of questions about U.S. history to measure my content knowledge. Once satisfied with my content expertise, they asked me, in English, if I could "teach history in Spanish." They never measured my Spanish proficiency or asked me what I thought about teaching a state-assessed course in Spanish.

Getting Ready for DL Instruction—A Personal Journey

Even though I received instruction in two languages during my elementary and secondary school years, I was not prepared to deliver instruction to DL students. I had no idea how differently these students had been educated in the DL program and had no knowledge about the best practices available to support their education. Based on my hiring interview, my understanding was that as a dual language teacher, my task was simply to teach U.S. history in Spanish.

The week before school started, I received a large set of books and ancillary materials to deliver instruction. The set included teacher textbook editions, colorful slides, CDs, and DVDs. All these materials were exclusively in English. Only one thin workbook was in Spanish, printed in black and white, with limited text and no illustrations. I soon found that this was not necessarily the experience of my DL peers.

While the sixth grade social studies DL teacher had a set of instructional materials mostly in English, the seventh grade teacher had abundant instructional materials available in Spanish. The textbook company that printed the sixth and eighth grade textbooks didn't have the Spanish versions fully available while the seventh grade company did. But the staff in charge of deciding which textbooks to adopt did not have the Spanish-delivered courses in mind when they made the decisions. Forced to develop my own instructional materials in Spanish, I gained a stronger ownership of the instructional process. The challenge also gave me the opportunity to plan and develop materials in collaboration with my Spanish language arts peers.

The DL Students

Based on my traditional schooling experience, I set up my classroom using obsolete practices. The desk rows were geometrically aligned and my classroom walls were filled with all kinds of print, exclusively in Spanish. When the bell rang and my DL students poured into the classroom, they started moving the desks that I had meticulously aligned. When I asked the students why, they replied, "Isn't this the DL classroom? This is how we sit." Nobody had mentioned to me anything about bilingual pairs. One student immediately claimed that the information placed on the walls was written in the "wrong color." I had used blue ink to print the classroom rules in Spanish, and according to the student, the Spanish text was supposed to be printed in red. Once again, nobody had told me anything about color-coding by language. I soon discovered that being a DL teacher in PSJA was much more than "teaching in Spanish."

My DL students were proud and performed well; they were eager to learn and demanded enriching instruction. Jaime is an example of DL students' high aspirations. During the first-week-of-school routine, in response to a questionnaire about student goals, Jaime assured me that he was going to be the valedictorian of his class. Throughout the year, Jaime worked thoroughly for each point to ensure a perfect score. Once in high school, Jaime continued his relentless effort. Four years later Jaime not only became the valedictorian of his class but also graduated from high school with an associate's degree and more than 100 hours of college credits. These accomplishments led to Jaime attaining admission and a full scholarship to an Ivy League school. Of course not all DL students are Jaime, and not all attend Ivy League schools, but all of the PSJA DL students have graduated from high school and their enrollment into college immediately after graduation is above 98%, double the national standard for all students, and almost four times the national percentage for Hispanic students.

Later, I was re-assigned to teach Spanish language arts to ESL students, where I discovered that the Spanish-speaking recent immigrants were not being placed in DL, Spanish-delivered courses. Based on the idea that "what these students need is more English," the students were placed in English-delivered courses regardless of their beginning stage of ESL acquisition, thus forcing them to be inefficient learners in a language they were still acquiring. Placed in an ESL pullout program, ESL-supported instruction was only available during one of the seven periods of the day. Recent immigrant students felt frustrated in classes where they couldn't understand the teacher and there was no other instructional support available. Other English learners who had been in U.S. schools longer, though more proficient in English, felt equally frustrated because they had gotten so far behind in content knowledge that they could not make sense of what the teacher was teaching. As a result, these English learners' self-esteem and academic confidence was lower than mainstream and DL students.

It took me 1 school year to convince the principal and the program director to allow Spanish-proficient ESL students to participate in DL courses and to become "non-traditional" DL students. Administrators were afraid that the incorporation of the ESL students would be detrimental both for the program and for the ESL students. Even the DL students were challenged by the ESL students' incorporation. Like other members of the school community, many DL students held a deficit perspective about Spanish-speaking recent immigrants. They thought the ESL students were ignorant and unwilling to learn.

The school eventually approved a new policy for the DL program to become the newcomers' program for Spanish-speaking recent immigrants. After a few weeks, the core DL students who had been in the program since early elementary grades not only accepted the presence of the ESL students in their classroom, but started perceiving them as peers and as linguistic and cultural assets. The active participation of the ESL students in the DL classrooms enriched the program. By the end of the school year the assessment data proved the decision correct—ESL students participating in DL instruction significantly outperformed their ESL peers not participating in the program on all standardized assessments, even though the assessments were delivered exclusively in English. They had benefited from more efficient learning of content in Spanish while they were acquiring English. A prime example of the transformational power of this decision is the story of Nestor.

Nestor entered the U.S. school system in fourth grade. By fourth grade all instruction in his school was delivered exclusively in English. Accustomed to being an excellent student in Mexico, by sixth grade Nestor was ranked among the lowest performing students at Liberty Middle School. His frustration eventually led to major misconduct. Before sending Nestor to an alternative education campus, the principal asked for the opportunity to place Nestor in dual language and Nestor became a non-traditional DL student in seventh grade. By eighth grade Nestor was in the top 25% of his class, but his academic achievement would become even more evident in high school. His story will be continued in the high school section below.

During my second year of teaching I met another important group of students—the students who left the DL program years earlier and now wanted to return. As previously mentioned, expanding the program into middle school was partially an act of faith. At the time, there was no empirical evidence to support the claim that the program was going to be successful. Therefore, some parents decided to remove their children from the DL program when they moved into middle school. Many of these students continued in the school district and were enrolled in the mainstream, English-delivered program at Liberty Middle School. However, when the DL program reached eighth grade, many of these students and their parents became aware of the academic benefits and the outstanding outcomes of the program. They wanted to be back in the program.

By then the program was immersed in a mesh of internal politics. For almost a decade, thanks to the Title VII grants, the DL program had enough funds to work autonomously from the bilingual department, and this autonomy eventually generated a rivalry among the program directors. The superior performance of the middle school DL students made the rivalry more acute. Consistent with the Thomas and Collier Graph (2012, p. 93), by eighth grade, the difference in academic performance between English learners participating in DL and English learners participating in transitional bilingual education was significant. On average, the DL English learners were not only outperforming the English learners not in DL but also outperforming their English-speaking peers not in DL. Additionally, all eighth grade English learners participating in DL had the opportunity to take the AP Spanish language arts class and test and gain up to 12 college-credit hours. In contrast, most English learners participating in the traditional program were not granted the opportunity to participate in AP courses due to the persisting deficit perspective.

When the grant funds ended, the district decided to continue supporting the DL program, placing it under the umbrella of the bilingual department. Now the rival programs were within the same department. Some decisions seemed to be impacted by this rivalry. Such was the case of the returning DL students. Arguing that the parents had their choice and that this decision was irreversible, the bilingual department rejected the idea of accepting the students back in the program. Fortunately, the school principal supported their participation and a significant number of students were able to return to the program by eighth grade. Eventually, the district decided not only to allow the reincorporation of former DL students, but allowed for other Spanish-proficient students to join the program in middle school. Now perceived as an enrichment program for Spanish speakers, the program soon attracted students who had never been in DL before.

Edgar is an example of this kind of student. Edgar was born to an immigrant family from Monterrey, Mexico. Though he was schooled in an early-exit transitional bilingual program, the family's frequent trips and long stays in Mexico allowed him to maintain his proficiency in Spanish. Back in the U.S. and eager for Edgar to maintain his Spanish academic proficiency, his family asked that Edgar be placed in DL in seventh grade. His placement was not immediately accepted. He was not a recent immigrant and he was no longer labeled an English learner. It was not until eighth grade that Edgar officially became a DL student. Eventually Edgar graduated third in his high school class and with an associate's degree. Thanks to his academic achievements, Edgar was granted a Gates Millennium Scholarship and attended Rochester University where he graduated with honors, and in the spring of 2017 he was recognized for his humanitarian efforts by UNESCO. Such success stories among non-traditional DL students are common.

A key challenge discussed previously is the deficit perspective that many stakeholders have about bilingual education, emergent bilingual students in general, and Spanish speakers in particular. The implementation of a DL program does not eradicate this problem. Many teachers, school administrators, and parents hold deficit perspectives about bilingual education and bilingual students that can eventually hinder faithful implementation of quality DL. An example of this bias impacted Jaime. As previously mentioned, Jaime was an outstanding student with a clear mission in mind—to become the high school valedictorian. By his sophomore year, his academic excellence was already evident. That year a new campus administrator joined the school. Amazed with Jaime's academic performance she asked, "Jaime, being such an amazing student, why are you still in the DL program?" Jaime confidently responded, "It's because I'm still in the DL program that I am an amazing student."

Another example occurred at Liberty Middle School when I was escorting my students to the cafeteria. Two of my recent immigrant students were walking in front of me. The students were speaking in Spanish—after all, it was lunch time, and they were DL students leaving a DL classroom on a DL campus that celebrated the Spanish language. A teacher walking toward them abruptly asked them, "When are you going to stop acting like fools and start speaking in English?" After a long conversation with the principal, the teacher apologized, claiming that she didn't mean to offend the students but to "motivate" them to speak English. Unfortunately, these types of cultural and linguistic microaggressions against bilingual students are common. Teachers might not be ill-intended but their actions are influenced by the deficit paradigms they hold in regard to bilingual education, bilingual students, and the use of Spanish at school.

The Outcomes

Although my first year of teaching in the DL program was filled with challenges, it was also highly rewarding. The DL students significantly outperformed the other students at both campus and district levels. Thanks to the advanced Spanish courses, Liberty Middle School DL students were accepted to participate along with high school students in the Pan-American Student Forum, a widely recognized Spanish-language academic competition taking place in Texas each year. This academic competition was originally organized by the Organization of American States "to offer students and teachers a better opportunity to learn more about all the Americas and the Spanish-speaking world, thus fostering cordial relations among these peoples" *(https://www.pasf.com)*. Liberty Middle School ranked among the five top-performing schools, even though their competitors were all high school students.

Perhaps the most important achievement of the middle school DL program was the amazing number of students attaining college credit before entering high school. All DL students took Pre-Ap Spanish Language Arts in seventh grade, and in eighth grade they were enrolled in the AP Spanish Language and Culture course. In May, all eighth grade DL students took the AP Spanish Language and Culture test with extremely high levels of success. On average, about 80% of all eighth grade DL students attained a score of 3 or higher on the AP test, enough to grant them from 6 to 12 hours of college credit, while the national average of Hispanic participation in AP courses at that time was 11%. The U.S. Department of Education identifies AP participation as a reliable measure of college readiness, a remarkable achievement for middle school students. Not surprisingly, when the DL program moved into high school, two of the three comprehensive high schools in PSJA asked for the opportunity to serve these amazing students.

Moving into High School

Expanding the program into two high schools implied doubling the number of teachers while reducing the number of DL students being served at each campus. In addition, there was no structured model to follow. The district decided to continue offering DL through social studies, Spanish language arts, and fine arts. During the planning year DL teachers were identified, materials acquired, and staff were trained and attended bilingual conferences. However, all these preparations did not prevent new challenges from arising.

The first challenge appeared as soon as the new school year started. While I had assured the DL students that the high school program would be provided through Spanish language arts, social studies, and an elective delivered entirely in Spanish, the DL students at North High School took my words literally and expected their DL coursework to be exactly like the middle school program. The eighth grade DL elective was drama; therefore, they enrolled in Theater under the assumption that it was going to be delivered in Spanish. When the school year began, the students realized they were wrong. Empowered by their higher levels of self-esteem and academic confidence, some DL students, led by Rigoberto and Andrea, "demanded" that the theater class be delivered in Spanish. Their request was denied. When the students learned that the school had contracted Disney's Aladdin Jr. for their musical for that year, they developed their own version.

Following the original plot of the musical, their version included two protagonists from different socioeconomic levels. The students added a language difference between the protagonists. Princess Jasmine spoke "the language of the wealthy and the educated"—Spanish. Yes, Spanish. While Aladdin, coming from a humble background, spoke the language of the poor—English. Inspired by their own linguistic background, the students were challenging the linguistic paradigms of the audience by changing the linguistic power balance in the musical. Suddenly, Spanish became the language of power. In their version of the musical, the wealthy Spanish speakers and the poor English speakers were segregated by a spell imposed by the mischievous Jafar. By distancing both groups through language, Jafar was able to control them because he was the only one capable of speaking both languages. Bilingualism was Jafar's source of power. Using metaphorical language, they conveyed the social value of a DL program through the plight of Princess Jasmine and Aladdin as they joined forces to defeat Jafar and to allow all members of their community to reap the benefits of being bilingual.

Though impressed by the students' creativity, the high school drama teacher claimed that the school was bound to a contract with Disney that impeded them from altering the musical in any way. Rigoberto and Andrea asked for support from their former DL teachers who asked the drama teacher to contact Disney. Surprisingly, Disney sent two professional scriptwriters to work with the students. The students' version of the musical became a campus success. While PSJA high school drama events typically include five to seven performances, the DL edition of Aladdin Jr. was presented more than 50 times. The Disney Company was so pleased with the new version that they took the students to Austin to present their version for one week, and during the summer took them to Orlando for 1 month to present the musical at Disney World. As part of the agreement, Disney kept the copyright for the bilingual version, and has since been presented in more than 20 languages and in more than 50 countries around the world. Keep in mind that this amazing feat was attained by PSJA DL students when they were in ninth grade!

PSJA High School also faced challenges at the beginning of the school year. Following the district's plans, PSJA High provided DL instruction in three content areas: Spanish language arts, social studies, and an elective. After two weeks of school, a representative group of DL students demanded that the social studies teacher be replaced, claiming their instruction was not as rigorous as they needed. The school was suddenly faced with a dilemma—retain the social studies teacher against the will of the students; water down the program by replacing the teacher with a non-Spanish-proficient teacher; or find a teacher willing and capable of delivering instruction entirely in Spanish in a different academic area.

They found their answer with an algebra teacher at PSJA High School who was both highly proficient and willing to teach in Spanish. The DL program director supported the idea even though it represented a new set of challenges. The first challenge was to speedily find textbooks and other instructional materials to deliver algebra instruction in Spanish. Another challenge was that in Texas, for students to graduate from high school, they needed to pass a high-stakes, state-developed algebra assessment delivered in English. Several key stakeholders were concerned that students would be "set up for failure" by receiving algebra instruction in Spanish and then tested in English. The DL director and several DL teachers reminded them that these DL students had already succeeded in assessments in English following instructional delivery in Spanish. In their eighth grade social studies course taught exclusively in Spanish, the DL students' average passing rate was significantly higher than school, district, and state averages. Based on this data, the district approved the algebra DL course.

This decision prompted a third challenge—the DL students had never been exposed to math instruction in Spanish because the DL math instruction for Grades K-8 had always been in English. When the students learned that the algebra course would be delivered in Spanish they panicked. One student claimed that "Math doesn't exist in Spanish." Fortunately, their anxiety was short-lived; after a couple of weeks, and thanks to the remarkable teaching skills of the algebra teacher, the students once again exhibited their academic strength.

The "math DL challenge" eventually proved highly fruitful for the program. The decision released the program from unwarranted content-delivery limitations. Schools could look for linguistically and academically qualified teachers willing to deliver instruction in Spanish, regardless of their content area. This academic freedom allowed schools to be more creative in offering DL courses in a variety of content areas to meet the complexity and diversity of the high school coursework offerings. Emboldened by the success of the "math DL challenge," both high schools decided to also include biology in their DL schedule. With time, it became normal practice to place all ninth grade DL students in DL Algebra and DL Biology. Almost 40 courses were eventually offered in Spanish, including several junior- and senior-level courses, and science soon became a key subject delivered in Spanish.

DL Success in Science

The decision to include biology in the DL course catalog proved highly fruitful. Participating students tended to outperform their mainstream peers. For example, DL students in the first two cohorts outperformed their peers by a significant difference. In the second year, when biology instruction was provided in Spanish, the average score of the DL students increased while the score of the mainstream students remained constant, and the score of the ESL students not participating in DL decreased (see Figure 5.1).

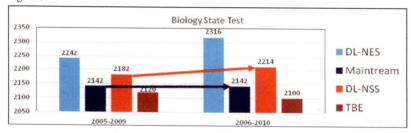

Figure 5.1

The students' performance on the biology state test (assessed in English) supported the decision to continue implementing DL science instruction at the next grade levels. Soon, both high schools were offering DL Chemistry and DL Physics. PSJA High also offered advanced DL courses in anatomy and physiology and medical microbiology.

Conscious of their superior academic performance, many DL students were eager to take more college-credit courses. Therefore, many DL students were not registering for the DL science courses so that they could enroll in AP Chemistry or AP Physics courses instead. To avoid losing students, the program searched for creative options. In 2012, Mario Ferrón, Jr. (co-author of this chapter, and I will now switch to "first person") became the first teacher in Texas to teach an AP chemistry course entirely in Spanish. These DL students' AP test-passing rate in English was significantly above the national average. The following year these students took the DL AP physics course with similar test results.

The expansion of the DL program into the field of science generated another amazing outcome. Nestor, the troublesome student who in sixth grade was en route to alternative education and eventually became a DL student, was now in high school. In ninth grade Nestor enrolled in my biology class. I soon noticed that Nestor was gifted in science. Therefore, when Nestor enrolled in my chemistry class the following year, I invited him to join a college research project. At the time, I was working on my master's degree in chemistry, serving as a research assistant for my professor, and conducting cancer research. Conscious of the academic capacity of my students, I decided to invite some of them to participate in the research project; Nestor was one of these students. Project participation implied a significant investment from the university because Nestor would be working with a sophisticated super computer and the license cost about $1,000. Nestor submitted his first research article to the American Chemical Society Conference in Boston, Massachusetts in 2010. Amazingly, Nestor attained this academic feat when he was only a high school sophomore.

Thanks to his participation in AP and dual credit courses, Nestor graduated from high school with more than 60 hours of college credit, many of them in science. His academic performance also granted him immediate admission to the University of Texas-Pan American where he graduated in just 2 years. By then, Nestor had published three articles in recognized peer-reviewed journals. Thanks to his academic accolades and his DACA documentation, Nestor is currently pursuing a Ph.D. in chemistry at Northeastern University.

In 2014, the valedictorian at the new PSJA Southwest High School was Omar, a recent immigrant participating in DL. Omar enrolled in a U.S. school for the first time during his freshman year with an English language proficiency level on the TELPAS (Texas English Language Proficiency Assessment System) of beginner. Four years later, and thanks to the opportunity to take 14 of his high school credits in Spanish, Omar graduated from high school as valedictorian, even though he was still labeled as an English learner according to the English proficiency test. Omar attained his Bachelor of Science degree (in English) at the University of Texas at Austin and is currently studying medicine at the University of Toronto.

Lessons Learned: Expanding the Secondary DL Program Districtwide

In March, 2012, the PSJA superintendent, Dr. Daniel King, asked Dr. Ferrón to become PSJA secondary schools DL coordinator. His main task was to expand the program districtwide: all elementary schools were to phase out their early-exit transitional bilingual program and to phase in DL instruction. At the same time, Dr. King asked all secondary schools to develop DL strands across all grade levels.

As the new secondary schools DL coordinator, my most important task was to ensure faithful program implementation. My first step was to identify and recruit students who could participate successfully in DL education. A key element for successful participation was for students to have some academic proficiency in Spanish. Therefore, I developed a multiple-question Spanish reading assessment. To give all students the opportunity to be identified, I tested all PSJA students in Grades 5-8. More than 10,000 students were tested and eventually 2600 students were identified and invited to join the program. More than 40 parent meetings were scheduled to inform parents about the goals, benefits, and challenges of the program. Of the 2600 students invited, only 70 (2.7%) declined the invitation.

Two things happened during the testing process: because PSJA tested all fifth to eighth grade students, the testing also included students who were already in DL. The DL students' scores provided the district with a minimum score that could be used as a benchmark to be invited to the program. In addition, the report also included the TELPAS scores of the English learners. The data exhibited a strong positive correlation between Spanish proficiency and TELPAS scores. These results support Cummins' claim (2000) that the more that students develop their first language, the more they show positive development of the second language. Also, Thomas and Collier's research findings (2017) illustrate that the best predictor of academic success in English for English learners is the quality and extension of instruction in the home language.

Once PSJA had enough students to implement the program at each grade level at each campus, the next task was to identify potential DL teachers. Meetings were scheduled at each campus to inform all teachers about the goals and challenges of the program. Each campus had at least one or more core content teachers who were able to teach in Spanish. Due to the substantial number of teachers needed, I recommended that schools recruit capable and willing teachers across all content areas. Based on my previous experience with the DL teacher-hiring process, I included teachers' DL knowledge and willingness to participate as critical aspects in the recruitment process. Even though their academic Spanish proficiency was a key element in the process, it was not an insurmountable requirement. As teachers they understood that academic proficiency can be developed through time and practice. To support teachers' academic Spanish proficiency development, I chose to deliver most of the DL professional development sessions in Spanish. In addition, to support program implementation, Dr. King also recommended the temporary hiring of teachers from Spain, most of them to teach high school math and science courses.

Once students and teachers were identified and recruited, schools were informed of their incoming DL students and the DL courses needed. Now the task was to monitor the process. Eventually this became the most time-consuming and challenging part of the task. Because most schools struggled to schedule students due to the complexity of the secondary-school master schedule, I recommended that counselors schedule the DL courses first. An additional challenge was to identify and acquire the instructional materials in Spanish needed to support instruction. By then, a variety of vendors were offering Spanish materials in a number of subjects and some vendors offered to import textbooks from Spanish-speaking countries if needed.

As the program progressed through the years, new challenges developed. Some counselors, based on their deficit perspective, were pulling academically successful students out of the DL program once they reached a specified level of English proficiency, thus limiting their continued development in both languages. Some campuses were scheduling students only in Spanish language arts or only in the Spanish-delivered core content course and many recent immigrants were not being placed in DL because "what they needed was English." Monitoring students' placement was an ongoing task. Student lists had to be reviewed and revised every month to ensure adequate and appropriate placement.

Another task was to provide the necessary support for the DL teachers to ensure faithful implementation. Lesson planning was a challenge for many DL teachers. DL teachers had to plan with mainstream teachers and such planning was done in English. DL teachers had to do double the work; first they had to plan in English with their English-speaking peers, and later translate everything to Spanish. To solve this issue, PSJA provided teachers the opportunity to network and plan together with similar grade level DL teachers from other schools. This collaboration proved highly successful. Another instrument used to improve instruction was to establish DL departments at each secondary school campus. DL teachers at each campus met periodically to analyze data and share information about the program at the classroom and campus levels. During these meetings, teachers would analyze student data and work together to support student progress. DL teachers developed an amazing bond; they felt empowered and supported.

Following the same line of thought, each campus developed DL student advisory boards, led entirely by DL students and sponsored by DL teachers. With representatives from each grade level, the student advisory board met frequently with the campus DL department to analyze student data and provide positive pressure to their struggling peers. They provided valuable feedback to teachers on how to improve their lessons. Some campuses also established DL parent advisory boards. Parents were supportive of the DL program and their advocacy became an important resource for most campuses. In conjunction with each campus' family liaison, DL parents helped teachers find resources, develop lessons, organize events, and monitor field trips. Many decisions made at the district coordinator level were guided by the feedback provided by these three structures.

More Challenges

One of the biggest challenges a DL program faces is its rivalry with the English-delivered mainstream program. Many teachers in the mainstream are used to seeing the bilingual program as a remedial program for English learners only that eventually feeds into the mainstream rather than a stand-alone program for all students. Many secondary English learners who have received a significant amount of schooling in their home country exhibit higher academic performance in comparison with their mainstream peers when they have reached enough English proficiency to exit the transitional bilingual/ESL services. Mainstream teachers don't want to lose these high-performing students. At the same time, many teachers feel their jobs are at risk if the DL program is expanded into the secondary school level because they cannot teach in Spanish. Unfortunately, the teachers' reaction can significantly hinder program implementation. Some teachers mislead students and parents about the benefits of the program. Some teachers see their DL peers as rivals and therefore reject collaborating with them. Many schools develop a "school within a school" mentality, where DL and the monolingual mainstream become rivals within the same campus. This environment can generate devastating effects—teachers competing for students and resources, programs openly criticizing each other, etc.

To solve this issue, we have learned that campuses interested in embracing DL need to adopt a campus-wide environment where all teachers are DL teachers, regardless of their language of instruction. All campus teachers and staff should thoroughly understand the program and participate in DL professional development. After all, DL instructional practices are highly effective regardless of the language of instruction (Thomas & Collier, 2017). When all staff members participate in cultural events and program celebrations it helps everyone to take ownership of the program.

But perhaps the most important challenge in the success of a DL program is to change the deficit perspective that surrounds bilingual education. All stakeholders must clearly understand the cognitive, academic, and socioeconomic benefits that an effective, enrichment program can bring to families, the school, and the community. They need to perceive Spanish proficiency as an academic and sociocultural asset and understand that the academic development of students' home language impacts their cognitive development and their mastery of the curriculum in both languages.

In summary, we believe that secondary DL instruction can be one of the most effective models of instruction. The beauty of dual language education is that it works and it works for all (Collier & Thomas, 2005). However, unless all key stakeholders change their paradigm, their actions will challenge effective program implementation. Schools and school districts interested in delivering DL instruction at the secondary level must be fully aware of the challenges and be fully prepared to meet them.

CHAPTER SIX
ILLINOIS: A SYSTEMIC APPROACH TO BUILDING A SECONDARY DUAL LANGUAGE PROGRAM:
THE STORY OF HIGHLAND PARK HIGH SCHOOL

DR. TOM KOULENTES—LIBERTYVILLE SCHOOL DISTRICT 70, ILLINOIS

Introduction by Collier & Thomas: *A passion for equity for all students is the theme of this dual language story from a high school principal in an affluent community with a diverse student population (22% Latino), 30 minutes north of Chicago's downtown. The neighboring K-8 school district with a strong DL program informed Highland Park High School (located in a separate high school district) to be prepared to receive DL students. In response, DL leaders at Highland Park High School developed the DL mission and core values of the program, invited key stakeholders to meetings, established a DL timeline for key decision making, identified high-quality DL teachers, established schoolwide DL professional development, formed DL parent and student advisory councils, and created the Highland Park High School Seal of Dual Language (with more rigorous requirements than the Illinois State Seal of Biliteracy). DL high school students (Latino and Caucasian) now enroll in many AP courses and achieve at higher levels than non-DL students on the ACT (college entrance exam). This is a White majority U.S. high school—a model for what U.S. schools can do.*

"It starts with a deep, unwavering commitment to equity for all students." That's what I tell folks who ask me how to start a dual language program. This answer surprises people; most think the first step to starting a dual language program is to hire high-quality instructors, or to develop academic courses that will be taught in a non-English language. But if the intent of dual language education is to create young adults who are fully bilingual, bicultural, and biliterate, how could dual language (DL) be built upon any foundation other than a commitment to educational equity?

In most school communities across the United States, the true goal of DL—to fully elevate a language such as Spanish or Chinese to the same academic and social status as English—is a radical idea. In far too many communities, it is canon that students must learn English, and any additional language a child speaks is certainly nice, but definitely not necessary. DL leaders must view themselves as equity leaders because any thoughtfully designed DL program confronts the notion of English linguistic superiority and explicitly creates a school environment where a non-English language is of equal value and status as its English cousin. Changing an English-dominant system and creating space and status for non-English languages in a public school environment is equity work, and in some communities where a monolingual English worldview dominates, it will be perceived as a radical and disruptive endeavor.

The fact that we were engaging in equity work was an important realization for our school staff. When we understood that our students' language and identity are inextricably intertwined, we learned that redesigning our school to systemically elevate the status of a non-English language simultaneously elevated the status of native speakers of this language within the larger school community. In that moment, our school community's long-held notions of White, English, racial, cultural, or linguistic superiority, as well as community beliefs about who schools are for and which students occupied honors courses, were upended in our new DL environment. Suddenly, our non-native English speakers were on the same level academically and socially as our native English speakers. For many communities, the idea of non-White, non-native English speakers occupying high-status academic realms such as honors or AP courses challenges a construction of reality that does not easily yield.

Resistance to moving from an English-dominant to a DL educational system can be fierce and DL leaders must stand firm against the pressure and criticism that will be hurled at them by those who will fight to maintain an English-dominant system. Despite a growing body of research to the contrary, for boards of education, parents, and community members with limited understanding of linguistics and with limited exposure to people from other countries, there may be a fear that DL programs threaten the overall quality of the school and the rigor of an education a child might obtain. Only those educators committed to equity and armed with the data about the positive long-term achievement impact DL has for **all learners** (Thomas & Collier, 2012) can remain stalwart and keep focus on the extensive restructuring that must occur to truly transform a school into a DL environment.

Despite the challenges, both politically and logistically, DL programs are being developed by a growing number of secondary schools across the country. Research on these programs continues to affirm that the academic and social benefits of a well-designed DL program affect all students who participate. Educators wishing to join this work can gather strength and wisdom from studying the trails blazed by those intrepid pioneers who have come before them. This essay is intended to be a road map written for those who, now understanding the full scope of the required curriculum and equity work, as well as the resulting educational benefits, choose to proceed.

Highland Park High School Dual Language Program

This chapter is a case study of the DL program that was designed and implemented at Highland Park High School (HPHS), a suburban Chicago school located approximately 30 minutes north of Chicago's downtown. Sitting along Lake Michigan's North Shore, the school is home to a diverse population of students. According to the 2017 Illinois School Report Card, approximately 70% of the students are *white,* 22% are Latino, and the remaining 8% are multiracial, Black, Asian, or Native American *(https://www.illinoisreportcard.com).* The school is well resourced, with property taxes from the highly affluent community accounting for approximately 90% of the revenue base and per pupil spending being over $20,000 per student. Despite being a wealthy community, nearly 15% of the school's students are from low-income households. Historically, HPHS has been one of the elite high schools in Illinois, with an average student ACT (college admission test) score of 26 (83rd percentile), and the vast majority of students attending 4-year colleges upon graduation. Within these impressive statistics, however, lies an achievement gap where Black, Latino, low-income, and special education students historically lag behind their White, middle-class peers in standardized test scores, enrollment in honors/Advanced Placement (AP) courses, and 4-year college attendance after high school graduation (www.illinoisreportcard.com).

It is within this school community that the staff of HPHS, a place where I worked as a teacher, bilingual program director, and principal for 22 years, has created and implemented a remarkable secondary DL program that currently serves approximately 200 students (10% of the school population) with core academic and elective courses taught either in English or Spanish. What follows is the story of how this program came to be, the challenges our staff confronted, and the strategies we used to completely transform our instruction of DL students in a period of 5 years.

Awakening

I remember the combination of excitement and embarrassment as I stared at the screen. It was the spring of 2012 and our community's K-8 elementary district, North Shore District 112, was presenting information about its DL program to our high school's bilingual team. Established in 1996, the District 112 DL program had, over the course of 20 years, grown into one of the preeminent DL programs in the nation, being recognized by the Association for Supervision and Curriculum Development in 2013 as a model school program. As partners in education, we had long known of District 112's program, but what struck me and my team that day was the sudden realization that nearly 700 students, approximately 100 children per grade level K-8, were DL students, and they would be attending our high school. These 700 children had a formal education that was 80% Spanish and 20% English from Grades K-3. Starting in about fourth grade and continuing through eighth grade the students were spending 50% of their school day with Spanish as the language of instruction and the other 50% using English. As a former bilingual program director with a strong background in language acquisition theory, I was thrilled to see that this cohort of kids was months away from coming to our school. As my mind raced with the possibilities for these students, a wave of embarrassment washed over me. Highland Park High School, one of the best public high schools in the state of Illinois, a place with a deep commitment to equity and excellence, had no formal curriculum or program to offer these students. These 100 DL freshmen, representing nearly one out of five of our ninth grade students, were about to move from a DL school system to a monolingual school system. Their formal education as emerging multilinguals was about to come to a screeching halt. As I looked around the conference room at our team, our eyes locked and we all knew what we had to do. We had to immediately set to work building a high school DL program worthy of our students and our community.

As I look back on it now, there were five key actions we took that were vital to our success. First, we set aside considerable time for strategic planning. Second, we were explicit and assertive in the recruiting and hiring of bilingual staff. Third, we differentiated our professional development offerings and put considerable resources toward professional development that taught our staff to work effectively with DL students by sheltering academic language and content. Fourth, we worked aggressively and proactively to educate our superintendent, board of education, and parent community about the academic and social-emotional benefits of high school DL programs for students. Fifth, we developed a Seal of Dual Language that required a higher level of achievement and language skills than our state's Seal of Biliteracy. In retrospect, all five of these actions were necessary for our success; had one been missing, our program would not have evolved in such an efficient or effective manner.

Dual Language Fridays: Allocating Time for Systemic Planning and Program Implementation

Perhaps the most challenging aspect of building a secondary DL program is the coordination of the communication, professional development efforts, and structural changes that need to occur to fully implement a schoolwide program and transform a high school. At the high school level, systemic change is extraordinarily difficult and complex. Traditional high schools are departmentalized, each often with its own school procedures, educational philosophies, and practices (Donaldson, 2006). Furthermore, high schools are often so large they contain many diverse stakeholders, and the best public high school reform efforts often fail due to their inability to fully capture the attention and sustained focus of such a large system.

To ensure that our school's DL program unfolded in a logical, thoughtful, and organized fashion, we created something called "DL Fridays." Each and every Friday, for a period of 2 years, we blocked out the last 90 minutes of our school day, from 1:30 to 3:00 pm to meet as a leadership team and discuss, plan, and orchestrate the implementation of our DL program across our entire school system. This commitment of time was substantial, so we purposely placed it at the end of each week, when most of the week's issues were addressed and managed, and at a time when few other meetings were pulling at our team.

The core group that met each week for DL Friday consisted of our world language chair, our English learner (EL)/bilingual director, our assistant principal for curriculum and instruction, and the principal (myself). In our school's context, these were the four most important people for curriculum change to occur. The department chair and EL/bilingual director were the direct supervisors of the world language teachers and EL teachers, and they were also the curriculum leaders of those departments. The assistant principal for curriculum and the principal were the curriculum leaders of the school as a whole; their presence in these meetings signaled that this was not a departmental initiative, but rather a "whole-school" initiative impacting all departments and programs.

The importance of the school principal being fully committed and engaged in the DL transformation cannot be overstated. In high school settings, research by numerous authors cite the importance of the principal serving as a curriculum leader (Chenoweth & Theokas, 2011) as well as maintaining organizational focus to protect the staff's time and ability to develop the deep structural changes that must occur for transformation to take root (Schmoker, 2011). In terms of working with DL programs, Thomas and Collier (2012) propose that it is the principal who must explicitly state that DL is an official, all-school initiative. The principal must support this effort with her attention, sustained focus on and allocation of resources to professional development, stakeholder communication, and defense of the program from critics. Absent the school principal's support, a DL program is at best a departmental initiative and at worst doomed to fail when resistance to it invariably begins to surface.

To sustain our focus and safeguard the evolution of our thinking, the "core four" leaders, meeting every Friday, kept a shared-notes archive using Google. The "DL Team Planning Archive" contained our running discussion notes, links to important resources, and any "To Do's" our team identified. Each week the archive grew with information and captured our team's thinking; all of us could contribute resources as we identified them. Six years later, this archive still exists and continues to serve as the historical record of the program's growth and development. New members to our school's leadership team do not need to wonder why specific strategies or decisions were made, it is all recorded and preserved in the archive. All formal presentations we have created and delivered to staff, the board of education, or community are contained there for quick and easy access. All our student-data reports, moving back several years, are warehoused here for longitudinal reference. Any and all formal communications with parents, students, and staff are also archived here for us to revisit the ways in which we helped shape our stakeholders support and understandings of our work.

Though we had our core four leaders who maintained the systemic focus and drove the development of the program, DL Fridays were intentionally designed to be highly inclusive. Each week the team met, we identified questions or topics that needed to be discussed for the next step in the program's design. We would group these questions into categories and then invite teachers or other administrators to our next DL Friday meeting to discuss these questions with our team and help us generate ideas. For example, when we were discussing the impact of our DL program on our Spanish for native speakers courses, we invited the world language teachers who taught our native speakers to attend a series of DL Fridays where we would discuss ideas and strategies for transforming this curriculum into a Spanish language arts course to better meet the needs of our DL program. Another example is when we invited our physical education (PE)/traffic safety department chair, and Spanish-speaking PE teachers to DL Friday for a series of meetings where we redesigned our school's PE curriculum to offer PE, health, and traffic safety classes taught in Spanish.

Inviting school stakeholders, teachers, and administrators to DL Fridays was an effective and essential strategy for our ultimate success. First, by including each stakeholder in discussions pertaining to his/her area, respecting their expertise and building trust, we were better assured of their investment in and support of the program, as these folks saw they had a hand in helping build it. Second, these conversations were vital to unearthing problems, obstacles or issues that our core four team may have missed. Identifying these issues well in advance of implementation allowed us the opportunity to make tactical adjustments and ensure our rollout was as smooth as possible. In addition, in a high school setting, when initiatives get rolled out staff members will naturally check in with the people they believe are most impacted by the initiative to determine their level of awareness and support for the project. By including our stakeholders, we ensured that these individuals would be informed and supportive of the initiative and would be equipped to educate their colleagues about the DL efforts when informal conversations occurred in offices, hallways, the staff cafeteria, or the parking lot after school.

Developing a Mission and Focus

As the core four met each Friday, we used Wiggins & McTighe's (2005) concept of "Backward Design" to organize our work. We started by asking, "What did we want from our DL program?" Our goal was to create the best DL program in the nation, as we believe our students deserve nothing less. With this as our goal, we next identified the characteristics that needed to be in place for our DL program to be considered the best in the nation. This took some time. We studied and read. We looked at the research about DL, read case studies of existing programs, and visited our elementary district to see what they were doing. We met with consultants. After several weeks of study, meeting, and discussion, our team adopted the following mission statement with our sending district (District 112) and identified the following actions as the core targets of the program we would create.

Mission: *We aim to become a DL school where children will become bilingual and biliterate while developing an ability to navigate multiple cultures.*

A few notes about our mission statement are worth discussing. First, it was important that we explicitly use the term "DL school" as we did not want DL to be perceived only as an EL program or only as part of the world language department. Our program was meant to be an all-school initiative. Every department would own and invest in our DL program, and our mission statement needed to emphasize this commitment. In addition, it was important to us to name three goals we had for our DL students in our mission statement. We were working to create students who are bilingual (able to speak in two languages), biliterate (able to read and write in two languages), and bicultural (able to navigate different cultural contexts). These three goals were vital to state, as every subsequent effort we made designing our program needed to support our efforts to meet these three primary goals.

After extensive research and discussion, our group developed the following core values and working agreements for our program. The Highland Park High School DL program would:

- offer academic courses in all subject areas in either program language, Spanish or English;

- aim to gradually build a program where 50% of the students' courses are offered in Spanish, and 50% are offered in English;

- utilize sheltered instruction in both Spanish and English language classrooms;

- conduct the "Bridge" in the target languages (Beeman & Urow, 2012);

- develop assessments that are designed to assess DL students' emerging skills as bilinguals, not simply translate monolingual assessments into one language or another;

- offer active-learning environments where students work collaboratively with one another to engage in problem-based learning; and

- use the obtainment of 12th grade literacy standards in both English and Spanish as the ultimate goal for all students in the program.

It is so important for a leadership team to create both a vision and core values. These became the road map for our team to follow and they were a vital tool for focusing discussions and efforts and filtering out distractions, noise, and ineffective efforts. With our mission set, we knew our program needed to move students through three pathways: one to build biliteracy, one to develop bilingualism, and one to nurture biculturalism. With the mission and vision clear and the core values set, DL Friday meetings became less about philosophy and vision, and much more about the practical and logistical details of working to implement this program across our system.

To keep our team organized and accountable to progress, we created an ambitious 5-year implementation plan that operated according to this timeline:

- **2013-14:** Transformation of our EL and world language course sequences; DL staff development. Create DL parent advisory committee.

- **2014-15:** Implementation of DL physical education courses; DL staff development. Create DL student advisory committee.

- **2015-16:** Implementation of DL social studies, health, and traffic safety courses; DL staff development.

- **2016-17:** Development of DL geometry, international business, graphic design and biology courses; DL staff development.

- **2017-18:** Comprehensive program review and audit. Suggestions for program improvement.

As you can observe in this timeline, we did not try to unveil a fully formed DL program in the first year. We understood that we were working to completely overhaul and transform our school curriculum and student programs. This work would take us multiple years and require substantial time. As administrators, we understood that we needed to outline the systemic changes that would occur and create a multiyear plan that would be used to organize and communicate all of the efforts. Looking back, the timeline we developed was remarkably accurate and it was an essential tool for helping to keep our entire school system, from the board of education to our district office to our school staff, connected to the efforts that were being taken to move our school's DL program from infancy to adulthood.

Identifying and Hiring High-Quality Dual Language Instructors

With the vision set and the wheels in motion to gradually implement a schoolwide DL program, our administrative team turned its focus to identifying and hiring the best possible teachers for our students to learn from. Our strategy for hiring started with bringing our entire administrative team together, including our assistant superintendent of human resources, and participating in training sessions where we identified the skills and characteristics necessary for being an effective DL teacher, as well as the ways in which we could identify these skills when we screened résumés and met with prospective candidates. Naturally, we were looking for teaching candidates who had high levels of Spanish proficiency. Every administrator heard directly from me, as principal, that I wanted a premium placed on candidates who had Spanish language skills, be those credentialed (i.e., Spanish majors/minors; bilingual teacher certifications) or un-credentialed (i.e., native Spanish speaker, fluent speaker without a degree). All else being equal, I asked our administrative team to hire Spanish speakers even if we didn't anticipate their initial assignments being in DL or bilingual classrooms.

In order to maximize our hiring pool, we would contact professors of education at area universities, inquiring if they had names of Spanish-speaking students in their education programs who may be looking for jobs. We attended national DL conferences, scouting talented educators from across the nation. We worked to build networks using social media, such as LinkedIn, to advertise that Spanish-speaking educators, of all areas of certification, were being sought in our school. As a means of ensuring this focus remained in place, all new hires had to be approved by me, the building principal, prior to moving forward. When non-Spanish speaking candidates were hired, it was only after I was satisfied that an extensive search for a Spanish-speaking teacher was conducted and the process did not yield one or the caliber of the Spanish-speaking candidate was significantly below that of the non-Spanish speaker. With this focused hiring effort in place, over the course of a few years our school was able to identify and hire Spanish speakers for every academic department, thus creating great flexibility for our school in the DL classes we could develop and offer. With our vision and implementation plan set, and our staff increasingly in place, our next step was to create sustained staff-development efforts for as many staff members as possible.

Coordinating Staff Development

The first step in our staff development plan was to create a schoolwide campaign to get as many staff members as possible ESL/bilingual certified. In the state of Illinois, an educator can take five to six graduate courses in language acquisition theory, sheltered language methodology, assessment of English learners, and other EL-focused courses, to obtain a professional certificate to be able to teach ESL or bilingual classes. At the time of writing, no such certification existed for DL courses, but much of the DL pedagogy is rooted in EL/bilingual education, and thus our school made an aggressive push to get our teachers enrolled in these courses to earn this certification. In order to entice our teachers to enroll in these classes, our district offered tuition scholarships, paid largely through our Federal Title monies, to any teacher who signed up for the courses during a school year. Our teachers wanted to accrue graduate hours, as doing so advanced them on their pay scale. When we offered tuition-reduced classes that counted for salary advancement to our staff, they responded with great enthusiasm. During the time period we offered this program, we would see as many as 20 staff members a year enrolling in courses to earn EL/bilingual certification. It is important to note that we encouraged this certification for all our teachers, regardless of whether or not we had plans for them to be in DL classes. Research demonstrates that EL methodology, such as Quality Teaching for English Learners® (QTEL, *https://www.qtel.wested.org/*), Guided Language Acquisition Design® (Project GLAD®, *www.ocde.us/ntcprojectglad*) or Sheltered Instruction Observation Protocol® (SIOP, Echevarría, Vogt, & Short, 2016), actually benefits all learners in a school (Thomas & Collier, 2012, 2017). Therefore, a teacher certified in EL instruction will be able to boost the achievement of all her learners, not just her English learners. Furthermore, national statistics indicate that by the year 2020, one of five children in public schools will be a non-native English speaker; having a staff equipped to work with developmental bilinguals of all stages is increasingly necessary to sustain effective programming for all learners.

In addition to the graduate courses, we utilized our school's professional development dollars to bring staff development workshops to our school during the summer and the school year. One of the most important workshops we offered was delivered by Cheryl Urow of the Center for Biliteracy, a 2-day workshop for approximately 50 members of our staff from all academic departments. This was designed to teach staff the basic philosophy and research of DL education, provide staff with guidance in practicing DL instructional methodologies, and teach staff the critical importance of "the Bridge"—an instructional strategy designed to help students transfer academic vocabulary from one language directly into another.

When we initially began to offer professional development in DL, we made the mistake of thinking that one curriculum would be sufficient to meet the needs of our entire staff. We quickly realized that a "one size fits all" approach to EL/DL professional development was a deeply flawed approach. Just as we ask our teachers to differentiate instruction for the diverse needs of students in their classes, so too is it important for administration to differentiate professional development offerings for staff who may be at various stages of teaching proficiency and, where DL is concerned, at various levels of proficiency with Spanish and English language skills. For example, when our team was working with Cheryl Urow, we studied the concepts of "simultaneous bilingual" and "sequential bilingual" explained in Beeman and Urow (2013). Simultaneous bilinguals learn both or multiple languages at the same time, usually in childhood where multiple languages are being spoken by various family members. In contrast, sequential bilinguals learn one language first and then another language later. Many of our teachers who were born in the United States, raised in an English-dominant household and school environment, are sequential bilinguals—they learned Spanish in middle school and beyond after already having a solid foundation in English. Many of our English learners, however, are simultaneous bilinguals (or multilinguals). These students were born in the United States to parents who spoke one or more non-English languages. As these children grew up, they were immersed in an English-dominant society while being spoken to frequently in non-English languages. Simultaneous bilinguals have always been operating in multiple languages and this has a profound impact upon the way they learn language (Beeman & Urow, 2013).

After we understood the concept, we began to differentiate our professional development offerings to target different types of language learners, applying the concept to our staff. In order to assess our staff, we created a master list of all of our teachers and teacher aides and organized it by each department. Next, we determined their language profile—we asked if they spoke any languages in addition to English and asked if they considered themselves sequential or simultaneous language learners. We then worked with our human resources department to determine which of our staff members had ESL or bilingual certifications in addition to their core content-area certifications. Though many variations exist, at the conclusion of this audit process we discovered four primary teacher profiles we were able to group our staff into. Each of these profiles was matched to a different professional development plan. (See Figure 6.1.)

Figure 6.1

Highland Park High School Staff Audit: Social Studies Department

Staff member	Language Profile Simultaneous or Sequential	Professional Certification(s)	PD Recommendation
Teacher A (Susan)	Not bilingual, speaks only English.	Social Studies Education	EL certification to serve EL/DL students in mainstream class with English as language of instruction
Teacher B (Monica)	Bilingual Spanish/English, Sequential learner.	Social Studies Education	EL/bilingual certification to serve EL/DL students in classes with English or Spanish as language of instruction. Spanish language courses to build fluency and confidence with Spanish language skills. History courses taught in Spanish to develop academic language in Spanish.
Teacher C (María)	Bilingual, native Spanish speaker, raised in Chicago, Simultaneous bilingual	Social Studies Education EL/bilingual certification	History courses taught in Spanish to develop academic language in Spanish.
Teacher D (Carlota)	Bilingual, native Spanish speaker, born and raised in Argentina. Sequential bilingual.	Social Studies Education, Spanish	EL/bilingual certification to serve EL/DL students in classes with English or Spanish as language of instruction.

The first teacher, Susan, was born and raised in the United States and never learned to speak Spanish. As a result, this teacher would initially think there is no place for her in a DL program. We disagree. At our school, we believe all students are language learners and every class is part of a DL school. While Susan will clearly not teach a social studies class where the language of instruction is Spanish, she will teach social studies classes in English where her students may be native Spanish speakers or English speakers from our DL program. As a result, it will be important for Susan to understand language-acquisition theory, sheltered English instruction, and how to differentiate instruction for English learners. In reality, the majority of the teachers at Highland Park High School have Susan's profile and it was very important for our administrative team to communicate to them that they have a critical role in our DL school. If the Susans on your staff do not believe they are included in DL programs, they will either actively resist the implementation of DL, fearing their jobs will be eliminated, or they will simply not invest time and energy in supporting the program. By communicating that every child in a DL school is a language learner, and by creating the expectation that all teachers will understand how to shelter academic language, you create the connection and urgency for your Susans to actively join and support the DL program.

The second teacher, Monica, was also born in the United States and is a native English speaker. Monica, however, became interested in Spanish and learned it as a second language when she attended middle and high school. Monica also studied abroad in college, spending a semester in Spain. While Monica has strong fluency in Spanish, we cannot assume she understands how children learn language nor how to shelter academic language for students. Therefore, our professional development plan for Monica will be for her to earn her EL/bilingual teaching certificate so that she is prepared to work with language learners. Next, we'll suggest that Monica take advanced Spanish courses to continue the development of her Spanish. As a native English speaker, Monica may not have a deep Spanish vocabulary and to continue to nurture her Spanish-speaking abilities will be important so that our native Spanish-speaking parents trust her ability to nurture the development of their child's language. Ideally, Monica would find a college-level social studies course that is taught in Spanish. Many sequential speakers, though fluent in conversational Spanish, often lack knowledge of the discipline-specific vocabulary required to teach an academic course in Spanish. Think about how challenging and specific the academic vocabulary of most high school courses is. As a sequential bilingual, if you took Spanish classes in high school and college you probably were not exposed to many of the words that a social studies, science, or math teacher must cover in a high school course. Words like: synthesis, analyze, thesis, debate, secession, treaty, alliance, and rebellion, which are common in a high school history course, may not be readily available to a sequential Spanish speaker. Participating in a history course where the language of instruction is in Spanish helps build Monica's vocabulary, fluency, and confidence to teach in Spanish.

Our third teacher, María, is perhaps the most complex identity. María was born in the United States to Spanish-speaking parents. María identifies as a proud Mexican-American and she is fluent in both English and Spanish. In addition, María has studied language acquisition theory and is EL certified. Initially, as a principal, I assumed that María would be perfectly comfortable teaching a social studies course in Spanish and that her professional development needs would be minimal. I was wrong. What I failed to understand was that María—having been raised in the United States where a monolingual English framework dominates schools and society—had her entire formal schooling in English. As a result, María lacks the Spanish vocabulary necessary to teach the academic language of school. Though María is a fluent native-Spanish speaker, her use of Spanish may have been limited to informal interactions with family and friends. These interactions would not have exposed María to the discipline-specific academic language we expect our teachers to use with our students. As a result, when it comes to teaching a high school course in Spanish, María's language skills may be no more advanced than Monica's. With this realization, we began working to get our Marías enrolled in college level courses where the language of instruction was Spanish.

Our fourth teacher, Carlota, was born in South America and was educated through college in her native language of Spanish. Carlota learned English in high school and college and immigrated to the United States after graduating college. Because Carlota was educated in Spanish, she does possess the academic language of high school social studies courses in this language and is perfectly comfortable teaching a course in Spanish. As a certified Spanish teacher, we don't need to improve Carlota's academic Spanish. However, because she lacks the EL/bilingual teaching certificate, we cannot assume Carlota understands how to shelter language for English learners and thus we'll ask her to obtain her EL/bilingual endorsement.

Using the strategy outlined above, our administrative team was able to create a detailed profile of our school's teachers in each academic department. This profile was then used to focus professional development opportunities to maximize their impact on each teacher's needs. In addition, this profile became a valuable tool for our hiring processes each year as it enabled us to evaluate how a specific candidate's language profile and certifications would help advance the development of our DL program.

Actively Educating our Superintendent, Board of Education, and Community about Dual Language

To build the case with our superintendent and board of education to prioritize district resources for the creation of a DL program, we created a rationale that combined our district's commitment to equity with academic research and Illinois school law. In Illinois, if a school has 20 or more students of the same language at one grade level, it must offer native-language support for students of that language group. At HPHS, we had approximately 300 Spanish speakers, thus necessitating the school to offer bilingual Spanish courses. Knowing that our district needed to offer a bilingual program, our argument to our superintendent was, "Why wouldn't we offer our students the best model for bilingual education?"

In a district publicly committed to equity and excellence, we pulled research from Thomas and Collier (2012, summarized on pp. 91-96) that compared the academic achievement of bilingual students exposed to a variety of language-acquisition programs. When one reviews this data, famously depicted in what is known among DL circles as "The Graph" (p. 93) it is clear that the only models of bilingual education shown to not only reduce, but eliminate, the long-term achievement gap between English and non-native English speakers are two-way and one-way DL programs. In addition, Thomas and Collier conclude that if DL students get continuing support through their primary language into the middle and high school years, they can reach even higher grade-level achievement in the second language. Furthermore, when they graduate from high school bilingual/biliterate/bicultural, they are prepared to fully participate as global citizens of the 21st century. Confronted with a state law mandating bilingual education and a genuine commitment to equity and excellence for all students, it became impossible for our superintendent and board of education to recommend any other course of action than to instruct us to build and design an outstanding DL program.

Now that we had taken the time to build the philosophical and structural support for the program at the school and district levels, it was time for us to activate our parent/guardian and community support. In this effort, we went back to our elementary district and constructed a collaborative communication and education campaign intended to reach an audience of pre-K to high school parents/guardians.

Each year, the elementary district held DL information meetings for parents whose children were preparing to enter kindergarten. The purpose of this meeting was to provide parents information about the DL program, the research supporting its implementation, the local achievement data of students enrolled in the program, and the specific steps parents needed to take if they wanted their kindergartner to become part of this program. In addition to this meeting, the elementary district ran a similar meeting for fifth grade parents to explain the ways the DL program would operate when their child moved to middle school and to reaffirm the parents' commitment to the program. Though these meetings were focused on elementary and middle school audiences, we began sending small teams of teachers and students to attend and speak at each of these meetings. Members of our core four would attend the meeting to speak about the high school's commitment to continuing the DL program. Most importantly, we would explicitly state that the high school would view all of our DL students as "gifted" when they came to us as ninth graders. This was so important to state because many of our DL parents feared that enrolling their child in this program would hurt their child's academic and social development. The fear of academic damage comes from a belief that all of the monolingual English children will have a more rigorous education in English, and thus, ultimately be smarter and more prepared for advanced academics than our DL students. The social fears are rooted in racist and xenophobic messages that have historically haunted this country since its founding. The parents of our White, middle-class students frequently express concern about putting their children with high numbers of Latino children (who in our community are largely from low-income families). This is why it is so important for every school and district to have a commitment to equity, to actively push back on these fears, and work to educate those who express them.

At these meetings, high school students who had been through the elementary DL program would also speak about the academic and social benefits they had realized as a result of their participation. Having our high school team present at these meetings was a powerful message to our parents. It signaled that our districts were working together to create a comprehensive K-12 DL program. We also created an eighth grade DL parent night. Like the other meetings, this one replicated the message that the DL students would be entering high school perceived as gifted and that the high school would be fully prepared to continue to nurture their development as bilinguals.

At all of these parent meetings, the elementary district and high school district worked to create and share longitudinal achievement data that demonstrated the DL program was not only building the students' language skills in Spanish and English, but that the students' reading, writing, and math skills were also developing at a level commensurate with their monolingual peer group. I strongly suggest that you use longitudinal achievement data when you present to parents, as only showing elementary achievement data may scare your concerned parents and board of education members into thinking the program isn't working. Research by Thomas and Collier (2012) shows that DL students often lag behind their monolingual peers when their reading and math skills are assessed between Grades Kinder to 3. This is to be expected, as DL students are learning to process information in two languages, while monolinguals have the advantage of only focusing on one. Interestingly enough, by fifth grade we see the DL students start to narrow the gap and by eighth grade gaps in reading and math between DL and monolingual peers are essentially eliminated. The achievement data that we have mined from our students over the years mirrors this trend. Most importantly, when one looks at national data, one sees it is during the high school years when DL students actually begin to exceed their monolingual peers in measures across the curriculum. This data suggests to parents that their children are engaged in deep and complex cognitive processes and that it is critical for parents to display patience in allowing their children's minds to sort out this complexity.

In addition to our formal parent presentations, we created both a DL Parent Advisory Council and a DL Student Advisory Council. The DL Student Advisory Council was composed of all the DL students in the high school and it meets three to four times per year during lunch periods. At each meeting, the students are asked about their experiences in our DL courses, and they are asked to provide us with insight and feedback about our program. Our student advisory council meetings are tremendously valuable. In asking for student feedback, we have been able to make immediate adjustments to aspects of DL courses that students did not understand; we were able to adjust our communication and marketing strategies to help students understand their development as bilinguals; and we were able to get feedback about which courses our students would like to see us develop and offer in the future. Most important, the DL Student Advisory Council communicated to our DL students that we viewed them as special and that we valued their input on the education we were providing them. The advisory built clear, positive and trusted communication between DL students and our administration.

To form the parent advisory council, we identified all the students in our school who were part of the DL program in middle school and invited their parents to participate in a series of four meetings that would be held at the high school during the school year. Each meeting was conducted half in Spanish and half in English. All parents had access to translation devices if they needed it. The purpose of our DL Parent Advisory Council was to educate our parents about DL research, understand the goals they had for their children, and gather their feedback about the ideas we had and the efforts we were making. Scott Russell, our world languages chair, and Jesse Villanueva, our DL/EL director, co-chaired all of the meetings, and I, as principal, attended as many as I could.

Our DL Parent and Advisory Council meetings were highly informative and were vital for the successful implementation of our program. First and foremost, it was critically important that we use each meeting to share research with parents and students about the long-term achievement benefits of DL education. In our experience, when many of our DL students arrive at high school, their parents begin to pull them from the program. Usually, this is due to the parents seeing their child has a firm grasp of oral fluency in L1 and L2 and the parent believing their child is fully bilingual and biliterate and no longer needs DL classes. At our meetings, we were active in sharing research by Thomas and Collier (2012) that demonstrated many of the most substantial academic gains for DL students occurs during the high school years in well-structured DL programs. Helping our parents understand that many of the academic benefits for their children were yet to be realized helped reinforce and strengthen our parents support and commitment to our program. In addition, when parents were no longer pulling their children from the high school program our number of DL students remained strong enough for us to offer multiple DL courses.

I cannot emphasize enough how important it is to educate your parents about the benefits of DL education. In the United States, where there is so much pressure on students to achieve and where English is the dominant language of business, academics, and power, parents of DL students face tremendous pressure to pull their children out of the program for fear that non-DL students will be better prepared for college. This fear is very real, especially in a community where English is the dominant language for the majority of families. By consistently sharing research with our parents that demonstrated the long-term academic gains of DL students we were able to successfully buttress their commitment to our program.

Our DL Parent and Student Advisory Councils also provided us the insight that our students and parents wanted our DL to be a fluid program, where students could opt in and out throughout high school. Rather than create a rigid DL program where all DL students needed to take the exact same courses, our community wanted a program that provided DL students a wide variety of courses they could take across the four years of high school. Students would be able to select which courses they would take in English, and which they would take in Spanish. This request actually provided fuel and energy to the original vision of the DL program we were attempting to build. Since its inception, we had always thought the development of multiple DL courses across multiple subject areas was the ideal design for our program. Having the parents and students officially express this desire gave us the support we needed to continue to push for the design and implementation of a wide variety of DL courses. With the student and parent feedback serving as our fuel, we began developing DL courses in science, mathematics, fine arts, business, physical education, and driver's education. Figure 6.2 shows the timeline of courses that were being designed at Highland Park High School in 2016.

Figure 6.2

Highland Park High School Dual Language Program

Grade Level	Spanish Language Arts	Spanish Content Courses
9th grade	Spanish Language Arts I Honors Spanish Language Arts II Honors	Patterns of World History Physical Education Introduction to Business (18-19)
10th grade	Spanish Language Arts II Honors AP Spanish Language	Physical Education Traffic Safety Introduction to Business (18-19) Art Studio (19-20) Civics (20-21)
11th Grade	AP Spanish Language AP Spanish Literature	Physical Education Biology (18-19) Art Studio (19-20) Civics (20-21)
12th Grade	AP Spanish Literature Seminar Honors in Spanish	International Relations (19-20) Biology (18-19) Art Studio (19-20) Civics (20-21)

State of Illinois Seal of Biliteracy Requirements	HPHS Seal of Dual Language Requirements:
• Proficiency in English equivalent to an Intermediate High level of proficiency. • Proficiency in a second language equivalent to an Intermediate High level of proficiency.	• 4 years of Spanish • 4 years of English • 4 content classes in Spanish • Dual Language Portfolio Presentation

Through the DL Parent and Student Advisory meetings, we learned that many of our students were torn between taking DL classes and the traditional honors/AP courses our school offered. We quickly realized that if students were forced to choose between AP/honors courses (which carried the benefit of a grade point average "bump") and DL classes, they would feel compelled to select the honors/AP course to create a transcript that would make them competitive for admission to highly selective universities. Our high school staff understood that if we wanted our DL program to grow and take hold in our high school, participation in DL classes had to convey the same status and weight on a child's transcript as the traditional honors/AP courses did. In order to ensure our DL courses had status and weight commensurate with AP and honors courses, HPHS worked to develop as many DL AP/honors courses as possible. When you review our curriculum offerings above, you can see that DL students are eligible for four honors/AP courses in world language. In addition, to create added status and transcript competitiveness for a DL child we created the Seal of Dual Language.

Seal of Dual Language

Like many states, the State of Illinois has recently adopted a Seal of Biliteracy to communicate to colleges and employers that a child is biliterate and bilingual in a non-English language. While we celebrate this action, and while many of our HPHS students are eligible for this seal each year, our school staff did not believe the Seal of Biliteracy effectively communicated the true depth of language that our DL students had acquired. We wanted to create something that conveyed the fact that our DL had become fully bilingual, biliterate, and bicultural, and had obtained college-level literacy in multiple languages. For this to occur, it became necessary for us to develop the Highland Park High School Seal of Dual Language.

The HPHS Seal of DL was inspired by the Albuquerque (New Mexico) High School (AHS) Seal of Dual Language, a school we learned about by attending La Cosecha Dual Language Conference in Santa Fe, New Mexico, in 2014. Like us, AHS wanted to communicate to colleges and employers that its DL graduates had developed advanced skills in both biliteracy and bilingualism, but that its students were also culturally competent and able to use language to navigate two cultures. With the AHS Seal of DL as a model, we worked with our students and parent advisory committees to construct a model for the HPHS Seal of DL. Unlike the state Seal of Biliteracy (which most of our DL students qualify for during their ninth grade year), the Seal of DL would be more challenging for students to obtain as it required students to demonstrate advanced proficiency in all three of our program's goals: bilingualism, biliteracy, and biculturalism. In order to be eligible for our Seal of DL, students needed to take four years of both English and Spanish language arts, and then take an additional four content courses in Spanish. While this selection of courses would accomplish the goal of making our students bilingual and biliterate, we also require that our students create a portfolio to demonstrate their authentic use of Spanish and English to navigate different cultural environments. This portfolio demonstrating a student's use of both Spanish and English affirms our goal of graduating students who can operate in both English- and Spanish-dominant environments. Students present their portfolio to the world language chair, the DL/EL coordinator, and a team of teachers and students at our "DL Fair" that we hold prior to graduation. When students qualify for the Seal of DL, we mark this accomplishment on their official school transcripts. Our school counselors and our school's college counselors make sure that the colleges and universities our students are applying to understand the prestige of the Seal of DL. Creating the Seal of DL was important because with it, our DL students are able to distinguish themselves from multilingual peers who have not dedicated their formal schooling to the pursuit of bilingualism, as well as their monolingual peers. The Seal of DL conveys considerable weight and status to colleges and employers and it incentivizes DL students to enroll in DL courses throughout high school.

Initial Achievement Data and Results

With our initial implementation of DL courses occurring during the 2014-15 school year, Highland Park High School is only now starting to collect the achievement data of its DL students. The following data was collected and prepared by Scott Russell, the HPHS World Language Department Chair.

Figure 6.3
Comparison of Eighth Grade DL & Non-DL Student Performance of Spanish Reading & Listening

ACTFL Proficiency Guidelines	ACTFL Performance Scale	AAPPL Measure Performance Score	Form
Advanced Low	ADVANCED	A	Dual Language Students Regardless of Background
Intermediate High		I-5	
Intermediate Mid	INTERMEDIATE	I-4	B
Intermediate Mid		I-3	
Intermediate Mid		I-2	
Intermediate Low		I-1	Non-Dual Language Students Regardless of Background
Novice High	NOVICE	N-4	
Novice Mid		N-3	
Novice Mid		N-2	
Novice Low		N-1	

8th Grade Performance on the Spanish Language AAPPL Exam (Listening & Reading) Dual Language vs. Non-Dual Language

Figure 6.3 compares the performance of eighth grade Spanish students on the Spanish Language ACTFL (American Council on the Teaching of Foreign Languages) Assessment of Performance toward Proficiency in Languages (AAPPL) test of listening and reading. This test was administered in the spring of 2015. As you can see, our DL students (native speakers of Spanish and native speakers of English) significantly outperform their non-DL peers (native speakers of Spanish and native speakers of English) in Spanish listening and reading skills.

Figure 6.4 shows a significant increase in the number of AP Spanish exams given at HPHS between 2011 and 2016. The increase in exams is due to the school offering both AP Language and Culture and AP Spanish Literature to students. DL students take AP Spanish Language and Culture during their sophomore year, and they take AP Spanish Literature as juniors. As you can see, the number of AP tests administered in Spanish increased dramatically when we began adding DL students to our courses, beginning in 2012-2013, and yet our school's test score averages remain very high. In fact, the average score for years 2014-2016 is significantly higher than the average scores for 2011-2013. This table is used as evidence to support the academic achievement of our DL students and is very powerful in gaining the support of the superintendent and board of education as increasing the number of AP students and raising AP scores is valued by most communities as a sign of academic excellence.

Figure 6.4
Increase in AP Exams and AP Scores for Dual Language Students

		AP Spanish Language and Culture		AP Spanish Literature	
School Years		N	Average	N	Average
2011		45	4.42	0	0.00
2012		47	4.47	0	0.00
2013		65	4.28	1	5.00
2014		77	4.73	0	0.00
2015		198	4.68	17	3.77
2016		86	4.30	43	3.70
		Total N	Weighted Average		
Pre-DL Years	2011-2013	157	4.38	—	—
DL Years	2014-2016	361	4.60	60	3.72
	Est. standard error =	0.096			
	t=	2.301			
	P<	0.05			

Figure 6.5
**ACT Performance of Native Spanish Speakers:
Dual Language vs. Non-Dual Language**

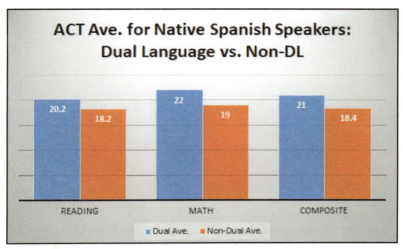

Figure 6.5 shows the 2015 ACT (for college admission) scores of native Spanish speakers who were enrolled in DL versus those of native Spanish speakers who did not enroll in our DL program. The data shows that our native Spanish speakers who are in DL outperform their non-DL peers on the ACT. This data suggests to our board of education and community that native Spanish speakers' academic achievement is greater when these students are enrolled in DL courses. This is powerful data that supports the district's commitment to equity, as it demonstrates that Latino students who receive intensive native-language instruction through DL outperform their Latino peers who do not continue their Spanish-language development. As we attempt to eliminate achievement disparities between different populations of students, this data strongly supports DL as high-impact instructional strategy.

Figure 6.6
**ACT Performance of Native English Speakers:
Dual Language vs. Non-Dual Language**

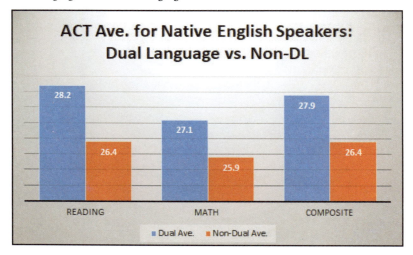

It has always been our contention that DL programs benefit all our students. This data refutes the notion that content instruction in Spanish hurts the achievement of native English speakers. As you can see in Figure 6.6, the ACT averages of our White, native English speakers who participate in DL exceed those of their monolingual peers. This data is important to share with the elementary schools because the parents of the White, native English DL students become fearful starting in third grade because they see their DL children lagging behind the development of the monolingual students. Data like this helps assuage a parent's fear they are "hurting" their child by keeping them in DL and it bolsters their confidence that if they are patient their children's academic achievement will actually exceed those of non-DL students by the conclusion of high school.

Figure 6.7
Comparison of 2015 ACT Averages Latino & White (Dual Language & Non-Dual Language)

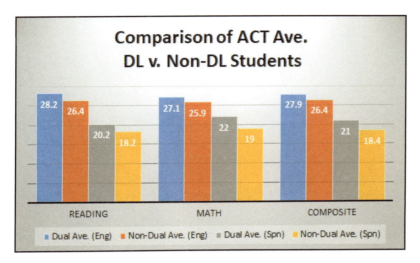

Figure 6.7 compiles the previous two and demonstrates that achievement disparities continue to exist between White and Latino DL students, as well as White and Latino Non-DL students. From this data our school learned that though our Latino DL students were achieving higher than their non-DL Latino peers, their achievement still lagged behind that of their White peers (both DL and non-DL) and therefore our school needed to continue its efforts to redesign our system to better serve all our Latino students.

Moving Forward

The five steps outlined above created an atmosphere at Highland Park High School where the implementation of the DL program moved forward in a quick and efficient manner. At the time of writing, this program continues to grow, evolve, and thrive. This year is the final year of the original 5-year plan the core four administrators created to get the DL program established. With the program now in place, the staff of HPHS is conducting a full review and audit of this program to determine the specific actions it will take to move this program to higher levels of excellence over the next 5 years.

Chapter Seven
Oregon: Woodburn School District—
Two Secondary Schools with Dual Language Programs

Dr. Victor Vergara —
Walla Walla Public Schools, Washington

Introduction by Collier and Thomas: *The school district of Woodburn, Oregon, is home to one of the first districtwide dual language programs in the nation, offering K-12 courses in Spanish/English and Russian/English. Their experienced secondary staff have grown the DL program with thoughtful, research-based, instructional and leadership practices that provide a truly welcoming school environment for their students. The school community is a unique mix of Latino, Russian, and Anglo heritages, with a large majority of the students starting school as English learners, mostly of low-income background. The Academy of International Studies at Woodburn High School now graduates over 90% of their English learners (whereas before the DL program the graduation rate for this group was 41%). This chapter, from a very successful principal's viewpoint in a model DL school district, covers many middle and high school DL leadership topics in detail. These topics include the DL middle and high school program structure, DL courses for each grade, curricular materials, assessments, professional development, ESOL courses, multicultural family and community involvement, the Seal of Biliteracy, DL courses for newcomers, and DL staff recruitment. Dr. Vergara was recognized as the 2012 Oregon Middle School Principal of the Year and 2016 Latino Principal of the Year for the state of Oregon.*

For 17 years I had the privilege of working in the Woodburn School District, located in the northern end of the Willamette Valley between Portland and Salem, in the state of Oregon.

The city of Woodburn has a population of approximately 25,000 consisting of thriving Latino, Russian, and Anglo communities. The three major languages of the community are Spanish, Russian, and English, and the multicultural heritages of residents are expressed in food, religion, music, dress, and language. A significant percentage of the Spanish-speaking residents are of Indigenous heritage from southern Mexico.

Through all of my years in the Woodburn School district I was exposed to the latest research, professional development, and best instructional practices around dual language (DL) education. Between 2005 and 2012 I had the privilege of leading Valor Middle School, first as vice principal and then as principal for 6 years. From 2012 to 2017, I served as the principal of the Academy of International Studies at Woodburn High School. With great effort and the incredible support of every single staff member at both schools, we were able to turn Valor Middle and Woodburn High around and offer a first-class multilingual education to all students. In this chapter, I will share some of the strategies that made these two schools among the best in the state of Oregon with their unique offerings of DL education for all students.

Woodburn School District (WSD) started developing bilingual education more than 20 years ago with the goal of providing students the opportunity to develop their bilingualism and biliteracy. Since then the WSD vision has been to become an outstanding multilingual school district, which motivates and empowers all students to succeed in learning and leading in a global society.

Woodburn School District Strategic Plan, Goal #3

In 2011 the WSD Board of Directors reinforced their commitment to offer the community of Woodburn a first-class education for its children, implementing a set of new goals for the strategic plan, including one specifically related to bilingual education: Strategic Goal #3 states, "WSD will implement a multilingual, multicultural curriculum to equip all students with the bilingual, biliterate skills, and knowledge critical to their success" (*www.woodburnisd.org*). The plan was to continue refining this program with the implementation of DL schooling, K-12, across the district. Along the same lines, WSD decided to utilize a theory of action tool, or evidence-based story that explains the specific changes they intend to make to improve teaching and learning (U of Washington, Center for Educational Leadership):

"If we focus on the K-12 **instructional core** within our biliterate/intercultural context, and

If we learn **collaboratively** at all levels, and

If we prioritize the use of **data** in our **cycles of inquiry,** and

If we align our K-12 system with a **proficiency-based approach,**

Then ... we will have high-academic achievement that is equitable for all students.

Valor Middle School

Valor History

Valor Middle School opened its doors in 1997 for 350 students, with the majority being English learners of Latino and Russian heritage. When I joined Valor in 2005, we had about 585 students, 74% Latina/o, 14% Russian, and 11% Anglo students. These included about 68% English learners and close to 85% participating in free/reduced lunch. At that time, behaviorally and academically, Valor was in chaos—we finished the 2004 school year with 1548 discipline referrals, only 8% of students passed the Oregon state writing test, 32% passed in reading, and 42% passed in mathematics. In terms of dual language education, Valor was piloting some class offerings and instruction in Russian and Spanish but without much direction and/or help. There were few secondary-school role models in DL education across Oregon and few knowledgeable leaders in bilingual education. We knew that improving DL education was going to be difficult, but were motivated by our desire to offer a first-class education to all our students.

Valor Middle School's vision was to create a "high performing learning community with strength of mind and spirit" (*http://www.woodburnsd.org/valor-middle-school/*). In order to achieve this vision, we focused first on discipline and then on academics, especially within our DL initiative. We had the pressure of receiving students from our two elementary feeder schools with Russian and Spanish bilingual and biliteracy skills, ready to continue their bilingual schooling at the middle school level. At the same time, we were receiving English learners in need of education in their primary language, either Russian or Spanish, while they were learning English. All these reasons led us to spend the first couple of years reading research, contacting and learning from national researchers like Kathryn Lindholm-Leary, Virginia Collier, and Wayne Thomas, and investigating and visiting DL program models in the United States, such as the K-8 Alicia R. Chacón International School in El Paso, Texas. During those first 2 years, administrators, teachers, parents, students, and staff came together to determine a new direction for the school, based on research and best practices. This is how we developed the following systems.

Valor Middle School Dual Language Program Structure

Multilingual development goal. We created a multilingual goal for our school with an emphasis on literacy support in three languages—English, Russian, and Spanish—and asked the district to support a K-12 curriculum alignment in the three languages. Furthermore, we agreed to increase the number of core classes in Russian and Spanish by implementing second-language techniques across the curriculum and increasing second-language options for native English speakers. We also incorporated parents as partners in improving achievement in biliteracy education. Our goal was for each student at Valor be given the opportunity to become bilingual and biliterate.

Biliteracy pathway. We adopted the DL model described below, to include the following components.

- Teachers and students would remain in the language of instruction during the entire class period.

- Sixth grade would offer three courses in Spanish or Russian, to include high-level core content and one required course in Spanish or Russian language arts, as well as English language arts.

• Seventh grade would offer two to three courses in Spanish or Russian, to include high-level core content and one required course in Spanish or Russian language arts, as well as English language arts.

• Eighth grade would offer two to three courses in Spanish or Russian, to include high-level core content and one required course in Spanish or Russian language arts, as well as English language arts.

See Figure 7.1 for a graphic of the course offerings.

Figure 7.1
Dual Language Middle School Model: Distribution of Languages by Subject in Each Grade

Subject	Grade 6	Grade 7	Grade 8
Language Arts	Spanish / Russian	Spanish / Russian	Spanish / Russian
Social Studies	Spanish / Russian	English	English
Mathematics	Spanish / Russian	Spanish / Russian	English
Science	Spanish / Russian	English	Spanish / Russian
Language Arts	English	English	English
Electives / ESOL	English	English	English
Electives / ESOL	English/ Spanish/ Russian	English/ Spanish/ Russian	English/ Spanish/ Russian

In the model presented above, sixth grade students had the opportunity of spending half of the day in the language other than English and in seventh and eighth grade they were able to take at least two classes in the other language. This approach was followed by about 70% of the students who came to Valor with some bilingual skills from the elementary level. The other 30% had the opportunity to take any of the three levels of world language classes in either Russian or Spanish.

Curriculum and instruction. As we were trying to figure out the best model for our program, the Valor staff worked together to develop a curriculum and the teaching strategies required to address Valor students' needs. Teacher collaboration was the key for this work. As principal, I was able to provide a common planning time in their daily schedule for the teachers of each content area to spend time analyzing standards and looking for an appropriate curriculum. They were able to follow a cycle of inquiry to produce common lesson plans that included the culturally relevant aspects needed for our students. Since the majority of students received literacy in Spanish or Russian and English at the same time, collaboration among these teachers was essential to ensure that they included all the standards while looking at possible transfer across languages of instruction without repeating lessons, materials, and assessments.

During my years as principal of Valor we were able to implement and refine the following curricular strategies.

- ALL DL students had access to at least two classes in either Spanish or Russian every day.

- Daily after-school interventions for English learners and students below grade level were provided.

- Saturday Academy School met two times a month for our English learners and those with disabilities.

- Course offerings of content classes in Spanish and Russian were increased significantly.

- English-only students were offered at least one class in Spanish or Russian as world languages which we labeled the English-plus track for the small percentage of students not enrolled in DL courses.

- Teachers increased school-wide implementation of instructional strategies and techniques for comprehensible input and for language development using the Sheltered Instruction Observation Protocol (SIOP®) lesson plan model for the delivery of instruction (Echevarría, Vogt, & Short, 2016).

- English language development classes for English learners were designed according to students' English language proficiency and grade level.

- In the content-area subjects, teachers increased implementation of instruction for strategy-based reading and writing.

- Literacy classes in three languages (Spanish, Russian, and English) were offered to students who were part of the DL program (almost 80% of our student population).

Curriculum requirements and options. In 2008, after completing our analyses of other DL model schools and reading the most current research, we decided to offer the following courses for our students in a seven-period day of 50 minutes each:

Figure 7.2
2008 Courses in the DL Program at Valor Middle School

	Required courses	Exploration courses
Grade 6	Literacy Language Arts in English Language Arts (Russian or Spanish) Social Studies Block (English, Russian or Spanish) Mathematics (English or Spanish) Science Physical Education/Health (English or Spanish) Advisory	Visual Art General Music Introduction to Theater Spanish as a World Language Russian as a World Language
Grade 7	Literacy Language Arts in English Language Arts (Russian or Spanish) Social Studies Block (English, Russian or Spanish) Mathematics (English or Spanish) Science Physical Education/Health (English or Spanish) Advisory	Visual Art Beginning Band Choir Language Arts through Drama Leadership Spanish as a World Language Russian as a World Language
Grade 8	Literacy Language Arts in English Language Arts (Russian or Spanish) Social Studies Block (English, Russian or Spanish) Mathematics (English or Spanish) Science Physical Education/Health (English or Spanish) Advisory	Visual Arts Choir Language Arts through Drama Leadership Spanish as a World Language Russian as a World Language

Due to the availability of bilingual Spanish and Russian teachers in other content areas such as health and physical education, students were able to take at least three classes in Spanish or Russian, equivalent to almost 50% of their day. Thus we included the "specials" in our instructional minutes provided in the partner language, as recommended by researchers (Thomas & Collier, 2012).

Materials. Searching for high-quality materials in Spanish and Russian was a difficult task, especially for the core subjects. We always looked for materials that were aligned to the Common Core State Standards and relevant to the partner language, teaching students as if they were native speakers and not using translations from English. Since Russian-language materials were particularly scarce and cost prohibitive, we spent large amounts of time and money translating materials from English to Russian in order to equalize the amount of instructional time in each of the two languages.

We introduced classroom libraries as a way to support our students' language development. The idea was to have a variety of books in different genres, levels, and languages connected to the content taught in each classroom, so students could easily expand their knowledge, take a book home, and continue developing their love of reading.

Assessments. During their daily planning time, teachers had the task of creating formative and summative assessments that were culturally relevant to our student population and would allow our students to demonstrate their understanding of the content in a variety of formats. We could then analyze student achievement in dual and non-dual classrooms. This timely feedback was critical for teachers—allowing them to better meet the diverse learning needs of all our students.

We piloted several language proficiency tools to assess students' listening, speaking, reading, and writing in Russian, Spanish, and English at least two times a year. After trying several published assessments, we ended up creating our own tools to measure these four domains. Assessing our students in two languages was time-consuming, but the data we gathered helped to inform and refine our instructional practices.

In the state of Oregon, every middle school student must complete an assessment in reading, writing, and mathematics in Grades 6, 7, and 8. Mathematics was the only state exam for which students could choose questions written in either Spanish or English; Russian was not available. For our DL students, especially those coming from the elementary DL program, the expectation at the middle school level was to be proficient in both languages. We expected them to be equally successful test takers in either language of the content assessment.

Professional development. One of our core beliefs was that teachers' professional learning was a key component of ensuring student success for all student populations. During my years at Valor Middle School we concentrated our professional development efforts in the following areas:

- refinement of sheltered content instruction with a focus on literacy;
- second-language instructional strategies for English learners;
- student portfolios showcasing student work in both their native and partner language;
- English, Russian, and Spanish language development;
- training in the proper scoring of reading and writing assessments in English, Russian, and Spanish;
- classroom curriculum, assessment design, and teaching for mastery strategies;
- support for the refinement of our bilingual program development and implementation;
- research, development, and integration of balanced-literacy instruction in English, Russian, and Spanish;
- assessment of literacy and effective use of classroom data in English, Russian, and Spanish;
- diversity and multicultural training;
- culturally responsive practices; and
- vertical and horizontal curriculum alignment (across and within grade levels).

To be able to support all these areas and hold ourselves accountable, we participated in regular learning walks in our English, Russian, and Spanish classrooms to look at the development of all the areas mentioned above (City, Elmore, Fiarman, & Teitel, 2009). At each cycle, teachers created a "problem of practice" connected to any of the above-mentioned areas. Teachers and administrators visited classrooms on a prearranged schedule, making non-evaluative observations and jotting them down in their notes. We analyzed the data and talked about next steps. It was extremely powerful for our teachers to participate and collaborate in refining their own teaching practices.

English language development. For our English learners, we offered English language development classes by proficiency level; ESOL I, ESOL II, ESOL III and ESOL IV. Students in ESOL III and IV attended regular core classes with ESOL-endorsed teachers with extensive training in second language acquisition. For our ESOL I & ESOL II students, we provided a specific program called the Multicultural Academic Program for Secondary Beginning to Early Intermediate English Learners. Since this program was developed for both middle and high school, I will explain this in more detail at the end of this chapter.

Multicultural families and community involvement. One of the keys to our success was family and community involvement; understanding the connection between family, students, and school was essential. Following the WSD vision, we engaged all members of our diverse community, encouraging them to bring their talents to support the achievement of our strategic objectives and mission. At the beginning of my tenure at Valor Middle School and after several meetings with parents, community, and staff leaders, we decided to focus on the following areas:

- Increased after-school programs in enrichment and extended learning options for students involving community partners who were willing to spend time with our students. Their focus was either content areas like literacy, math, or science, or sharing other skills they had such as music or art.

- Following WSD community and partnership goals, increased opportunities for parent involvement in the six key areas of Epstein's model (2017)—parenting, communicating, volunteering, learning at home, decision making, and collaborating with the community.

- We held at least two nightly parent meetings a month related to our school-improvement goals. Valor teachers and staff facilitated weekly activities for families, from dances to learning sessions and physical-activity nights to integrate families with the opportunity to learn from each other's cultures. On any given Thursday we had between 60 to 200 families participating.

- We hired a parent-involvement site coordinator to facilitate activities and make sure to reach all families and community stakeholders.

- The creation of the Valor Connection Center (parent room) offered extensive learning and volunteering opportunities for parents and community members any time during the day.

Hard work at Valor paid off. Building systems around bilingualism, biliteracy, and the understanding of multiculturalism were the keys to our success. Valor went from being one of the lowest-achieving schools in Oregon in 2005, to being recognized by the state as one of the top 10 performing middle schools in Oregon in both 2010 and 2012. This long journey taught us that it is possible to close the achievement gap by offering world-class bilingual education.

Dual Language High School: Academy of International Studies (AIS)

AIS History

About 15 years ago (around 2003), Woodburn High School was considered one of the lowest performing high schools in the state of Oregon, with high pregnancy rates, severe discipline issues, and an ongoing increase in gang affiliations. The Gates Foundation presented Woodburn High School with the challenge and financial support to transform from a comprehensive high school to four smaller academies or schools. This is how the Academy of International Studies (AIS) opened in the fall of 2007.

AIS serves 350 students in Grades 9-12—95% are of Hispanic heritage (the majority are now fluent English speakers who attended the DL program at elementary and middle school levels in Woodburn), 25% are English learners, 18% are migrant students, and 91% are economically disadvantaged (Oregon Department of Education, 2014).

Beginning in 2010, 3 years after AIS opened, three out of the four small academies or schools started showing academic improvements, with some of the highest graduation rates in the state (Oregon Department of Education, 2013). However, the Academy of International Studies was not yet showing that level of success. When I decided to accept the position as principal, we had about 60% of our students graduating. Again, with hard work and incredible collaboration among teachers and staff fighting for an equal opportunity for our students and their families, we were able to reach high academic success, getting to just above 90% graduation rates for 4 years in a row (see Figures 7.3 and 7.4).

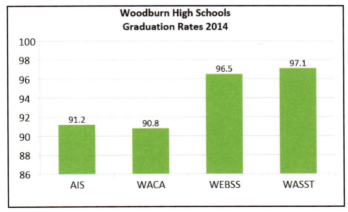

Figure 7.3
2015 Oregon Department of Education Report Card

Figure 7.4
2015 Oregon Department of Education Report Card

AIS's mission was to cultivate global relationships in a bilingual environment of academic excellence that inspires and promotes social justice. Our school vision was that ALL students would graduate from AIS prepared for college, work, and citizenship; empowered to act in a better world; and literate in more than one language. Through programs such as the International Baccalaureate (IB) and the bilingual/DL program, AIS provided students with a rigorous curriculum, standards, and expectations that promote intercultural awareness, holistic learning, bilingualism, and communication.

AIS High School Dual Language Program Structure

The majority of our students went through the DL program at the elementary and secondary level. AIS also served all the English learners and most of the reclassified students (former English learners) of the four district high schools. Those last two subgroups represented a total of 78% of our student population. It was critical for AIS to have well-developed instructional programs and effective instructional strategies to support the learning and growth of these students. It was equally important to honor our students' native languages and cultures and create opportunities for them to be proud of their bilingualism. We offered students the ability to get an IB diploma, and made it possible to learn a third language. Along the same lines, we were one of the first schools in the state to pilot the seal of biliteracy on our graduation diploma, an initiative created by the Oregon Department of Education. We were proud and excited about this new opportunity to honor our students' bilingualism.

Multilingual development goal. At AIS, we created a multilingual goal similar to the one at Valor Middle school, with an emphasis on literacy support in three languages—English, Russian, and Spanish. We agreed to align our courses with the middle school offerings and decided to increase core classes in Russian and Spanish. We also implemented second-language techniques across the curriculum, increased second-language course options for native English speakers, and incorporated parents as partners in improving achievement in biliteracy education.

Biliteracy pathway. We adopted the dual language model presented in Figure 7.5.

Figure 7.5
Dual Language High School Model: Distribution of Languages by Subject in Each Grade

Subject	Grade 9	Grade 10	Grade 11	Grade 12
Language Arts	Spanish / Russian	Spanish / Russian	IB Spanish / IB Russian	IB Spanish / IB Russian
Social Studies	Spanish / Russian	English	IB English	IB English
Mathematics	Spanish / Russian	Spanish / Russian	IB English	IB English
Science	Spanish / Russian	Spanish / Russian	IB Spanish/ English	IB English
Language Arts	English	English	IB English	IB English
Electives / ESOL	English	English	English	English
World Languages	Spanish/ Russian	Spanish/ Russian	Spanish/ Russian	Spanish/ Russian

In this model, students had the opportunity to take up to three classes in either Spanish or Russian at each grade level About 70% of our students followed this model. The other students had the chance to take world languages classes in Spanish or Russian.

Curriculum and instruction. At AIS we focused on creating and developing a curriculum that included culturally responsive practices, understanding identity and issues of social justice, bridging languages, and the use of technology with an eye towards the future of our world. At the beginning of my tenure at AIS, teachers spent many days collaborating on the creation of culturally relevant annual work plans for their content subjects. Annual work plans included the following components:

1. Scope and sequence of the course
2. Development of units
    A. Unit description
    B. Student-expected prerequisite knowledge
    C. Unit learning outcomes
    D. Standards
    E. Essential questions for the unit
3. Daily lessons
    A. Essential questions
    B. Expanded learning targets including content, language, and product
    C. Alignment to text
    D. Formative assessments
4. Summative assessment

During our Wednesday late-start professional development time, we were able to meet regularly in professional-learning communities/data teams to follow a cycle of inquiry (Figure 7.6) to analyze our instructional practices in greater depth based on student data.

Figure 7.6
Cycle of Inquiry: Educational Excellence Organization

www.educationalexcellence.org/home.html

Curriculum requirements/Biliteracy pathway. At AIS, we looked at all incoming end of year eighth grade students to place them into the appropriate course sequence, especially for literacy. We had a seven-period day offering six 50-minute core classes and a 55-minute advisory period. DL students were placed in at least two courses in their non-English language. Many courses were

Figure 7.7

offered in Spanish, Russian, and English (see Figure 7.7):

	Required courses	**Electives**
Grade 9	Science (offered in English and Spanish) Algebra (offered in Spanish or English) English Language Arts Spanish or Russian Literacy 1 Physical Education Health (offered in Spanish or English) Advisory	Multicultural Art Leadership Choir Mariachi Band World Languages Spanish Russian
Grade 10	Science (offered in English and Spanish) Geometry (offered in Spanish or English) English Language Arts Global Studies (offered in Spanish or English) Spanish or Russian Literacy 2 Physical Education Health (offered in Spanish or English) Advisory	Multicultural Art Leadership Choir Mariachi Band World Languages Spanish Russian
Grade 11	IB Science (offered in English and Spanish) Algebra 2 (offered in Spanish or English) IB Mathematics English Language Arts IB Language Arts in English IB History 1 IB Spanish Lit. 1 IB Russian Lit. 1 Physical Education Health (offered in Spanish or English) Advisory	Multicultural Art Leadership Choir Mariachi Band World Language Spanish Russian
Grade 12	IB Science (offered in English and Spanish) IB Mathematics Language Arts in English IB Language Arts in English IB History 2 IB Spanish Lit. 2 IB Russian Lit. 2 IB Theory of Knowledge Physical Education Health (offered in Spanish or English) Advisory	Multicultural Art Leadership Choir Mariachi Band World Languages Spanish Russian

AIS was one of the first schools in Oregon to start granting high school course credits based on a measurement of language proficiency as well as subject knowledge. The table above shows a regular path for students, but we had many DL students who completed course requirements for graduation in advance and started as juniors taking college-level classes such as Advanced IB Spanish, Math, or Science.

Materials. Every year we had to refine our materials, specifically the ones in Spanish and Russian. At this school we translated several materials trying to adapt and connect them with the Common Core State Standards and their expectations. It was a lot easier to find core class materials like math, language arts, science and history in Spanish than in Russian. Throughout the years we were able to create a book room and classroom libraries, purchasing books in the three languages of our DL program.

Assessments. Teachers created formative and summative common assessments to measure student progress. Teachers teaching the same content but using a different language were able to collaborate, with data on the table, about best instructional practices and how to improve, regardless of the language of instruction. Along the same lines, many assessment questions were translated into Spanish and/or Russian to facilitate access for our students, especially when teachers were measuring content and not language. Every year we piloted different language-proficiency assessments that might provide us with a good understanding of where our students were in the four domains of listening, speaking, reading, and writing. At the time I left the school, we were still trying to find the right tool. Students in Oregon take a state writing, language arts, and mathematics tests at 11th grade, and only the mathematics test was offered in Spanish. The science test was optional but we encouraged students to take it to measure their academic progress in this content area. At the same time, students taking IB classes were able to take the IB assessments with the possibility of earning college credits.

Professional development. At AIS we focused our professional development following four essential questions:

1. What do we want students to learn?

2. How do we know if they have learned it?

3. What do we do if they don't?

4. What do we do when they do?

We believed if we framed our work with these questions in mind, we would be able to focus and strengthen our abilities to benefit our students. This was the work that continued helping ALL of our students. In conjunction with our teachers, we decided to create a vision for our professional development system:

> To continually improve student achievement in any language by providing high-quality professional development in research-based practices supporting the instructional core, and by fostering a collegial and collaborative environment ensuring students' success while at AIS and in postsecondary endeavors.

At AIS we used a cycle of inquiry (see Figure 7.6) to focus on our instructional core by collaboratively:
1. planning for proficiency with learning targets, assessments, and instructional strategies;
2. teaching with effective instructional strategies and assessments; and
3. reflecting on student evidence and the effectiveness of those instructional strategies.

Then we decided to focus on six different initiatives, following up with a long-term plan under each. The following three initiatives pertain to DL education.

1. Literacy across content areas in English, Russian, and Spanish (writing & reading)
   a. Professional development for selected teachers in reading strategies that can be applied across content and are aligned to Common Core State Standards
   b. Learning targets for writing in all classrooms
   c. Continued refinement/alignment of the curriculum of literacy classes for ESOL students
   d. Monthly meetings of teacher leaders, IC, and principal to plan cycles of inquiry based on writing across content
   e. Professional development for teachers in how to establish, develop, and effectively use classroom libraries at the secondary level
2. Sheltered Instruction
   a. Teachers participate in sheltered-English strategies trainings and work with teams to integrate the strategies into their classroom instruction.
      i. Learning targets with embedded language
      ii. Formative assessments
      iii. Self-reflection and assessment using the Sheltered Instruction Learning Target Rubric (*http://www.cal.org/siop/about/*)
   b. Instructional coaches provide training in sheltered instruction during late starts and with individual teachers.
   c. Principal, IC, and teacher leaders participate in quarterly instructional walks to observe sheltered instruction strategies in action.
3. Professional Learning Communities (Data Teams)
   a. Cycles of inquiry based on CCSS English, Spanish, and Russian language arts & literacy (writing), in history/social studies, science, and technical subjects. Each PLC will complete three cycles of inquiry in a year.
      i. September - December
      ii. January.-March
      iii. April-June
   b. Instructional coach will provide regular facilitator training and support in the use of protocols and tools, including identifying a problem of practice, creating mini lessons, and supporting best instructional practices in classrooms.

English language development. Our ELD instructional program consisted of appropriate educational services in two areas: ESOL and grade-level access to the core academic content curriculum. ESOL class periods are where students receive ESOL instruction during a regular class period. The Sheltered Instruction Observation Protocol (SIOP) was the framework that provided language support for content instruction to help make content comprehensible and accessible to English learners. For our ESOL I & ESOL II students we had a specific program called Multicultural Academic Program for Secondary Beginning to Early Intermediate English Learners. I will explain this in more detail at the end of this chapter.

Multicultural family and community involvement. Family involvement at the high school level is extremely difficult, particularly because many Latino families have the cultural expectation that school personnel are responsible for the education of their children and that they should not interfere in the process. With that in mind, we decided to be strategic and scheduled at least one activity a month with specific topics/activities for parents to choose from. We provided dinner, translation services, and childcare at each meeting. The idea was to increase parent participation in our school and facilitate the interaction among families of different cultures and backgrounds.

Seal of Biliteracy

The Oregon State Seal of Biliteracy was established to recognize high school graduates who had attained a high level of proficiency in listening, speaking, reading, and writing in one or more world languages in addition to English. The state of Oregon approved the seal in early 2015. AIS was one of the first high schools in the state to implement such an important recognition. The purpose of the Oregon State Seal of Biliteracy is:

1. to encourage students to study languages;
2. to certify attainment of biliteracy;
3. to provide employers with a method of identifying candidates with language and biliteracy skills;
4. to provide post-secondary institutions with a method to recognize and give academic credit to applicants seeking admission;
5. to prepare students to be college and career ready;
6. to recognize and promote world language instruction in public schools; and
7. to strengthen intergroup relationships, affirm the value of diversity, and honor the multiple cultures and languages of a community.

A special Woodburn High School (AIS) ceremony is held every May to award certificates and medals to graduating seniors who successfully complete the bilingual portfolio and interview process for the seal of biliteracy.

In only a few years, The Academy of International Studies showed incredible progress, graduating more than 90% of its students every year from 2014 on and following up with the remainder of the students until they graduated. There is an enormous respect for all teachers and staff at AIS who build strong relationships with families and students, helping to positively change their lives forever.

Dual Language Courses for Newcomers to Secondary Schools

Two initiatives that are districtwide and deserve attention, especially in the development of a comprehensive bilingual program, are English language development and L1 content courses for newcomer students, and the recruitment of minority staff who understand how to work in bilingual settings (discussed in the section that follows this one). Due to the necessity to better serve our English learners in Woodburn, especially at the secondary level, we developed the Multicultural Academic Program to serve new arrivals just beginning to learn English. This program was designed for secondary beginning- to early-intermediate level English learners. When students are provided instruction that acknowledges their current English proficiency level or previous formal education, then schools will be able to prepare them to achieve challenging educational goals.

The Multicultural Academic Program in Woodburn School District provided sixth through 12th grade ESOL 1 and ESOL 2 students with (a) ESOL instruction, (b) Spanish, Russian, and English literacy development, (c) Spanish- and Russian-language content courses (e.g., social science), (d) English-language content courses specifically designed for students learning English at the beginning to early intermediate levels, and (e) access to sheltered instruction courses in art, physical education, and technology. Because this program would serve students who have not been in the U.S. very long, part of the program's purpose was to acclimate students to their new community and the U.S. school system, while countering the isolation and confusion these students often experience (Short & Boyson, 2004). An intercultural advisory class was a key component in developing students' understanding of the U.S. school system, developing cross-cultural competency, adapting to, and thriving in their new home.

Additionally, having a centralized middle and high school program designed for beginning to early intermediate students maximized staffing resources at the secondary level. For example, between the two middle schools, in any given year we had about six to seven beginning-level students and an average of 30-40 early-intermediate students. Having a teacher at each school for the few beginning students did not make economic sense, while spreading the early intermediate students between the two schools did not ensure that students would receive a complete program with courses that they could understand. Furthermore, beginning to early-intermediate students often need access to the same courses (e.g., Spanish or Russian literacy for those 2 years or more behind grade level, Spanish mathematics, etc.). Creating multiple sections of courses for small groups of beginning to early intermediate students in multiple schools was not an effective use of personnel and instructional resources for our school district.

The goals of this program were developed based on student needs:

1. Goals for Students Who Lack a Formal L1 Education:
    a. Develop students' native-language skills (Spanish).
    b. Develop students' English skills in listening, speaking, reading, and writing.
    c. Provide comprehensible content-area instruction to access core curriculum.
    d. Validate students' cultures as they learn to participate in the U. S. school system.
    e. Develop students' language-learning and study skills while developing their ability to advocate for themselves.

2. Goals for Students with Formal L1 Education, on Grade Level:
    a. Maintain and improve students' native-language skills (Spanish).
    b. Support students in acquiring beginning English skills in listening, speaking, reading, and writing.
    c. Provide comprehensible content-area instruction.
    d. Validate students' cultures as they learn to participate in the U. S. school system.
    e. Develop students' language-learning and study skills while developing their ability to advocate for themselves.

The Multicultural Academic Program is a short-term program that students exit once they demonstrate intermediate English proficiency, i.e., moving into ESOL 3. The amount of formal education a student has in his or her primary language directly influences his or her English proficiency (Collier, 1995), with those lacking a formal education taking longer to acquire academic English proficiency. The DL program at middle and high school then continues to serve these students.

Staff Recruitment at the Secondary Level

Recruitment and retention of culturally and linguistically diverse teachers is a focus of the Oregon Department of Education as well as the Woodburn School District, along with several other school districts that have offered bilingual education for many years. The state has continued to identify as many potential opportunities as possible for recruiting minorities to our teaching force. In 1991, Oregon passed the Minority Teacher Act, since updated and now called the Educator Equity Act, with the goal of reducing the gap between the number of educators of color and the minority students we serve. The successful recruitment and support of instructional assistants of color to prepare them for teaching and later administrative positions, is one approach to help underserved minority students succeed in public schools.

Twenty-six years after the creation of the Minority Teacher Act and after one amendment in 2013, these efforts have had a negligible impact on an achievement gap that continues to widen. According to the Oregon Educator Equity Report (2016, p. 4), while a third of Oregon's students are people of color, only 10% are teachers of color.

The possibility of partnerships between educational organizations, school districts, and universities to collaborate around teacher- and leadership-preparation programs that focus on equity is essential. One organization addressing this need is the Aspiring Administrator Program of the Oregon Association of Latino Administrators (*OALA, www.oala.info*). This organization was created 14 years ago with a vision "to create a forum for Latino administrators and educational leaders that promotes equity in leadership positions throughout the state of Oregon." OALA's general mission is "to promote Latino educators, both current and aspiring, into positions of leadership through mentorship, networking, and professional development. OALA will affect the educational interests of all students in Oregon, particularly those of Latino heritage, in order to ensure their educational success." OALA partners with institutes of higher education to prepare these future social-justice leaders to fight inequalities that still exist in our schools. OALA's vision and mission provide a clear message of support to minority Latina/o educators in helping to close the gap of racial disparities within our schools.

One example of a university preparation program is Portland State University, which, for the last several years, has adopted a focus and a mission on equity in all their programs related to education preparation. As stated on their Graduate School of Education webpage, "GSE Vision: Preparing professionals to lead life-long learning and development within our diverse communities." (*www.pdx.edu/education/*). This institution partners with OALA and Chalkboard to make sure we have well-rounded social-justice teachers and leaders in our schools, especially those with a large population of minority students.

Summary

Over the past 20 years, Woodburn School District has made great gains in achievement test scores, graduation rates for English learners, and AP/IB course credits achieved by Latino and Russian-heritage students. The DL program has now expanded into almost all of the WSD schools, along with the majority of the coursework offered. An even more dramatic impact is the effect the dual language program has had on the community. This success has led to confident and capable students whose parents are extremely proud as the students become bilingually proficient adults—ready to use both of their languages in their post-high school jobs, schooling, and personal lives. As a result of their leaders' and staff's vision to provide a first-class education for their students through dual language education this mostly low-income, small-city, and rural community has benefited enormously from the transformations that have occurred in their local schools.

Chapter Eight
Texas: Houston Independent School District Dual Language Expansion to Secondary Schools: Challenges and Successes in a Large Urban School District

Dr. Virginia Elizondo

Introduction by Collier and Thomas: *Among the largest urban school districts in the U.S., Houston Independent School District (HISD) is one of the dual language success stories. The bilingual staff of every school district in the country typically acknowledge that they are "a work in progress," but, as we found in our 7 years of research working with HISD, the Houston schools have certainly accomplished a tremendous amount in a school-choice context serving a very diverse student population (Thomas & Collier, 2002). Author Dr. Virginia Elizondo elaborates on issues encountered during the second expansion of DL to many more HISD campuses beginning in 2013, and the challenges that come that expansion. Topics in this chapter include providing appropriate secondary DL core content courses for both the continuing DL students and newcomers, challenges with leadership changes in a site-based management school district, master-schedule planning, DL curricular materials, DL feeder patterns from elementary to secondary, DL staffing, and DL professional development.*

The Houston Independent School District (HISD) is the seventh largest school district in the nation and the largest school district in the state of Texas. There are roughly 214,000 students within this district of eight early childhood centers, 159 elementary schools, 38 middle schools, 38 high schools, and 41 combination schools for a total of 284 campuses. The ethnic makeup of the school district is .17% American Indian Alaskan Native, 24.02% African American, 4.05% Asian, 61.84% Hispanic, .07% Native Hawaiian Pacific Islander, 1.16% Multiethnic, and 8.7% White. Over 40% of the students in the district are in the elementary grades of one to five. The district's overall student population includes 74.93% qualifying for free or reduced lunch. HISD's English learner population is 67,393 (31.5% of the total number of students), with over 42,000 of those students participating in a bilingual program. The ESL program supports over 26,000 students. Dual language programming is offered at 20% of the district's campuses.

A brief review of the history of HISD dual language education shows that in the early 1990s HISD had two elementary campuses implementing two-way dual language for native Spanish and English speakers to study the full curriculum together through their two languages. When Drs. Thomas and Collier analyzed and reported on the data from these two high-achieving schools, the superintendent in 1995-96, Dr. Rod Paige, strongly recommended expanding this model to multiple campuses and the first wave of expansion of one-way and two-way dual language schools in HISD began. Conducting collaborative longitudinal research in HISD from 1995-2002, Thomas and Collier found that by 2002 the Latino, African American, and White students attending these classes in multiple schools were, by fifth grade, scoring above grade level in both English and Spanish on difficult norm-referenced tests—the Stanford 9 and the Aprenda 2. (Summaries of these research findings are published in Collier & Thomas, 2009, pp. 73-80; Thomas & Collier, 2002; 2012, pp. 60-61).

The desire to have bilingual or multilingual children was, and still is, a popular sentiment in our Houston school communities. In response to this interest, HISD moved forward with a second massive rollout of elementary dual language program expansions in 2013-2014. These programs began at the lower grade levels of pre-kindergarten, kindergarten, and in some cases first grade. As of 2017-2018, our first cohort of this expansive rollout is in third grade. In 2017, the Association of Two-way and Dual Language Education named Houston ISD as a recipient of the District of Distinction award to celebrate and recognize the district's commitment to dual language education.

Within only 2 years, many elementary campuses began to offer dual language (DL) programming. Major time allocations, dedication, hard work, creativity, collaboration, and commitment to providing our students access to bilingualism and biliteracy made this possible. With so many campuses, students, and their families engaging in our elementary DL programs, the need to expand our middle and high school DL offerings was the next logical step. Since the early focus of the rollout was at the early-elementarylevels, we were afforded the opportunity to be proactive. There were a limited number of DL campuses at the secondary level. Unlike the newly expanded campuses at the elementary level, there was not yet a districtwide plan for a secondary DL curriculum that was aligned with both the elementary DL schools and general-education coursework at the middle school. This led to our focus to create curricular alignment across all secondary programs and add additional middle and high school DL campuses as needed.

We also had to recognize that in a district as large as ours, there are many options for students to choose from. We are a district of school choice which means that families can request a transfer to any of the schools in the district. Options equal competition. Although we have large numbers of students in our DL elementary program, we cannot count on all DL families to choose for their children to continue attending the program at secondary level. In this chapter, I will take you through the issues that we encountered on our journey to expand our secondary offerings. The reflections include research from other district and state programs, as well as our own.

Dual Language for All: Programming

Let me start by giving you a little background information about our state's policy and how it influences programming decisions. In Texas, according to state policy, bilingual programming other than DL is not permitted after fifth grade for English learners. However, we know that secondary English learners who have not participated in elementary DL classes but who may still be in need of linguistic and academic support could benefit from courses taught in their first language (L1). DL programming allows English learners this opportunity. In addition, we have a second group of many biliterate DL students who have participated in DL programming in their elementary years. Now that they are in secondary schools and have achieved cognitive advantages from elementary DL, they require challenging courses and continued advanced development of their biliteracy. The goals for these two groups are different and school districts need to determine the purpose and goals of their secondary DL programming during the planning stages. Districts must decide how to meet the needs of both of these student groups. Do they schedule both student groups together? If so, how does the teacher ensure the rigor to challenge the advanced biliterate group while ensuring the scaffolded rigor required for students still acquiring their second language (L2) and continuing literacy development in their L1?

Both student groups can indeed work together, but this is a consideration that will need to be addressed. Districts may decide to offer specialized DL courses that address each student group's particular needs. Some programs create the DL courses as Advanced Placement (AP) or Pre-AP. The structure of these courses is fast paced and typically covers the content of the current grade level as well as a significant portion of the following school year's content. This sometimes leads to the erroneous belief that they can only allow students into the program who have previous DL experience. Districts should ensure that both levels of DL courses be explained to students and parents. Transparency in the programming goal is essential and ethical.

We have two campuses that offer DL at the secondary level and both have very good reputations for their programming. Some of the secondary courses are designed for students who have become biliterate through the elementary DL program. The other DL coursework is designed to help English learners who have not yet acquired enough English and who have participated in a variety of L1 courses in previous transitional bilingual programming. In a transitional bilingual class, the amount of students' L1 that teachers utilize in instruction is based on student need for the L1 support. Having multiple DL courses with different goals could benefit a campus to ensure that all DL students' needs are met. If there is more than one level of DL programming, then there is room for struggling students to continue in the program. The school must do what it takes to help each student succeed. DL programming is for everyone and should not be reserved only for students who received DL in elementary school.

Site-Based Management

Supporting teachers and discussing newcomer programming with campuses in a district with site-based management is very challenging. School leaders are encouraged to be innovative and create the path required to ensure student success. However, school leaders can have various perceptions of the definition of best practices for English learners. In discussions with leadership I have found that, absent research-based training and knowledge, these perceptions come down to the leader's personal beliefs regarding how language is acquired, which are often based on personal experiences or "common sense." Some principals have experienced having to develop English in school themselves. They look back at their English-only school experience and think, "This is what they did to me, and look at me—I learned English and I am successful." Some think, "The problem is that we do not immerse them in English first." But neither point of view is supported by research.

With site-based management, bilingual program decision making at each campus is up to the discretion of the principal. Beyond the incorrect foundational beliefs stated above is the potential for a lack of consistent DL programming for the students when the leadership changes, as it frequently does. For example, when the principal decides that all students should test in English in fourth and fifth grades, this decision does not acknowledge that each student has started acquisition of English in a different time frame, since new immigrant arrivals are constantly entering the school district. The teachers often respond to the testing decision of the principal by feeling that they should increase the instructional time in English. But more time in English does not lead to higher test scores if the students have not yet mastered the curriculum in the language that they know best (Thomas & Collier, 2012; also see Chapter 1).

Student mobility is another issue to be addressed across campuses. A student may begin one program in one campus and then transfer to a different campus and experience a different bilingual program. Mobility issues are at times something beyond our control, but consistent student experiences with bilingual programming across campuses is something that site-based leadership can provide but frequently does not. When students experience these inconsistencies in elementary campus practices, they are adversely affected as they move into secondary DL programs. As we move forward we need to establish firm commitments from district leadership to seek principals supportive of DL programming who subscribe to a common definition of secondary DL.

Master Schedule: Common Planning

When visiting secondary DL programs, we found some campuses providing a very minimal version of DL. It included mainly world language courses, taught traditionally. Students would take the Spanish for Native Speakers course and then proceed to an AP course in order to take the Spanish AP exam in the middle school years. Somehow, successfully passing the Spanish AP courses had become the measure of a successful DL program. However, any student, regardless of whether they participated in DL, can successfully pass this exam. The exam does not reflect the knowledge and skills that native Spanish speakers command, essentially making native English speakers' Spanish proficiency the standard for native Spanish speakers. DL students are capable of so much more because of their past academic coursework taught and learned through Spanish.

We also found that campus leaders were avoiding offering the middle school core content courses in Spanish, especially when these courses were to be tested in English with the State of Texas Assessments of Academic Readiness (STAAR). They believed the students must be exposed to the content in English to be successful on the state assessment, even though this is not what DL research findings say (Thomas & Collier, 2017). Educating campus leaders on the profile of an entering DL student and setting up formative assessments to monitor student progress could gain the campus leaders' confidence to offer more core courses in the partner language. DL elementary students moving into middle school already display the advantages of having moved into high-cognitive levels of academic achievement through the DL program. When interviewing middle school teachers, we found that they clearly could see the higher achievement and cognitive development of their DL students in comparison to their students from other classes. The middle school DL program must offer core courses in Spanish, even if that content is to be tested in English, since DL students can master the subject equally well (if not better) in Spanish. DL research shows that secondary DL students are quite capable of taking a core content course in Spanish and, when tested on this subject in English, scoring higher than students who receive all instruction in English (Thomas & Collier, 2014, 2017).

For a variety of reasons, the master schedule in secondary schools is always a challenge. First, secondary campuses have many other initiatives and programs that compete with DL. Second, working common planning periods for the DL teachers into the schedule is not always easy. But I cannot stress enough the importance of DL teachers having time to work together. They need to plan across the curriculum, have time to discuss and process the DL staff development they are receiving, and to confer regarding meeting the needs of all the students in their DL classes. Third, DL courses in the non-English language must be scheduled in the available time slots, assigned a physical space, and staffed with qualified bilingual teachers. This adds substantially to the master schedule's complexity and requires a very competent and flexible scheduling person to balance all of the competing scheduling needs.

Materials

Spanish materials or no Spanish materials—that is the question. This has been a debate at the secondary level in our district for a while. For those of us who have ventured out in the world of bilingual materials we have found one thing to be true—vendors (at least for Texas) rarely produce materials beyond the sixth grade for DL programming at the secondary level. So the question to ask is, "Is it necessary to have Spanish materials in high school for a DL classroom?" Will the programming suffer at this level without these materials? The answer depends on who you ask. Some teachers want every aspect of their classroom in Spanish, while other teachers say the materials are for reference anyway so the language in which they are written is unimportant. I would say that I would not stop DL programming because I could not find a Spanish textbook for that grade level. But keep in mind that I am in Texas and The Lone Star state likes to do things "our way." In states that do not follow the Common Core State Standards (e.g. Texas), materials can be scarce because vendors are more likely to produce materials following the Common Core.

Feeder Pattern and Recruitment

The idea of enrolling DL students at the middle school is attractive to some administrators because they are aware that these students coming from the elementary DL program will outperform other students. They want to have the DL students feeding into their schools. We have not had many DL middle schools, and of those, only one was a continuation of elementary DL. As we opened two new programs, we included a policy that the students had to have elementary DL experience to enter the program. However, this immediately caused debate over the issue of middle school English learners who were newcomers. Some schools wanted to include these students in the program, so initially we left it to the discretion of the campus principal.

However, our district policy now is to include newcomers in the DL secondary program as often as possible. One of the great benefits of secondary DL programs is that there exists flexibility in the students' schedule. Whereas DL teachers may have a student who requires an additional course for English language development and another who does not, these students will not be given the same schedule simply because they are participants in the DL program. This creates an opportunity for ESL support courses for newcomers who may struggle in a DL course taught in English, but for whom the courses in Spanish are usually quite appropriate, as long as the newcomers have had opportunities to attend school in their home country.

The debate then arose as to why we refused to include native English speakers with no DL background into the secondary DL program. Parents of native English speakers saw participation in DL as an opportunity for their children to learn a second language. The concern is that at this level in DL programming we are trying to challenge the students who are already biliterate. This is why it is important in the secondary DL course offerings to focus on core content courses offered in Spanish and not just world language courses that teach the language but don't teach content in that language. A native English speaker who is not proficient in the language would struggle, as the DL course is not scaffolded sufficiently for second language learners at the beginning level. There are supports, but not enough to support a non-Spanish speaker. As previously mentioned, newcomers who need ESL support are afforded additional ESL content courses in middle and high school, so this allows them to participate in the DL program.

Status of the Spanish Language in the Southwest U.S.

In one of our middle school DL programs we have found that the students do not want to speak Spanish. This is the case for both the English- and Spanish-speaking students. Obviously, this is in opposition to the fundamental intent of DL courses. When we asked students their thoughts, Spanish speakers stated that they now knew English so they no longer needed to speak Spanish, and the English speakers stated that they really did not need to speak Spanish. One student stated that the only time they could use their Spanish was to speak to people in the service-related industries, a particularly poignant example of the community's perception of power relations between English and Spanish speakers. From the beginning of the DL program and throughout every grade we need to reinforce the belief that speaking Spanish is an asset, and that there is real value in the language (see Thomas & Collier, 2017, pp. 15-16). We need to stress the importance and the substantial difference between understanding the language at the fifth grade level and what it looks like to be proficiently bilingual in eighth grade and in 12th grade. We need to pull our DL students away from believing that fifth-grade proficiency is all they need and want. Our English learners may feel this way because Texas state criteria require English tests in fifth grade to meet exit criteria (reclassification as fluent in English) requirements. This may make all students feel that fifth grade is the natural stopping point for their DL participation. But in fact, the state reclassification criteria only defines a minimum proficiency level in English. DL students who continue their studies into their secondary years routinely achieve much more.

Student Admission to the Secondary DL Program

When we began to expand DL programming into secondary schools, we had to start small. We based the expansion on the number of available students. One challenge with continuing the program in secondary is the competition with other programs. The challenge becomes greater in the transition from middle to high school. Our district offers many programs and specialty campuses, especially in high school.

A second challenge is DL student attrition between the elementary and secondary years. Because of the attrition that will occur, we kept the DL expansion small in the past. Now that we have opened over twenty new DL elementary campuses, we monitor their progress and will open additional middle and high school DL programs as the need arises. The goal is to have established feeder patterns for each area where our elementary DL programs are located.

Third, we are a school-choice district, although we do establish DL school feeder patterns. Parents from other geographical areas of the city may send their children to our DL schools without applying for approval. Our current elementary DL programs are in areas of town that are popular for parents to choose for their children. The first middle school expansions are in these areas as well. However, because of school choice, we cannot accurately predict ahead of time how many students will sign up for the DL program in a particular school. We try to admit all eligible and willing English learners to DL, but we typically have more native-English-speaking applicants than we can accommodate. Therefore, we have established a lottery process for the native English speakers who choose DL. Inevitably, there will be some campus programs that are more popular than others, and so we need to ensure that we are transparent and fair in our selection process.

Transportation

The transportation policy in HISD states that a student is granted transportation if they are located two miles or more from their zoned school. Their zoned school is determined by district-created boundary lines that designate certain streets to specific schools for the students to attend. The district also provides transportation to students participating in magnet programs. We have a policy that we provide transportation to English learners who are attending their non-zoned school for bilingual programming services while they are classified as English learners.

This places many of our secondary DL families in a predicament. Most English learners entering in the early grades of PK and K are reclassified as proficient in English by the time they leave elementary school. Unless the secondary DL campus is a magnet school, the students whose families cannot provide their own transportation would not be able to continue their DL education. What is needed is for the school board to fund transportation for DL programs even though they are not magnet programs.

Newcomers

There is debate among district staff as to whether instructing newcomers in Spanish (as occurs in a DL program) is the best option, considering the shortened time frame that secondary students have in school. Each child enters our schools at varying levels of literacy, math, and English development. In Texas, students entering at ninth grade are placed into a graduation cohort. The expectation is that the student will graduate on pace with students who have been in Texas schools their entire academic career. The students are placed on a personal graduation plan. No considerations are given to students who are new to the Texas curriculum, English, or the U.S. school system. The expectation for all high school students is that the student will graduate "on time" with the other students in their graduation cohort. In the case of newcomers, this puts extra pressure on students, teachers, campuses, and district leaders.

Also, when newcomers enter the school system they do not always have transcripts. If they do, their transcripts are reviewed to determine if any of the courses can give the student credit toward their high school course requirements. These issues cause stress, concern, and much debate when considering placing newcomer students into existing DL programs. This has led us to pilot a high school newcomer DL program. In this program two thirds of the class will consist of newcomers while one third of the class will consist of existing DL students. The frameworks for professional development, course content, and supplemental materials are currently being created. Our hope is that this pilot will provide insights on how to best support newcomers in the DL program, and to better understand in what specific ways DL programming helps those students achieve academic success while they acquire English language proficiency.

Leadership Changes

Leadership changes are a reality, especially when working in a larger school district. It makes sense for all school leaders to be knowledgeable of, and a proponent of, the type of programming occurring on their campuses. Most often the new principal has little experience with DL, and even less coursework in DL schooling. At this point one might say, "Wait a minute, for a DL campus, why would you hire a principal who does not have some DL experience?" Keep in mind that often a campus has a strand of DL programming, but that is not the only program on the campus. The campus leader may have been chosen because of his/her ability to develop personnel, improve student data, or engage the community. The district could have had a specific targeted goal for the campus, and DL was not on the top of that list.

Campus leaders new to DL need support. Without help from DL support staff, they can be overwhelmed by the number of decisions required, as they will be receiving information from all sides once they step into their new role. To illustrate, I was working with a secondary school to initiate new DL classes. Just as we had set things in motion to begin this process, two key people including the campus principal abruptly changed. I met with the new principal. In the discussion with the former staff, one of the key people explained why the school had committed to this DL plan. The new principal agreed to continue with the DL endeavor, but was concerned as to the support the campus would offer. Soon thereafter, the school's accountability rating fell below satisfactory, and with that the idea of introducing the new DL program died. The principal was not willing to attempt any new programming because of the adverse rating. There would have been major scheduling and curriculum conflicts and language of instruction concerns. DL should not be forced upon a principal. We are going to continue discussions, and he left the door open to the possibility of implementing DL the following year. I see this as giving us longer to plan.

DL Staffing and Professional Development

Finding teachers with partner language proficiency is a first step in DL staffing. At the secondary level you will find teachers who teach languages other than English who are academically proficient in the partner language. Then the next step is to find bilingually certified teachers for the content areas for which you plan to offer DL courses. Setting up a training plan for the teachers is an imperative next step. It is during these training sessions that you discover the potential of each teacher to be a DL teacher by helping them to define their underlying beliefs about the DL program. Some, you may find, have serious conflicts with their beliefs about language acquisition, language transfer, or bilingual programming in general. Be sure to include staff development sessions that inform the teachers of the type of DL programming the students have experienced in their DL elementary school classes, so they can see the alignment with the secondary program and the benefits the students will receive from continuing to participate in DL courses.

Teacher Cohesiveness and Compatibility

At some of the new secondary campuses we began with only two partner language teachers participating in the DL program. The ideal would have been to have designated English-course teachers assigned to collaborate with the partner-language teachers to plan together. As we added DL teachers, new working relationships needed to be formed. DL central office staff in HISD do not control whom the principal hires. But it is important to have central office DL staff serve on the interview committee for the hiring of DL positions.

Helping the teachers bond can also be a role that central office DL staff can help facilitate. While the new DL teachers are learning about DL practices, it is important to have someone familiar with potential campus challenges to work with and to discuss the components of the DL program. Some of our secondary ESL teachers do not have anyone to plan with as they may be the only person on campus teaching ESL. When campus staff are assigned to be a cohesive unit that works together, all of these staff—ESL teachers, DL teachers who teach the courses in the partner language, and English language arts teachers—can more effectively plan courses to meet the needs of the students. The DL content teachers must also be included in the staff meetings organized by curricular departments for the content courses taught in English that are not part of the DL program.

Culture

Part of teaching children the value of another language is teaching them the value of cultural differences. Examples for young adults in middle and high school could include building positive relationships, bullying prevention, community building, conflict resolution, and social-emotional skills. At the secondary level, it is even more important to teach students about equity, fairness, respect, and inclusiveness. In their lives outside of school, our students are often exposed to a rhetoric that demeans all cultures except the dominant culture. That has been a historical reality in our country. The only way to change that message is to teach students openness to many varied cultural patterns through which people experience life in diverse regions of all the countries in which the partner language is spoken, including the U.S.

When Spanish is the partner language, and the DL program is located in the southwest U.S., Spanish is routinely associated with immigrants, which are often associated with poverty, lack of education, menial jobs, and sometimes considered separate from U.S. society. Students experience these disconnects and this added negativity makes it even more difficult for students to stand with their head held high in pride for being bilingual in Spanish and English. A well-implemented DL program will address these issues and help students overcome them by developing students' self-concept, and by training teachers and other school staff to promote appreciation of a multilingual and multicultural identity.

Where We Are Today

HISD expanded into two new DL middle schools these past few years. We were fortunate that one principal dove right in and had some incredible teachers on staff who stepped up and did an outstanding job. That school soon will be graduating its first cohort of eighth graders. In the recent period of DL expansion, we had an interim superintendent who decided to halt DL expansion. However, one of our principals who had tremendous support from the community to begin DL programming on campus decided to move forward. The program is doing well. Our next superintendent supported the expansion of secondary DL schooling, but changes have again occurred, and the reality is that a new superintendent may or may not be supportive of DL programming. We try to build capacity at our DL campuses, provide professional development on multiple platforms, and write and influence local policy. Our DL programs need to be well implemented, successful, and sustainable so that they outlive us as individuals. That is the advice I send forward for those of you who may experience this type of leadership change in the midst of efforts to expand your successful DL programs into the secondary years. Remember that the overarching goal of your secondary DL program is to bring even higher achievement and adult-level proficiency in two languages to all of your DL graduates.

CHAPTER NINE
CALIFORNIA: NORTON SCIENCE AND LANGUAGE ACADEMY ADVENTURES IN DUAL IMMERSION: GROWING A MIDDLE SCHOOL WITHIN A WHOLE-SCHOOL TK-8 DUAL LANGUAGE PROGRAM

ERIN BOSTICK MASON, TEACHER

Introduction by Collier and Thomas: *This chapter is unique, as the only description in this book of a public school dual language program that exists in all classrooms, at all grade levels. This whole-school model has many advantages over the dual language strands that exist in most schools throughout the U.S. Author Erin Mason presents her perspective on how "a whole-school design fundamentally impacts the way staff work together, the students' educational experiences, and the students' expectations for the larger world they help shape each day and will reshape throughout their lives." The school is stable and supportive. The students' multilingualism/multiculturalism is so strongly developed by everyone in the school that "learning languages is as normal as breathing for these students." The DL program is for students of all ethnicities, social classes, special needs, and interests. In a whole-school program, DL middle school classes must offer the broad choices and electives that other schools offer, with flexibility and creativity. This chapter is packed with ideas for creating the "dream" DL school, while facing the challenges that come as each new grade level is added to the school.*

A Fairy Tale Begins…

Once upon a time a group of about 200 5-, 6-, and 7-year olds embarked on a journey at a new public charter school called the Norton Science and Language Academy, (originally the Norton Space and Aeronautics Academy). As they grew up, they blazed the path to middle school graduation. San Bernadino, California, where this story takes place, is a socio-economically, culturally, and linguistically diverse community. Families, teachers, administrators, and community leaders dreamed of a whole-school dual language, or as it is called in California, dual immersion education for their under-served students. The program would serve transitional kindergarteners (TK), students who turn 5 years old between September 1 and December 31, all the way to twelfth graders. In fact, with the promise of learning English, Spanish, and Chinese, and a special focus on science, the dream was so captivating that it attracted students and families from all over the region. Teachers and staff traveled from near and far to join this brigade of dual immersion torchbearers who were committed to building the first whole-school TK-12 dual immersion (DL) campus in the region.

However, as any fairy-tale reader (or DL supporter) can attest, these brave educators and families would face many challenges that tested their resolve, teamwork, and creativity. They embarked on a journey that would require courage, innovation, and stamina at every turn. Although the tale of this school community continues to evolve, there have been many lessons learned in their quest for K-12 DL education for all. The journey of creating the middle school has been especially eye-opening and worthy of reflection. This tale is the story of their adventures and some of the lessons learned along the way. This chapter will focus on how a whole-school DL program impacts middle school.

Many Roles, One Theme

If you have helped envision and initially implement a DL program, you may find yourself relating to the fairy-tale analogy. On the one hand, DL is 100% research-based, proven, and attainable. At the same time, it often feels like it requires a bit of magic to make it come to life. Our belief in the vision of multilingualism, multiculturalism, and academic success for all creates that magic—that is to say the systemic energy to persevere. It empowers us with the flexibility and stamina that long-term implementation requires from all parts of a system.

The 2017-18 school year marks the 10th anniversary of our school and provides an opportune moment to reflect on the story of our founding and some of the lessons learned. Throughout this first decade, my involvement with the school has taken many forms and has provided me with a variety of vantage points from which to observe and experience the school community's journey. Originally, I served as the school's DL coach in my role as English learner program manager at the offices of the San Bernardino County Superintendent of Schools. I helped shape the DL vision and trilingual program design for the school's charter. Once the first principal was hired, we helped train and coach him as he learned about DL, hired staff, recruited families, and planned for the school's opening. For the first several years I served as the school's coach from the county office, working with teachers in the classroom, supporting administrators, and training parents.

As the school and my own family grew, I joined the community of Norton in a new, more personal way by enrolling my children, who by the 10th anniversary of the school were in the elementary and middle school grades. In 2013, I seized the opportunity to join the staff as the instructional coach for the school. In 2018, after 16 years of serving as administrator, coach, researcher, and professor, I decided to join the fourth-grade teaching team as a classroom teacher. Each of these experiences provided me with a new perspective on the development of the school. Yet, through each of those roles, I have consistently witnessed how the decision to pursue a whole-school design fundamentally impacts the way staff work together, the students' educational experiences, and the students' expectations for the larger world they help shape each day and will reshape throughout their lives.

Impact on Staff

Some of the aspects of a whole-school environment may be quickly visible, such as the impact on staff. Whole-school programs offer a unique opportunity for support and teamwork. Without having to balance the needs of monolingual and multilingual programs in one school, stakeholders can harness all energy towards solving common challenges, such as curriculum, assessments, communication, facilities, and scheduling within the parameters of a common vision of biliteracy, academic success, and multicultural proficiency for all. The whole-school environment facilitates a unified sense of identify around the vision. It makes the identity clear when recruiting and training new staff. The critical mass of support needed for DL is stable and supportive. It quickly becomes self-perpetuating in the sense that DL is intrinsic to the identity of the school community. It is front and center to any new administrators, board members, authorizing agencies, staff, families, and students. The school is less vulnerable, although not immune, to debates over the value of multilingual education.

Impact on Students

However, the most powerful impact is directly on the students. Many students in our whole-school DL program grow up thinking all students in all schools have access to these programs. They cannot imagine schooling any other way. Their lives at school are so consistently multilingual and multicultural for so many years that they understand all students can learn languages and build multicultural proficiency, even when they see or hear contrary ideas at home or in the community. In many ways, they take their multilingual abilities and environment for granted in the best possible way. They accept multilingualism and multiculturalism as the norm instead of the exception. DL is not an exclusive program for any particular subset of the population, such as only students identified as gifted and talented, only those in general education and not special education, only Latino and Caucasian students, only middle-class students, or any other demographic groups that may exist. It is open to any student who enrolls in kindergarten or first grade. By middle school, continuing elementary school students, partner-language speakers, and recent arrivals from partner-language countries are all open to participate no matter their ethnicity, special needs, socioeconomic level, or interests. It is a program FOR ALL and the students live that every day.

Furthermore, it impacts students' expectations for society beyond school. They hold a high expectation for society to continue with this level of pluralism and hold their communities accountable for improved race relations, socioeconomic relations, and linguistic policy and practices. They are not naive, in that most have witnessed or experienced a variety of forms of discrimination in life, including racism, linguistic profiling, economic marginalization, and other societal forces. However, learning languages is as normal as breathing for these students. They learn perseverance, how to understand ambiguity, how to identify patterns, and all the other benefits as described in much of the DL research. They leave school knowing that a peaceful, multilingual, multiculturally proficient society is possible and requires ongoing reflection and perseverance from community members.

Appealing to Students

Students have a stronger voice in deciding their own future in middle school and logistics plays a major role in determining their options. To be truly inclusive of all students, DL education needs to offer the complete secondary experience in the eyes of the students. Since most students initially enroll in DL programs in kindergarten or first grade, families and parents are the ones who make the decision to join the program and commit to the first 6- to 7-year timespan. However, by the start of middle school, students are more involved in the decision to continue in the program or not. Since many school districts have distinct elementary, middle, and high school campuses, each transition triggers the same conversation again, whether to stay in the program or leave. If the DL programs are well established in a district, the guidance staff may automatically direct students to continue. If the program is relatively new or staff are new, it may be easy for long-time DL students to get lost in the master-schedule shuffle.

Socially and emotionally, students in middle school are at a pivotal juncture in developing their ideas about who they are, their talents, and which paths to pursue. At the same time, the logistics of middle school scheduling (classes, transportation, sports, etc.) have a tremendous impact on the choices available to them. A whole-school program ensures that students do not have to choose between being a dual language student and any other identities that they may want to explore or develop. For example, in many middle schools, the master schedule pits DL against athletics, arts, music, or leadership programs. Since DL secondary programs offer two to three periods in the partner language, many schools offer one of the DL classes as the student's elective, as a zero and/or a seventh period. This has implications for pick-up and drop-off times for families, the student's participation in athletics and clubs, etc. In some schools, the English learners may be forced to miss one of the DL periods in order to enroll in English language development. In other cases, intervention classes such as English language arts for struggling readers may trump DL classes. It can be increasingly difficult to accommodate the students' paths unless all parts of the system are working in harmony, and even then it sometimes takes compromises on the parts of families, students, and staff to make it work.

The whole-school DL approach partially eliminates these challenges because all students are part of the program and a K-8 or K-12 campus further smoothes the transitions by providing continuity. However, whenever there are other options for schools in the local area, K-8 and K-12 programs still face challenges as students transition from one stage to another. Whole-school programs must offer what students define as the complete middle school or high school experience, which typically involves student-selected electives, expanded opportunities in the arts, athletics, including school sports leagues; clubs; technology and student leadership. Our campus decided it was essential to rise to the challenge of providing a broad middle school experience in the eyes of our students. As we have grown, reflected, and reinvented our middle school, we have made it our objective to provide the broadest middle school experience possible so that they do not have to limit their own budding identities or any typical opportunities during their multilingual, multicultural journey.

Balancing Commitment and Flexibility, While Maintaining Stamina

Once again we return to the quest of our intrepid DL adventurers at the Norton Science and Language Academy. Commitment, flexibility, and stamina were required from the start. Commitment served as our compass, specifically a dedication to the research and possibilities for DL, as well as our team's abilities to make those a reality. Flexibility to find creative solutions in the face of ever-changing needs and resources allowed us to succeed where there were multiple opportunities to stop short or give up on our goals. Finally, emotional and institutional stamina continues to allow us to thrive over a 10- to 15-year period of growing each grade level.

Taking time to recognize our intermediate successes and make upgrades to our program from good, to better, to best, allows us the energy and morale to stay in the game for the long haul. Annual staff reflection, weekly professional learning communities, and trimester planning must include dedicated time to reflect on our short-term and long-term goals, with special attention paid to the celebrations along the way. A constant focus on what has not yet been achieved leads to burnout. In fact, it is imperative that our community school as a whole nurtures a focus on our successes. It is easy to always look at what remains to be accomplished. School leadership must find ways to make celebration of intermediate successes clear for all to see. Publicly recording those successes in our meetings, school plans, websites, newsletters, and conversations rejuvenates us all and increases our personal and institutional stamina.

Appreciative inquiry can take many forms. On a regular basis our professional collaborations make time to recognize the positive accomplishments in our ongoing work together. Our grade-level professional learning communities, school site council, academic leadership team, multitiered systems of support team, and classified staff team meetings all include regular attention to intermediate successes. In addition, we have longer-term cycles of reflection. For example, our school voluntarily committed to WASC accreditation (Western Association of Schools and Colleges) in our original charter, starting in elementary school. Some wondered why we would voluntarily choose to add this additional process of review and scrutiny to our K-8 institution before we created the high school. However, it has proven to be a very supportive and gratifying process for our school community. It has been refreshing and energizing to hear such positive feedback from a recognized external body. The feedback has recorded our growth, challenges, and successes in a regular cycle. It is one of the ways that we build time for reflection and celebration into our cycle of institutional development.

Adapting Plans, While Staying on Course

Initially, the school intended to have a space and aeronautics focus, thus the original name, the Norton Space and Aeronautics Academy. It was hoped that local aeronautics partnerships would flourish since it was located near the former Norton Air Force Base in San Bernadino. However, several educators and community leaders involved in the planning of the charter school recognized the opportunity to create the first whole-school DL program, as well as the first trilingual program model in the region, based on the 80-10-10 model used at Alicia R. Chacón International Elementary School, in the Ysleta Independent School District in El Paso, Texas. The partnership between the San Bernardino County Superintendent of Schools, which was the authorizing agency of the charter, and the Lewis Center for Educational Research, which was the local education agency, resulted in the decision and commitment to make this dream a reality, focusing on English, Spanish, and Chinese. It would be designed to meet the needs of underserved populations from across the region, with the promise of eventually providing K-12 DL education schoolwide.

Over the years, many other components were added and adapted under the unwavering umbrella of whole-school DL. Due to the challenge of finding enough qualified Chinese-speaking teachers long-term, the idea of an 80-10-10 model was quickly adapted into a 90:10 Spanish/English DL program, with a strong Chinese FLES (foreign language elementary school) program. Chinese language and culture instruction were offered for 30 minutes a week to every student in Grades K-5 and offered as an elective to middle school students. The campus also added a transitional kindergarten for students who turned 5 years old between Sept. 1 and Dec. 31. At the time of the 10th anniversary, the school had grown to approximately 800 students and the plans for the high school and land acquisition to expand the campus, were also in progress.

The School Community

One of the benefits of being a public charter school was that this school was required to have substantial agreement from a variety of stakeholders in order to get the school up and running. Families had to go out of their way to enroll their child since there was not an automatically designated geographic zone that funneled students to the site. It was a new school that was an addition to the existing schooling options in the area. Parents specifically chose it knowing it was whole school DL and K-12. However, this did not result in a predominantly affluent population or one that had been traditionally empowered in public school systems. In fact, the school was successful in attracting a traditionally underserved population from across two counties, including many families who qualified for free and reduced lunch, had felt underserved or unsuccessful in their local school, and/or were searching for a site where a range of siblings, relatives, and friends could attend the same school long-term. Families were interested in the multilingual, multicultural vision within a safe community of long-term relationships.

Staffing

Staffing was one of the first challenges. Many of those involved with the founding of our campus were not experienced in DL education prior to joining this effort. For many of the teachers, this was their first job after their bilingual credential program at the University of California, Riverside or the California State University, San Bernardino. For others, this was their first position in DL.

However, as much of the DL research supports, even one or two individuals with experience can be enough to light the spark and guide a willing team to DL success. In this case, one lead teacher was wisely recognized by the principal for her expertise as both a DL teacher and former administrator at a school with a DL program. Her knowledge of DL and organizational management allowed her to play a key role in coaching the other new teachers and helping the principal shape the school. Eventually, she served as teacher in various grade levels and then returned to the role of vice principal, helping to lead and shape the middle school.

The initial teaching staff who opened the school are reverently and warmly referred to as the Original Teachers. They pitched in and embraced extended professional duties well beyond their classrooms. They faced the challenges of helping to recruit the first cohorts of students, as well as a growing classified and certificated staff over the years. Similarly, the teachers who helped establish each new grade level, especially the middle school, required a unique set of skills. They committed themselves to a constant cycle of planning, implementing, and reflecting on each system they put in place. Moreover, they embraced all of this work within the context of a 1950s school site that was in an ongoing state of refurbishment and construction in order to accommodate each growing cohort of students. Together, the staff who blazed the path for the first year of each grade level are appreciated and recognized for their joint commitment, flexibility, and stamina. It requires an expanded set of skills to thrive in that kind of innovative, ever-changing environment.

Reflecting and Restructuring Middle School

It may be cliché to say that middle school is full of challenges. Yet, this statement is rooted in the very real experiences of students, families, and staff over time. For decades, generations have lived middle school experiences that are shaped strongly by rushed daily schedules, curriculum and instruction silos, secondary school systems that are locked into place by facilities and transportation factors, and the biological experiences of 11- to 14-year-olds. Moreover, the typical social-emotional roller coasters that are felt by so many students, families, and staff in the middle school years are often exacerbated by all of the previous elements listed above. It can be a perfect storm for frustration on the part of all stakeholders. Negative middle school experiences are so common in our society that many are convinced that it is an inevitable part of growing up. Many joke that those who teach middle school must either be saints or blessed with superpowers to survive students at this age and the fossilized middle school structures that are often in place. Likewise, many adults and children believe it is a necessary evil that students must grin and bear, as if "getting through" is the best possible outcome. However, the structures and approaches in our schools can either exacerbate the challenges or soothe them. It is up to our DL stakeholder teams to create the most supportive systems for each evolving step in our communities' journey.

As DL research has repeatedly shown over recent decades, it is not sufficient to add multilingual instruction to ineffective school systems. Implementing ineffective approaches in two languages instead of just one language is not beneficial. DL requires comprehensive reflection regarding most aspects of traditional monolingual, hegemonic schooling. DL is at its heart enriched, additive, multilingual education for all. On the one hand, it is essential to take the time to conduct some appreciative inquiry in order to identify the current strengths in one's school system and strategize how to use those strengths to find solutions to other challenges the school community faces. On the other hand, the school community must find the time and energy to reflect on how well each component of the school system supports the vision of multilingualism, multiliteracy, and multicultural proficiency for all and be ready to change and adapt where it is not yet working.

Furthermore, these reflective processes are not activities that can be checked off a list and filed away. There is a continual process of reflection and refinement. It is not as much a linear process as a spiraling process, in part because policies sway, community and political attitudes fluctuate, curriculum shifts, assessments change, and the needs of populations evolve. However, this reflective process is also a way of life for DL school communities because it is too exhausting and, often, ineffective to try to reassess all parts of a system simultaneously. As a result, strength of vision, dedication to program models, and knowledge of research is necessary but not sufficient. As research in organizational management, such as the work of Margaret Wheatley's classic book Leadership and the New Science (2006) illuminates, relationships, identity, and access to information are essential for the long-term stamina and resilience of your growing DL community at the secondary levels. Leaders must hold the vision of DL for all to see, and at the same time, be willing to move from good, to better, to best as the program grows over the years. The challenge is to remain true to the DL model while refining the components of the larger school system.

As we return to the journey of the Norton Science and Language Academy, the first lesson is the essential importance of a visible commitment to DL, combined with flexibility in how to make that happen with each year's growth. As the school celebrated the 10th anniversary of its opening, the need for these two ingredients was more apparent than ever. Getting a middle school up and running in those ever-changing first few years is a unique challenge. It provides opportunities to shape and reshape the structures, vision, and systems with unique frequency before they become institutionalized and considered the normal way of operating. When there is no "way we have always done it here," the possibilities for reinvention are wide-open. For example, Norton tried a few calendars before establishing a vacation schedule that suited the many binational families traveling to and from Mexico during the year. Norton also tried a variety of middle school schedules and teacher qualifications within the first 3 to 4 years of the program. Each year, there was new feedback on how the system was working and adjustments were made accordingly.

However, too many or seemingly random changes can trigger a sense of instability for staff, families, and students. A program has yet to become firmly established until it has been implemented at each grade level and graduated the first few cohorts. Since middle school DL programs are less numerous than elementary DL programs, new DL middle school programs may face the challenge of being unproven locally, especially if it is the first of its kind in the region.

Ongoing communication with all stakeholders is key. As with the creation or re-creation of any organization, restructuring schools takes cyclical, repeated reflection from a wide variety of stakeholders. Furthermore, the assumptions and past experiences that are ingrained in us, and are often unquestioned, will join us in this new planning process and may only be revealed well into the reflective cycle (after months or even years). A cyclical process of reflection will require both visible commitment to creating a research-based DL that works for all local stakeholders, as well as ongoing flexibility regarding how to stay true to the model with ever-changing resources. Small initial student cohorts, changing needs for facilities, evolving ideas of curriculum and instruction, and a variety of student experiences necessitate continual feedback and reflection.

It is rare to have all of the components in place to begin the ideal school all at once. Furthermore, due to the nature of language development and the corresponding design of DL, secondary DL programs typically grow out of an existing elementary program. The first few years require especially visible, vigilant commitment and flexibility since communities must grow the program over multiple years, until they have enough students in each grade to establish stable, reliable cohorts year after year.

As we know, DL research shows that a long-term commitment of 5 to 7 years is needed to close the achievement gap and develop biliteracy and bilingualism (Thomas & Collier, 2017). As a result, families at Norton were aware of this commitment and had agreed to do their best to stay until the end of elementary school at fifth or sixth grade. Moreover, this public charter school is a regional DL school, drawing students from a wide geographic region. Many students or families are drawn to consider the pros and cons of attending a regional school versus their local school by the time they reach middle school, especially if the middle school is not yet proven and established.

As the first student cohorts at Norton reached third and fourth grades, staff began to survey parents and estimate how many students would choose to remain at the school for Grades 6-8. Public relations play a key role early on in demonstrating commitment and flexibility to the secondary experience. Some students and families specifically wanted the K-8 or K-12 experience in order to have the social and emotional stability of long-term relationships with peers and staff. Many families spoke of the increased sense of safety that resulted from staff, families, and friends knowing one another well and supporting one another over years of child-rearing and partnership in education. Students spoke of the confidence gained from knowing the social and academic terrain of their school long-term instead of attending different schools for primary and secondary. Yet, they also expressed the need for some of the typical middle school opportunities that their local middle schools offered, like a sports league, electives, and deeper experiences in the arts. They did not demand that these elements all be present on the first day of middle school. Rather, stakeholders wanted a commitment that these would develop quickly in the first couple of years.

Most of all, the commitment to developing the middle school had to be clearly visible to all stakeholders. It was written in the school's charter but that was not enough. Plans in official charters and annual reports are often not as reassuring as the community "buzz" of ongoing communication. The details regarding the commitment to secondary DL needed to be repeated over many years in informal conversations, as well as formal settings such as board meetings, the parent teacher organization, the school site council, meeting agendas, in the newsletter, and the website in order to have the secondary plans spoken of with assurance and confidence by families and staff. With a clear commitment on behalf of the staff and leadership and a clear desire on behalf of the families and students, the community began the process of choosing the key components of the middle school system and shaping a middle school that could adapt over the transitional years before achieving full enrollment in Grades 6 through 8.

Transitioning from Elementary to Middle School

When the first student cohort reached sixth grade, the students stayed in self-contained classes as part of the elementary school. In fact, the first two cohorts only had enough students to form one class each. The school decided it was a priority to maintain separate language role models. Therefore, one fifth- and one sixth-grade teacher team taught. One provided half of the day in Spanish to her homeroom class and the other half of the day in Spanish to the other grade's class; and the other teacher provided the English component of the curriculum for the two grade levels. Team teaching across grades was a true sign of commitment and flexibility.

The First Iteration

The first iteration of the middle school included the atypical decision to create the middle school with Grades 5-7 for 1 year and then transition to the more common Grades 6-8 the following year. This was the best option that could be found at the time, until the first cohort reached eighth grade. This required special agreement from the families and students since most students do not switch classes until Grades 6 or 7 at most middle schools. Furthermore, the first year of middle school followed a traditional six-period approach to the school day. A zero period offered a few optional electives. Only some students chose to participate due to the early start time. Technology classes, specifically robotics, were the most popular. Zero period also hosted the required English language development class for a remaining group of long-term English learners and any newcomers that might enroll. A seventh period offered additional intervention supports, such as math tutoring in small groups. The grading system changed from the K-4 system of a three-point rubric to traditional A-F grades. To the students' joy, the school also joined a sports league and offered multiple team sports each season. School dances were enjoyed each trimester and students attended overnight science field trips in Grades 7-8. One of the favorite trips was a camp-out at a marine institute in Dana Point, California, where students learned to operate submersible rovers to explore the sea floor.

Credentialing

The decision was also made to pursue teachers with single subject credentials to fill those subject-specific teaching positions. This required flexibility and commitment from the leadership in the business services and human resources departments, since it meant that class sizes would sometimes be very small (15-20 students) or larger (up to 35) to accommodate emerging student enrollment in the two oldest cohorts. The class sizes had to be adjusted in order to make it feasible to teach content areas separately for each grade level. As a result, families, staff, and students needed to be understanding since one student's class might have 35 enrolled and her/his sibling might have 15 in his/her class depending on the unique numbers of these first two cohorts. Likewise, teacher pay would be the same for those very different class sizes. Commitment to the vision, understanding that this was a temporary (3 to 4 year) time span for transitioning to a well-established middle school, and ongoing collaboration/communication between staff, families, and students soothed frustrations that arose. By the time the first eighth grade class graduated, there were just over a dozen students. The second graduating class had a few more. Eventually, the school's standard enrollment of five kindergarten classes (120 students) would feed into about three fifth-grade classes (with typical attrition for student mobility), and form two to three solid classes of 60 to 80 students total in each grade at middle school.

However, the school quickly realized how difficult it can be to find single subject credentialed teachers who also have bilingual certification. As a nation, we need to grow more certified bilingual, biliterate secondary teachers! (See Chapter 15.) To address this, some districts choose to establish pipelines with student teaching programs at their local universities. Norton did this for Grades K-5 with several universities in the region. They often served as long-term substitute teachers who were later hired. Others completed student teaching at the school site and were hired directly after graduation.

Many secondary teachers choose single subject credentials because they enjoy the focus on a single content area. They may not think of getting the bilingual authorization or may have specifically been told it is not a necessary or worthwhile investment for secondary teachers. In many regions of the United States, dual language or bilingual education is largely perceived as an elementary school program. Credential programs for secondary teachers may or may not encourage them to take the time and money to invest in completing the coursework and exams that cultivate and attest to their bilingual/biliterate abilities. Even when our school found math or science teachers with bilingual abilities in Spanish, most did not have the official bilingual certification. Therefore, human resources needed to give them opportunities to develop those certifications. Again, this is an example of the commitment and flexibility that may be required from all parts of the system.

On the other hand, many teachers were not ready or interested in the level of flexibility and initiative that these first few middle school years required. Teachers needed to be able to teach, scout curriculum and materials, and collaborate with staff across grade levels and content. Middle school teacher turnover (loss of staff) became a major challenge. Several teachers taught for a year or less, accepting positions in established middle schools with large middle school subject-matter departments and established curriculum. Norton's situation was further exacerbated by an economic shift from an employers' market, where teaching jobs were scarce, to a teachers' market, where districts had regained more financial stability and were competing for staff through higher salaries and better benefits.

Our growing, whole-school DL middle school needed teachers who were willing to work in a changing environment, take lots of initiative in their teaching and in evaluating materials, and collaborate beyond their classroom in two main ways. In one sense, they were juggling grade levels and content. Teachers might be the only one teaching their subject matter and grade or they might be teaching multiple grades and subject matter. Both scenarios can be a challenge. In another sense, they were teaching in a shifting context and were asked to reflect and reshape those contexts based on their experiences and those of their students. This included some physically changing environments. When construction on new classrooms took longer than expected, teachers and students had to be temporarily placed in the library or multipurpose room until their permanent location was ready. For some it was days and for others a couple of months. Regarding curriculum and instruction, we were creating the syllabi, designing pacing schedules, purchasing materials, training our teams, and rethinking grading and classroom management in each of those first few years. We knew the goal was bilingual, biliterate, multiculturally proficient students who achieved at and above grade level. We carefully implemented each stage, monitored progress, and re-evaluated if changes were needed. It was a deliberate, yet daunting, experience that required extensive personal and institutional stamina, as well as time for collaboration.

Reflecting After Years One and Two

Strengths in our middle school. In the first year, the fifth through seventh grade students provided extensive feedback verbally and through their achievement. On the one hand, they appreciated being recognized for this new stage in life and in school. They had new uniform colors, a separate part of the campus where their classrooms were clustered, and a new schedule. The relationships among the students and staff were clearly a main strength as well. The athletics program was a budding success. Furthermore, beginning in fourth grade each student received a laptop computer, enabling tremendous potential for innovation in middle school. Special education services were also a strength of the school, with a bilingual speech therapist, bilingual resource specialist, bilingual school psychologist, and bilingual school counselor full-time on campus for TK-8. However, in the first year, the fifth grade students were challenged by the six-period schedule and its requirement for increased executive functioning and student independence on their part. Fortunately, we knew this would last only one year, so staff created support systems that included increased communication with parents about assignments. Assignment journals and calendars were also modeled and supported in class.

Challenges with the six-period schedule. At this same time, the sixth through eighth graders taught us that not all the issues were age related. In the second year of middle school, most structures stayed the same, but with Grades 6-8, instead of Grades 5-7. After the second year of middle school, the school had feedback from a six-period day with older students. The basic traditional middle school six-period structure was not working as well as we hoped. Tardies increased tremendously, with six chances a day to be late. There was no morning recess or nutrition break and lunch period was a short 30 minutes. Moreover, the middle school started at the same time as K-5, but offered a zero period. The sixth period ended after the K-5 students. A seventh period also existed for tutoring. Some required subjects and some electives were taught in the zero period, with academic support in the seventh period time frame. However, not all students could take electives due to this schedule. In addition, many of our students who participated in free or reduced breakfast lost instructional time. Many zero period students spent most of their days leaving class early to get breakfast in the cafeteria, which followed the K-5 breakfast schedule. These classes also had higher rates of absenteeism. Families shared it was hard to drop off and pick up students at different times. Students and staff shared that the systems we put in place the first two years needed to be reviewed and reconsidered.

Homework and grading. The bond between teacher and student is pivotal. That bond needed to be enhanced, not strained. We also needed to carefully calibrate where and how to invest students' and teachers' energy, since both groups were reporting some signs of burn-out and frustration. We needed staff to have the opportunity to work with fewer students. Students also needed the opportunity to build deeper relationships with teachers. Teachers shared that the number of students and the number of separate content-area assignments was a strain on both students and staff. At the time, homework counted as part of the grade. Grading and keeping track of homework took valuable time and energy away from more valuable teaching investments. It also resulted in highly concerning rates of D's and F's. Any D's and F's are cause for concern; however, by analyzing our data we confirmed that missing homework was significantly impacting grades. Even though students had laptops to take home, many did not have internet access or an adult/mentor to support them at home in the evening. Others had significant family responsibilities, including caring for younger siblings while parents worked. Some stayed up late to finish assignments and then lacked the sleep to make the most of the next instructional day.

As a team, we reviewed the research on homework and grading. We concluded that it was most beneficial for student learning if we scheduled some class time for assignments while teachers met with small groups, providing differentiated instruction. We also determined that designing interdisciplinary assignments or project-based learning would better align to the Common Core, increase the levels of depth of knowledge, provide fewer assignments for students to complete, and fewer assignments for teachers to grade. For example, one cross-disciplinary project or essay could evaluate mastery of history or science, as well as multiple language arts standards. This would free students and teachers to engage in more complex, real-world learning, while deepening their relationships, and minimizing time spent on assignments that may or may not accurately reflect the students' current abilities.

Time in the school schedule for teacher collaboration. Finally, it needed to be easier to fill positions and retain teaching staff. We needed collaboration time and flexibility with the types of credentials we sought. As previously outlined, the teachers were asked to work in a very innovative setting, where they were constantly taking initiative and acclimatizing to a changing environment. This makes collaboration time and support even more essential. Traditionally, teachers in secondary schools have individual preparation periods for each subject they teach. In our first 2 years of middle school, we had not been successful in figuring out how to provide that with the student enrollment, staff numbers, and facilities we had available. We realized that this was a major contributing factor to teacher stress and strain.

As a school, we all had an abbreviated teaching day on Wednesdays that provided opportunities for a cycle of staff meetings, professional development, grade-level planning, and teacher preparation each month. Our kindergarten classes were all full-day, yet they still finished one hour earlier than Grades 1-5, providing multiple opportunities for weekly collaboration. In addition, the school created further opportunities for enrichment for our students and dedicated weekly professional learning community time for our TK- 5 teachers by implementing a rotation schedule with part-time classified teaching staff. This was achieved with four classified staff who taught a few hours a day. Each grade had one day a week that was their enrichment day. In that time, the Chinese language and culture, art, music, and physical education teachers each taught for 30 minutes. When sandwiched on either side of the lunch break, this provided 2 hours and 45 minutes of collaboration time for grade levels each week. In order to build strong relationships and trust for the teaching teams at each grade level, the teachers went off-campus to lunch for an hour during this time. This is nearly unheard of in most school settings. Yet, it proved to be highly effective in creating strong teams of colleagues who felt safe to innovate, give and receive feedback, and analyze student data openly. As a result, we committed ourselves to finding a way to provide this when we restructured our middle school.

Single subject and multiple subject credentials for teachers. With regard to the debate of single subject and multiple subject credentials at middle school, we realized we needed flexibility. There is a place for both. We wanted to integrate subject matter, which suggests a multiple subject background would be most suitable. It is also easier to find multiple subject credentialed teachers with bilingual certification. On the other hand, being bilingual in the middle school level is not necessary for all teaching positions, since students have significant levels of bilingualism by that stage in the program. However, it is essential to have an understanding of first and second language development, as well as an understanding of how your school's languages compare and contrast. This is typically within the repertoire of teachers who were trained in a single subject credential program. Plus, we had one or two content areas that needed to be taught separately due to our enrollment and facilities. Therefore, a single subject teaching credential position needed to remain a choice for our school. Furthermore, Norton uses Guided Language Acquisition Design (Project GLAD®), as well as other methods that rely on extensive professional development and a long-term coaching model, rather than a more prescriptive curriculum. It also means that you have to grow your own teachers to a certain degree. Longevity is essential at our site, since we build these skills over many years. We needed to be able to attract appropriate teachers and retain them for years to come.

Reinventing our Middle School Structure

We began researching, reflecting, and planning to create a new structure for our middle school during the winter of the second year. Planning the middle school structure and a flexible growth model included voices from families, students, and staff. In the end, staff reviewed the benefits and drawbacks of many options. The leadership team debated the merit of these and visited other school sites as examples, when possible. They called colleagues and networked to get ideas. The various middle school options reviewed included a self-contained classroom model for all Grades K-8, with multiple subject teachers and students staying with one teacher for Spanish and one for English each day, as in Grades K-5. A second model was a commonly used block schedule that took the same six-period division of subject matter and extended the time for each period up to 90 minutes, with each period meeting a few times a week instead of each day. This model relied on single subject teachers and had different schedules depending on the day of the week. The research on smaller learning communities was also reviewed, and we decided that it was a strong match for our community's value of long-term relationships.

Essentials for our middle school. In the end, a third option was created, modeled on a variety of research that met certain needs of our students, families, and teachers. It was decided that instructional periods needed to be longer to allow for differentiated instruction (English language development, Spanish language development, re-teaching, intensive support), interdisciplinary instruction, and longer class projects (project-based learning, science labs, theatre productions, etc.). We agreed that our middle school needed:

- common start and end times for school in Grades 1-8, with no zero or seventh periods;

- time for differentiated instruction;

- student-selected electives for all;

- common breaks for staff and students;

- collaboration and common prep time for teachers;

- integrated subject matter that matched the Common Core's interconnected approach to learning;

- optional after-school clubs based on students' interests;

- fewer teachers for students to get to know;

- fewer students for teachers to get to know;

- common yearly scope and sequence that made the links across subject matter clear to teachers, students, and families;

- common templates for syllabi;

- common grading and weighting policies across all courses;

- focus on grading classwork and not homework;

- maximized class time for assignments and a focus on health and well-being at home; and

- common classroom management strategies.

New middle school schedule. We took the daily schedule and redesigned it from start to finish. Time that had been lost each day due to transition time between each period was reconfigured into a nutrition break in the morning, as well as daily start and end times that matched elementary grades. Zero, sixth, and seventh periods were eliminated. School start and end times now matched for all Grades 1-8, eliminating the need for sibling care in Grades 1-5, ensuring breakfast without loss of instructional minutes, and ensuring attendance in ELD and academic support times. We wanted teachers in the middle-school blocks to have the flexibility to conduct, for example, a science experiment one day that would last longer than the traditional 45-minute period, with a follow-up integrated writing assignment the next day. Likewise, when it was time to focus more heavily on language arts, we wanted our students to have time to perform a play or meet in small groups for Spanish or English language development and not be interrupted by a bell after 45 minutes. As a result, we redesigned the middle school daily schedule to include five periods:

- approx. 90-minute period for integrated Spanish language arts and social science taught by a multiple subject teacher,

- approx. 90-minute period for integrated English language arts and science taught by a multiple subject teacher,

- approx. 45-minute math period taught by a single subject teacher,

- approx. 45-minute physical education period taught by a single subject teacher,

- approx. 35-minute elective taught by classified staff, and

- a 15-minute nutrition break and 30-minute lunch.

Scheduling teacher collaboration time. Student-choice electives for all students have been a key element in appealing to students and retaining them. Collaboration time and prep periods have been essential in supporting and retaining teachers. By connecting these two needs, we found a joint solution. We placed classified staff in elective teaching positions and freed our certificated teaching staff to have a common collaboration and prep time daily for almost 45 minutes. This enabled us to have time to build common classroom-management practices, grading policies, scope and sequence, and a team identity. We placed the elective right after the first instructional block and placed the nutrition break adjacent. This enabled students to get a boost in engagement in an area that interested them and then a break outside for the bathroom, a snack, and socializing with peers. Teachers then have about 45 minutes a day to work together. The middle school team uses the time to collaborate in a variety of ways. They balance weekly discussion times for teachers who shared the same students, for teachers who teach the same content, for teachers who teach the same grade levels, and for general middle school planning such as dances, fundraisers, and classroom management techniques. Some days are just for individual prep time.

Staffing the electives. To achieve this tandem dream, we had to be innovative in our staffing for electives and it has proven beneficial in multiple ways. Three of the four classified teachers from elementary school also teach the electives in middle school including more specialized art, music, and Chinese classes. Other classified staff teach electives such as technology (robotics, coding, etc.), yearbook, and study skills. As a result, students now have relationships with staff that previously may have had limited or narrowly defined roles with students. Members of the Information Technology department often teach the technology elective. This gives them insight into the students' needs and interests. It also gives them feedback directly from students on the effectiveness of various software and devices on campus. The counselor or counseling interns sometimes teach the study skills class, which focuses on communication and personality styles, identifying one's strengths, and building executive functioning. Finally, there is a teaching-assistant elective which has proven popular on our TK-8 campus and requires no additional staff. Middle school students are matched with a TK-5 classroom and work with that teacher to support the daily learning of younger students. Many students enjoy the mentoring relationships they build with younger children, the exploration of a career in teaching or designing educational materials, and the opportunity to be mentored by another teacher who is not currently in charge of their grades. I am often surprised how much and how often my teaching assistants ask to stay and talk with me, share their personal news, and ask me about my life, even when this elective was not their first choice.

Summary

In the end, we had to get the middle school up and running for a year or two before we could reinvent it. The cyclical process of reflection is necessary due to our deeply imbedded, often unquestioned beliefs, and our finite emotional stamina. The process of inventing and reinventing can be emotionally and physically exhilarating and exhausting all at once. There are only so many hours in a day, staff meetings in a year, collaboration sessions in a month. Research, reflection, and planning take time and energy. It cannot all be achieved at once, even when the desire is unified in your community. Our school is a whole-school dual immersion public charter school that makes local decisions and has little bureaucracy with which to contend. None of these debates or challenges involve the need to defend or convince anyone about the value of bilingualism or biliteracy. Even so, it has taken about 5 years to establish the structures and systems that we find more effective for our middle school.

This is not the end of our reflection or refinement. Our adventures will continue in middle school and beyond. Building our high school is next on the horizon. Each school community's journey will include different obstacles. Our journey required creativity regarding scheduling, facilities, curriculum and instruction, and staffing. In the end, we all require commitment, flexibility, and stamina to make our fairy tale a reality and last us through the challenges we face in our dual immersion adventures. The research in this book and the relationships we all create through our collaboration are the greatest tools we have to empower and rejuvenate us in this ongoing adventure of secondary school dual immersion education. Thus, may we remember the source of our fairytales' magic, that vision of multilingual, multicultural, and academic proficiency for all our students.

Chapter Ten
New Mexico: Albuquerque Public Schools
La historia de dos escuelas bilingües:
Bilingual Seal Development

Mishelle Jurado, Lisa Harmon-Martínez, and Dr. Gabriel Antonio Gonzales

Introduction by Collier and Thomas: *This chapter tells the story of the development of the bilingual seal in Albuquerque Public Schools, New Mexico, with the focus on two dual language high schools. Preparing for and receiving the bilingual seal is the culminating activity, the pinnacle, at the end of all the dual language coursework in students' senior year. These three authors express with passion all of their hard work to provide this experience for their bilingual students and to guide their students to success with the celebration of this important credential on their diplomas. They show how the process of bilingual seal development influenced and drove both the evolution of the dual language high school programs and the assessment process to for awarding the bilingual seal. As a result, the central role of the bilingual seal led to more equitable relationships in use of the two languages in academic contexts, more rigorous courses offered in both languages, meaningful department and collegial collaboration, and more connections with family and community.*

> To be bilingual to me, means to have my two cultures, my two identities, and my two nationalities. The program at Atrisco has helped me grow as a person, to keep my language and culture while I learn a whole new one. I cannot imagine a world where I lose my Spanish or a world of not knowing English.
>
> Edmarie, senior, Atrisco Heritage Academy High School (2017)

A bilingual seal is so much more than an emblem added to a diploma or a sash worn at graduation; for the students who earn the seal and their families, it is a way to recognize and validate their bilingual identity as well as their proficiency in two languages. For Albuquerque Public Schools, the pathway to earn a bilingual seal has driven the evolution of the district's dual language offerings and vice versa. The seal has been a driver of improved processes, student outcomes, and institutionalized practice.

The school district of Albuquerque Public Schools (APS) is a large urban district of 84,000 students, of whom 67% are Hispanic, 21% are Caucasian, 5% are American Indian, 3% are African American, and 2% are Asian. There are 28 middle schools and 14 comprehensive high schools in the district. As the largest school district in the state of New Mexico, APS is the recipient of most of the state-funded bilingual education monies. In 1973, when the New Mexico legislature funded bilingual provisions in our state's constitution, schools were able to apply for financial support for bilingual programs that would serve the state's large heritage and active Spanish-speaking student populations. Of the 14 comprehensive high schools in APS, six of them offer bilingual or dual language programs that intentionally support the Spanish and English language development of their students.

Many of those Albuquerque high schools with bilingual or dual language (DL) programs have long considered ways to honor the language proficiency and academic achievement of students involved in a bilingual program. In 1998, Río Grande and West Mesa High Schools became two of the first high schools in the nation to test and certify bilingual proficiency. That year, bilingual coordinators Carlos Chávez of Río Grande and Pilar García of West Mesa devised their own recognition of those students who achieved high levels of English and Spanish proficiency by establishing criteria for attaining a bilingual seal on their diploma. Students were required to achieve a certain score on tests in listening, speaking, reading, and writing in both English and Spanish. They were also expected to pass a minimum of four core classes in Spanish, such as math, science, and social studies, plus two elective courses, as well as the required courses in English (Albuquerque Tribune, 1990, May 22). Other district high schools later adopted similar requirements, but the practice remained particular to each high school.

In this chapter the authors will focus on two high schools—the oldest and newest in APS—and the path they took to formalize program expectations and bilingual seal requirements and processes: Albuquerque High School (AHS) and Atrisco Heritage Academy High School (AHAHS). In addition to describing the ways that the evolution of both the bilingual seal and the high school course offerings influenced each other, we will also offer a discussion of how equity of languages, rigorous courses, physical space, and department standing resulted from the central role of the bilingual seal in our schools' DL program.

Los principios — The Beginnings

Mishelle Jurado (author), currently the biliteracy coach at AHAHS, taught for a number of years at Río Grande High School in their maintenance bilingual program where students signed up for bilingual seal consideration during their senior year and completed an interview with the bilingual staff along with the oral portion of the assessment. The bilingual staff scored the interview and oral assessment with a rubric that they developed to assess the students' proficiency in English and Spanish. If and when the student passed the interview and oral test, they were allowed to complete the reading comprehension and essay portion of the assessment. The exam was typically administered during the school day and consisted of three components: students read passages in both English and Spanish and answered comprehension questions, wrote an essay answering questions related to the reading, and responded in Spanish and English to interview questions. There was a great deal of camaraderie among the teachers and the bilingual office; everyone pitched in to score exams, help with interviews, and basically do anything else needed to support the students and the bilingual program. At the end of the school year, everyone came together to celebrate the students, parents, teachers, and community. When Mishelle became the bilingual coordinator in 2011 at AHS, the bilingual seal development process continued to evolve.

El sello bilingüe — The Bilingual Seal at Albuquerque High School

From its beginnings in the late 1800s, AHS served a community that encompassed both the country-club area as well as the large rural tracts that surrounded the small city. Today AHS is located in the downtown and university area with a student body of 1,703: 77% are Hispanic, 14% are Caucasian, 3% each are African American and Native American each, and 65% of all students receive free or reduced-price meals.

In her first 2 years as bilingual coordinator at AHS, Mishelle found a great ally in Lisa Harmon-Martínez (author), an English language arts teacher and English department chair. During those initial years they formed a close working relationship, sharing language arts strategies across languages. With similar approaches and goals, they envisioned and worked toward moving AHS' maintenance bilingual program to a balanced DL program. They were given permission by the principal to co-coordinate the bilingual program. An extra shared planning period allowed them the opportunity to reach out to other educators regardless of their language of instruction in order to further develop the DL program at AHS. This collaborative program-coordinator model was built into the master schedule.

At first, AHS followed the same general bilingual seal procedures Mishelle had experienced at Río Grande. However, in succeeding years bilingual professionals from the community were invited to conduct the interviews with the students rather than relying only on the bilingual staff at the school. New readings and essay questions for the reading and writing portion of the assessment were developed by a committee made up of district bilingual coordinators from area high schools and the team at APS' Language and Cultural Equity Department. The results were mixed. The students worked hard. Some passed because they knew how to take a test. Others missed the cutoff by only one point. It was heartbreaking to inform students and their families that they did not pass the assessment by a single point. A current janitor at AHS still recalls missing his opportunity for the seal more than 10 years earlier after being short only one point from a passing grade. In the last year of using the district-produced exam for the bilingual seal at AHS, students were asked to respond to questions about the new Pope's role in the world. One young woman with deep proficiency in Spanish could barely answer the question because she did not have the cultural knowledge. This student ultimately did pass the assessment but it was difficult to watch her struggle. A change was needed to better validate students' language development and measure their bilingualism more effectively.

Expanding Spanish language arts requirements. At that point in the development of the bilingual seal at AHS the exam was envisioned as the culmination of coursework; the students had to successfully complete one Spanish IV or higher class and any four content courses taught in Spanish. Students were taking only one year of Spanish language arts, and while this could indeed be a high-level class, it did not require students to develop their Spanish academic skills in a language arts class all 4 years of high school, as they were required to do in their English language arts classes. In 2011 when Mishelle was first assigned to teach Spanish language arts for 40 students from Grades 9-12, Mishelle and Lisa realized this needed to change. They created a plan for the DL students to take 4 years of Spanish language arts along with the four classes of English language arts required by the state. To establish equitable expectations in regard to Spanish-language development and its place in a DL program was groundbreaking in APS. (See Figure 10.1 for AHS' DL course offerings.)

Figure 10.1

Dual Language Enrichment Program Course Offerings 2017-2018

	Spanish Language Arts	English Language Arts	Spanish Content	English Content
9th Grade	• Spanish Language Arts I (Pre-AP Spanish Language Arts 9)	• English 9 • English 9 Honors • English as a Second Language I-IV	• Biology • Analytical Biology • Algebra I • Algebra I Honors	• Biology • Analytical Biology • NM History, Health • Algebra I, Algebra I Honors
10th Grade	• Spanish Language Arts II (Pre-AP Spanish Language Arts 10)	• English 10 • English 10 Honors • English as a Second Language I-IV	• World History • AP World History • Geometry • Honors Geometry • Chemistry	• World History • AP World History • Geometry, Honors Geometry • Chemistry
11th Grade	• AP Spanish Language and Culture	• English 11 • AP English Language and Composition • English as a Second Language I-IV	• US History • AP US History • Physics	• U.S. History • AP U.S. History • Physics
12th Grade	• AP Spanish Literature and Culture	• English 12 • AP English Literature and Composition • English as a Second Language I-IV	• Economics, 1 semester • Government, 1 semester • Anatomy and Physiology	• Government, 1 semester • Economics, 1 semester

• ESL students with an ACCESS score of 5 or higher can be placed in an English Language Arts class with a TESOL certified teacher; students may take no more than 3 content credits in Spanish, including Spanish Language Arts.
• ESL students with an ACCESS score of 5 or lower must be placed in an English as a Second Language class with a TESOL certified teacher; students may take no more than 2 content classes in Spanish, including Spanish Language Arts.
• The AHS Dual Language program expects balanced instruction with Spanish and English throughout all four years of high school. Students should have no more than three content classes in Spanish each year, including SLA.

It took 2 to 3 years for everyone to understand and support this new requirement, from school personnel to parents and students, but before long more Spanish language arts sections were needed. Students wanted to be in the DL program and receive the bilingual seal; 4 years of Spanish language arts was now considered an integral part of the program. Freshmen soon learned of the DL program and enrolled in record numbers. Data collected at AHS over the past several years validates this curricular decision, in that students who take 4 years of Spanish language arts have higher grade point averages (GPAs) than students who do not (see Figure 10.2). In the DL schedule, priority is given to the offerings of Spanish language arts sections to ensure that students can take a Spanish language arts course each year and meet the seal requirements. In the master schedule, however, Spanish language arts is listed as an elective course and must compete with other electives on campus for schedule allocations. Since students must sacrifice an elective each year in order to fit Spanish language arts into their schedule, the fact that our applicant numbers continue to grow affirms the importance of the bilingual seal in our students' minds.

Figure 10.2
AHS Spanish Language Arts (SLA) and Grade Point Average (GPA) Correlation

School Year	2014-2015	2015-2016	2017-2018
GPA of students with 4 years of SLA	3.32	3.09	3.0
GPA of students without 4 years of SLA	2.61	2.54	2.53

The portfolio process. The next steps involved new requirements for the bilingual seal portfolio. At an event hosted by Dual Language Education of New Mexico, presenters from Ysleta Independent School District in El Paso, Texas, shared their assessment process in which students presented a bilingual portfolio in their senior year based on a community-service project that they designed and implemented. Inspired by the Ysleta portfolio process, new requirements for the AHS bilingual seal were established. Because parts of the new bilingual seal portfolio were modeled after a similarly structured, established AHS senior exit portfolio, staff members readily accepted the new process. They already understood its value, with some even accepting the portfolio seal score as a final exam grade in the second semester. This option had been offered to senior exit portfolio participants for many years. Teachers across the curriculum could opt to count all, or part of the portfolio score as their final exam, further validating the portfolio as an academic assessment. There was also greater buy in among the students and a great deal of excitement to pilot this new process for the bilingual seal.

In 2013-2014, the new requirements for the bilingual seal were modified from the original senior exit portfolio requirements to include a section on language reflection and to lengthen the student presentations to 45 minutes. In an effort to move away from the view of bilingualism as solely an economic endeavor, the AHS bilingual staff developed alternative questions. The new questions were designed to elicit deeper student reflections regarding the way their two languages complement one another at school and in their personal life, the relationship between the students' languages and their sense of identity, and how they planned to continue developing their languages. Students were required to respond to two of the questions but it was recommended to the evaluators that they ask students the other two questions in either language if further evidence of language proficiency was needed. Evaluators could ask any follow-up questions that they saw fit.

A senior at AHS describes the importance of developing both languages simultaneously. Marcus is a heritage language learner who is revitalizing Spanish in order to connect with his family members. He describes how essential his two languages are to his identity:

> Learning Spanish has allowed me to experience new ideas and views on everything from my family life to immigration and has made me more open minded when learning about different values and beliefs. Bilingual people often speak of the duality of personality that accompanies learning another language and while I have experienced this to a certain extent, I believe that my personality is shaped by both my languages working in tandem as opposed to each language creating a distinct portion of my personality. (Bilingual Seal portfolio reflection, 2018)

From the class of 2016, Alí, who grew up speaking Spanish at home, reflects on her identity:

> … I have struggled for many years to identify myself with my ethnicity, being that my mother is American and my father is Mexican, the challenge to integrate both cultures has been hard for me…. Growing up a güerita in Martineztown was not always easy for me because of my appearance and the way I speak; but then once starting [in the DL program], I realized I was not the only white girl speaking Spanish [who] had an accent in English…. *Yo me identifico como mexicana americana y nadie me lo puede quitar.* [I identify myself as Mexican American and no one can take that away from me.] (Bilingual Seal reflection response, 2016)

Assessing the two languages. In this first year of development and implementation, the goal was to establish a holistic rubric to use during the students' portfolio presentation. Mishelle and Lisa sought to validate the linguistic identities of their students by developing a portfolio that would assess students' use of the two languages simultaneously, instead of evaluating English and Spanish as independent of one another. Susana Ibarra Johnson, former Director of Bilingual Education at Bernalillo Public Schools, helped clarify their thinking:

> Working with Lisa and Mishelle while they developed a more holistic rubric for students getting the seal was invigorating. The bilingual students were asked to structure a presentation with a portion delivered in English and Spanish (language-specific); yet they were allowed to employ translanguaging (García, Johnson, & Seltzer, 2017) when needed to better make their point or convey math or science ideas or concepts. This new perspective had to do with what Mishelle and Lisa heard and saw in their classrooms—students who flexibly use both of their languages to demonstrate their knowledge, a more holistic communicative way of viewing language. (personal communication, 2017)

Assessing students' holistic use of language, rather than assessing English and Spanish as disparate parts, required training and calibrating with evaluators in the first year and each year since, as new evaluators have joined. The evaluators readily understood the idea that bilinguals use languages simultaneously, as they are bilinguals themselves, but the question of how to assess this was problematic, as some students' use of one language seemed to be more developed than the other.

> No two English language learners/emergent bilinguals are the same, and so the way they acquire language will not be the same either. These students do not move up a "ladder" of language learning in lockstep. Rather, they develop their language capacity from their own starting points and in their own timeframe as they engage in content-area learning. (Valdés, Menken, & Castro, 2015, p. 260)

Students are seen as being on a unique trajectory of language development in both languages, but there is still an expectation of a minimal level of proficiency in both languages. Instead of penalizing students for what they could not do, evaluators were asked to assess what students could do.

In spite of best efforts to ensure calibration among evaluators, there is still a propensity to compare one student against another. Some ideas that have been developed over the years to better support evaluators in this process is to create videos for evaluators to watch in advance of the presentations that include scoring guidelines and commentary. The presentation-day schedule has been modified to include more time in the morning to educate evaluators about the philosophy inherent in this portfolio assessment and how to use the rubric. An additional 15 minutes after each presentation have been added for calibration among evaluators.

In the reflection portion of the portfolio, students are asked to reflect on their high school career and what their bilingualism means to them. Teenagers enjoy talking about themselves, of course, but this process means much more than that to them. Community volunteers are coming to hear their personal stories and to listen to their experiences as DL students. Most importantly, this is an opportunity for students to share their greatest triumphs and struggles.

To support the students, workshops are held during office hours for students to complete and organize the written portion of the portfolio. Students are also offered time in class to edit and practice their oral presentations and receive feedback from their peers and their teacher. Given that the culminating Spanish language arts class at AHS is AP Spanish Literature and Culture, teachers support the portfolio development to some extent in this class. While balancing the demands of the AP-required reading and portfolio development is a continual struggle, best practices in language development, including oral presentations of required literature throughout the school year, offer students great opportunities to develop presentation skills.

The intention in developing this new portfolio assessment was to provide students an opportunity to truly show off their linguistic and cognitive skills, while also providing them a chance to learn from their missteps by revising the portfolio if necessary. With this new model, students who did not pass the portfolio process were permitted to present their portfolios a second time. Depending on their linguistic need, those students had to commit to meet with Mishelle or Lisa to revise their portfolios in a purposeful way. In these meetings, the scoring rubrics made available to all students were reviewed, and attention was given to their oral and written language. By revising the portfolio, students could learn from their shortcomings and further develop their skills. It is contrary to the very philosophical foundation of the new seal process to deny students' bilingualism—an essential part of their identity—simply because of a single assessment point; however, students can and have failed the portfolio process. Briana, an AHS graduate from the class of 2014, who is a heritage language learner and who was unsuccessful in the portfolio process during its first year of implementation, describes what it felt like:

> When I failed my bilingual seal the first time I attempted it, I felt really disappointed in myself.... I failed ... because I was scared that I was going to do a bad job if I ... really tried. What if my Spanish wasn't good enough? What if they didn't like what I had to say about my high school experience? So I decided to speak as little Spanish as possible and to give a cookie-cutter presentation. Obviously, it blew up in my face. So, when I tried again, I really told the truth about my high school experience. I showed my vulnerability. And I also spoke more Spanish, even if it meant nervously stuttering though it. (personal communication, 2018)

The majority of students did pass the assessment and evaluators were very impressed by the quality and content of the presentations. In the first year of the portfolio process, community evaluators included bilingual employees of a national computer processor manufacturer, DL educators from K-12 schools, college professors, and the director of multicultural education for the state of New Mexico. The evaluators were so impressed with the students' command of academic language that several offered internships, mentorships, and even jobs to the students at the end of that first week. The success of the new process clearly illustrated the value of a portfolio presentation in which the topic is meaningful to students. Alondra, one of the first students to complete the portfolio presentation explains how the new portfolio process supports a student's sense of self:

> Modern day programs like the bilingual program in Albuquerque High School help establish a pathway for bilingualism to become a historically legitimate practice, allowing myself and many others to establish our languages as an earned, expert certification. The portfolio is an extremely individual assignment allowing each student to explore their own strengths and pushes them to take credit for their accomplishments, finally receiving written legitimacy of their language skills. (personal communication, 2017)

No longer was earning the bilingual seal contingent upon a snapshot assessment; instead students now spend weeks and even months preparing their written and oral portfolio presentations. Despite the increased rigor of the portfolio process, the number of students completing the bilingual seal requirements continues to grow (see Figure 10.3).

Figure 10.3
Number and Grade Point Average (GPA) of Students Receiving the Bilingual Seal at AHS

Year	Number of Students	GPA	Assessment Tool
2011	20	2.75	test
2012	31	2.99	test
2013	19	3.23	test
2014	48	3.24	portfolio
2015	51	3.09	portfolio
2016	64	2.92	portfolio
2017	63	2.96	portfolio

El sello del estado de Nuevo México — The New Mexico State Seal of Bilingualism-Biliteracy

In the spring of the first year of implementation of the new portfolio process at AHS, the state of New Mexico passed House Bill 330 (HB 330), ultimately becoming NMSA 22-1-9.1, New Mexico Diploma of Excellence, State Seal for Bilingual and Biliterate Graduates. By August 2014, in the second year of implementing the AHS portfolio process for the district seal, Mishelle and Lisa were selected to serve on the state task force to write the rules for implementing the State Bilingual-Biliteracy Seal HB330, which allowed four pathways to the Bilingual Seal.

1. Tribal Non-Regulatory Guidance: Certification by an individual tribe, as Native American tribes are granted absolute autonomy in the state, and their languages (Diné, Apache, Keres, Towa, Tewa and Tiwa) are often taught in local schools

2. Units of Credit and Assessment: Four units of credit earned with a C or better in a language other than English and an assessment of language proficiency, such as AP, IB, or CLEP (College-Level Examination Program)

3. Units of Credit and Alternative Process Portfolio: Four units of credit earned with a C or better in a language other than English and an alternative process portfolio option, including both receptive and expressive language

4. Assessment and Alternative Process Portfolio: Assessment and alternative process portfolio option, combining portions of Options 2 and 3

The portfolio and coursework pathway to the state seal not only validated the work done at AHS over the previous year, but it offered students an additional option for earning a seal. This was an exciting time to work with diverse educators from kindergarten through postsecondary across New Mexico representing a variety of linguistic backgrounds.

El sello bilingüe de las Escuelas Públicas de Albuquerque — The APS Bilingual Seal

In 2017, 3 years after the initial implementation of the portfolio process at AHS, and with the new state seal requirements, Albuquerque Public Schools began to revise their existing bilingual seal process to include the portfolio process. The district established a committee of teachers and principals from K-12 DL schools to identify new requirements for the coursework and portfolio that would align with the newly approved New Mexico State Seal. This process also inspired committee members to establish bilingual seals and portfolio assessments at elementary and middle school sites, a practice that has now become formalized by APS.

In addition to adding the portfolio presentation to the assessment, the committee also increased the minimum requirements of coursework to earn the APS seal.

- 4 years of Spanish Language Arts with a combined average of C (2.0) or higher
- 4 years of English Language Arts with a combined average of C (2.0) or higher
- 4 content credits taught in Spanish with a combined average of C or higher
- 4 content credits taught in English with a combined average of C or higher

For the honors seal, students must earn a 3.0 GPA and take and pass at least 1 AP course. To meet the 4-year requirement of Spanish language arts, students are required to take AP Spanish Language and Culture or AP Spanish and Literature by the end of their senior year.

Other changes were also made. In an effort to elicit deeper reflection, the committee asked students to select a minimum of one academic artifact in each language and write a reflection regarding the academic growth demonstrated in that artifact. This required some guidance from school staff to educate students as to what a reflection might include. This is especially true if they selected a non-traditional artifact to reflect on in their writing, such as a dance piece, a music composition, a science experiment, a presentation in class, a work of art, or something similar.

Just as in the original portfolio process at AHS, students were also asked to reflect on their evolving understanding of cultural competency by answering the following questions in depth.

- What is the relationship between your languages and your identity?
- How do Spanish and English complement one another in both your educational and personal lives?
- How will your identity, or understanding of yourself, help you relate to others as well as succeed as a contributing member of society after graduation?

Schools also have the option of writing an additional question that they feel would provide further information needed to assess their students' growth. Offering each school this kind of autonomy validates the diverse student populations across the district.

In order to begin the portfolio process, student eligibility for the various seals is determined. An analysis of students' transcripts should be completed at the end of the junior year when final grades have been posted so that students can be advised as to what classes they still need to take in their senior year. It is also recommended that a streamlined worksheet be provided to students so that they can record their credits earned throughout high school and plan their schedules accordingly each year this also serves as a self-advocacy tool. By October, students apply for the bilingual seal portfolio process, making an agreement with a teacher for support in English or Spanish throughout the school year as they develop their portfolios (see Figure 10.4).

Figure 10.4

Name: _____ ID Number: _____

This Bilingual Seal Application and unofficial transcripts are due Friday, November 21.

Bilingual seal requirements: In addition to meeting the requirements listed below, Bilingual seal candidates must also pass a portfolio presentation during which oral and written English and Spanish will be assessed.

Application checklist:

- Completed Bilingual Seal Application (this form)
- Letter of eligibility for the seal OR a letter of recommendation from a teacher

Seal Requirements Checklist: if you meet all requirements, you may earn up to 2 seals.

Albuquerque Public Schools Bilingual Seal	New Mexico Seal of Biliteracy and Bilingualism
- AP Spanish Language and Culture and/or AP Spanish Literature and Culture (complete credit) - 4 content credits taught in Spanish: 1. _____, Grade: ___ 2. _____, Grade: ___ 3. _____, Grade: ___ 4. _____, Grade: ___	- Any 4 Spanish language, language arts, or content credits taught in Spanish, with a C or better (list the class and grade earned below) 1. _____, Grade: ___ 2. _____, Grade: ___ 3. _____, Grade: ___ 4. _____, Grade: ___

Honors bilingual seal requirements checklist: In addition to the credit and portfolio requirements, Bilingual Seal candidates can earn the Honors Cord.

- 3.5 GPA or higher, GPA: _____

- At least 1 AP course taught in Spanish, course title: _____

List ALL of the schools and grades in which you took language arts and/or content classes in Spanish:

Elementary School	
Middle School	
High School	

Mentor Contract:

To help you through the portfolio process, you must select a teacher or staff member to help you. Please provide their name and contact information below.

Mentor name: _____ Room number: _____

Mentor email: _____

Describe where and how often you will meet with your mentor to develop your portfolio and presentation.

Join the Remind 101 for updates and reminders about workshops:

The portfolios are presented in March or April so that students have ample time to write and practice their presentations. This also provides the time required to process scores, notify students and families about passing or failing, allow students who did not pass the opportunity to revise their portfolios, and organize a bilingual seal ceremony before the schools' commencement ceremony in May. Bilingual seal ceremonies are delivered only in Spanish, with English language translation for parents, teachers, and students in the audience who may need it. This tradition was adopted to disrupt the English-dominant practices in our public schools. In the last 2 years, the ceremony has become a *convivio* with a family potluck after the ceremony. This provides parents and students an opportunity to celebrate a journey that many of them started in kindergarten.

Student portfolios are collected one week prior to the portfolio presentations. Some students develop elaborate, artistic scrapbooks while others turn in streamlined notebooks. Some students have created online portfolios by developing websites to showcase their artifacts and written reflections. (See Figure 10.5 for the AHS Bilingual Seal Scoring Rubric.)

Figure 10.5

Student name:

Bilingual Seal Scoring Rubric: 2013-2014
This rubric is intended to holistically assess oral and written language,
taking into account the use of both English and Spanish.

Essential Question: How has Albuquerque High helped you make connections academically, linguistically, and personally that impact your future plans?

Area	1	2	3	4	Oral	Writing
Discourse: all-encompassing language organization	Ideas and events are present; minimal connections are made	Ideas and events are somewhat clear; somewhat sequential and connected	Contains a clear series of events or ideas that are connected	Logical and effective sequence in clearly developed and connected series of events or ideas		
Content: Answers essential question, as it relates to bilingualism	Minimal relevance in reflections; lacks point of view and voice; reflections were unclear or unfinished	Relevant reflections; voice and point of view are apparent in some parts of presentation but not throughout	Relevant and well-developed reflections; voice and point of view are apparent throughout	Relevant, thorough, well-developed reflections, examples were given with supporting details		
Vocabulary: Social and academic word choice	Reflections provide definitions only; words and phrases are repeated	Reflections describe information with repetitive phrases	Reflections use comparative/contrastive and sequential language; explanation is detailed and content-specific	Reflections include descriptive language, negotiation of meaning, use of idiomatic language		
Fluency: Ease of expression and command of grammatical structures to convey intended meaning	Repetition of basic syntax; sentence structure and length are not varied; word choice is labored and halting	Syntax is varied, with apparent errors; word choice interferes with meaning	Evidence of control of a variety of structures and idioms, although a few grammatical errors will occur; word choice conveys meaning	Control of a variety of structures and idioms; occasional errors may occur but without pattern or limiting understanding; word choice deepens meaning		
Grammatical Conventions: Spelling, subject-verb agreement, pronoun antecedent, paragraphing, and punctuation	Grammatical conventions that interfere with meaning	Grammatical conventions are consistently misused, in patterns	Some control of the conventions of language	Significant command of the conventions of language		
Total Points Earned:	/ 20	/ 20				

There will likely be some difference in scores between students' written and oral language as they develop at different times. Students may also experience translanguaging, speaking in one language and writing in another, as a means to process content and concepts. (García, 2009)

Presentation Elements Checklist

Organization

Presentation Materials (slides/video/art/music) are effectively organized in a notebook for evaluators to reference throughout the presentation	1
Presenter is on time, dressed for success, has great eye contact, projects confidence, and manages presentation time wisely (does not exceed 45 minutes, not including time for questions at the end)	1

Academics

Transcript Analysis: analyze transcript for core classes taken in Spanish and English	.5
Standardized Test Results: Reflect on standardized test scores	.5
Includes two writing samples with reflections: one writing sample in English and one sample in Spanish	2
Includes two critical-thinking projects with reflections: one critical-thinking project in English and one in Spanish	2
Includes two favorite assignments with reflections: Assignments are in either language and written in either language	2
Include a course-of-study reflection for four core academic subjects (English, math, science, social studies): two of the required core reflections in Spanish and the other two in English	4
Include a course of study reflection for your elective subjects: written in Spanish or English	1

Personal Accomplishments, to include interests, hobbies, and community service

Includes evidence of school involvement	1
Includes life goals and aspirations	1
Includes a letter of recommendation from a community member (non faculty/non family)	1

Section 3: Self Reflection

Recognition of a teacher or staff member who made a difference in your education	1
Influence of AHS in academic, social, emotional, and cognitive growth discussed	1
Influence of AHS in career and/or lifetime goals discussed	1
Influence of meaningful experience at AHS discussed (field trip, work study, etc)	1

Section 4: Language Reflection Questions: students must answer at least 2

How do Spanish and English complement one another, in both your education and your life?	2
How do you plan to continue your language development growth in both languages?	2
Where do you see US bilingualism in the next ten years?	2
What is the relationship between your language and your identity?	2
Total points earned:	25

To organize the evaluator panel, Mishelle and Lisa typically contact their DL feeder schools for help in attracting potential evaluators. They also reach out to local businesses, community colleges, and universities. To recognize their participation as volunteer evaluators, certificates are provided for educators to use as evidence for their professional evaluations. A minimum of three evaluators are sought for each presentation. Many return year after year, as they are invigorated by the passion of the students and impressed by the quality of language used and the content shared in the presentations. Informal feedback is requested from the panel when we meet during the lunch hour (volunteers cannot be paid but can be well fed) and evaluations are collected at the end of the process to inform planning for the next year.

The Albuquerque High School Dual Language Program

Visibility. AHS's DL program is extremely visible on the school campus, as is the Spanish language on school signage and student-created coursework hung in the hallways. Through the advocacy of administrators and the bilingual coordinators on campus, the bilingual office, which combines the programs for English learners and the DL program, has occupied a set of offices that are centrally located in the school building. DL students often refer to this space as their "home." Students have lunch, celebrate birthdays, and complete school projects here. The increased informal interaction has given staff members a way to identify struggling students and provide resources for them. Informally, the older students mentor the younger students. The bilingual office is also where the Family Language Acquisition Center is housed, inviting parents of students enrolled in the DL program and those enrolled in ESL classes to attend language-learning sessions. This space for students and parents exemplifies the philosophy of "transcaring," defined as "a common collaborative 'in-between' space that transcends linguistic and cultural differences between schools and homes" (García, Woodley, Flores, & Chu, 2012, p. 799). This is not just a physical space but a physical manifestation of the importance of home language in the school setting. Once more space and visibility for the DL program was provided, the program grew very quickly. Students and staff became more aware of the program, teacher and administrative engagement increased, and students became more involved.

Combined language arts department. A significant result of Mishelle and Lisa's collaboration is the formation of a combined AHS Language Arts Department, in which English and Spanish language arts teachers collaborate across languages to support students' development in both languages. Lisa served as the English language arts department chair for some time, and with her advocacy with school administrators, AHS Spanish and English language arts teachers began to meet in after-school department meetings to create cross-curricular plans across the two program languages and to address student needs. English and Spanish language arts eventually became one cohesive department. English and Spanish language arts courses are listed on the same section of the master schedule, solidifying the systemic change to incorporate English and Spanish language arts teachers into one department.

Official state AP content courses taught in Spanish. Other exciting administrative changes have been made. Although AHS has long offered AP classes in social studies taught in Spanish as part of their DL courses, in the 2016-2017 school year, the New Mexico Public Education Department approved an official bilingual course number for AP World History and AP U.S. History taught in Spanish for school use, allowing for the credit to be listed as "Bilingual" on students' transcripts. This helps attract and keep high-performing students in the DL program. The bilingual seal drives course offerings at AHS, but for a time, high-performing AP students were dropping bilingual classes in the upper grades because the official honors and AP bilingual offerings were limited. Now colleges can see rigorous, college-level coursework in Spanish on student transcripts.

Equity and empowerment. One of the main themes that has surfaced, as increased program expectations and course offerings have been developed, is the need for equity at all levels. Honors and AP classes, Spanish language arts, content classes conducted in Spanish, school space, access to families and the community are critical to a sense of parity of program and program languages. With parity comes empowerment. Students are anxious to share their new-found sense of identity and recognize the role that the DL program has played in fostering and developing it. A student-leadership club, *Mentes abiertas,* was formed to promote bilingualism at AHS and in the community. Student members began to present at La Cosecha, the annual DL conference sponsored by Dual Language Education of New Mexico. Similar leadership groups formed in other secondary schools across New Mexico and led to the formation of the annual Student Leadership Institute—a day-long event that takes place during La Cosecha and provides students and their adult sponsors opportunities to network, learn from each other, become anchored and connected to sociocultural and linguistic realities, and recognize those realities as assets and as leverage points to inform current and future leadership efforts.

Atrisco Heritage Academy High School, continuing the work

In 2016 Mishelle left AHS and became the biliteracy coach at AHAHS, Albuquerque's newest comprehensive high school. AHAHS is currently home to more than 2700 students; over 80% are Hispanic, the majority of whom are Spanish speaking. Lessons learned at AHS have been carefully studied and efforts have been made to develop a similarly strong, well-rounded DL program that best serves the school's large bilingual student body.

In 2011-2012, 3 years after first opening their doors, there were no content classes taught in Spanish at AHAHS. The pathway for the bilingual seal was in place but it only focused on Spanish language arts and AP Spanish language and literature classes. The school already had a mandatory requirement for all students to take 3 years of a language class, but there were no additional course offerings in Spanish. In 2012-2013, the DL program began to offer enough Spanish content classes for students to be able to fulfill the course requirements for the APS District Bilingual Seal (at that time, four content classes in Spanish and one Spanish language arts class). They began to recruit and build classes for Algebra I and Geometry taught in Spanish. Because no currently employed teachers at AHAHS had the endorsement to teach math classes in Spanish, the school recruited a teacher from Spain on a 3-year visa. In 2014-2015, the AHAHS DL program began to offer social studies and science classes taught in Spanish. While successful in finding local teachers to teach some subjects, the school had to continue to hire teachers from Spain.

For the first time, AHAHS offered the portfolio process to the graduating class of 2017 with 23 recipients. Having learned from her experiences at AHS, Mishelle carried many of the successful elements of the portfolio process to AHAHS. For the class of 2018, 75 students presented their bilingual portfolios, 74 in Spanish, and one in Navajo, earning the Seal of Biliteracy from the state of New Mexico and the Bilingual Seal of Albuquerque Public Schools. The goal now is to properly staff Spanish language arts and other content classes taught in Spanish and to continue to educate all teachers to best serve emergent bilingual students. (See Figure 10.6 for the current AHAHS Bilingual Course of Study and Figure 10.7 for an overview of the DL program at AHAHS designed for parents and students.)

Figure 10.6

ATRISCO HERITAGE ACADEMY HIGH SCHOOL
RECOMMENDED BILINGUAL COURSE OF STUDY
TO OBTAIN THE APS AND STATE OF NEW MEXICO BILINGUAL SEAL
2017-2018

FRESHMAN YEAR	SOPHOMORE YEAR	JUNIOR YEAR	SENIOR YEAR
Appropriate English Language Arts Class: • English 9 • ESL I-IV • English 9 Honors	English Language Arts Class: • English10 • ESL I-IV • English 10 Honors	English Language Arts Class: • English 11 • ESL I-IV • English 11 - AP Language	English Language Arts Class: • English 12 • ESL I-IV • English 12 - AP • Literature
• Spanish Language Arts I 9	• Spanish Language Arts II 10	• AP Spanish Language 11	• AP Spanish Literature 12
Target language of instruction is Spanish: • Algebra I • Algebra - honores • Biología	Target language of instruction is Spanish: • Geometría - AP/regular • Historia del mundo - honores/regular • Química	Target language of instruction is Spanish: • Algebra II, AP/regular • Historia de EEUU - honores/regular • Física	Target language of instruction is Spanish: • Gobierno AP • Economía, • Física AP
Target language of instruction is English: • NM History • Health • Biology • Physical Ed.	Target language of instruction is English: • Chemistry • AP/World History • Honors/Regular • Geometry/Chemistry	Target language of instruction is English: • Chemistry, • AP/World History • Honors/Regular • Geometry/Chemistry	Target language of instruction is English: • AP/Regular • Government/Economy • 4th year of Math
• One Electives	• Two Electives	• Two Electives	• Two Electives

It is encouraged that students take the following electives: Mariachi, French, Dual Credit UNM/CNM, Ethnic Studies, and/or CEC classes.

ESL Enrichment Program
Students with an ACCESS score of 1.0-4.9 will be placed in the appropriate ESL class, a Spanish language arts class according to grade level, and one content class taught in Spanish in math, science, or social studies.

Dual Language Enrichment Program
Students will be placed in the appropriate Spanish language arts class according to grade level and two content classes taught in Spanish in math, science, or social studies.

ESL Non-Spanish Speaking Enrichment Program
Students with an ACCESS score of 1.0-4.9 will be placed in the appropriate ESL class, together with the support of sheltered content instruction in English.

Figure 10.7

Dear Atrisco Heritage Academy Parents/Guardians,

The Atrisco Heritage Academy Dual Language Program is designed to support emergent bilingual students in their academic, biliteracy, cultural-identity, and linguistic growth within their 4 years of high school. Research today tells us that when students have access to their home language and a rigorous English curriculum they perform better in school and their adult life. It is our goal that our students, your children, have the skills and language for a very successful future in our community. This program is available for all students.

Students will need a total of 16 units of study, or more, eight in English and eight in Spanish with a C or better in their 4 years of high school. The units of study include but are not limited to: Spanish Language Arts I, II, AP Spanish Language and Culture and AP Spanish Literature, English Language Arts/ English as a Second Language (ESL) 9-12, mathematics, science, and social studies. Students are encouraged to participate in Baile Folklórico, Mariachi, and/or Mexican-American Studies/Ethnic Studies, or any other electives while in the Dual Language Program.

The AHA Dual Language Biliteracy Portfolio is a 30-45-minute presentation that highlights the 4 years of academic, biliteracy, cultural-identity, and language development. Students are encouraged and assisted in maintaining records of their work in both languages to use as examples of their growth. The Portfolio is presented in front of a bilingual community panel.

Required	Required	Recommended	Required
Spanish Language Arts I	English or ESL 9	Mariachi Baile Folklórico Mexican/ Ethnic studies (any year)	AHA Dual Language Biliteracy Portfolio (Spring senior year)
Spanish Language Arts II	English or ESL 10		
AP Spanish Language	English or ESL 11		
AP Spanish Literature	English or ESL 12		

An important component of our Dual Language Program is English as a Second Language (ESL). If your student requires ESL services, they will be placed according to grade level, ACCESS scores, and academic history. If you decide that your student should not be placed in ESL, we will schedule a conference with you to discuss your decision. We strongly encourage parents and students to work with our new approach as we plan to work extensively on academic English language development.

Students who successfully complete the Atrisco Heritage Academy Dual Language Program and Portfolio will earn the Albuquerque Public Schools District Bilingual Seal, the State of New Mexico Diploma of Excellence Bilingualism and Biliteracy Seal, and will have the opportunity to receive college credit through the Spanish Language and Culture AP and Spanish Literature AP exams.

- The University of New Mexico grants six credit hours for a score of 3, and 15 credit hours for a score of 4 or 5.

- New Mexico State University offers up to 6 credits at the 300 level for scores of 4 or 5.

These are just some of the potential benefits our program offers, however one of the truest benefits is the lifelong skill of bilingualism and the strength that brings to our families and community.

As the great Sabine Ulibarrí once said, "*Si olvidas de dónde vienes, ¿Sabes tú a dónde vas? Si has perdido tu pasado, ¿dónde está tu porvenir?* Our goal is that our students learn about themselves through the process of engaging in Testimonios[1] of their families, community members and others, giving the students the agency to identify areas of growth and development for themselves, academically, culturally, linguistically, and professionally.

[1]Testimonio pedagogy is teaching and learning that does not disconnect theory from praxis. It "brings together critical consciousness…to take action to connect with others with love and compassion to bring collective healing" (Bernal, Burciaga, & Carmona, 2012, p. 368).

Physical-space considerations are part of AHAHS' move toward building a strong, well-rounded DL program. Efforts are underway to make a home for bilingual students where they can eat lunch, seek help from staff and from each other, and complete school projects. Equitable signage is available for Spanish-speaking families and guests as a visible and respectful way to exemplify the school's sense of cohesion and inclusivity.

Recomendaciones para el futuro — Recommendations for the Future

The dual language programs at both AHS and AHAHS work to provide a rigorous college-preparatory program that will prepare all students for the benefits and challenges of post-secondary education and the workforce. The implementation of strong DL programs is a factor in pushing students to aspire to greatness.

The first recommendation involves the implementation of a bilingual seal portfolio process. The bilingual seal offers graduating seniors a unique opportunity to be recognized for 4 years of linguistic achievement in a rigorous curriculum in two languages. These accomplishments, and students' ability to articulate their pride in their learning, can be readily used to complete college and scholarship applications. The portfolio process gives our students agency and voice and ensures that students are rewarded for their proficient bilingualism and biliteracy—while simultaneously validating their identities.

A second recommendation is to mentor teachers and staff so that they can advocate for DL program development and needs. This should not belong solely to the people in charge but should be a common goal for all stakeholders. AHS' combined Spanish and English language arts department, their shared planning and consideration of student learning, the place the bilingual seal portfolio has taken alongside the senior exit portfolio, and the heightened visibility of the bilingual office and the Spanish language in the school have raised the school community's awareness and pride in the DL program. Administrators, teachers, and staff are better informed and better equipped to advocate for the program. Jessica, a veteran teacher at AHAHS, talks about her professional growth in the DL program and what it means to collaborate with her DL colleagues:

Through this collaboration with other DL faculty, I have begun to contribute to the implementation of new dual language programming, new biliteracy seal pathways, and the restructuring of our ESL program. Being able to contribute to the implementation of new and improved learning and achievement opportunities for students has been an amazingly fulfilling process. These changes are energizing and inspire me to take on new challenges.
(personal communication, 2017)

It is through meaningful relationships that permanent change can happen. No program should depend on one person. DL programs bring together the stories of who we are. The students, teachers, and families create bonds that go beyond the simple *adiós* after graduation. Strong ties are built from programs that serve to establish even stronger community ties. "It is a process that brings together critical consciousness and the will to take action to connect with others with love and compassion to bring collective healing (Rendón, 2009)" (Bernal, Burciaga, & Carmona, 2016, p. 368).

It is these *conexiones* that will cement a strong program for our bilingual youth and community. The evolution of the DL program class offerings at AHS and AHAHS were directly influenced by an understanding of the academic language and content needs of students. Best practices for assessment emerged in collaboration with colleagues and experts to develop a bilingual seal process that reflects students' growth in language and literacy development, academic achievement, and cultural competence in two languages. Essential and related considerations of ways to elevate the DL program processes, staff, courses and students, as well as the partner language, included a focus on rigor, on physical space, and department standing.

The effort to make these considerations a reality has positively impacted AHS and AHAHS and has influenced the development of both the Albuquerque Public School Bilingual Seal of Distinction and the New Mexico State Seal of Bilingualism-Biliteracy. Investing in and growing secondary dual language programs can ensure the future of our bilingual communities in a way that embraces all of our identities and brings awareness of the bilingual language practices that many of us live with every day.

Chapter Eleven
Florida: The School District of Palm Beach County
Show Me the Way: One Practitioner's Path to Success in Secondary Dual Language Immersion

Dr. David Samore—Okeeheelee Middle School

Introduction by Collier and Thomas: *Okeeheelee Middle School is featured in this chapter highlighting a successful dual language program in the 11th largest school district of the U.S., Palm Beach County, Florida. Okeeheelee's principal, Dr. David Samore, strongly encourages the development of more secondary DL schools, as he analyzes factors that have inhibited DL expansion in the past and proposes strategies that can help DL schools flourish at secondary level. His perspective originated with his experience as a world language teacher, so he uses the term "immersion" from the world language perspective, which insists on no switches to the other language, presenting a contrast with other chapters in this book that describe contexts where students grow up in a bilingual community. Okeeheelee Middle School was recognized in 2013 as an International Spanish Academy Middle School of the Year for North America, by the Ministry of Education of Spain. Dr. Samore was recognized as 2008 and 2015 Florida Principal of the Year and in 2017 was selected to be a member of the Florida Commissioner's Leadership Academy of state school leaders.*

Throughout the U.S., K-12 schools experience diminishing gains in academic achievement as students become older. After more robust learning gains at the elementary level, secondary schools have seen student academic achievement level off (LoGerfo, Nichols, & Reardon, 2006). Given the compelling consistency of this phenomenon, it would seem likely that secondary schools would be keenly interested in discovering a strategy that would extend greater learning gains from elementary through secondary education. One proven strategy to maintain learning gains K-12 is dual language immersion. Due to its relatively low cost and typically high return on investment, dual language immersion (DL) has a long track record of maintaining academic growth throughout Grades 6-12.

Many DL schools in the U.S. are K-5, the large majority of them stopping abruptly at the end of the elementary school experience with no secondary DL programming in sight. This abandonment of DL at the secondary level occurs even though research has shown its success when implemented with fidelity over the K-12 continuum. The popularity of DL in the elementary arena has continued to blossom, yet in spite of its continued growth K-5, the brakes are applied upon transitioning to middle and high school.

What are the conditions at the secondary school level which discourage DL implementation? How can we stimulate the growth of DL programming at the secondary level? While many inherent structural and cultural differences exist between elementary and secondary schools, with the implementation of quality DL K-12, schools can increase student achievement, improve social and emotional learning, and enhance the cultural competence of all participants.

As an experienced practitioner of secondary DL, I have learned many lessons. With few templates of secondary DL schools to imitate, most of these lessons are self-taught and learned with the help of a few colleagues who understand second language acquisition. My own experience as an International Baccalaureate (IB) student, coupled with professional experience as a world languages teacher, proved very helpful as well. In a very real way, I came upon DL almost by accident.

My own secondary education was a typically American monolingual experience until the end of 10th grade. I was admitted to the United World College of the Atlantic in Wales, one of the first IB schools in the world. As an IB student, I boarded with 385 students from 65 countries. Surrounded by many languages, I saw that a wide variety of languages all lived and breathed, manifesting their respective cultures. As one school friend from Germany told me, "Language is nothing more than organized noise." My international classmates managed at least two or more languages and I discovered my German friend was right. The excitement of seeing them transition easily from Italian to German to English was breathtaking and I wanted to be a part of it. Why do we in the U.S. seem to perceive second language acquisition as so daunting?

By the time I graduated from university with a master's degree in Spanish language and literature, I was fluent in Spanish and had also studied French, Italian, and German at advanced levels. Brought on as a middle school modern languages teacher, I was given the assignment of teaching high school Spanish I and II as well as French I and II to native English-speaking middle school students *who had never studied a word of either Spanish or French until they entered my classes.* My principal, a strong leader and adept risk-taker, believed that I could find a way to do this successfully. She supported me unconditionally and gave me the confidence to do what no middle school world languages teacher had ever done before in our large school district. It occurred to me that if I was going to succeed, I had to do something "new," so I chose to immerse my students in their new language. How did I, as a young teacher with no dual language experience, succeed in compressing an immersion experience into a one-year course with students who had never been faced with a language other than English? I structured my lessons so as to creep to full immersion over a 36-week school year comprised of four nine-week grading periods. I made the students aware of this plan from the first day of class. At first they seemed daunted, but as the first few days and then weeks transpired, they realized that language was, in fact, "organized noise." They just needed to learn new conventions.

First nine weeks. I used only the target language in speaking, but used a mix in written forms. If the student did not comprehend the term or expression, I gave them the English translation. The students were permitted to use English as they wished. The use of the target language in all forms was encouraged, but not required.

Second nine weeks. I used only the target language, in both written and oral forms, and used no English at any time. When the student did not comprehend, I re-explained in the target language. *I never resorted to English.* My commitment to total immersion was a sort of blind faith, but was so convincing to my students that they, too, adopted this faith in their own collective capacity. This did create some anxiety initially, but the students quickly adapted once they realized that they could find ways to understand what was going on. The students were permitted to use English as they wished, but were encouraged to use the target language.

Third nine weeks. I continued to use only the target language exclusively. Each time a student used the target language, he/she was awarded either two or four points, depending on whether they used a combination of the target language and English (two points) or only the target language (four points). I insisted that they use complete sentences, however brief. To this, too, they adapted quickly. To keep a tally of the quality of their participation, I kept an omnipresent clipboard holding the class roster with me as I taught. As they adapted, I gained confidence in my faith, which was by now not blind at all. The key to immersion success was clear: *the teacher's commitment must be to remain in the target language at all times.* Also, the teacher must exude comfort in code-switching outside of the classroom, such as in the cafeteria and in the hallways, so they grow comfortable with the immersion teacher's bilingual skills. This period of time is especially crucial since it is when U.S.-born English-speaking students "make the leap of faith" and realize that they can indeed operate in a second system of "organized noise."

Fourth nine weeks. By this time, we were in 100% one-way immersion. *English was prohibited entirely.* Students could offer help to one another in the target language, liberally. Students would *lose* two points for each instance of non-target language use. They learned and employed pat phrases such as *Ayúdame, ¿Cómo se dice eso?* or *¿Qué significa eso?* and listened carefully to the explanations of their peers. It is imperative that the immersion teacher not make the common mistake of repeating her students' commentaries or answers. It is preferable to ask students to repeat their responses in a louder voice. This helps them learn to manage their acquired language in a variety of ways, but the main benefits are two: (1) students have a chance to rephrase their response better and (2) the mutual respect and dependency among students increases. The *esprit de corps* and collective efficacy of the class was breathtaking: seeing that their teacher was not backing away from his commitment to 100% immersion, they banded together to commit as a class. This is especially helpful in outside-the-classroom contact when their monolingual friends are amazed at their peer's growing bilingual abilities, exclaiming, "You actually understood what he said?" Their happy reply: "Sure, I'm bilingual now!" They felt immense accomplishment in being in a class where they learned and shared in a language that was not native to them. It was now "cool" to be bilingual.

Additionally, the Spanish I/II and French I/II high school students went on to great world language success in high school. Though their high schools were initially incredulous that an incoming ninth grader could be prepared for Spanish III or French III, they quickly learned that not only were they successful, they were among the best they had ever seen. In short, I learned through first-hand experience that immersion can be successful in middle school with the proper commitment and support.

A personal note: my immersion experience as a teacher completely altered my life. After teaching one-way immersion (for native English speakers learning a partner language), my wife and I became parents to two sons who are now bilingual adults (they are grown men of 31 and 27). I researched bilingual families and found that if both parents were not bilingual and determined to raise bilingual children, at least the one who is bilingual should commit 100% to one language while the other, monolingual parent speaks the dominant language.

When my wife became pregnant with our first son, I immediately began speaking Spanish to her midsection. As our children grew she would speak English, while I continued to speak only Spanish, even in front of their friends and others, 24 hours a day. No matter the circumstance, whenever I interacted with our children, they heard only Spanish from me. When the oldest was in the throes of peer pressure as a middle schooler, he would ask me to use English instead of Spanish in the presence of his monolingual friends. Remembering my immersion teaching experience, I refused to back away from my commitment to Spanish. Incidentally, his friends all thought it was special that our son was bilingual. As a byproduct of my commitment, he gained social rank with bilingual classmates, so popularity among his peers increased as a result. To this day, when I communicate with our sons, I continue to use only Spanish. Our eldest son, now a father himself, uses both Spanish and English with our grandson (he is married to a monolingual English speaker). I, however, remain committed to using only Spanish with our grandson as his parents delight in seeing their son's comfort with code-switching between Spanish and English.

Okeeheelee Middle School

As the principal of a dual language two-way immersion middle school in South Florida, I have had my share of successes and setbacks that mark 14 years of our school's secondary DL journey. Our school, Okeeheelee Middle School, is one of 32 middle schools in the School District of Palm Beach County. As part of a larger collection of 39 municipalities which comprises Palm Beach County, we are located in the city of Greenacres. Our county coincides with the school district with over 190,000 students, making it the 11th largest school district in the U.S. We are 65 miles north of Miami, part of the three-county megalopolis that includes Palm Beach, Broward, and Miami-Dade counties.

Our school is one of five DL schools in our district which carry the title "International Spanish Academy." An International Spanish Academy (ISA) is affiliated with the Ministry of Education, Culture and Sports in Madrid, Spain. A branch of the *Ministerio de Educación, Cultura, y Deportes is the Consejería de Educación,* with education offices in consulates of Spain throughout the U.S. and Canada. It is through the *Consejería* that schools in the U.S. and Canada may be deemed an ISA. The Spanish Ministry of Education seeks North American schools that have shown a commitment to K-12 Spanish-English DL. Currently there are 134 ISAs in North America with five in the state of Florida. All five ISAs are in the School District of Palm Beach County: three elementary schools, one middle school, and one high school.

We began our dual language odyssey 14 years ago as the first ISA in the United States. Elementary and high school ISAs quickly followed as we established our K-12 ISA dual language family. From the initial three ISAs we have added two more elementary schools. For over a decade, we have hosted ISA leadership meetings three times per year. These meetings are modeled after the meetings of ISA principals we met while in Alberta, Canada, at a conference. We saw how their meetings created a bonding and collective efficacy among the ISA schools. Since then, we, too, have replicated their cohesion and strength that comes from working closely together.

During our meetings, stakeholders from across our large school district are invited to come and share in our K-12 DL journey. This broad group of district representatives continues to come to each meeting because they find the meetings both relevant and purposeful. Since we have representatives from the central district offices of budget, human resources, senior administration, technology, and choice and career options, "things happen"—our ISA Leadership meetings yield movement and results. Decisions and recommendations are made during the meeting based on proposals and lively discussion which is, at times, provocative. While there are others from whom we have much to learn, our ISA team has breadth and length of experience, leading to the following six questions.

1. Is There a Place for Secondary Dual Language Schools?

There is definitely a place for secondary DL schools. The establishment of a K-12 DL continuum has very few drawbacks and many advantages. Secondary DL schools are, in some respect, a "sleeping giant." If implemented with fidelity, secondary DL schools, combined with committed school district leadership that provides appropriate support, will quickly see substantial results. Though there are fewer models of bona fide secondary DL schools to review than for Grades K-5, those that do exist have strong supportive data.

For example, we discovered within our first 2 years that our two-way model of DL that we offer to both non-native and native Spanish-speaking students is powerful. Our ISA is made up of mainly two categories of students: (1) those who are not from Spanish-speaking homes and (2) those who identify themselves as "Hispanic" and who speak Spanish in their homes. Not all students from the latter category are fluent in Spanish, but their families are keen for their children to reclaim the language of their heritage.

2. How Does Dual Language Compare to Other Strategies to Raise Student Achievement?

Educational leaders in the U.S. spend millions of dollars annually to raise student achievement. DL has the lowest cost ratio to high return on investment of any school strategy designed to enhance student achievement. DL raises overall student achievement for a fraction of the cost of other programming options (Thomas & Collier, 2017).

Successful DL is largely a result of commitment to mission and making adjustments in hiring and retention practices in human resources. Research has consistently shown that, of the variables controlled by schools, the most influential variable is the classroom teacher. The second most influential factor is the school administrator. This is true in all K-12 educational settings, and certainly no less true in a DL environment.

Finding highly qualified teachers of any kind is difficult. Currently, recruitment and commitment of teachers is a significant challenge, given the fact that the number of people choosing a career in education is in decline. It is fair to assert that recruiting and hiring high-quality DL teachers is even more challenging. The human resources office in the district must adopt a posture of continuous recruitment and even recruitment of teachers from countries other than the U.S. There are a number of good organizations which assist in this process. These non-U.S. teachers must obtain a visa, typically the

J-1, which is accomplished in collaboration with the U.S. federal government and can be facilitated by the state government as well, in states that provide support for dual language programs.

The visiting DL teachers are not hired as additional, above-allocation teaching vacancies, but instead fill regular, allocated teacher vacancies. In most districts, vacancies are increasingly harder to fill, so these recruitment efforts satisfy the growing need to identify high-quality teachers. Since there is a nationwide shortage of teachers (especially in culturally diverse regions of the U.S.), this is less problematic than if non-U.S. DL teachers push out local teacher candidates. Since the salary is the same as though they came from down the street, and the class sizes and student-teacher ratio are the same, there is no additional cost. Costs associated with retention of non-U.S. teachers can be expected to be slightly higher, since districts will need to invest in intake strategies, such as cross-cultural training to ensure that these teachers adjust to local cultures as well as regional varieties of the partner language that are present in the community.

3. Which Students Gain Most from Dual Language Education?

Every student gains from DL education. Period. DL is value-added for all students who participate in it. Any student, regardless of his/her cultural heritage, will gain from a well-implemented DL education.

DL education helps all students perform at a higher level than non-DL students. Whether the students are heritage learners of Spanish or learners who come from heritage homes with no Spanish language, operating in two language systems will increase their cognitive development and learning capacity. This phenomenon has been seen in studies comparing students of both heritage and non-heritage speakers (Thomas & Collier, 2012, 2014, 2017).

My own school bears witness to this phenomenon. Very shortly after we began our two-way dual language immersion program, we tracked the success of our students as compared to students who were not enrolled in our International Spanish Academy (ISA). It became clear within 2 years that the DL students were yielding statistically identifiable benefits on English-only standardized tests. Students who had had almost no command of English as sixth graders in the ISA outperformed non-ISA students on the Florida Comprehensive Achievement Test by eighth grade after 3 years in the ISA. Remember, this is on a high-stakes test entirely in English. Students in our school continue to achieve at high levels on the current Florida Standards Assessments.

4. What Are the Root Causes of Unsuccessful Dual Language Schools?

There are many highly successful DL K-5 schools in the U.S. However, based on the conversations I hear during my attendance at conferences, such as NABE, ACTFL, and La Cosecha, I suspect there are also many less-than-successful DL K-5 schools. Conference attendees commonly express frustration that their schools could be more effective. The conditions that exist for these less robust DL schools are created by some of the factors I describe below. Let's examine three factors that discourage secondary school leaders from attempting to implement DL education.

Lack of strong elementary DL feeder schools. To experience success, a secondary school considering DL must have vibrant and successful K-5 DL feeder schools for secondary DL to work. Even if there is an administration that is willing to support one-way secondary DL for new arrivals, two-way DL cannot be started in sixth grade, since the native English speakers continuing in DL at middle school must be able to take rigorous content courses in the partner language on grade level. Therefore, high-quality K-5 DL is a prerequisite to secondary dual language success.

Other curricular choices at the secondary level make 6-12 DL harder to sustain. Due to the proliferation of charter schools and non-public choices, most secondary schools in the U.S. are compelled to see themselves as entrepreneurial, as there is keen competition for students and for qualified bilingual teachers. Secondary schools fervently believe that to compete with their peer secondary schools, they must package their school's curriculum and programmatic offering as innovatively as possible to appeal to the community, hence the creation of choice-themes. Parents are often attracted to the idea of their secondary child being in "Pre-Med" or "Pre-Engineering," or "Pre-Law." These choice-theme names appeal to middle- and upper-class parents who, pondering an uncertain future for their children's career prospects, believe that their child needs a competitive edge in order to be successful post-high school.

The current landscape of secondary schools has spawned the creation of courses that are very similar to trade-specific courses such as culinary arts, replete with gleaming steel kitchens and pre-med clinics with costly medical equipment. In many if not most cases, though the choice-theme course offerings are packaged expertly and marketed well, the choice-theme courses are often very similar to those of most other nearby competing secondary schools. It is as though these parents do not understand that their child can become a medical professional or engineer or lawyer without attending these choice programs. In fact, thousands of students each year do exactly that. The reality is that very few higher learning admissions offices give consideration to whether or not an applicant attended a choice theme high school. The majority of the students who do not participate in high school choice-theme curricula are admitted to graduate schools to become doctors, engineers, and lawyers.

Many thousands of high school students go on to universities to study something other than what interested them (or their parents) when they were 14-year old eighth graders and applied to these choice-theme high schools and in the process passed up the opportunity to become bilingual/biliterate doctors, engineers, and lawyers. For example, if fifth grade students do not enroll in a secondary school with a pre-med program, their potential to be admitted into a pre-med university program after graduation is not adversely affected. However, if a fifth grade DL student does not continue in a legitimate DL secondary school, their two-language development will be stunted and they may never become bilingual/biliterate. Their option of becoming a bilingual medical professional is almost certainly eliminated.

The lack of understanding of school administrators who control support of DL programs. It is difficult to lead something you don't understand. This is perhaps the primary reason why many DL schools are not successful at any level and is also likely the primary reason secondary DL schools are not created. Well-intentioned district administrators impose their culturally inaccurate understanding of language acquisition on school programming. To them, DL is counterintuitive: since they themselves struggle to manage a second language system, how can children be successful? After all, administrators have advanced degrees, so how could the brain of a child possibly manage it when a highly educated professional cannot? When DL is unsuccessful, it is almost always a result of two factors, neither of which has to do with fiscal investment. These two factors are: administrators' lack of understanding and lack of vision and political support. A lack of understanding is usually due to lack of effort or opportunity to find out more about DL education or misperceptions about DL. That is, the school district leaders simply don't know the compelling research that indicates the quick educational return on the DL investment.

Most district administrators and school principals are functionally monolingual. Their only exposure to a language other than English was perhaps a few courses studied in high school and/or university. In either case, these monolinguals typically were not expected to perform at a high level of oral communication and therefore regard DL from a very different standpoint than those who fluently speak more than one language. As a result, monolinguals operate under a paradigm of thought evinced by people who understand only one language system. This understanding, or perhaps misunderstanding, holds that the human brain can only effectively manage one language system. This is not true. These monolingual administrators are impressed when they encounter a bilingual or multilingual person because, to them, speaking more than one language proficiently is a marvel which borders on miraculous.

Curiously, no matter how many bilinguals a monolingual witnesses, most fail to understand that being bilingual is not the result of some miracle, but rather the result of opportunity and motivation. These monolingual district administrators chalk up the language skill of bilingual speakers as exceptional since their life experience has typically not exposed them to large numbers of bilingual and biliterate people. Of course, being bilingual is not a sign of intellectual superiority at all; it is a sign of accessible opportunities. How does one explain finding a shop girl in a small village in Finland who speaks five languages and has never attended college? Or the multilingual taxi driver who barely made it out of secondary school in Athens? They have both had the exposure and the motivation to become skilled in languages. They have both had opportunities accessible to them (multilingual communities in which they live) and circumstances to motivate them (selling a product requires speaking the language of your customers).

A lack of vision and political support usually results from the broader community's predisposition to the myth that studying a second language somehow is subtractive to the first. This too has been shown to be false since DL research and experience shows that the study of a second language is additive, not subtractive. That is, the study of two language systems yields greater and more complex learning since the systems are not discrete—they borrow and interact from one another as the brain seeks to make meaning of both language systems (Cummins, 2000).

5. How Do I Know What a Successful Dual Language Program Looks Like?

To create a successful DL secondary school, you must know what a great DL elementary school looks like. While traveling to a successful dual language school may take considerable effort, there is no substitute for it. If you don't know where one is, access *http://www.duallanguageschools.org*. While virtual visits are better than nothing, you will never understand what makes a system work if you do not ensconce yourself in that system. When you visit a successful dual language elementary school, pick their brains, discover their triumphs and challenges. Visit classes, meet and talk with teachers. Try to determine how your secondary school can avoid their mistakes and capitalize on their successful strategies. Watch their actions, listen to their issues, and learn from their experience. School culture is something we feel first hand and you cannot feel it if you are not there during the school day when children and teachers are present.

The nature of differences that exist between elementary and secondary schools comes into play on the matter of school culture. Scope and size push secondary schools to establish more silos that isolate sections of their campus, whereas elementary educators are often more inclusive. Secondary educators, in their quest to create viable DL options, would be wise to enter a successful elementary DL school with an open mind. That is, elementary administrators tend to be more willing to consider ideas that emanate from their secondary peers than vice versa. Secondary administrators should try to discern the worthwhile aspects of elementary DL that can "flow" into their secondary schools.

6. Is There a Secondary Dual Language Template that Can Be Replicated Successfully?

Strong secondary DL schools exist. Some good examples are presented in the chapters of this book. Your peers at these schools are usually very happy to share their road map to success since there are so few of them. Though the spirit of generosity prevails, know that your DL school will have to be "tailor made"—all programming requires some level of adaptation to your local circumstances and context. While each school community may share many aspects, they are ultimately unique and require some customized accommodations. What makes your school community unique? How do those unique aspects play a role in the implementation of your dual language secondary school? How can these unique traits be developed into assets? If you see the uniqueness of your school community as a liability, bring some fresh views and eyes to the table to see how best to capitalize on your uniqueness, not overcome it.

I assert that secondary DL programs should establish **principles** to guide the implementation process. While the list could be long, I have chosen to discuss five principles that have guided decision making at my school:

Principle #1: The Identification of the DL Leader Is a Deciding Factor.

Leadership counts. The identification of the school leader at any K-12 DL school matters a great deal. When I left education to go into the private sector years ago (only to return to schools and commit my lifetime work to it), I was frustrated by the general lack of appetite of public school administrators to "get outside the box." Even though educational leaders extol the value of taking risks, very few school leaders are actually those who follow this advice. Playing it safe becomes their modus operandi. Keen to be in an environment that encouraged visionary bold decision making, I left the world of public education and went into private enterprise where playing it safe meant you risked going out of business. My supervisor guided me to take risks, counseling that if my team did poorly, then my leadership was largely responsible for that performance. This also applies to DL leadership.

Core characteristics of the successful DL leader include humility, self-reliance, and resourcefulness. The school leader must envision success through DL in spite of doubters among the ranks since much of DL seems to be counterintuitive, especially to the monolingual. An example of this is the pressure you will be under to reduce or minimize DL in the face of high-stakes assessments. In the era of high-stakes testing, school leaders are highly pressured to remove any possible perceived obstacle that might reduce student achievement. Since high-stakes tests are in English, many educators ask themselves how a student could succeed when half of the DL student's classes are taught in a language other than English? Thus, to those unfamiliar with the research, DL is seen as a risk, not as an opportunity to raise achievement scores. To many educators, it just doesn't make sense to keep teaching science in Spanish, for example, if the state science test is in English. How could DL students do well on the high-stakes test?

Yet that is exactly what occurs. Students, both native English speakers and English learners receiving academic instruction in, say, English and Spanish, do in fact excel in high-stakes tests in English even though they have received their academic instruction in both languages. Research and best practices support this experience—any child who is educated in a purposeful, bona fide DL environment will perform better than if they had not been in that DL environment. Period. Gifted children become more gifted. Children of poverty perform better and their futures are enhanced. DL is the tide that lifts all boats.

Strong, visionary leadership must prevail, even in the face of those who repeatedly voice their doubts based not on research, but on "common sense." DL enhances achievement for all students and levels playing fields. For example, in our school we have different groups of students enrolled together in DL. Some students have been raised in homes where the only language spoken is English. Others have been raised in homes where the only language spoken is Spanish. Still others have been raised in families where neither English nor Spanish is spoken at home (for example, Haitian-Creole or Finnish). These students are in 50:50 classes where academic instruction is in Spanish 50% of their day and in English the remaining 50% of the day. Every spring all of our students take the high-stakes test, the Florida Standards Assessments (FSA). Though only 43% of our entire school population of 1,500 are enrolled in our DL/ISA, they are the highest performers on the FSA, a test given entirely in English. Even the eighth grade ISA student who arrived from Colombia as a sixth grader with almost no knowledge of English outperforms his U.S.-born, non-ISA peers on the FSA.

What happens in many school districts in the absence of DL? For the English learner, the absence of DL education can mean being left behind and shunted to the corner of the classroom. "I don't know what to do with her. This computer program is supposed to be good. I'll just have her sit over at that table and do it." Then the English learner, instead of acquiring academic language in both English and Spanish, falls further behind and performs poorly on state assessments. For the student whose first language is English, the absence of DL almost certainly means that learner will be deprived of the value-added advantage, academically achieving at a lower level than they could have with DL. Worse, the opportunity to be bilingual and biliterate, almost a guaranteed benefit in the workplace, may never be realized.

Principle #2: Be Prepared to Hunt for High-Quality Dual Language Teachers.

Finding qualified DL personnel is key. The success or failure of a secondary DL program rests almost entirely on the quality of teachers hired to teach it. Finding highly qualified teachers of any kind is a challenge. For those schools who are just beginning to consider DL, many school districts are already actively "in the hunt," especially at the secondary level. Schools with the same hope of recruiting and hiring high-quality dual language teachers are possibly ahead of you on the recruitment trail. The prospect of seeking and finding bilingual and biliterate faculty who can operate at an academic level beyond Grade 5 is a daunting task, and the demand is far greater than the supply. Nonetheless, high standards in dual language teachers is a requisite, not an option—your DL program will never fulfill its mission without top teachers who are masters of their instructional content area(s) and fully academically proficient in their language(s) of instruction.

A word of caution: since so many school administrators are monolingual English speakers, they can be impressed by candidates who claim to be "bilingual" and use a few phrases with a convincing accent. A DL teacher not academically proficient is more likely to retreat to English during instruction instead of remaining 100% in the non-English language in which they are actually contracted to teach, and this will reduce the DL program's effectiveness. So what is the best way to identify qualified bilingual teachers? If you are a monolingual English speaker, make sure that you conduct your interviews along with bilingual leaders in your school district who are qualified to assess the academic proficiency of the teacher candidates. Secondary DL instruction typically operates at high levels of cognitive demand and DL teachers must be able to deliver high-quality instruction with high levels of academic proficiency in the subject being taught.

The truly high-quality DL teacher must command the Spanish language at the level that a university student in a Spanish-speaking country would speak, in the subject in which that teacher is certified. This includes the fluent use of academic language and the ability to understand a high-level, academic presentation with advanced academic vocabulary. Part of your interview process should include a **writing sample** on a topic related to what the candidate will teach. This gives you a chance to determine if the candidate utilizes accurate orthography and syntax at an appropriate level. Be sure to include a live teaching component in your interview process in which the candidate steps into a classroom with students and **teaches a DL class.**

If local teacher candidates are not available, you may have to recruit internationally to find the high quality DL faculty you need for the secondary level. A number of governments operate programs permitting their country's teachers to live and teach in the U.S. For Spanish-English DL programs, Colombia, Costa Rica, México, and Spain are among the countries that encourage this type of teacher exchange. The hunt for high-quality DL teachers is a requirement, not an option. Every opportunity that you get to fill another position, work on hiring your next bilingual staff member.

Principle #3: Be Patient.

You will probably want to progress faster than the school community is capable of progressing. You will face people inside and outside your organization who perceive that a DL academic teacher (for example, math, science, social studies) is a "Spanish teacher." These folks will need to be told gently and firmly (and probably more than once) that the new DL math teacher from Puerto Rico teaches *math*. Spanish just happens to be the language of instruction.

The DL leader can expect to encounter "cultural myopia" as one endeavors to forge ahead in the implementation of DL education, feeling surrounded by people with a lack of understanding of what DL education actually is. Try to perceive these as growth opportunities. As you educate others about DL, your goal must be to minimize the friction with a patient re-telling of what DL is and that, if they can join you in being patient, they will come to understand that DL is very effective and to be pleased with the results.

The DL leader must remain steadfast and committed to have those hard conversations with colleagues, parents, supervisors, and board members who do not yet fully understand how and why DL works so well. The fact that you must have these corrective conversations at so many levels is fundamental to giving birth to a legitimate DL school. It will be frustrating many times. Nonetheless, the end result, where DL students are excelling in a bona fide DL environment, justifies all the hard work and your dedicated patience.

Principle #4: Remaining in the Language

This is a principle that we follow at my school. At secondary level, all DL classes are in either English or the partner language. I will use Spanish as my example for the partner language. Teachers who teach in English never offer any language other than English. Those who teach in Spanish never, and I mean never, use anything other than Spanish. It is the DL teacher's commitment to the language that makes DL work properly. If a student in a DL Civics class does not understand a term in Spanish, should the teacher give the student the term in English? Absolutely not. Define and explain the term in Spanish. Act it out. Draw pictures to illustrate it. *But never use English!*

It is this commitment to the language of instruction that makes DL successful. Every time the teacher uses the "other" language, the student takes a step backward. This is not a matter of political correctness, but rather a matter of effective teaching. This backing off of language commitment hamstrings the student to constantly rely on his/her stronger language. This reliance slows the student's mental and emotional commitment to the weaker language, thus slowing their quest for true bilingualism. Immersion works in this DL context. We know immersion works because all of us, regardless of the culture or heritage, learned our first language through immersion. Did we learn our first language by someone explaining terms and expressions to us in some primitive, baby language? Of course not. The brain makes sense of disparate noises and seeks meaning in its shape, syntax, and repetition. DL is very much the same process.

Principle #5: Language Assessment for a Dual Language Secondary School

What are the skills required for exit from a K-5 DL school and entry into a secondary dual language school? The instrument we use to measure student progress in Spanish is *LAS Links Español*. This instrument measures listening, speaking, reading, and writing, with scores on a scale of one to five, the score of five being the highest. This assessment of language acquisition is a deliberate, laborious, and careful process. A similar process is conducted in English. These scores help determine which courses students are qualified to take.

Additionally, our school is committed to the use of the Common European Framework of Reference for Language (CEFRL) regarding language skills. The CEFRL was created by the Council of Europe between 1989 and 1996. The purpose of the CEFRL is to provide a method of learning, teaching and assessing all languages in Europe. There are six reference levels which are, essentially, rubrics designed to measure language acquisition in all four language competency areas, resulting in a learner's language skill level being A1, A2, B1, B2, C1, or C2. I have listed these in ascending order, that is A1 is the most rudimentary level while C2 is the most advanced. For example, a speaker with native fluency who possesses the academic language of a graduate university student might be C2.

We administer a detailed assessment of all four language competency areas to all prospective ISA faculty. This includes an interview and an essay. Our expectation is that the ISA teacher must command Spanish at the B2 level (as a required minimum) and a C1 as a preferred minimum. Our school has bilingual teachers from Colombia, Cuba, Guatemala, Honduras, México, Perú, Puerto Rico, and Spain. Our experience has been that these teachers command strong academic Spanish coupled with strong preparation for teaching in a classroom. This protocol has worked well for us as it both legitimizes the skills of the DL faculty through the use of a vetted European language standard (CEFRL) and establishes a clear and legitimate metric for all DL students to achieve *(Diplomas de Español como Lengua Extranjera, Advanced Placement Language and Culture exam, and LAS Links Español)*.

As you set your sights on creating, developing and implementing a successful secondary DL program, you will know that, though not yet common, there are successful templates to emulate. Further, you are not alone in this endeavor; the secondary DL family is made up of a community of learners and innovators who are always ready to share ideas and explore options at your side. You have only to seek them out and ask.

Chapter Twelve
New York: South Bronx Community Charter High School
High School Dual Language, Science, Technology, Engineering, and Mathematics (STEM) Classes, and Visionary Education

Mario Benabe, Teacher

Introduction by Collier and Thomas: *This chapter is distinctive in its focus on teaching strategies (rather than administrative issues) in a dual language high school in our largest school district of the U.S., New York City. At this diverse school in the South Bronx, students receive instruction that is directly connected to their cultural and linguistic roots. In an extended example, Mario Benabe describes for us how he instructionally emphasizes the Prism model's sociocultural dimension for his dual language students who are of primarily Latino, Indigenous, and African American backgrounds. Readers whose schools are similarly diverse can gain insights and suggestions for their own secondary dual language instructional contexts.*

The sample instructional project illustrated here is based on the Inca quipus or "talking knots," which was an amazing Indigenous base-10 analog data system for storing information used for administering and governing their cities and empire. Similar systems were used by the ancient Chinese and Hawaiian cultures. Quipus contain the basic characteristics of modern digital databases and spreadsheets, but in an analog form from the 1500s. They represent an example of Indigenous wisdom and innovation used in a dual language instructional setting.

Author Mario Benabe was honored in 2016 for his approach to teaching and learning in STEM by the White House Initiative on Educational Excellence for Hispanics under the Obama administration.

At the South Bronx Community Charter High School (SBCCHS) we implement four approaches to teaching and learning. These approaches are evident throughout the students' experience, in each learning environment and every learning process. The high school promotes learning by doing, with the students designing solutions to everyday problems. Students are surrounded and supported academically, linguistically, culturally, socially, and emotionally, to ensure active engagement as they navigate a self-paced, challenging learning environment. Our first approach is a *competency-based framework,* a multi-layered approach to teaching and learning that involves measuring students' progress by what they know and can do, rather than the time they have spent in class. At SBCCHS, the focus of teaching and learning is to help students learn, practice, develop, and demonstrate 19 competencies that indicate their academic, personal, and professional readiness. This approach is centered on clear, actionable learning targets—called attainments—that students use to create, apply, manage, and understand the world around them.

Our second approach is centered around *culturally responsive education* as a way of providing justice to our students. We believe that achievement is anchored in one's existing strengths and in full engagement of one's self and lived experiences. Within our school, the context, content, and means for learning may vary according to individual needs while the goal for self-awareness and connection is shared and consistent. It is the school's goal that all students and staff feel safe, supported, empowered, and important.

Our third guiding principle is *human-centeredness.* We place value on the notion that thinking through designing is a human-centered approach to innovation and a child's central way of learning through doing. It involves a commitment to understanding individuals' needs, recognizing that lived experience is legitimate and instructive, and thus, students build and revise solutions as needed to achieve increasingly better outcomes for all.

Our fourth approach is *integrating social and emotional learning.* As a school we understand that we need to broaden our idea of college and career readiness to include integrated academic, social, and emotional skills that enable students to achieve personal meaning and success as productive, proactive, well-rounded, and fulfilled agents of change. We focus on asking ourselves a larger question: what do students need to experience, feel, think, and do in order to both achieve a meaningful life and solve the increasingly complex challenges of an interconnected world?

As the founding Science, Technology, Engineering, and Mathematics (STEM) educator at SBCCHS, I work primarily with culturally and linguistically diverse students, some of whom are students with disabilities. My role is to think critically (in the sense of Freire's critical pedagogy, 2014) and design a dual language (DL) learning environment that is STEM focused. I then anchor the DL-STEM curriculum with the appropriate scaffolds that support each individual young person's reality and that are centered around his or her language(s), culture, identity, and history.

Our learning environment at our high school draws from Dr. Christopher Emdin's *Pecha Kucha* talk, *A Stem with No Root Bears No Fruit* (2015). In this talk, Dr. Emdin argues that in order to create science communicators we need to focus on "the type of work that scares us, and that we perceive as having no value." Creating larger STEM-focused academic viability in classrooms involves going deeper into the roots of a student's history, language, and culture. Thus, it is of critical significance that educators who engage in this work are STEM-minded and not STEM-blinded.

Another talk by Cely (2017) argued that "STEM education is more vulnerable to the blindsidedness that white-supremacist culture and colonialism has developed around and within this discipline." The work with students then becomes to de-colonize STEM fields so that we can recognize and learn from the depth of cognitive rigor around and within a child's cultural, linguistic, and pluralistic identities. When we erase the historical, cultural, and linguistic capital of young people and communities, we create the conditions that foster invisibility against the very things that sustain them. If there isn't consistent revision to our own practices in STEM teaching and learning, and if we largely focus on domains outside of those things that sustain our children's roots, we cannot "bear fruit"— or have successful STEM fields. In our learning environment we have designed a setting that invites the infinite wisdom already embedded within the cultural and linguistic reality of our students. We have been able to shift the understanding around dual language teaching and learning practices so that our studies look deeply into our students' ancestral bases—from knowledge of Indigenous and African roots–and call forth those traditions to teach STEM.

The aim of this chapter is to present three essential features within our dual language (DL) STEM learning environment that provide a unique experience for students whose roots are from linguistically and culturally diverse contexts. The first is the need for DL programs to explore, utilize, and build a learning environment that is centered around Indigenous and Afrocentric practices and traditions, especially for students whose heritages include these roots. The second feature of our learning environment involves sharing one significant social-justice project that utilizes an Indigenous mathematical tool to address a community issue. The essence in sharing this project is to argue for secondary dual language programs to move towards a project-based learning experience. Lastly, I make a recommendation for a structural support shift in DL settings that speaks to the need to authentically support culturally and linguistically diverse students with disabilities.

My recommendation pushes for a triangular support and services model where a combination of three educators from diverse licensing and teaching backgrounds work together in one learning environment. In a secondary educational setting across content areas this pushes for the need to have a general education, special education, and a bilingual/ESL certified teacher to be positioned within the same environment. This has the potential to reform collaborative teaching from a traditionally binary perspective to a dynamic ternary one. This teaching model both challenges and addresses existing paradigms that can make it difficult for schools to design a program that can accommodate culturally and linguistically diverse students with disabilities.

Utilizing Indigenous & Afrocentric Rituals in Dual Language Settings

"No one leaves his or her world without being transfixed by its roots, or with a vacuum for a soul. We carry with us the memory of many fabrics, a self soaked in our history, our culture; a memory, sometimes scattered, sometimes sharp and clear, of the streets of our childhood, of our adolescence; the reminiscence of something distant that suddenly stands out before us, in us." (Freire, 2014, p. 24)

Our STEM learning environment utilizes two cultural and ancestral rituals, an opening ceremony, called libations and a closing ceremony, In *Lak'ech*. *Libations* is an Afrocentric ritual consisting of pouring water from one vessel to another. It helps us to prepare the environment as safe, sacred, and spiritual before we engage in learning. We practice an abbreviated version of the full ritual. We primarily use *libations* to build a deeper connection to our ancestors.

Before we begin class we watch a STEM-related video that depicts cultural experiences or practices existing in our world today. An example of a video would be the building of the *Q'eswachaka* bridge over the Apurímac River. In Peru, four Quechua communities: the *Huinchiri, Chaupibanda, Choccayhua,* and *Ccollana Quehue* come together every year to build a 124-foot-long rope bridge. The yearly tradition has existed for hundreds of years, dating back to the Incas. When the video is over, we frame a dialogue around initial student reflections. We use a handmade wood carving of a jaguar as a talking piece to facilitate our dialogue. The jaguar is said to be the gatekeeper to all that is unknown. We use this artifact as a way to empower one person to speak, and the entire group to listen.

After everyone shares their initial reflections, we discuss the science around the ecological knowledge that the Quechua communities exhibited using *Jarava ichu* (Peruvian feathergrass) taken from the earth to design the bridge. We also discuss the engineering concepts that impact the design of the bridge, and the mathematics needed to complete their traditional practice. The purpose of this opening ceremony and activity is to allow our students to build an ethno-mathematical understanding of the cultural and ancestral knowledge of Indigenous or Afrocentric communities across the globe.

Over time, students have taken ownership of this lesson format and have investigated inherently STEM traditions within their own cultures to share with our learning community. If it is possible to replicate any of the materials or methods they discover, then we feel it is our duty to include them in our project-based learning model. In the next section, you will see how an Indigenous mathematical communication tool, *Quipus* (an ingenious information system and calculator using knotted ropes) was used by our students to address a community injustice through a project-based learning experience.

Next, to complete the ceremony, we pour *libations* by using affirmations or quotes. For this ritual we use a clear glass half filled with water, and a tribal bowl to pour the water into after each quote or affirmation is recited by a student. After each student recites his/her words, as a group we say in harmony, "we pour, and we say *ashe*". *Ashe* is a Yoruba word that means measure carefully and reflect on what has been said. For the *Q'eswachaka* bridge example, the narration of the pouring of *libations* was as follows:

"In honor of recognizing las comunidades de los Huinchiri, Chaupibanda, Choccayhua, and Ccollana Quehue de Perú para mantener sus tradiciones culturales,

we pour and we say, ashe."

"Este momento es para dar respeto y amor a nuestros antepasados,

we pour and we say, ashe."

"We are often looking for treasure far away, when in fact there are acres of diamonds in our own backyards; to this, and discovering our hidden gems,

"we pour and we say, ashe."

"We pour and we say, ashe."

"We pour and we say, ashe."

This ritual around creating a sacred space in a classroom reflects peacekeeping and self-reflection. Montessori (1949) shared that "an education capable of saving humanity involves the spiritual development of man, the enhancement of his value as an individual, and the preparation of young people to understand the times in which they live" (p.30). The way we utilize *libations* in our STEM-learning environment allows for our young people to explore layers of their Indigenous and African roots while drawing deeper ties to the STEM content.

In Lak'ech is a Mayan principle which means "you are my other self" (Fregoso, 1993). Aldama, Sandoval, and García (1993) report that In *Lak'ech* reflects an Indigenous ontology that views all people, all beings as related to each other in an intricate web of life. Luis Valdez, the father of Chicano theater (el teatro campesino), adopted this Mayan precept in a poem titled, *Pensamiento Serpentino* (1971) that we use for our closing ceremony.

In Lak'ech

Tú eres mi otro yo.

You are my other me.

Si te hago daño a ti,

If I do harm to you,

Me hago daño a mí mismo.

I do harm to myself.

Si te amo y respeto,

If I love and respect you,

Me amo y respeto yo.

I love and respect myself.

At the end of class, we gather in a circle, and recite this poem together. This is a way for students to take ownership of and share ancestral teachings within our STEM learning environment. In summary, these two rituals have allowed for our community to internalize concepts of empathy and love for the interconnectedness of humanity.

From Project-Based Learning (PBL) to Pro Black/Brown Learning (PBL)

Within our STEM project-based learning experience students have an opportunity to look deeply into various Indigenous tools, knowledge, and perspectives on mathematics. The intended outcome of this project was to have students design an interactive math lab which would function as a museum exhibit. The exhibit was named Indigenius Mathematica which speaks to the mathematical genius Indigenous communities across the globe have by virtue of their deep connections to the land and nature. This project gave participants the ability to learn about various mathematical tools and systems developed by multicultural groups represented in our community and within history. See Table 1 for the project's essential questions and Table 2 for the challenge description.

Table 1
Essential Questions

1.	How have different cultures used math to make sense of the world around them?
2.	How can we investigate multiple narratives around mathematics?
3.	How has math from different cultures been both adopted and lost over time?

Indi*genius Mathematica*

Table 2
Challenge Description

Goal	Students will be able to create models of Indigenous and Afrocentric math tools and systems.
Student's Role	Ethno mathematician and Researcher
Audience	Students, teachers, educational institutions, family, friends, and community members.
Situation	You are being asked to design an interactive math lab museum exhibit that allows participants to learn about the mathematical tools and systems developed by multicultural groups represented in our community and within our history.
Product	Model and description that users can explore independently to learn about the tools and systems of indigenius math.
Criteria for Success	Rubric grading will be based on our competency-based instruction. See graded attainments: I can take a real-world problem and express it in mathematical form. I can plan and carry out investigations. I can formulate a sound argument based on evidence. I can value diversity. I can work collaboratively with others.

Our students became deeply interested in learning about the Incas, specifically around their use of *quipus*. Ascher (1981) explains that a *quipu* is "a collection of cords with knots tied in them. The cords were usually made of cotton and were often dyed one or more colors. The records referred to by Pedro Cieza de León (Spanish conquistador and chronicler of Perú) were on *quipus*. In earlier times, when the Incas moved in upon an area, a census was taken and the results were put on *quipus*. The output of gold mines, the composition of work forces, the amount and kinds of tribute, the contents of store houses—down to the last sandal, says Cieza—were all recorded on the *quipus*. At the time of the transfer of power from one *Sapa Inca* (Emperor) to the next, information stored on *quipus* was called upon to recount the accomplishments of the new leader's predecessors" (p. 10).

Bazin, Tamez, and Exploratorium Teacher Institute's Math and Science Across Cultures (2002) resource guide and activity gave us the ability to practice the deep creation of quipus. Our students were able to design their own quipus to communicate the narratives of their community in the Bronx. As part of their project they identified one issue that impacted their community negatively and provided suggestions for ways to heal the injustice.

Quipu Project Map Display at South Bronx Community Charter H.S.

In the example above, students told the story of the Bronx Community District 4 (on the left side of the image) and Community District 3 (on the right side of the image) using quipus. In New York City, this is the High Bridge and Concourse, Morrisania and Crotona region of the Bronx. The guidelines for this project are provided in Appendix A, and one group's final report in Spanish on Bronx Community District 3 is provided in Appendix B, as well as a translation into English.

Paris (2012,) says:

> Our pedagogies [must] be more than responsive of or relevant to the cultural experiences and practices of young people—it requires that they support young people in sustaining the cultural and linguistic competence of their communities while simultaneously offering access to dominant cultural competence" (p. 94).

This project allowed our students to conjure up the spirit of a mathematical tool that has existed for hundreds of years and use it to communicate a social-justice message regarding change in their communities. In addition, we opened the exhibit to family and community members to observe our students' work. Lastly, we worked to extend our audience to include policy makers. We intend to present to local government the issues within our community using the *quipus* as an anchor for the dialogue between our students and these stakeholders. This will invite a new lens through which we advocate for changes in our community. We are providing a doorway to empower our students to be agents of change within our society through an ethno-mathematical approach.

Designing Programming to Support Culturally and Linguistically Diverse Students with Disabilities

Innovation is when things that have traditionally been distinct collide to create an avenue for new possibilities. The idea of having a triangular support and services model to bring together three educators with diverse licensing backgrounds in a single learning environment came directly from a recommendation students provided to improve their own learning. As a school we have a revision period during which students reflect on the prior project-based learning experience and provide recommendations to improve the next one. This gives students the opportunity to make decisions that best support their academic, social, and emotional needs. It also speaks to an understanding that we as staff have potential blind spots that only students themselves can see. This period is where the seeds of innovation are planted in our school.

We always frame the recommendation component of the conversation to use two protocols. The first is "Yes, and ..."or "Sí, y ...." This protocol validates every idea generated and provides support to build onto any initial suggestion or thoughts. The second protocol is framed as, "no idea is too big." This empowers the group to feel they could share any idea in their imagination to better their learning experience. There were multiple suggestions shared in this one experience but the one that resonated with the group was when a student asked, "What if we had three teachers in our room?" The entire room took on a different energy when the student shared this recommendation. Multiple students started snapping their fingers in support of the idea. Others went on to discuss which teachers they would want in the same room. Students started communicating joyfully about how different teachers might work together to make different learning environments. It was at this very moment that I observed what Scott (1990) describes as the *hidden transcripts*. Creating this space for students to recommend gave teachers and staff the opportunity to listen deeply to topics and suggestions that young people might otherwise have kept hidden. With that came an understanding that there are some power structures that need to be dismantled so that young people can resist and voice their concerns when their needs are not met. Making this suggestion a reality for our students went a long way toward validating their spirits' request.

I have had many conversations with educators across the New York City (NYC) district, with charter schools, as well as educators across several states. One consistent concern was how to provide appropriate educational experiences for students who are English learners/multilingual learners who are also students with disabilities. In the same way I observed the *hidden transcripts* of my students, I felt another concern arise among educators who felt that their administrators provided a disservice to this population of students. In NYC public schools alone, according to the *English Language Learner Demographics Report* for the 2015-16 school year, there were 35,256 children who were identified as culturally and linguistically diverse students with disabilities. At the same time, an alarming number of them, 79.1% (n = 27,897), received instruction in English only. While there are growing numbers of dual language, transitional bilingual, and English as a new language programs in the NYC Department of Education, the rate at which we are moving to provide appropriate pathways for culturally and linguistically diverse students with disabilities is stagnating.

Collier and Thomas (2007) developed the Prism model to summarize the factors that influence the process of second language acquisition in a school context. The Prism model "has four major components that drive language acquisition for school: sociocultural, linguistic, academic, and cognitive processes. To experience success in second language (L2) academic contexts, L2 students who are not yet proficient in English need a school context that provides the same basic conditions and advantages that the English-speaking group experiences" (p. 334). One of their examples of the Prism model for English learners receiving English-only instruction shows the significantly negative effect this can have on children. They argue that when learning English is the first goal, "the Prism model of language acquisition for school is reduced to mainly one dimension, development of one language (L2) and the other half of that component is missing— the continuing development of L1 (first language). This has unhappy consequences for the student in three out of the four Prism model's components" (pp. 337-338). (See Figure 12-1). Figure 12-2 illustrates the full Prism with all components being supported through both the students' primary as well as the second language.

Figure 12.1
The English-Only Perspective: Learn English First!
A Common but Misguided View of Many Policy Makers

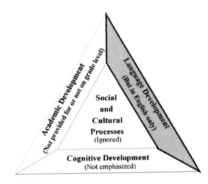

Copyright © 2003-2009, Wayne P. Thomas & Virginia P. Collier

Figure 12.2
The Prism Model for Bilingual Learners

Copyright © 2003-2009, Wayne P. Thomas & Virginia P. Collier

Collier and Thomas (2007) stated the following:

> All of these four components—sociocultural, academic, cognitive, and linguistic—are interdependent. If one is developed to the neglect of another, this may be detrimental to a student's overall growth and future success. The academic, cognitive, and linguistic components must be viewed as natural developmental processes. For the child, adolescent, and young adult still attending formal schooling, development of any one of the three academic, cognitive, and linguistic components depends critically on the simultaneous development of the other two through both first and second language (p.336).

We can no longer mistreat our students and push them towards an injustice because by design we will only replicate harm. I am calling for what Paris (2012) describes as **culturally sustaining pedagogy,** in which it is required that the pedagogies that support culturally and linguistically diverse students with disabilities be more than responsive of or relevant to the cultural experiences and practices of young people. It requires that they support young people in sustaining the cultural and linguistic competence of their communities and inviting those as markers of success. Coulter and Jiménez-Silva (2017) state that "historically, deficit theories and mandates have oppressed (and continue to oppress) children and families at the intersections of race, class, gender, and ability through means of narrowed language and literacy curriculum, English-only policies, tracking, and segregated schools" (p. 211). For me, the creation of a classroom context that hosts three teachers with diverse licensure is a push towards desegregation. It ends the process of separating environments that provide only the program's goals instead of sustaining the whole child and providing the appropriate support and services related to his or her disability and legal rights. Bhabha (1994) speaks to the notion of *hybridity,* a deep discourse whereby cultures are blended, remixed, and remade, giving way to alternative cultural production (Ikpeze, 2015). Similar to our STEM dual language program, I argue for a mixed-aged, group fusion, *hybrid* learning environment between special education and the major types of programs for English learners in which there is an adoption of a competency-based, culturally sustaining, and project-based learning model that is centered around the four major components that Thomas and Collier (2007) describe in driving language acquisition.

Conclusion

"The cycle of dysfunction in education is rooted in our adoption of the language of innovation, within a culture that fosters stagnation and fear of revolution." (Dr. Christopher Emdin, 2017)

For several years, I have been thinking deeply about visionary education and models to consider or create in our teaching and learning practices as educators. Throughout this chapter I have shared insight into potential shifts that we can adopt in order to provide new possibilities for DL programs across the nation. I want to share one last story that could also shift our unit of analysis of visionary education in DL settings so that we could focus on the importance of looking at the home as another source of power in a child's development. The implication for educators is that we should actively seek to involve and encourage home values and infuse the cultural context of families into our students' education.

The story begins by sharing my grandmother's role in my development of learning. I remember vivid images of when I was ill growing up, my grandmother's response, and the practices she undertook to make me feel better. For example, she would sing songs for me in Spanish that her mother sang to her in Puerto Rico to make me feel better. She would prepare something hot for me to drink using a combination of *hierba buena, hierba menta, y hierba mejorana* with a spoon of honey if I had stomach pains. She would also mix *Superior70 Alcoholado* con una *plata ruda* if I had a fever. Everything she did worked; I was suddenly healed overnight, and sometimes in the moment.

In those moments when I was ill, she was able to practice a type of teaching that valued deep cultural rituals that manifest through lived experiences. She was able to tap into her inner visions and consciously create the ritualized practices that healed her when she was a child. I think deeply about teaching and learning practices that are visionary or revolutionary and that are equipped to provide the same form of healing to other children in schools that my grandmother gave me at home. For example, Montessori (1949) when addressing the second plane of development, ages 6-12, states: "During this period of social interest and mental acuteness all possibilities of culture are offered to the child, to widen his outlook and ideas of the world" (pg. 4). My grandmother, *mi abuela*, did that by virtue of living and existing in her full cultural self. She didn't teach me the culture; I observed and absorbed it until it became ritual.

There are such deep artifacts present in the home that provide a layer of development to children that meet us as educators at the intersections of culture and education. I remember my grandmother engaging in the cultural practices of ancestral movement in our living room. She would center herself and dance as her body moved freely to the accompanying drumming. We gathered to form a circle around her—my brothers, sister and I would try our best to move as freely as she did. She created the impressions necessary for us to understand what an expression of freedom looks like, feels like, and sounds like. She would chant lyrics to songs in a language distinct from Spanish, and although we didn't know what she was saying, we still felt that connection to it.

In order to be visionary and revolutionary educators, we must deeply value the child's home and find ways to interact with it because it is an important part of their development. Montessori (1967) gives insight into understanding that "development is a series of rebirths" (pg.17). We have to also acknowledge that linguistic and cultural rites of passages that are present in the home and/or the community of our students can be forms of rebirth. Through her daily cultural practices, *Abuela* made a consistent effort to ensure the well-being of our home, and everyone who lived in it. Similarly, we want to prepare a learning environment that best serves the well-being of the child, so we must invite the home-related layers of a child's identity to run fluidly through our classrooms.

One last deep impression I have of my grandmother was her ability to have an infinite cognitive rolodex of ancestral old sayings. I would tell her about an experience that brought me a bit of pain, and she was able to provide a proverb that gave me so much perspective about life. She was able to summarize my long experiences within just a few words. Many times this came with references to the earth's elements like animals, water, fire, mountains, etc., all for the purposes of sharing the interconnectedness of humanity. Deep cultural oral traditions can also be present within the homes of our students, and our DL schools should nurture these in order to increase student engagement with school. As Cely (2017) explained in a speech at the Communities of Learning Summit,

> Storytellers who are truth tellers are collectively ignored in our schools. If we don't invite them in, we lose the cultural and localized knowledge that young people witness daily. These stories can be pivotal in awakening a child's interest in school. These stories carry a unique marker of our students' identity.

And we can greatly increase our effectiveness as educators by incorporating these into our schools' DL programs.

In our practices we must push ourselves to not just rely on reading and writing, but speaking and practicing deep listening. If we invite these storytellers in as curators of wisdom, listen deeply to what they share, we allow for the transfer of localized and communal knowledge to be shared within the DL classroom that, in other traditional school contexts, have been rendered invisible. My grandmother did nothing more than engage with her ancestry to foster in me a love for humanity, interconnectedness, and peacekeeping. As educators we play such an important role in this world, where we are helping our students do the excavation work of self-discovery with a concerted effort to look into the mirror and see their cultural roots. In addition, we all must look into the mirror, and crack into our own ancestry to dismantle sexism, white supremacy, racism, and other oppressive systems and structures. We must also learn to feel what we want to teach.

I have always considered my framework, *Do The Right Thing Pedagogy*, to be the application of collectively ignored localized knowledge to teaching. This is a model that is forever evolving when we work to coach ourselves out of awful teaching and learning practices that don't approximate students' reality. We must tap into the infinite wisdom of our ancestors that is principle-based in nature and lived experiences in order to use it as a *Dialectical Opposite* [Do] *To Heal Education* [The] that invites *Reality, Immersion, and Good-Hearted Teaching* [Right] *Through Historical, Indigenous | Afrocentric | Aboriginal and Native Grounds* [Thing].

Appendix A

(Translated)

Final Task: Identifying Community Social Issues and Representing Them Using Quipus

Task Description: This final challenge includes completing three tasks that are designed for your group to use your knowledge around building quipus to communicate the narrative of a Bronx community district of your choosing. In the first part of this challenge, you will look closely into several data points that represent an overview of your district. In the second task you will represent these data points using quipus. Finally, included within these data points are injustices that affect the Bronx. You will focus on one of these injustices and provide a recommendation to support a better outcome for our community. As a group you will report this information through a final report. Included throughout each section are links and resources to support your learning.

Part 1: Selecting an Issue

In the groups you have been working with throughout the year, select a Bronx community district using this link [NYC Community Health Profile]. Please choose an area in the Bronx that your group identifies most with to complete the table below.

1. Write the name of your group.	
2. Write the name of your chosen district.	
3. What was this location's population in 2015?	

4. What are the percentages of ethnic groups of the district? [Include percentage, and include the conversion to identify the exact population]	Hispanic: ___ Black: _____ White: _____ Asian: _____ Other: _____
5. Population by age:	0 - 17: _____ 18 - 24: _____ 25 - 44: _____ 45 - 64: _____ 65+: _____
6. Life expectancy:	
7. Adult educational attainment within the selected district:	College Graduate: _____ High School Graduate or some college: _____ Less than High School: _____
8. Income in selected district?	Poverty: _____ Unemployment: _____ Rent Burden: _____
9. Incarceration rates in selected district?	_____ per 100, 000 adult ages 16 and older
10. Access to health care:	No Health Insurance - Ranked: _____ Went Without Needed Medical Care - Ranked: _____
What does the data tell us about these issues in the South Bronx?	
How does this issue also affect the immigrant population in the South Bronx? (You may have to do outside research for this!)	

Part 2: Representing These Statistics Through Quipus

Now that you have selected and understood several key statistics related to the Bronx district of your choosing, it is now time to represent them using the Incas' mathematical tool, Quipu.

Directions: (1) divide the parts amongst your group (2) build the quipus (3) bring everyone's quipus together onto one main rope.

Supporting Material

How to make a figure-eight knot? (video)

How to make a long knot (video - 1st minute only)

Single knots are the ones most people practice when they tie a knot.

Part 3: Final Report

Product: Our goal is to create a map of the different Bronx districts using Quipus! Use the template below to complete your final report.

Title:

```
[                                    ]
```

Introduction: Your introduction should include some of the Incas' history. Information you should include: What are some general information/facts about the Inca Empire? Why was the *quipu* created? Who were the *quipucamayocs*? What was the purpose of the *quipus*?

```
[                                    ]
```

Resources for Introduction: Inca Empire History ; *Quipus* History [Spanish] ; *Quipus* History [English] ; Relevant information on *Quipus* ; *Quipus* [video] ; Inca facts [video]

Body paragraph 1: Describe each part of the *Quipus*, different types of knots, and different types of cords. What are the building blocks of *Quipus*? [Resources: Building on Indigenous Knowledge Systems]

```
[                                    ]
```

Body paragraph 2: Fill in the missing information using the community district you selected.

> In this example, we looked at specific data items from the Bronx community district _____, _____ section of the Bronx. We had to research the following data from this section of the Bronx and recreate those data points with the *Quipus*.

Body paragraph 3: Use the table information from part two of the final task for this section.

1. Location	
2. District.	
3. Population	
4. Ethnicities of the district?	Hispanic: __% = _____ Black: __% = _____ White: __% = _____ Asian: __% = _____ Other: __% = _____
5. Population by age:	
6. Life Expectancy:	
7. Adult educational attainment within the selected district:	College Graduate: High School Graduate or some college: Less than High School:
8. Income in selected district?	Poverty: _____ ; Unemployment: _____ ; Rent Burden: _____
9. Incarceration rates?	___ per 100,000 adult ages 16 and older (city-wide) - This district is ranked #___
10. Access to health care:	No Health Insurance - Ranked ___ : ___% = _____ Went Without Needed Medical Care - Ranked ___ : ___% = _____

Body Paragraph 4: The first sentence is given to you as a support. Explain how the quipu can be read using the information from the previous resources. Use all of these words [principal cord, subsidiary cord, lower level, single knot, figure-eight-knot, long-knot, upper level, place value]

> In order to understand how to read each cord, we needed to investigate how our ancestors designed the principal cords.

Body Paragraph 5: Provide an example for participants to understand.

For example: If you look at the first-cord on the left, in this example, it represents the population: _____.

Ones Place (Lower Level)	__ (long knot) or (figure-eight knot)
Tens Place	__ (single knot)
Hundreds Place	__ (single knot)
Thousands Place	__ (single knot)
Ten Thousands Place	__ (single knot)
Hundred Thousands Place	__ (single knot)

If you look at the _____-cord from the left, in this example, it represents _____ : __% = _____.

Ones Place (Lower Level)	__ (figure-eight knot) or (long knot/s)
Tens Place	_____ (single knot)
Hundreds Place	_____ (single knot)
Thousands Place	_____ (single knot)
Ten Thousands Place	_____ (single knot)
Hundred Thousands Place	__ (single knot)

Conclusion: Explain why it is important to keep the Inca culture alive through *quipus*. Describe an area of the data that you think was an injustice to you and/or your community and explain its significance as it relates to the Bronx. How would you address this injustice?

Appendix B

Student Exhibit of Bronx Community District 3:

Uso de Quipus para contar la historia de Morrisania y Crotona en el Bronx

Es difícil de entender una cultura cuando no hay mucha evidencia que sobrevive, o cuando no somos capaces de tener una comprensión completa de las pistas dejadas atrás. Quipus se puede describir como "cuerdas anudadas" utilizados por los incas para el mantenimiento de registros. En mis ojos se relaciona con lo que ahora llamamos codificación.

Cuerdas con nudos no son la forma más obvia de empezar a explicar una cultura, pero los quipus pueden ser la verdadera complejidad de la comprensión matemática de los incas. La estructura de un quipu se complica muy rápido. La base de cada quipu individuo comienza de la misma manera, pero el cuerpo se vuelve más complejo a medida que se complica el asunto estudiado.

Los componentes básicos de un quipu son las cuerdas que se hacen de forma individual y luego ensambladas. Estas cuerdas individuales que se construyen, cuando se ponen juntos en un quipu, cada uno tiene una función específica.

En este ejemplo, nos fijamos en los elementos de datos específicos del Bronx Community District tres, La sección Morrisania y Crotona del Bronx. Tuvimos que investigar los datos siguientes de esta sección del Bronx y volver a crear esos datos con una herramienta indígena [Quipus].

1. Ubicación	Morrisania y Crotona
2. Distrito.	Distrito 3
3. Población	81,698
4. Grupos étnicos del distrito?	Hispanos: 59% = 48,201.82 Negros: 38% = 31,045.24 Blancos: 1% = 816,98 Asiáticos: 1 = 816,98% Otros: 1% = 816,18
5. Población por edad	0- 17: 30% = 24,509.4;18 - 24: 12% = 9,803.76;25 a 44: 27% = 22,058.46;45 a 64: 22% = 17 973;65+: 8% = 6,535.84
6. Esperanza de vida:	75
7. Adulto logro educativo dentro del distrito seleccionado:	Graduado de la universidad: 18% = 14.705 Graduado de escuela secundaria o alguna educación superior: 44% = 35,947.12 Menos de escuela superior: 38% = 31,045.24
8. Ingresos en el distrito seleccionado?	Pobreza: 44% = 35,947.12; Desempleo: 20% = 16,339.6; Alquiler Carga: 61% = 49,835.78

9. Tasas de encarcelamiento?	371 por 100,000 adultos mayores de 16 años (en toda la ciudad) - Este distrito es el número 1
10. El acceso a la atención médica:	Sin seguro de salud - el puesto 16: 23% = 18.790,54 Sin atención médica necesaria - nº 24: 11 % = 8,986.78

Para entender cómo leer cada cuerda, se necesita investigar cómo nuestros antepasados diseñaron los principales cordones. Cada cable se descompone por valores de lugar con el fin de contar con los elementos. En el nivel inferior hay dos nudos diferentes que podrían ser utilizados. El nudo de ocho y nudos grandes.

La forma de ocho-nudos representa el número (1) mientras que el nudo grande representa los números (2 - 9). Una vez que un número llega a diez, un solo nudo se crea por encima del nivel inferior. A medida que cada nivel aumenta esos valores representan valores de lugar.

Por ejemplo: Si nos fijamos en la primera cuerda a la izquierda, en este ejemplo representa la población: 81, 698.

Unidades Lugar (nivel inferior)	8 (a largo nudo)
Decenas Lugar	9 (nudos individuales)
Cientos Lugar	6 (nudos individuales)
Miles Lugar	1 (nudo individual)
Diez Miles Lugar	8 (solos nudos)

Si nos fijamos en el segundo cable de la izquierda, en este ejemplo representa la población de hispanos: 59% = 48,201

Unidades Lugar (nivel inferior)	1 (en forma de ocho nudos)
Decenas Lugar	(espacio fue dejado en el medio Ya que no hay decenas lugar)
Cientos Lugar	2 (nudos individuales)
Miles Lugar	8 (solo nudo)
Diez Miles Lugar	4 (solos nudos)

En conclusión, debemos valorar la historia de nuestros antepasados en las clases de matemáticas. La diversidad de las culturas y las herramientas matemáticas indígenas y afrocéntricas podrían ayudar a desbloquear los secretos de nuestra historia que fue destruida. Este *quipo* representa aspectos de este barrio en el Bronx, y algunos de los datos impactaron nuestro grupo. Esta comunidad ocupa el primer lugar en los índices de encarcelamiento. Esto tiene que cambiar, y el gobierno local aquí en Nueva York debe invertir en prácticas de justicia restaurativa para ayudar a curar esta injusticia. La gente en mi comunidad son detenidos diariamente y la educación puede arreglar y mejorar este lío. Como grupo, vamos a escribir una carta a los políticos locales para asegurarnos que están apoyando a nuestra comunidad a mejorar. Espero que podamos crecer como una comunidad, y aumentar nuestras tasas de graduación.

(Translation into English)

Student Exhibit of Bronx Community District 3:

Using Quipus to tell the story of Morrisania and Crotona in the Bronx

It is difficult to understand a culture when not much evidence survives, or when we fail to have a full understanding of the clues left behind. Quipus can be described as "knotted-string" used by the Incas for record keeping. In my eyes it predates and relates to what we now call coding.

Cords with knots are not the most obvious way to begin to explain a culture, but quipus may hold the true complexity of the mathematical understanding of the Incas. The structure of a quipu gets complicated very fast. The base of each individual quipu begins in the same manner, but the body becomes more complex as the matter being recorded gains complexity.

The building blocks of a quipu are the cords which are individually made and then assembled. These individual cords that are constructed, when put together into a quipu, each have a specific function.

In this example, we looked at specific data items from the Bronx Community District Three, The Morrisania and Crotona section of the Bronx. We had to research the following data from this section of the Bronx and recreate those data points with an indigenous tool [Quipus].

1. Location	Morrisania and Crotona
2. District.	District 3
3. Population	81,698
4. Ethnicity of the district?	Hispanic: 59% = 48,201.82 Black: 38% = 31,045.24 White: 1% = 816.98 Asian: 1% = 816.98 Other: 1% = 816.18
5. Population by age:	0 - 17: 30% = 24,509.4 ; 18 - 24: 12% = 9,803.76 ; 25 - 44: 27% = 22,058.46 ; 45 - 64: 22% = 17,973 ; 65+: 8% = 6,535.84
6. Life expectancy:	75
7. Adult educational attainment within the selected district:	College Graduate: 18% = 14,705 High School Graduate or some college: 44% = 35,947.12 Less than High School: 38% = 31,045.24

8. Income in selected district?	Poverty: 44% = 35,947.12 ; Unemployment: 20% = 16,339.6 ; Rent Burden: 61% = 49,835.78
9. Incarceration rates?	371 per 100, 000 adult ages 16 and older (citywide) - This district is ranked #1
10. Access to health care:	No Health Insurance - Ranked 16th: 23% =18790.54 Went Without Needed Medical Care - Ranked 24: 11% = 8,986.78

In order to understand how to read each cord, we needed to investigate how our ancestors designed the principal cords. Each cord is broken down by place values in order to count items. On the lower level there are two different knots that could be used. The figure-eight knot and long knots.

The figure-eight knot represents the number 1, while the long-knot represents the numbers 2- 9. Once a number reaches 10, a single knot is created above the lower level. As each level increases, those values represent place values.

For example: If you look at the first cord on the left, in this example, it represents the population: 81,698.

Ones Place (Lower Level)	8 (long knots)
Tens Place	9 (single knots)
Hundreds Place	6 (single knots)
Thousands Place	1 (single knot)
Ten Thousands Place	8 (single knots)

If you look at the second cord from the left, in this example, it represents the population for Hispanic: 59% = 48,201

Ones Place (Lower Level)	1 (figure-eight knot)
Tens Place	(space was left in between Since there's no tens place)
Hundreds Place	2 (single knots)
Thousands Place	8 (single knots)
Ten Thousands Place	4 (single knots)

In conclusion, we should value the history of our ancestors in math classes. The diversity of cultures and Indigenous and Afrocentric math tools could help us unlock the secrets of our history that was either destroyed or taken away from us. While these quipus represent aspects of this neighborhood in the Bronx, some of the data was shocking for our group. This community ranks number one in incarceration rates. This needs to change, and the local government here in NYC should invest in restorative justice practices to help heal this injustice. People in my community are arrested every day for things that education can fix. As a group, we are going to write a letter to the local politicians to make sure that they are supporting our community for the better. I hope we can grow as a community, and increase our graduation rates.

Chapter Thirteen
California:
Tearing Down Walls, Building Bridges, Lessons Learned!

Dr. Michele Anberg-Espinosa – Simpson University, Redding, CA

Introduction by Collier and Thomas: *This overview chapter, summarizing several points made in the ten chapters of Part II, examines the challenges that are especially present in large urban multilingual school contexts. Dr. Michele Anberg-Espinosa recounts some of her experiences in multiple school districts and discusses issues that school leaders need to address when implementing and expanding dual language programs at the secondary level. Lessons learned include empowering disenfranchised communities without alienating others; involving parents, teachers, students, community members, board members, and administrators in collaborative DL decision making; motivating secondary DL students to continue enrolling in DL classes; providing PK-12 articulation meetings; addressing DL curriculum development and teaching challenges at secondary level; ensuring continuing resources for secondary DL; and making equity and social justice in DL programs a priority, including enrolling newly arrived English learners, retaining African American students and other diverse groups in the DL secondary program, and developing culturally relevant pedagogy. The bottom line is that clear communication builds bridges.*

Lessons Learned from Secondary Dual Language Implementation in Urban Multilingual Contexts

I had just started a new job in a large urban multilingual community with several dual language programs. "Will you get in touch with this board member?" my boss requested. "She is part of this language community and is inquiring about the status of the program at the middle school level. The students are now entering sixth grade, and the community wants to hear about our plan for the program expansion into secondary. The parents are anxious; the students are anxious" (subtext—I am anxious).

Leadership at central office and at the dual language (DL) school site had changed, and although the parents had been promised continuity of the program, action steps that would ensure transparent communication and a well thought out plan had gotten lost along the way. As I did my homework, I found that due to administrator turnover, there had been limited communication between central office, parents, and teachers about the nuts and bolts of DL expansion to the middle and high school. A teacher had not yet been found and the board member, although extremely polite, respectful, and forgiving, wanted to ensure that the promises made to the community were fulfilled. The lack of transparency created fear and concern among key stakeholders.

Promises fulfilled ... how easily forgotten are the promises made in DL programs with excited kindergarten parents. Rosa Molina (Association of Two-way and Dual Language Education) has always said, "It's a K-12 conversation!" The dialogue must not only involve parents of kindergarteners but also the stakeholders down the line as these kindergarteners become middle and high school students.

But how can we ensure that these promises are fulfilled? Having board policies in regard to K-12 DL education is critical for sustainability, especially to ensure financial support for a program where administrators and teachers on special assignment can be assigned specifically to support the implementation and expansion of the DL program. It is also essential to ensuring that these guidelines are articulated for all to see and be informed. Board policy, administrative guidelines, school site program guidelines, counseling manuals, and publications for parents are all important for sustainability. However, bold policies need to be tempered with financial foresight, as a district can be caught up in the excitement of championing new DL programs without the financial wherewithal to support them in the long term. My story offers highlights of some important lessons learned in the process of secondary DL expansion at multiple sites in multiple languages. It also highlights the importance of equity.

Dual Language Leadership

Who oversees DL programs? Is there a person at the school or district level who is well informed in DL research-based practices who will coordinate the administrative effort? Wherever a DL program exists there should be site support for the teachers, including DL instructional coaches and schoolwide and districtwide collaboration. This requires resources and knowledgeable leadership at all levels within the school district.

Parents need to understand that DL is a commitment through high school, but it is the teachers, schools, and central office staff who build the long-term and sustainable infrastructure and frame support that unites rather than divides the communities we seek to serve. Parent advocates, school site councils, and school boards must navigate many complexities. For example, there is a tension between responding to White, empowered parents who come out in force and drive the dialogue at school site councils and board meetings, and responding to partner-language parents and communities who are often without a voice. Despite the fact that so many English learners or re-designated students (including those from marginalized populations) are served through these programs, we discovered that one fear of social justice-minded central office leadership or school boards was that conceding to the dominant community could be seen as giving it permission to "run the show" But when the partner language communities expressed demands, often the message was dismissed or not fully heard because the delivery format and style of the message was not what central office leadership or school boards were accustomed to; communication styles were different. This was a mixed message.

Decisions about the DL program must be based on principles, not on fear and a perceived potential loss of power. Indeed, it is possible (particularly when funding is involved) to be so committed to a so-called "social justice" that districts and school boards can go overboard, and unintentionally communicate an 'anti-White' agenda, indirectly denying justice to the very communities we seek to empower. One way we eventually learned to get stakeholders on the same page was to present needs together as a community (with both English-dominant and partner-language representation), and to communicate with stakeholders about needs before they were voiced in public. It's a delicate dance to provide leadership to empower disenfranchised communities without alienating others. It takes wise leadership and transparent communication among stakeholders to navigate the complexities of this tension.

Informing Stakeholders

The journey into secondary DL programs involves many components and layers. One particular layer has to do with the challenges that may emerge in the actual process of expansion into secondary, requiring a significant level of coordination and collaboration among personnel and the community. Parents, teachers, students, community members, board members, and administrators must be informed and involved in decision making. It's not just coordination between the English learner department and the middle or high school. A lot of footwork is required to involve all these stakeholders; it's not just a meeting that happens once. It requires significant collaboration at different points in the process.

In one particular urban professional context, we began with a proposal for DL expansion into secondary based on community needs, parent input, and staffing. Once this proposal was accepted by the district, we followed a 3-year implementation plan with dates, benchmarks, and deadlines. This plan involved gathering key stakeholders together at different intervals. For example, at first, the community was involved in conversations about the possibility of expansion. Once this was established, there were needs-assessment conversations with principals where it was determined how prepared the sites were to receive the program. As time progressed, teachers, speakers of the language in the community, and others became involved in the conversation. Once involved in the process, they often expected to receive updates and be involved in subsequent conversations.

With so many other pressing issues, communication between central office staff assigned to DL programs and middle or high school personnel is often considered low priority. We found that because urban schools tend to have a high degree of turnover of staff and administration, as well as significant student concerns, administrators often found themselves in "survival" mode. Therefore, our discussions about DL expansion were understandably not first on their list of priorities. Since the expansion only impacted a few classes at the beginning, it required persistence to encourage school sites to prioritize orientation meetings for expansion that didn't seem pressing on the surface. ("It's two years away."). The expansion would inevitably sneak up on staff and principals, regardless of the proposed lead time. Since the amount of time it took to plan the first cohort of DL sections was significant, it was difficult to find a time in which the staff and principals were available and prepared to do necessary follow-up to complete the action steps as indicated on the timeline.

We found the best way to address the communication disconnect was to involve district leadership in charge of principals, such as assistant superintendents, so proper steps could be taken in a timely manner to build awareness around the requirements for expansion, especially in regard to staffing and curriculum. Having one dependable contact at the secondary level who was not the principal, but had the ear of the principal, was ideal, such as an assistant principal in charge of curriculum. In addition, we found that most high school principals did not come from language-education backgrounds, and therefore building awareness about the DL programs needed to be part of the discussions so the principal or other staff who would be promoting and representing the program at their site could do so accurately and effectively.

Not all folks, and especially not those in positions of central office leadership, were aware of the steps for expansion. They were somewhat removed from the day to day planning, but nonetheless held important keys for program success. Central office awareness and support was critical for the proper functioning of the program, from staffing, to budgeting, to oversight of principals who led these programs. Parents also had to be informed in a timely manner. Stakeholders didn't want to be told what was going to happen; they wanted to be given an opportunity to weigh in on the decisions being made. It required foresight to schedule meetings with the different stakeholder groups and a concerted effort to publicize and organize them.

Strengthening Vision and Purpose

The shift to DL in middle school is a transition that must not be taken lightly. Students often choose the middle school DL program due to parents' insistence to fulfill their commitment to the program to gain the most benefits. Many students find themselves just going through the motions. There needs to be a bigger motivating force and focus for students to stay in DL besides the research that shows that the greatest gains are evident in later grades.

Student motivation. DL educators need to transform their approach to motivation at the secondary level. Often, middle school students experience decreases in motivation for schooling as they progress in age, either because they don't feel confident or because tasks are not engaging or relevant to them (Association for Middle Level Education, 2017). How often do effective middle school practices take place in DL classrooms? There is so much emphasis in just finding personnel to fill classes that the critical component of student motivation takes a back seat.

Staying in a DL program through high school takes endurance and persistence. A key component of student retention and resiliency is ensuring that middle and high school students' interests and passions are addressed. Students are becoming more independent and self-determining as they leave elementary school. Although there is a paucity of research regarding the non-negotiables and best practices of secondary DL, according to authorities in middle school education, there are many key points we do know about educating young adolescents. These include valuing the students through engaged and active learning with challenging, exploratory, integrative, and relevant lessons that use multiple learning and teaching approaches, and varied assessments (Association for Middle Level Education, 2013). As DL educators we must ensure that we incorporate these concepts as baseline best practices.

Encouraging high expectations. High expectations are a key component of effective middle and high school programs, but students must be motivated to embrace these high expectations. For example, James Orihuela, middle school teacher extraordinaire in Southern California, gives a motivating speech about the importance of college credits in high school as a student motivator. He speaks about how this is especially critical for our disenfranchised students who may not otherwise consider college. By taking some classes for college credit prior to the end of high school, the likelihood that these students will attend college greatly increases. He imbues his students with the expectation that they will pass the Advanced Placement (AP) exam in Spanish at the end of eighth grade. With over 90% of his students on average passing the AP test, his students can enroll concurrently in local community colleges with the goal of obtaining the equivalent of a minor in Spanish prior to leaving high school.

Building Bridges between Elementary and Secondary Teachers: It's a PK-12 Conversation.

There are so many steps to just getting the DL program offered in secondary. Among these precursor steps are the important conversations regarding program planning and implementation that should occur between middle and high school bilingual and ESL teachers, world language educators, and elementary DL educators. There is so much more to DL program expansion than just making sure classes are offered!

Professional development, conferences, and support for DL programs have understandably focused on K-5 programs. Unfortunately, the stakeholders who have the biggest potential for impact—the secondary teachers—are frequently not included in the dialogue. So expansion often takes place without vertical conversations with those charged with its implementation. This creates significant tension when a teacher is being asked to implement a program they may not fully understand or support. In addition, the impact that the DL program has on secondary master scheduling is another major challenge. So, PK-12 teachers coming together to discuss the vision, goals, and day-to-day implementation of this expansion is of utmost importance. Communication with these key stakeholders is critical for "buy in" and impacts student placement, curriculum, graduation requirements, communication with parents, continuity of the program, and so on.

We found PK-12 articulation meetings to benefit the entire language community. After an initial adjustment period, these meetings created a support network and shared vision for teachers. A real solidarity evolved that empowered teachers to become leaders instead of followers in the effort to make their DL programs successful; connected across elementary, middle, and high school; and the best possible option for students. Teachers assumed ownership to improve their programs, and even proposed and participated together in community multilingual, cross-cultural events. These meetings changed the dynamic of communication with stakeholders from defensiveness to celebration, because our focus changed from trying to convince stakeholders that we were doing enough to support the program to proudly sharing the genuine progress we were making in creating a more cohesive DL program.

Secondary expansion also has an impact on secondary teaching assignments because the DL students enter with superior language proficiency and higher achievement than non-DL students, impacting course loads, prep periods, and scheduling. Because some world language teachers may lose their positions (e.g., lesser taught languages might be displaced because a large number of incoming world language students are from the middle school Spanish—or other—DL program), we must treat those who serve our students in our secondary programs in the same way that we honor those teachers who are displaced at the elementary level when bilingual staff are needed. Middle and high school teachers must be treated with the utmost of professionalism and transparency in regard to how the language pipeline PK-12 will impact them.

A world language teacher's job is highly impacted when the incoming student population consists of students who are more skilled in the language, and in ways that do not match the continuum of language development that many of these teachers are accustomed to expect. For example, a big complaint that world language teachers had in our district was that non-native students coming out of elementary and middle school DL programs may be fluent speakers, but have 'issues' with grammar that are typically taught in the beginning level world language classes. Notwithstanding language learning theories and approaches that should be taken into account, there should be much more emphasis among PK-12 teachers about student language "assets" rather than "deficits." One way we addressed this was through language testing for students in eighth grade. We facilitated the creation of an exam for each language, designed by our middle and high school teachers, to determine placement in different high school classrooms. Although the tests were not perfect, they created the expectation that students who had been in a DL program needed to be placed appropriately, not in introductory language classes like Spanish 1! There was pushback from our world language teachers but they eventually accepted our efforts to have and use a consistent placement test, and they began to recognize that they needed to shift their own paradigm of teaching to accommodate the DL students. We also began working towards an online testing system to obtain a more standardized measure of student proficiency.

Whereas elementary and secondary DL teachers may have a different perspective on best practices for language learning, there is much they have in common—a passion for language learning and cultural awareness, a commitment to social justice, and more. Whereas world language teachers may agree at some level about the pedagogy in the younger grades, they may be intimidated by students coming to secondary with 6 to 9 years of second language (L2) development and with wide variation in skills and needs in their L2. This can be overwhelming because differentiation for individual students' needs soon becomes hugely important, perhaps something they've not needed to worry much about in the past. At the same time world language teachers are experts at supporting world language students who are completely new to the language (such as an English-only student learning Spanish for the first time). So there is great potential in vertical articulation meetings to mutually reinforce strategies and practices. Offering PK-12 articulation meetings for districtwide consistency in practice and expectation goes a long way toward building awareness of each other's contexts. Done well, it can create a united vision which builds momentum for each language community as a whole, creating opportunities to promote language learning and cultural awareness as a community of learners.

But articulation for PK-12 isn't enough. Collaboration with community colleges and universities plays a key role in student motivation. Providing secondary courses with concurrent enrollment with local higher-education campuses is an attractive feature for students and their families. Investing in collaborative meetings with community colleges and universities to establish a pipeline for DL students is key to the long-term success of the DL program (e.g., see Chapters 2, 4, 5, and 6).

Curriculum Development and New Secondary DL Teachers

DL program expansion requires curriculum development. This is ideally done collaboratively and in advance of the start of the school year. However, in most districts summer work is optional. In addition, given the teacher shortage, the credentialing requirements at the secondary level for both content and language proficiency, and the small pool of DL instructors, hiring was often not possible until immediately prior to the start of the school year. Therefore, new secondary teachers were faced with simultaneously developing and delivering a new curriculum, often without colleagues with whom to collaborate and without a textbook, since it was a completely new course.

Most often we had to hire a new DL teacher with little prior experience in planning, who, for the most part, was isolated from other staff members. We had originally hoped that plans developed by one DL teacher could be kept in the archives and disseminated where applicable, such as when another teacher was hired as new sections were added. But we saw it was not realistic to use the plans of a very new teacher. Even for a seasoned teacher, it was burdensome to document every curricular step when what was needed at first in the expansion was excellent teaching.

When a DL class was offered for the first time, the program usually required only one or two classes. This was problematic for a few reasons. One, there weren't enough sections in the DL program to justify a full-time teaching assignment. This meant that either a teacher was hired part-time, would teach at more than one site, or would have to teach other classes—which increased the amount of time needed to prep for classes. We found none of these options was ideal and contributed to a significant amount of burnout. There was also an additional stressor in that new DL teachers worried that complaining would impact their evaluation. If they didn't complain, however, they were left on their own to figure out their own support. Without a network of support, they would likely burn out. Our newer teachers who took on roles in DL expansion classrooms truly struggled, and they compelled us to provide better support networks.

We tried curriculum development at the district level, and a baseline level of curricular support was definitely helpful, but it became somewhat unsustainable over the long run for a team to focus on just one course given the numerous districtwide demands on staff. We were most often faced with a teacher who was passionate about the program but new to teaching and to curriculum development, and without much lead time to prepare. We advocated that each teacher in charge of a DL expansion class be given an extra preparation period for the first year of implementation of that particular class, so the teacher would have a better opportunity to develop this curriculum.

Ensuring resources were allocated in advance was key to DL program support. We advocated strategically with a detailed budget to relevant stakeholders in advance of deadlines, because we were well aware that support for DL expansion competed against other very important programs. Therefore, expansion had to be handled with much sensitivity and political savvy, never lacking the critical data, facts, figures and a crystal-clear rationale to provide at a moment's notice. The resource discussion usually had to take place in January and February of each year for the following school year. Ideally, resources were to have been committed as decisions were made for DL expansion, but we discovered that changing personnel and leadership within the different stakeholder groups required revisiting and reminding leadership of the financial commitment to the program. Keeping the information available at any moment for a discussion with stakeholders needing a refresher of the rationale was key. We found that the first thing to go when leadership changed was the assurance of funding for our DL programs.

In summary, when we expect teachers, especially a first- or second-year teacher, to take on classes which are new to their experience, we must consider the kind of support they are offered. We found that they needed the collaboration with job-alike colleagues, and we set aside time for them to collaborate and share lesson plans with fellow teachers. We built this into the infrastructure because teachers requested this from year to year. And lastly, we consistently advocated for resources.

Moving Beyond Strictly Language Goals Toward Equity

For me the most important issue with the greatest societal impact for participating DL students and their families and for transforming communities is ensuring equity and social justice in our programs. Bilingualism and biliteracy are the first two goals of DL programs. There is also a third goal, often referred to as multiculturalism or cross-cultural awareness—I like to call it equity. With so much involved in setting up the language component of the program, it's not uncommon that the third goal is overlooked, glossed over, or presented in superficial ways. Given the fact that this third goal is not as clear or as easily measured as a student's ability to read, write, or speak in a second language, it's easily swept under the rug in the daily grind. To me, this is the hidden curriculum in our DL programs!

Many of those teaching language at the secondary level (all levels for that matter) would consider themselves advocates for social justice. In fact, on any given day there's no doubt we would agree to march with signs saying the third goal is really important. But our passion doesn't create equity. We demonstrate what we value through what we spend our time on, what we invest in. So moving from what we *say* we value to actually demonstrating that we value an equity- or social-justice-focused curriculum is the crux. It's common yet naïve to believe that if two or more populations of students are together in a classroom (or two or more parent groups are at a meeting), and they have the common goal of learning languages together, we can check off the equity or social justice box of our DL 'things to do' list. But diversity in population is not equity! Being intentional with equity is really our only choice. What if the curriculum (especially at the secondary level) hinges on how students view and can transform themselves and their environments through informed perspectives on race, culture, and language, as a way to move toward identity development? Just as we must make implicit language learning explicit and intentional for all students, so must we be explicit and intentional about conversations and activities that promote equity.

Needs of students. In the planning process towards implementation of a DL program which aspires to promote equity, we must analyze the needs of all groups of students to determine if we are offering everyone equitable opportunities. One question that came up continually was what to do with native speakers of the language who haven't been educated in that language. Here is where the binary language models we assumed in elementary school no longer apply. First, because DL students are much more skilled bilingually by the time they reach the secondary level, it's sometimes not even relevant to say that they are English- or Spanish (or other partner language)-dominant. Spanish-speaking English learners who have not had the privilege of being in a DL program should be included in the class, provided that they are aware of the level of expertise and language proficiency of their classmates and the teacher scaffolds instruction.

Having native speakers of the partner language in DL classes is a win-win. Students who haven't participated in the DL program should be given the support to be successful in a high-performing program. Language in this context should be viewed as a collective skill set among students in the class. Rather than scrutinizing the grammar of, say, a newly arrived Latino student, and "problematizing" the student's language skills, we must consider their linguistic and cultural experiences as resources. The experiences of all members of the class are valid, go beyond speaking and writing skills, and enrich the class knowledge base. Students also need to know how to navigate varied sociolinguistic contexts, which can be advanced through interaction with their diverse peers. Nonetheless, according to teachers of DL language classes, it's naïve to believe that native speakers can be grouped together in a DL classroom without a plan to support them. Since the skills of some native speakers who have not received any schooling in their first language can vary greatly, some sites found that offering them an introductory native-speaker class prior to entry into DL classes had very positive results.

As we analyzed our practices in DL courses, we discovered that 25% of the students attending our Spanish for native speaker classes were long-term English learners who may not have had any formal schooling in Spanish, although they were fluent orally. In other words, we had students at the high school level who spoke Spanish at home, were still developing their English, and had chosen to study Spanish to satisfy their world language requirement. We knew that we needed to try to bridge Spanish language arts and English language arts to address these students' development of literacy skills. So we used the Common Core State Standards en español, and began the work of aligning our lesson plans for native-speaker Spanish classes with Spanish language arts, which was consistent with the curriculum used to address the English language arts standards. It made good sense to link English and Spanish language arts, since they were the same standards but in two languages, and they would therefore complement and reinforce one another, giving our Spanish-speaking Latino students an extra boost. Forging collaboration between the Spanish and English departments was what we considered essential for our Latino students' success. (See Chapter 10 for another example of the power of collaboration between the English and Spanish language arts departments.)

Is Dual Language for ALL? Who are your students and why? Do you know the trends? What are you doing to ensure that there is equal representation, or at least equal opportunity in your program? If this isn't embraced when your students are in elementary it won't get any easier in secondary school. How do we ensure that students who enter our DL programs remain, especially students who are underrepresented? There will be some attrition in any program, but analyzing data around success and the reasons students want to remain in the program (as well as attrition) is necessary for any secondary program. Unfortunately, teacher, administrator, parent, and community beliefs and expectations about who will be successful in DL programs don't always match the population of students whose parents chose to enroll them in the program in kindergarten. We noticed educators in particular tended to have preconceived notions about how students should naturally fit in a program as opposed to offering support to meet the needs of all students. In the name of equity for English learners, some faculty/staff truly believed that serving underrepresented students who are not English learners in a DL program (for example African American students) were second priority. So, how can we ensure staff have what they need to support students to have equal opportunity? Much can be gleaned from successful work with students in non-DL programs. How familiar is your staff with the following approaches to successfully engage students: connections, culturally relevant pedagogy, valuing multiple cultures, among others? Teachers must have high expectations for all students and embrace all students, not just English learners. How can this be accomplished? One critical piece is to take time to obtain input from communities of learners.

An ongoing debate has involved those who believe that African American students from low income communities (and presumably who may need more linguistic support in the academic English register) are better served in an all-English classroom. But research has shown that African American students can greatly benefit from attending K-12 DL programs (Thomas & Collier, 2002, 2014). In some cases, these students are "given the opportunity" at the beginning of a program, and then after a few years in the program, they are "counseled out" by well-meaning teachers, specialists, and administrators. Who will your students be and will the population of students who began in your kindergarten program be the same students in secondary? If you'd like to be sure your program is successful for all communities, including African American students, what will you do?

A case study about African American student longevity. My doctoral research involved a case study at a K-8 Spanish/English DL charter school in which I interviewed African American students and their parents about their perspectives of and experiences in the program. I was interested in finding out the reasons students remained in the program and if there was anything that could be enhanced to better serve African American students and families at the site. I found that longevity was a result of several things. Students were content overall with the program and they had great friendships (which were primarily cross-cultural). They also wanted to learn Spanish for the societal benefit. Parents were satisfied with the program and kept their children in it because of the positive family-like school climate. Interestingly, despite satisfaction with the program, both students and parents desired a more culturally inclusive school, one that included more African American-themed learning experiences, and in particular, more students and staff representing underrepresented groups and cultures, especially African Americans.

I learned that in order for the program to better serve their African American students, there was a need for an increase in instructional strategies and techniques that would best facilitate the acquisition of Spanish as a way to ensure high levels of academic achievement, since Spanish was not their first language. They had all received some additional support, but the inclusion of more instruction in Spanish within the regular school day needed to increase in order to facilitate success in all academic areas. They also desired an incorporation of more cultural elements (especially those relating to African Americans such as Black History month) in the curriculum to create a more inclusive learning environment and prepare students to be global citizens. Additionally, an increase in strategies to address the very specific interests and needs of the African American parent population and their participation in the program was important.

Although this research focused on a K-8 program, many principles can be applied to middle and high school environments. One such example is to ensure inclusion of cultures and backgrounds other than what is represented by the partner language. For example, one non-negotiable is to highlight Black History month within the DL program, especially in communities where African American or students of African descent are represented. All too often, we hear the following, "We celebrate all cultures all year long." We must ask ourselves honestly, "Is this accurate?" Deceiving ourselves by suggesting we do it all year long actually promotes a watered-down curriculum that never ends up celebrating any culture in any significant way. In listening to the African American students in my dissertation study, their perspective was, 'everything all year long is celebrating Latino culture.' It was unmistakable that they were thirsting for some identification with their own culture. One teacher at the school where I did my research had an 'aha' moment when she realized that in the effort to celebrate and raise the status of Latinos they could potentially isolate other cultures, such as African Americans. It was clear that culturally relevant pedagogy specific to cultures in the classroom (not just for the DL partner language and corresponding partner-language culture) was a non-negotiable for the students. Also, visual and performing arts like drama and African dance and/or drumming through which students could freely express their culture were identified as contributing very positively to the experiences of this group of African American students in a DL program.

Unfortunately, by and large, programs around the U.S. are not capitalizing very much on the rich potential for dialogue and discussion that Afro-Latino history and Afro-Latino Spanish speakers afford. In another professional context, I led the DL teachers at our school site (where the student population was almost entirely African American) in a dialogue and discussion about what kind of response we as a staff should have for a parent who said her African American child didn't have family or close family friends who looked like him and spoke Spanish. We discussed ways in which we could make sure that our African American students might see themselves represented among Spanish speakers by doing a project on famous Afro Latinos. Here's an example of a teacher who decided to take a stand with her first graders. The students found information on Afro Latinos, such as Graciela Dixon, Supreme Court justice in Panama. They wrote a short report and presented in class.

How much more in depth could discussions and dialogues be around the rich Afro Latino intellectual, linguistic, and cultural histories at the secondary level! What better way to unite communities than to discuss their common background.

Beyond language into changed communities. One very important aspect of achieving equity is not often discussed in our DL circles, but it is what I would consider the "Holy Grail" of DL programs. It's deep and complex, not for the faint of heart, and relevant only to programs where equity is a priority, not a product of lip service. We must move beyond competency in the language simply for the purpose of a better job. There's no mistaking that there should be some monetary benefit if a student has studied for so many years. However, if we don't move beyond this, we will fall short of what our programs were truly intended to sow into the next generation. We must have as an overall goal in our DL programs (starting at kindergarten) to promote learning language and cross-cultural skills for the purpose of developing agency, civic responsibility, and community transformation. The whole point of equity is not to just have it in our schools, but to duplicate it in society. The only way this can happen is if this generation of students values it to the degree that they will assume this leadership responsibility. The will happen only when it's a priority in our DL expansion planning and curriculum from the get-go. How can we ensure that this takes place?

In secondary DL, this would mean moving beyond simply preparing for the Advanced Placement exam to deeper engagement with students and communities. The minimal expectation of a secondary DL program should be facilitating deep dialogues among staff members, within classrooms, among parents and the overall language communities, and then providing opportunities to put language and cross-cultural competency skills into action in meaningful contexts. We must begin with learning to understand one another's cultural perspectives at a basic level without making assumptions.

Some DL programs around the country seek to offer practical opportunities that emerge from bilingual skills—for example, medical translation. This is a worthy goal, but we would be remiss if we did not require the deep dialogue around societal inequities in health care and a student's role in transforming his/her own environment. Unless we engage in these dialogues, the medical translation program becomes another résumé builder to get families interested in the program or to get a great job. What does it take for a community to be transformed? The way secondary DL programs are framed and implemented is critical if what we want are not just producers/consumers of the language but global citizens committed to serving their community and making the world a more just place to live.

Getting race on the table. Our high school classrooms reported that discussions related to race, equity, and identity were extremely motivating and students were fully engaged. So if this engages students, and we know it's essential to create an environment of equity, how do we go about promoting this kind of dialogue? It's not surprising that our students talk about race, identity, and language all the time. How comfortable are we in participating in, leading, or promoting discussions about race and identity? If we as adults resist this charge, we are denying students the very thing that has potential to transform relationships in our communities. But there is a way to do it effectively and in a manner in which all parties feel safe. Practically speaking, what might this look like? Glen Singleton's work around "getting race on the table" is a good reference for safe facilitation (Singleton & Lifton, 2012). Done well, structured opportunities for conversations about race facilitate individual transformation, build cross-cultural communication, foster understanding, and require a response to inequities that emerge in the course of the conversations.

According to Singleton's perspective, to create a safe place for difficult discussions when it comes to structured conversations about race, four agreements of what he calls "Courageous Conversation" must be in place: *1) Stay engaged, 2) Speak your truth, 3) Experience discomfort, and 4) Expect and accept non-closure.* Having participated in these well-facilitated types of conversations and professional development sessions at the school and district levels with multicultural and multilingual colleagues, we grew significantly in our ability to listen to one another, to appreciate each other's perspectives, to gather data on "focus" students, to build awareness, to take action, and to be motivated to continue the dialogue for the good of our students, their families, and our community.

Racial identity development. As a goal of these important conversations, identity development and racial-identity development must be a priority of the program for ALL DL students and for discussions around race. Identity discussions inherently involve race, despite the discomfort these conversations may cause the adults leading them, and sometimes even the students engaged in the discussions. We must create the proper forum in order for all parties to feel safe. How does this apply to White families? In every way! In fact, White racial-identity development is a fruitful and necessary component of awareness if our multicultural communities are truly going to be transformed into peaceful communities. As an overall DL community, it's a daily struggle to figure out how to encourage White students and their families to understand the perspectives of students of color and English learners, and balance the demands and perspectives of the White community with those of our partner-language communities. But I believe that in doing this, we are treating the symptoms as opposed to really going to the source of the issue. Just as there is a plan to empower every student of color and English learner, there must also be a plan to develop identity in every White participant in the DL community.

Howard (2016) highlights the importance of White racial-identity development in his book *We Can't Teach What We Don't Know.* One of his main points is that we must, as professionals, be willing to become aware of the different identity orientations in order to support ourselves and our students to move along the continuum towards a transformation mindset. He posits that "Whites need to acknowledge and work through the negative historical implications of 'whiteness' and create for ourselves a transformed identity as White people committed to equality and social change. Our goal is neither to deify nor denigrate whiteness, but to diffuse its destructive power" (p. 17).

Regardless of race/ethnicity, the takeaway is that there are different points along the continuum, and our students, teachers, and families will be at different places. The goal is to become self-aware and to continue moving as individuals in order that together we can create a synergy of transformation in our own mindsets. However, in all cases, this work is arduous and requires long-term commitment, skilled facilitation of dialogues (which first take place among staff), and a passion to incorporate racial-identity development into the curriculum at all personal cost. Nonetheless, this work is life changing, especially because it will drive conversations at the classroom level with students, and in so doing become part of the program's DNA. This is what we need to create truly transformational DL programs.

Concluding Thoughts

Throughout this chapter, I've discussed the lessons learned around implementation of dual language programs in the multiple contexts I've been blessed to be a part of. In each of the examples, the overarching theme to improve our programs has to do with clear communication, which builds bridges among individuals, groups, and communities. Listening to stakeholders in my opinion is the single most important high-leverage strategy, whether it is listening to students, parents, teachers, administrators, board members, or others. In addition, making equity a priority by 1) ensuring we are creating equitable opportunities for all students leading up to secondary; 2) ensuring that in the secondary DL classroom we are being equitable through culturally relevant pedagogy; 3) reaching our fullest potential through a commitment to racial-identity development for staff, students, and their families and related discussions; and 4) as a by-product of these discussions, reaching out to others in student spheres of influence (e.g., medical-translation settings, etc.) in culturally sensitive ways to make our communities a better place. Hopefully, application of these takeaways will assist you in the implementation of a program which builds bridges, not walls, and takes bold steps to go beyond what few other programs have been able to accomplish—true equity and social justice.

PART III

Graduates Speak, Teacher Preparation, and a National View

Chapter Fourteen
Secondary Dual Language Graduates Speak Up: Experiences, Impact, and Advice

Elizet Moret, Texas Education Agency, and Irán Tovar, Dual Language Consultant

Introduction by Collier and Thomas: *When it's time to evaluate how well a dual language program is working, dual language student graduates have powerful tales to tell. The authors describe how to best collect and use dual language graduates' feedback for purposes of program improvement. In addition, they share rich information from interviews with students who have attended K-12 dual language programs and are now young adults using their bilingualism in their continuing studies and in their personal and professional lives. The interviews focus on these graduates' experience in dual language classes and their recommendations for program improvements for dual language educators and current students. These dual language graduates also share specifics about the very positive impact that the dual language program has had on their lives.*

Dual language research has consistently shown that programs across the nation have positively impacted students' academic performance. We often hear students' stories from the perspective of teachers and administrators, but we have yet to explore the first-hand experiences of students who go through such programs to hear how their participation has impacted both their personal and professional worlds after high-school graduation. In an effort to learn more about the effects that dual language (DL) programs have on students, we reached out to colleagues to locate and interview representative young-adult graduates of DL education programs to share their experiences as participants of such programs. This is a pilot study, designed to develop appropriate and meaningful questions of DL graduates and to field-test data collection and analysis procedures. We recommend strongly that each DL high school program set up procedures to follow its graduates and interview or survey them at least a year after graduation so that they will have had sufficient time to reflect on their high school experience.

We decided to center our questions around what would be most relevant for readers who are working to establish or fortify their DL programs. The questions are meant to provide insight and guidance in learning more about the benefits and needs of programs, as determined by student participants. Our purpose for these interviews is to provide an understanding of DL graduates' perspectives and to make their voices heard as they share their experiences and advice with current administrators of DL programs.

We developed a list of questions that we presented to the participants and asked them to answer and elaborate on each. We then compiled the answers to provide a synopsis of their experiences. As we analyzed their responses, other questions emerged that needed answers. Strong DL secondary programs will impact the academic, social, and language-learning opportunities of our students and accompany them on their personal and professional journeys for years afterwards. These young adults can help us design secondary DL programs to be more responsive to students' needs and to enhance long-term benefits.

The format chosen to present the information in this chapter is to provide the question followed by a synopsis of answers, as well as several quotes from the students. We hope to have done justice to the depth and complexity of information that was gathered. All participants were very enthusiastic about the possibility of providing insightful contributions to future program implementation as a result of this chapter. We are forever grateful to each and every one of the student graduates for taking the time and giving thoughtful dedication to their responses. The student graduates we interviewed attended DL classes throughout all years of schooling, Grades K-12, in Texas, Oregon, and North Carolina.

1. Thinking about your secondary experience (middle & high school), as a participant in a dual language education program, what was most enjoyable?

The graduates we interviewed had one common enjoyable experience—they all felt that they had each gained a new "family" thanks to their participation in their school/district DL education program with their DL peers and teachers. They enjoyed growing not only academically with their new "family," but also with all of the other students' families who participated in their DL program. One of the students shared that the DL students in his middle school created an organization focused on Spanish language and culture with the help of one of their DL teachers for the sole purpose of continued growth and support within their DL community. The student organization transitioned to high school along with the DL students and this had a great impact on students' academics, while also providing a vehicle for maintaining communication with their "academic family" across the two high schools housing the DL program. The DL teachers and administrative staff also saw the students "... as part of a larger family ... and enriched the bridges between the academic space and the home."

Another DL graduate commented on how much she enjoyed the commitment everyone had to their DL program, which made everyone feel welcome and gave them a sense of belonging to something exceptional in their community. She shared that parents of student participants became involved in their learning and how this helped many of the students, particularly those who were first-generation students graduating from high school. This particular student shared that one of the most enjoyable moments for her was graduation day, as she realized that no one had dropped out of the program; they had accomplished their goal together. "We were all there," she proudly stated, referring to her peers in the DL program.

Some DL graduates spoke with excitement regarding their studies of different cultural contexts and learning through authentic literature and history. They enjoyed listening to stories from every student, as each of them, depending on their upbringing and background, would look at things through a different lens or understand history differently due to the stories shared by their parents and grandparents. Some of the graduates pointed out the great impact that school trips to a Spanish-speaking country had on them, as they were able to apply their learning and engage with cultural and historical knowledge building through talking with locals and practicing "real-life" experiences outside of the classroom." One student explained that "Learning a language does not mean much without understanding its history and the people."

2. What core curricular courses did you take in the partner language in middle and high school?

We compiled the courses that students took in middle and high school into the following figure to provide a breakdown by level of course offerings with Spanish as an example of the partner language. We discovered that participants had different options according to their district's program selection of courses and thus the participant experiences varied greatly by program.

Figure 14.1
Dual Language Courses Taught in Spanish Taken by Graduates

Middle School	**High School**
• Spanish 1 • Spanish 2 • Introductory level Spanish 3 • Texas History • United States History • World History • Math • Physical Education • Theater • Dance	• Spanish for Native Speakers 1-4 • Spanish 3 • AP Spanish 5: Language and Culture • AP Spanish 6: Literature • Spanish 7 • Science • Math • Geometry 1 • Geometry 2

Note: Spanish courses and levels vary, depending on how these are structured by districts across the country. Levels represented in this figure were kept as part of the answers provided by students, but higher levels were specific to Advance Placement courses and beyond.

3. Did the dual language program at your district provide other activities (after-school, extracurricular, clubs, etc.) that promoted the dual language program and exposed students to the cultural aspects of the program?

The graduates' responses indicated that more extracurricular activities are needed for the integration and interaction of DL students. The bullet points that follow summarize the information provided by the students interviewed, but it is clear that a greater integration of DL students in extracurricular activities is needed, and the development of specific areas of interest for students must be adequately considered, based on cultural interactions, language development, and social and academic needs.

- The Pan American Student Forum integrated DL students and newcomers. The organization was first created in middle school, but was later extended to the high school level so students could continue to meet together and share common goals.

- School and parent communities hosted German and Chinese festivals/carnivals, through which they would showcase language, culture, and traditions through dances, poetry presentations, and singing.

- Two students from two different states mentioned the creation of dance teams that focused on learning traditional Latino dances so they had the opportunity to learn more about cultures and traditions from Latin America and Spain by being part of these groups.

- Language clubs were also mentioned by some of the students. Graduates shared the important roles these clubs played in their academic language growth, as they focused on more activities in the partner language that went beyond the classroom walls.

- The creation of a sports program, which allowed for district-level interaction of all DL student participants.

- Two school bands with many DL student participants shared a band teacher which facilitated more interaction across the two schools.

4. What advice would you give students who are considering continuing their dual language program participation at middle and high school?

Trust the program. All students interviewed encouraged DL students to "trust the program." Students shared that at times they felt pressured, frustrated, and scared, thinking that they would not be able to perform academically as expected, since they felt the rigor of language and academic content greatly increased at the secondary level. One student was concerned that his math course in Spanish would be measured by a state-required assessment in English. "This seemed crazy at the time and I was furious to know that our expectations were not just to pass, but to excel. At the end of the day, I missed one question in the exit level TAKS (Texas Assessment of Knowledge and Skills)." He added, "Whenever the teachers and administrators tell you that you have the potential to do something that you do not see yourself doing, trust them and keep doing what you are doing. You will be surprised with the end results!"

Reasons for continuing in DL. Several graduates stressed the importance of continuing in a DL program at the secondary level to learn more about other cultures, embracing both the similarities and the differences. Students agreed that "participating in a DL program opens your eyes to a world out there and opens the doors to many possibilities in your life and future careers." Additionally, graduates shared that when taking courses in the partner language in high school, they had the opportunity to gain college credits. Graduates who were non-native speakers of the partner language advised students that continuing in the DL program provided them the opportunity for constant use of the language, as it is only in practice and communication that one is able to keep the language active and proficient. "It's a gift to be able to speak more than one language and keeping up with the language is much easier than relearning it later in life."

5. What advice would you give to administrators of dual language programs when considering the development of such programs at middle and high school?

Stay true to the program and be flexible. Two main topics emerged from summarizing graduates' responses in regard to their advice for administrators. While they recognized the difficulties that exist for administrators and districts in developing an effective DL program, they emphasized the importance for administrators to stay true to the program and to be flexible when needed. An example provided by one of the students was in regard to scheduling courses. She and her peers needed a course to be offered in the afternoon instead of in the morning due to constraints with other courses, but the response to this request was, "It's been done this way for so long." This response was not taken well by the DL students. They emphasized the need for educators to be a lot more flexible and more willing to adapt to changes. They want to remind administrators that they themselves have had to be flexible to adapt to a program in which they learn in two languages.

Hire native-speaking DL teachers. Graduates also shared the importance of hiring native-speaking teachers of the partner language. "They have an authentic accent and, more importantly, cultural experiences to share …. I got to hear various accents, learn different colloquial/regional expressions, and learn of life in those countries. This type of information is irreplaceable."

Respect regional varieties of the partner language. At the same time, several graduates stressed the need to have teachers who are open minded in regard to regional varieties of the partner language and uses of code switching. An example provided by some students was that of the hiring of teachers from Spain. While they loved the opportunity to learn and interact with them, some teachers made them feel as if their Spanish was not good enough because it was not the Spanish spoken in Spain. The teachers constantly corrected their border-town Spanish, when in essence the differences had more to do with the cultural ways the language was being utilized. One graduate explained, "Not only is there a history of power among people from Spain and those of us from Latin America through colonization, but there is also a discrepancy between authenticity of the language which creates tense learning environments." Graduates who were native speakers of the partner language advised that teachers who come from other Spanish-speaking countries be given professional development opportunities in regard to the culture of their new environment and community. At the same time, students interviewed felt that bringing teachers from other Spanish-speaking countries added rich cultural knowledge as teachers would share their stories with them and they could learn how traditions and culture played a different role in every Spanish-speaking country.

Offer rigorous DL content courses in a wide range of subjects. Lastly, graduates shared the importance of developing courses with highly proficient, rigorous uses of the partner language.

Differentiation should still be done at the secondary level, as every student learns at a different pace and level, but a wide range of DL courses should be offered. While the courses should continue to advance students in the partner language, some felt that too much emphasis was put on grammar. This reduced opportunities to truly learn more about cultural patterns and the different uses of the partner language, including in personal and professional contexts.

6. Were there any classes/courses you had to give up in middle and/or high school to continue in the dual language program?

Flexibility for electives and core DL classes. The majority of the students denied having to give up any courses. Their program had been developed in a way that either embraced multiple-language requirements or the schedule for students in the DL program was put together to avoid those issues. On the other hand, a few students had to give up electives in order to maintain their courses in the DL program. Choosing between dual-credit classes, Pre-AP, or DL classes was also an issue for other students; while all three choices were of benefit to them, they were only able to choose one. One graduate summarized, "I recommend flexibility of electives and core classes. I was into sports, so I knew I could only choose one elective. Make sure that DL students have options beyond just one elective in their schedules."

7. What courses would you like for an administrator/school district to consider for dual language program participants?

Graduates offered an array of suggestions for possible courses to be made available for students in DL programs. A common thread was to incorporate courses that focused on the cultural aspects of the partner language. The importance of understanding the context and history of a language was essential for many of them. "My favorite Spanish classes weren't the ones where I was solely learning verbs, vocabulary, or grammar. They were the ones where we learned about the history, art, and architecture of Spain and the current social issues facing Latin America," expressed one participant. For districts in or near border towns on the U.S.-Mexico border, participants suggested identity courses such as Latino studies or Mexican American studies that go beyond literature and dig deeper into cross-cultural life experiences. There was also interest in core classes in the partner language to promote command of that language across content areas and diverse contexts. Keeping up with the market and offering business, business computer-information systems, or global-business courses was another suggestion.

8. What do you think administrators can do to further assist dual language teachers in supporting the academic success of dual language students?

Professional development in DL for all administrators. Graduates shared several ideas for administrators to assist DL teachers in supporting the academic success of their students. The consistent message was for administrators to become knowledgeable about DL programs. There was a shared acknowledgment that not all administrators could be or become bilingual, however, it is essential that they be well-informed about the research and best practices in DL education. Along with this, it is important for administrators to "keep up" with requirements that prepare students for the 21st century, thus making sure that ample up-to-date and rigorous classes are created as part of the DL strand. This would create choices for students in the program instead of having to "give up" a desired class because it is not part of the DL program. In addition to the standard curriculum, these

DL graduates suggested that school districts provide teachers with some funding to buy books and films that have cross-cultural value for their courses.

Professional development in DL for all secondary teachers. Another way to assist DL educators was to provide targeted professional development for educators, focusing on topics that are relevant to the needs of the DL students they serve. One student commented,

> "I think that it is essential that every teacher attend training sessions about the identities of the students. As José Martí (1891) mentions in his famous essay Nuestra América, we cannot govern a people that we do not know. Thus we cannot educate students that we do not know."

The student then pressed on to the importance of providing teacher professional development that addressed issues ranging from ethnicity, class, gender, sexuality, weight, and other factors that contribute to the makeup of the students in the program. All these are viable means to support teachers as they develop a deeper understanding of their students, and in turn helps strengthen the cultural competency of the DL program.

9. What specific experiences during your participation in the dual language program at the secondary level made the biggest impact on your life?

Bonds with speakers of the partner language and with family. The experiences that graduates described varied greatly but were positive overall and personally rewarding. Student-teacher relationships were formed and for many still remain strong. Some of the experiences that had the most impact were the opportunities to communicate with native speakers in the partner language at different stages in their lives. Some participants credited the program for helping them establish a rich cultural connection with their immediate families claiming that they felt closer to their roots as they embraced their language and culture at school. "It has always kept me grounded, for I am always taken back to my family and my community."

International travel, scholarships, and employment opportunities. Several of the graduates experienced immersion into the cultures of their program's partner language as they traveled as part of their program to countries where the language was spoken. One student shared that "The greatest compliment of my life came when one of the staff members at our hotel asked what part of Spain we were from because of the quality of our accents and our Spanish!" Exposure to other cultures and being able to take part in exchange programs as well as becoming candidates for scholarships and employment opportunities overseas became a reality for some. Appreciation and understanding of other cultures was a sentiment shared by DL graduates who had entered the program as non-native speakers of the partner language.

10. How has your participation in the dual language program impacted your professional career?

Using their bilingualism in professional contexts. Some of the graduates we interviewed were enrolled in college while others were in professional roles, all utilizing their second language as part of their professions. The sentiment towards their second language came through as gratitude for the opportunity to acquire and/or fortify a second language as part of their educational programs. All students credit their participation in their district's DL program as being an influential component of their current and future achievements. Employment opportunities, as well as college and university choices, broadened as a result.

A student proudly shared, "I will be moving to Munich, Germany, to work for one of the world's leading orthopedic engineering companies. I would never have had this opportunity had I not learned German!" Another, now a bilingual teacher, stated —*Ahora soy maestra bilingüe enseñando en español, de hecho, yo quería ser maestra de alemán*— "I am now a bilingual teacher teaching Spanish; however, I wanted to be a German teacher." explaining that she was trilingual and through the DL program she not only strengthened her native Spanish, but also acquired both German and English. —*Estoy aquí tratando de dar la misma calidad de educación a mis alumnos que me dieron a mí cuando yo fui alumna en el programa dual.*—"I'm here trying to provide the same quality of education for my students given to me when I was a DL student."

11. In reflecting upon your overall experience, how has your participation in the dual language program made an impact on your life?

The DL program inevitably left an empowering mark on all of the participants. Everyone shared positive experiences and the opportunities they have had as a result of their participation in a DL program. As they reminisced on their younger selves and the fears and challenges they faced as they acquired a second or third language, their collective feedback indicated that everything was worth the end results. We feel it is appropriate to share some of the many comments to represent the voices that have spoken throughout this chapter.

"The DL program implanted this seed that came to blossom in college and through it I found a voice that was not only appreciated in English, but also in Spanish." (This student is now pursuing his Ph.D.)

"The DL program has impacted my professional career in helping me gain opportunities I would not have had if it weren't for being bilingual. I saved time and money in college by having most of my credits fulfilled for my language, which is now my minor."

"I traveled with a mission group, acting as their interpreter, giving me a unique experience not only of the Cuban culture but also in getting to have a real, practical use of the skills and abilities that were taught to me in the DL program."

"Although it was scary and uncomfortable at first, it was an incredible learning experience, in the language itself and in the associated culture. I fell in love with the Latin culture and still actively use Spanish, perform in a Latin dance group on campus, and plan on studying abroad for a semester in Spain."

"The DL program has allowed for me to be placed in a high-level Spanish course, allowing for my minor in Spanish to be much easier and quicker to complete."

"It has changed my life completely. I feel as if Germany is a second home and the language comes very naturally to me."

"*Nada más,* believe in the program, embrace the program, do it right and students will succeed. Both my kids speak English and Spanish, but at home they speak to me in Spanish. Make sure that the language does not get lost within generations. Stay true, be bilingual, trilingual, multilingual; it is important to the future of our kids. It's important for them to not only speak both languages but also to be truly biliterate."

Closing

All of the graduates we interviewed were delighted to share the impact that their DL program had on them and their professions, as well as the advantages in their university-level studies. By sharing their stories we were able to get a closer look at how students in DL programs view such programs and the long-term effects and contributions to their lives as adults. We hope that the information reported in this chapter will be of benefit to future programs. The graduates' rich experiences have brought up questions that will encourage further and deeper analyses of students in DL programs and how these programs have impacted them as adults. There is so much more information that we were not able to capture since we wanted to keep our focus on supporting up-and-coming secondary DL programs. We feel we barely scraped the surface of the content, knowledge, and cultural aspects that DL programs provide for students. We hope that this study will inspire future research that can be shared through the lens of the students.

Chapter Fifteen
Transforming Secondary Dual Language Teacher Preparation

Dr. Joan R. Lachance—
University of North Carolina at Charlotte

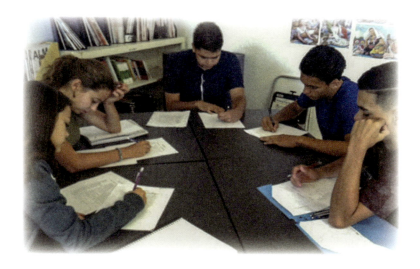

Introduction by Collier and Thomas: *Our next steps in expanding dual language programs at secondary level must be closely coordinated with the universities that serve the surrounding communities of each school district. Dual language teachers and administrators are in great demand. In this chapter, Dr. Joan Lachance challenges the field to expand secondary teacher preparation with specialized coursework that prepares dual language teachers to teach effectively and serve students with many diverse needs. Dual language pedagogy must include biliteracy development, rigorous multilingual/multicultural coursework, use of meaningful dual language materials across the subject areas, and authentic assessment.*

The National Dual Language Teacher Shortage

While research confirms that dual language programs strongly support academic growth for all students, the U.S. faces a national dilemma regarding the availability of qualified teachers who are prepared for the unique requirements of dual language teaching (Center for Applied Linguistics, 2012, 2017; Lachance, 2017a; Thomas & Collier, 2012). Numerous states across the U.S., including North Carolina, aim to expand dual language (DL) programs and simply cannot find enough DL teachers from their local areas, regions, or nationwide (U.S. Department of Education, 2015). DL teacher shortages often result in states continually being forced to use alternative licensure options (Center for Applied Linguistics, 2017). Therefore, state education agencies look to other countries to fill DL teacher vacancies as best they can (Associated Press, 2008; DeFour, 2012; Modern Language Association of America, 2007; Rhodes & Pufahl, 2009; Wilson, 2011). While there are cultural and linguistic benefits to having native-speaking teachers in U.S. DL classrooms, there are also noted challenges associated with this dependence on temporary international faculty (Hutchison, 2005; Kissau, Yon, & Algozzine, 2011).

In some cases, international teachers do not adapt to their post in the U.S., resulting in reduced classroom effectiveness, which in turn causes declined program enrollment or program elimination (Haley & Ferro, 2011). School, district, and state-level DL program administrators, while invested in supporting program expansion, are challenged with using additional human resources and limited time to provide professional development for visiting DL teachers. These same stakeholders are frequently dismayed when visiting teachers they have supported return to their countries earlier than planned due to maladjustment (Collier & Thomas, 2014). DL school administrators continue to search with desperation to find bilingual teachers who can deliver states' content standards in a language other than English with academic and pedagogical alignment and with full academic and cognitive rigor (Lachance, 2017b).

As U.S. schools produce increasing numbers of graduates of K-12 DL programs, this bilingual teacher shortage will diminish. School districts with long-term DL programs are now hiring their own DL graduates. Some school districts are creating DL program structures at high school level for students to enroll in dual-credit coursework for preparing teachers, with incentives to be hired in their local school district when they complete DL teacher preparation programs at the university (see Chapter 4).

The Unique Nature of Dual Language Academic Development in Secondary School

Central elements in language education include the notion that language learning with higher order cognition is developed through student-to-student interaction (Vygotsky, 1978; Walqui & van Lier, 2010; Zwiers & Crawford, 2011). Students' successful use of collaboration and collective learning in varying contexts is considered fundamental for cognitive, metacognitive, and metalinguistic advancement (Beeman & Urow, 2013; Cummins, 1991; Molle, Sato, Boals, & Hedgspeth, 2015). More so, middle and high school students' learning and language development requires specialized scaffolding (extra support to understand the meaning), which should include significant peer interaction with teacher-structured attention to language functions (Gibbons, 2015; World-class Instructional Design & Assessment, 2012). In content-based DL instruction with middle and high school students, collaboration and dynamic activities within students' zones of proximal development (the next steps that students are ready to take in their learning process; Vygotsky, 1978) are substantial key points to support increased language demands associated with rigorous secondary school classrooms, high-stakes testing, and states' graduations requirements. Based on human-development research, adolescents and young adults are entirely and highly capable of complex analytic thinking. However, they need specialized support to process and accommodate peers' cultural and linguistic needs for successful academic learning through two languages in secondary school (Calderón, 2007; Lindholm-Leary, 2012).

In conjunction with the need for specialized scaffolding for secondary DL learning, van Lier (2004) maintains that students' self-concept greatly impacts learning and thinking processes. Adolescents and young adults see themselves in a certain way, forming an *internal* sense of self. Students also consider the *external* sense of self, simultaneously giving merit to others' opinions of how they are viewed and accepted (Ryan & Shim, 2008). Long-standing research supports the point that adolescents' notions of self, both internal and external, are intensified as adolescent and young adult learners pass through this momentous period in human development (Purkey, 1970; Vars, 1969). Uniquely, secondary school learners are also advantaged with having amplified imagination and higher levels of abstract thinking (Joseph, 2010; Manning & Bucher, 2012). For DL learning, secondary students' intellectual development and broad spectrum of thinking serves to fundamentally support biliteracy development in changed ways from elementary school settings (Grosjean & Li, 2013; Molle, Sato, Boals, & Hedgspeth, 2015). With this in mind, the continuation of DL programs from elementary to secondary school settings is crucial for metalinguistics and academic language development. Additionally, secondary school DL teachers can tap into their students' abstract, intellectual strengths to solidify students' collaboration. Teachers' use of such unique cognitive-developmental features further supports the higher demands of academic language development in secondary school (Cummins, 2014; Manning & Bucher, 2012).

Recommendations from Dual Language Educators in North Carolina and New Mexico

Given the research-based conclusions that DL education supports all students' learning, along with the national shortage of DL teachers, I chose to conduct a 3-year qualitative study to gain insights regarding teacher preparation from current DL educators' perspectives, K-12. In this study, I interviewed 34 DL educators from North Carolina and New Mexico to identify beneficial and unique teaching strategies in DL teaching, so that the findings of the study might inform the coursework needed in U.S. teacher education programs. This study, along with my experience in higher education with DL teacher preparation, informs my recommendations in this chapter for secondary DL teacher preparation programs.

The study was situated in the southeastern state of North Carolina and the southwestern state of New Mexico. North Carolina DL programs are expanding based on a formal policy of the North Carolina State Board of Education (2013). New Mexico was selected for the study because DL programs have been in place there for several decades. Both states also have some form of bilingual endorsement or seal for high school graduates (New Mexico Public Education Department, 2016a, 2016b; North Carolina Department of Public Instruction, 2017; U.S. Department of Education, 2015). The study's 34 teacher and administrator participants worked in DL programs with English- and Spanish-speaking students. While other partner languages were available in North Carolina's DL programs, this study focused on language-minority and language-majority students in Spanish/English program settings. Both interview data and classroom observation data were collected and analyzed. (See the Appendix at the end of this chapter for a short summary about the study participants, interviews, classroom observation, and data analyses, and see Lachance, 2017c, for details of the methodology of the study.)

Study participants expressed detailed examples of their educational backgrounds, prior teaching experiences, and the individual pathways that led them to be in DL education. While there was variation within participants' years of experience, location of post-secondary education and degrees, and current roles in DL programs, they all provided invaluable insight regarding the uniqueness of DL teaching and learning. More to the point, they provided very specific details for teacher preparation programs aligned with the study's goals and three research questions. These are: (1) What do you as DL educators conceptualize and identify as beneficial and unique in DL teaching and learning? (2) How were your conceptualizations developed during pre-service education program coursework? And, (3) What recommendations do you make to educator preparation programs/professional development programs to address the explicit needs of DL education? These experienced DL educators' recommendations are incorporated into the guidelines for secondary DL teacher preparation in this chapter.

The following sections, Core Themes One and Two, will explain concepts for preparing secondary DL teachers, while keeping our students at the heart and center of recommended pathways for teaching. Sociocultural theory is embedded throughout each individual topic (Vygotsky, 1978). DL teachers must be entirely committed to the fact that students' relationships with each other and with their teachers have a direct impact on the learning processes (Collier & Thomas, 2007). Likewise, while the topics are presented in linear fashion, it should be noted that they are all vastly interconnected. The last section of this chapter provides a suggested list of specialized coursework for secondary DL teachers.

Core Theme One: Preparing Teachers to Transform DL Classrooms

The following topics are categorized as areas that DL teachers will experience in the field. Above and beyond teachers' managing of daily routines and standard curricular procedures, DL teachers require specialized training unique to DL in order to fully demonstrate pedagogical and content-specific DL competencies.

Dual language pedagogy. For decades, researchers in various aspects of scholarship related to best practices with English learners, emergent bilinguals, and other language learning student populations have focused on the importance of specialized pedagogies for increased language acquisition. Frameworks such as Guided Language Acquisition Design (Project GLAD®) and the Sheltered Instruction Observation Protocol (SIOP®) model focus on peer-to-peer interaction and multidimensional pedagogies that facilitate students' use and application of new language in the context of school (de Jong & Bearse, 2014; Echevarría, Vogt, & Short, 2016; Orange County Department of Education, 2018). In the case of DL classes, these elements of student-centered interaction and strategic connections to content-based concepts in meaningful ways are literally doubled, given that students are acquiring two languages in oral and written form. DL teachers' considerations of students' communicative patterns related to meaning and content are essential while designing collaborative classroom activities (Collier & Thomas, 2007). Other specialized pedagogies include DL strategies for oral language development to support increased content-based writing skills across all subjects of the curriculum (Walqui & van Lier, 2010; Zwiers & Crawford, 2011).

An additional aspect of DL pedagogy includes national standards that serve as guiding principles for states' content and language development standards. In teacher preparation, institutions of higher education are required to demonstrate that teacher candidates are learning and later demonstrating pedagogical competencies that align with the content they will be licensed to teach.

One critical missing component in this mixture is the absence of national DL teacher preparation standards, which is addressed in detail at the conclusion of this chapter. Therefore, teacher preparation courses must focus on how said pedagogies are unique in DL settings, with special attention given to the interaction between content and language in DL classroom experiences and to the many varying needs of students attending DL classes.

Biliteracy development. The topic of biliteracy development also merits specialized attention in DL teacher preparation courses. In fact, it could be argued that this topic is so significant and multidimensional, it is worthy of an entire course even while it is simultaneously conceptually embedded in other coursework. K-12 DL teachers need to be ready for many variations in students' backgrounds with regard to prior learning patterns connected to literacy. In secondary classes some DL learners may have entered the DL program with some literacy basics in one language, others in two languages, and still others may have no foundational aspects of literacy in any language. Therefore, DL teachers must be prepared to support literacy development in two languages with all types of students (Flores, Sheets, & Clark, 2011; Guerrero, 1997).

At the secondary level, these different literacy levels may be greatly challenging to address, given the nature of high academic levels of each content area and the smaller number of years left to complete high school graduation requirements. Literacy development across the academic subject areas of science, social studies, mathematics, art, music, and physical education, as well as electives, require unique approaches to teaching (Collier & Thomas, 2014; Escamilla et al., 2013; Thomas & Collier, 2012).

Research confirms there is a robust, binding relationship between a reader and the text materials with which the learner is interacting (Bunch, Walqui, & Pearson, 2014). Therefore, DL teachers need to understand their students' cultural and linguistic backgrounds as well as varied linguistic repertoires and tap the resources and knowledge that the students bring to the classroom. This allows teachers to gain insights into the students' development of cross-disciplinary literacies in two languages. Figure 15.1 provides an example of aspects of content concepts, language materials, and contextual factors such as program location that shape student comprehension.

Figure 15.1.
Curricular support in a middle school science classroom

Multilingualism and rigor. Principles of metalinguistics and metacognition, as well as brain development, indicate the importance of rigor for all the DL content classes, including when taught through students' second language (Zadina, 2014). In order for students to master difficult and challenging content-based concepts, they must be taught through specialized DL pedagogies and highly individualized scaffolding (Gibbons, 2015), while being given ample opportunities for high levels of language use in the classroom. With states' graduation requirements and increased rigor within the high stakes testing processes, DL teachers will need to be amply prepared in their subject areas and be ready to provide many support systems for the rigorous concepts and text materials of each subject.

Authentic dual language materials. DL teachers need a wide range of academic text materials to support students' constructions of meaning (Calderón, Slavin, & Sánchez, 2011). Text materials combined with specialized pedagogical skills are necessary to facilitate students' comprehension and rich application of two languages while also attending to students' increasing proficiency in both academic languages (DeFour, 2012; Lindholm-Leary, 2012). DL teachers must recognize how sociocultural elements embedded in text materials and learning tasks influence DL learners' successful literacy development (Escamilla et al., 2013). These specialized skills are related to students' identities, level of reading comprehension, textual challenges, academic language development, and sociocultural communicative domains of secondary school language (Echevarría, Vogt, & Short, 2016; Walqui & van Lier, 2010; Zwiers & Crawford, 2011).

In addition to understanding the relationship between the reader and the text materials, DL teachers will need preparation to address the shortage of authentic DL materials in the field. Translating or modifying colossal quantities of existing texts and materials is no longer the only strategy (Bunch et al., 2014). Often times DL teachers will encounter schools and districts that approach DL resources by adapting monolingual curricular materials. In other words, districts may purchase a text book series that was originally written in English, and the translated versions of the text are exactly the same in the partner language, even though the curricular points to be made are quite different across the languages. Recent theory cautiously advises teachers to remember the deep, multifaceted relationship between the reader and the texts with which they are interacting. To choose authentic texts in the partner language, DL teachers will have to consider aspects including text features, the context of the reading materials, and the reading tasks themselves knowing they all greatly shape students' overall reading comprehension (Gottleib & Ernst-Slavit, 2014). In the case of DL learners with multilayered, dimensional language ranges (e.g. regional varieties, influence of socioeconomic status, first-generation or fifth-generation heritage speaker, and many other linguistic variations of experience with language use), literacy development is even more intensified when texts and materials are presented in highly contextual environments like those found in secondary-school classrooms (Molle et al., 2015). Therefore, pedagogical solutions to these complex learners' needs must honor varying linguistic ranges and adapt materials in authentic ways, and DL teachers must be prepared for the tasks at hand in working with diverse learners (Gibbons, 2015).

Authentic assessment. In K-12 classrooms, much attention has been given to high-stakes testing. Teachers, schools, and districts are often "graded" on effective education programs by examining students' standardized test results. However, there is also great emphasis placed on the mismatch between standardized testing and language learners (Herrera, Cabral & Murry, 2013). DL teachers must be prepared to discover a wide variety of ways to authentically capture what students know and what academic skills they can demonstrate in relation to content standards, academic language, and meeting graduation requirements. This is no easy task given the fact that states' high-stakes testing requirements will be superimposed on the assessment processes, often by measuring students' knowledge and skills with assessment tools designed for monolingual students (Gottleib &

Ernst-Slavit, 2014). Even when bilingual assessments of content are available, DL teachers will need dedicated preparation that supports the deconstruction of the assessment systems in their teaching environments, that understands layers of bias within whatever assessment tools are utilized, and that requires creative, potentially self-made options to compensate for assessment gaps in DL settings. Much like the topic of biliteracy, there should be an entire course dedicated to authentic assessment.

Core Theme Two: Transforming Dual Language Teacher Preparation

This next set of topics encompasses skill sets and areas of knowledge that should also be included in DL teacher preparation programs in university courses as well as in school districts' ongoing professional development. While they are not necessarily topics that manifest within the classroom context, each topic does in fact shape DL teachers' practice.

Teachers as ongoing learners. Language development is ever-changing and ongoing. Just as students are continuously expanding and deepening their language repertoires, so are DL teachers! It is crucial for DL teachers to always look for ways to enhance and strengthen their own language development in both languages. For some DL teachers, this may include things like traveling to other countries during summer breaks, with a specific language-learning goal attached to the traveling experiences. Other DL teachers may expand their language repertoires by intentionally reading advanced levels of literature or their subject specialty in their second language.

DL teachers may also need to prepare to teach at different grade-levels or schools. Even when teachers remain in one school and/or grade-level, they will certainly interact with DL learners with new needs on a regular basis. Therefore, it is always wise for teachers to "brush up" and stay current with subject-specific language that is associated with a current or new teaching assignment. DL teachers will also need to be prepared to evaluate new texts and materials for use in their classrooms.

Dual language program structures. The scope of DL programs across the United States is vast! Some states have a majority of their DL classrooms representing Spanish and English as partner languages. Other states have DL programs that include partner languages such as Arabic, Cherokee, French, German, Haitian Creole, Hindi, Japanese, Korean, Mandarin Chinese, Portuguese, Russian, Urdu, or Vietnamese. In addition to these linguistic variations there are also programmatic structural tenets that determine how much time and what portion of an instructional cycle is dedicated to instruction in English and which subject areas are taught in program partner languages. Many DL programs in the early elementary grades follow a 90:10, 80:20 or 50:50 division of instructional time in each language while secondary programs are organized by number of courses offered in each language. There may be variations for one-way and two-way DL programs. In each variation of the program structure options, DL teachers need to be prepared for the contexts in which they will work.

Likewise, they may also be asked by administrative teams and other district-level decision makers for recommendations on how to construct secondary feeder patterns for optimal K-12 articulation. This means middle school teachers must stay in touch with elementary and high school teachers, and vice versa. Eighth grade students often leap into graduation requirements in ninth grade, and many other connections across grade levels must be taken into account. Given that the majority of the current DL programs are at the elementary level (Center for Applied Linguistics, 2017) and that larger numbers of "accelerated" DL students will soon be coming to middle school, secondary DL teachers will need to develop new strategies with regard to vertical K-12 alignment.

Program evaluation and learner assessment. Parallel to the concepts associated with authentic assessment, DL teachers will need to demonstrate skills and competencies in DL program evaluations based on learners' outcomes. In order to be prepared to explain the advantages to parents and the school community, school and district administrators need teachers' insights as to how the secondary DL program benefits students. Immense pressures are associated with student levels of academic performance as a result of any given education program, but especially so with DL. To name a few, there are high school graduation requirements, biliteracy seal competencies, skill sets facilitating global readiness when entering the workforce, grade point averages for college admissions, and cost-effective educational solutions to closing the achievement gap. With all these in mind, DL teachers will need to demonstrate that they can collect, analyze, and articulate student outcomes to express short- and long-term academic and linguistic gains.

Historical/community factors. Another area of DL teacher preparation that is shaped by the broad scope of DL programs throughout the United States is that of historical and community factors (August & Hakuta, 1997). DL teachers will need to know how the school/program in which they work is situated in the community, including in-depth understandings of things like 1) community values associated with DL, 2) perceived benefits of DL for communities and families, 3) the history behind DL programs in the community, and 4) inclusive versus exclusive family/community member involvement in DL programs. Deep-seeded connections to culture, identity, language and power, systemic bias, and "white-washed" curricular patterns must be examined in DL teacher preparation courses. These are often quite sensitive in nature, yet must be addressed in honest and transparent ways, evoking social advocacy for equitable DL education programs.

Educators' sociocultural influences. All DL teachers need aspects of their preparation to include the examination of their own cultural, linguistic, and sociocultural backgrounds. Only then may they understand how to fully support students' sociocultural factors in the context of DL learning. Similarly, DL teachers need to understand how parents, school administrators, and other community members view the role of "the teacher." Cultural and community variations on the perceptions of teachers' roles will greatly shape ways in which DL teachers will approach parents, students, and the community at large. For example, a native English speaker who is teaching in a high school DL setting where the majority of the students' parents are native speakers of Spanish will need to know methods of communication that work well with the families. The same principle applies where a native Spanish-speaking teacher is living and working in a DL community that is primarily English speaking. Is an at-school "parent-night" preferred over an informational emailed newsletter? Should the teacher reach out to parents in social settings to reinforce relationships that therefore strengthen conversations about academics? Or not? What other community factors influence how parents perceive teachers? An awareness of these and many other sociocultural factors should be included in preparing DL teachers.

Parents: Demystifying dual language. Another equally important layer of DL teacher preparation and sociocultural considerations specifically points to demystifying DL programs with parents. After DL teachers closely examine their own sociocultural influences, as well as that of their students, they will need to understand how parents view DL education. The societal connections between language and power may shade and skew the "hows" and "whys" behind parents' election for their children to participate in DL classrooms. And teachers need to be prepared for many delicate and complex layers to this topic. Teacher preparation courses must address some controversial questions like these: Are language-minority parents viewing DL education as a "fix it" so their children will superficially retain a home language yet outwardly demonstrate a preference to English as the language of power? Will only the "advanced placement" language-majority students be seen as qualifying for DL in high school? What about native English-speaking students who are also classified as within racial minorities—will they have equal access to secondary DL programs? These areas of consideration and others must be included in DL teacher preparation courses.

"Home-grown" teachers. Teaching in DL programs requires special skills and knowledge, especially in the areas of academic language development and disciplinary literacies (Lachance, 2017c). As mentioned earlier in the chapter, there is a national shortage of DL teachers. In many states, the only way DL programs have been able to survive is because of organizations that invite international teachers to come to the United States on temporary employment work permits to teach in DL schools (Kissau, Yon, & Algozzine, 2011). Foreign-born faculty bring many valuable qualities to U.S. DL classrooms. Rich language repertoires, wide-ranging cultural influences, and adventurous personalities are only a few of the benefits of international visiting teachers. Yet, there are also some noteworthy challenges associated with an over-dependence on such teachers to keep DL afloat (Hutchison, 2005). Pedagogical disconnects with student-centered, standards-based (and often assessment-driven) instruction have proven difficult for many international teachers. The variations in needs among DL learners, who include English learners, emergent bilinguals, heritage speakers of the partner language, and native speakers of English, are often times new to teachers from outside the U.S. Even with specific faculty-orientation programs that attempt to help visiting teachers adjust to their US classrooms, many do not fulfill their teaching contracts, even though they are temporary (Boyle, August, Tabaku, Cole, & Simpson-Baird, 2015; Hutchison, 2005).

An even more important reason for DL teachers to learn about this topic is so that they themselves can become ongoing recruiters in the field. They are in perfect positions to help secondary DL students understand the crucial shortage of DL teachers and help them learn about post-secondary options that may be available to them. School districts are proud to "grow their own" bilingual teachers (see Chapter 4). Higher-education faculty from the local universities may apply for grant programs to fund dual-credit courses for high school students interested in preparing to be teachers. A cohort approach establishes an ongoing pattern of multilingual secondary DL students entering teacher preparation programs and then returning to their home districts to "carry the torch" as new DL teachers. As such, and for additional reasons, the topic of clinical partnerships is a vital component of DL teacher preparation (Clarke, Triggs, & Nielsen, 2014).

Institutions of higher education (IHEs) and school district collaboration: Clinical partnerships. Just as students who are learning languages need practice and application, so do teachers. Solid, ongoing partnerships between IHEs' teacher preparation programs and successful DL schools are imperative for new teacher mentorship (Darling-Hammond, 2012). DL teachers need numerous valuable clinical experiences with inspired cooperating teachers throughout the teacher preparation program. Real-world application of newly learned DL pedagogies should be present throughout teacher-preparation courses as opposed to an isolated semester of student teaching upon completion of all required coursework—just before teacher candidates are recommended for licensure. This is a challenge! DL teaching is a difficult task in any given situation, and especially for a clinical-teacher candidate. Practicing DL teachers who are willing to provide such mentorship will also need support in a variety of forms. School administrators will need to be creative in order to provide the necessary logistical frameworks for such partnerships. Keeping this in mind, IHEs intending to prepare DL teachers should be exceptionally deliberate about how clinical partnerships are formed and with whom.

Proposed Coursework: A Thematic Crosswalk

As a culmination of the previously mentioned topics, with in-depth descriptions of their impacts on shaping DL teacher preparation, this chapter also presents potential options for specific coursework to address the specialized practices of DL teachers. This portion of the chapter is not an exhaustive list of courses for pre-service DL teachers but rather conceptual options for future considerations in teacher preparation. Consequently, they may also serve as areas for in-service DL teacher professional development. These specialized courses focused on dual language teaching could be offered combining teachers for Grades K-12, but when the teacher preparation program has a sufficient number of students for DL at secondary level, each course should move to a secondary DL focus. All of the courses listed below should be combined with licensure coursework for the age group that the teacher plans to specialize in.

Biliteracy and Second Language Acquisition in Dual Language Teaching. The focus of this course or courses would be for teacher candidates to fully explore the specialized processes of the development of reading and writing in two languages for the young adult. In the context of secondary programs, DL teachers will need dedicated learning to grasp the deep, inseparable relationships between secondary content concepts and young adult literacy patterns. Analyses of academic language demands, contextually dependent language functions, language progression, and developmentally appropriate cognition are a few of the concepts that may be found within this course. The topic of authentic DL materials also is embedded here.

Authentic Assessment for Dual Language Learners. DL teacher candidates require a course dedicated to student-centered, content-based learning and the measurement of language progression, over time, in two languages. As previously discussed, DL teachers will need to deconstruct existing systems of assessment and grading patterns in their DL setting and then reconstruct creative and innovative ways to capture students' academic and sociocultural gains. This course will explore these competencies. In the context of secondary programs, this course must also investigate the relationship between assessments and DL learners' graduation requirements.

Dual Language Methods and Advanced Pedagogies. DL teachers must demonstrate innovative ways to design and deliver dynamic student-centered instruction that facilitates DL learners' application and practice with new language. This means that DL teacher candidates will learn what students need to be engaged and actively participating in curricular concepts that encompass many levels of cognition, metacognition, and metalinguistics. This course will showcase student-centered methodologies via unit planning, including considerations for authentic assessment and other teaching and scaffolding strategies such as project-based learning—with grade-level nuances in mind.

Dual Language Clinicals and Internship. As referenced earlier, DL teacher preparation must include many entry points and various scenarios for teacher candidates to apply new theories, teaching methodologies, and freshly acquired DL pedagogies throughout their preparation (Lindholm-Leary, 2012; Reyes & Kleyn, 2010). Great consideration for strategic clinical experiences, with specific learning tasks and capstone assignments must be embedded across the coursework continuum. Ample clinical practices with leading mentor DL teachers in the field will support new teacher candidates in ways that will give them hands-on experiences that may not be learned in theoretical isolation. Simply put, teacher candidates must actually use best practices and new pedagogical concepts with students, in the context of a real DL classroom.

Teacher Preparation and Accreditation: A Call for National Dual Language Teacher Preparation Standards

As the popularity of DL programs in the United States rises and programs proliferate (Center for Applied Linguistics, 2017; Dual Language Schools Directory, 2018), there is no nationally systematized approach to preparing teachers to serve in DL settings. In most states, teacher preparation programs focus on developing competencies and skills to teach in English-medium classrooms or in classrooms where native-language instruction is provided as a temporary support while students acquire English (U.S. Department of Education, 2015). Even in the small portion of states that have established bilingual teacher preparation standards and defined pathways to bilingual teacher certification, it stands to reason that programs may need additional structure to authentically prepare DL teachers. DL pedagogies encompass highly specialized competencies to support secondary literacy and rigorous grade-level core content in a language other than English, along with the cross-cultural goals of DL programs (García, 2009; Howard et al., 2018).

In the absence of national DL teacher preparation standards, leaders in higher education across the country are left to work in an ad hoc fashion to meet increased market demands for teachers to serve in the growing number of DL schools. Many states, with excellent intentions, have resorted to designing DL teacher education "packages" of coursework that supplement another area of teacher licensure. For example, a teacher candidate may seek an initial elementary or secondary generalist credential supplemented with a concentration or minor in bilingual studies or a world language. Another common practice is for certified teachers already serving in the DL classroom to enroll in a certificate program at a university, with coursework in the area of DL education contributing toward a master's degree or continuing education credits. While these options serve to support the practice, it's argued that neither sufficiently prepares the DL teacher for the rigors of teaching core content in two languages to students from diverse linguistic and cultural backgrounds. What is needed is a set of national DL teacher preparation standards, framed by theory and best practices identified in the research. Theory and practice specific to DL should serve as the basis for DL teacher preparation curricula, benchmark assessments aligned to national accreditation standards, and full initial teacher certification in the area of DL education.

To conclude the chapter with an all-encompassing stance, it is increasingly vital to address the specific nuances of DL teaching and learning in ways that connect to national standards (Lachance, 2017b; Knight, Lloyd, Arbaugh, Gamson, McDonald, Nolan, and Whitney, 2014; Darling-Hammond, 2012; Herrera, Cabral, & Murry, 2013). In doing so, the numbers of formally prepared DL teachers may increase, affording the expansion of more DL programs nationwide. With this in mind, the field of teacher preparation needs to further address the specialized pedagogies associated with DL teaching and learning, such as those mentioned in this chapter. It stands to reason that the establishment of national standards for DL teacher preparation may facilitate potential pathways leading to accredited, stand-alone licensure programs (Council for the Accreditation of Educator Preparation, 2017; U.S. Department of Education, 2017).

Appendix
Overview of study participants, interviews, classroom observation, and data analyses

(See Lachance, 2017c, for more details on the methodology of the study.)

Study participants. The teachers and administrators interviewed had a minimum of five years of experience in K-12 education. Several participants serving secondary schools had prior teaching experience at the elementary level and were thus able to identify nuances with regard to secondary students' development and collaborative learning that are unique to secondary DL. The data sources from each of the participants included face-to-face interviews in Spanish and English and participant observation in classrooms and work settings.

Figure 15.2
Participants

	Female	Male	Role in Secondary school	K-12 DL Teacher	DL Administration/Other
North Carolina	17	3	9	12	5
New Mexico	12	2	5	9	3

Note: All study participants were from DL programs with Spanish and English as the partner languages. The Administration/Other category included school principals, a DL organization director, state education agency curriculum consultants, and state-level professional development coordinators.

Interviews. Semi-structured, audio-recorded interviews were conducted on-site with all participants, ranging from 60 to 90 minutes in duration. The interview questions were based on the *Guiding Principles for Dual Language Education* (Howard et al., 2018), to explore current dual language educators' conceptualizations of teacher preparation. The interviews were conducted in the participants' language of choice and transcribed in both languages as the researcher is fully biliterate in English and Spanish.

Classroom observation and data analyses. Data sources also included 60-90 minute observations with teacher participants in their schools and classrooms both in North Carolina and New Mexico. Anecdotal records from teachers' classrooms were kept to capture details regarding classroom configurations, teacher-generated and district-adopted curricular materials, ancillary language supports across the content areas, and other visible resources for literacy and content development in both languages. The study results included participants' conceptualizations associated with academic language and content development in DL classrooms. Most importantly, the participants articulated strong recommendations for the field of teacher preparation.

Chapter Sixteen
Secondary Dual Language Education: A National View

Dr. Wayne Thomas and Dr. Virginia Collier

A transformation of U.S. education has been underway for almost 20 years and it is gathering momentum! We refer to the developing national phenomenon of dual language education moving into all grades PK-12. Dual language education is an American innovation that predates the 21st century, since this inclusion form of bilingual schooling was first tried in the 1960s for the benefit of Cuban students in Florida whose families anticipated a quick return to the homeland. They wanted their children to remain proficient in their home language of Spanish while living in the English-speaking environment of the U.S. mainland. Educators at Coral Way Elementary school in the Miami metropolitan area chose to invite native English speakers to join the bilingual classes and this integrated model is now known as two-way dual language education. This program model is now rapidly spreading to all regions of the U.S., but two decades ago this was not yet happening.

The Past 20 Years

Gap closure research. Beginning in the late 1990s and continuing into the new century, a movement in some states to eliminate the most common form of bilingual schooling supported by federal and state funds (labeled "transitional") peaked when three states—California, Arizona, and later Massachusetts—declared that they would emphasize English-only instruction for English learners and move toward elimination of transitional bilingual education. However, during the same period, a number of large-scale research studies and meta-analyses from many different sources were conducted at the national level that provided clear and incontrovertible evidence that "bilingual is better, and dual language is best" (Thomas & Collier, 2012, 2017). Innovative school districts took notice of this emergent solid body of research that strongly reinforced the findings of previous research studies in favor of enrichment bilingual education and began to promote one-way dual language (one language group receiving schooling through their two languages) as a powerful means of achievement gap closure for English learners, as well as two-way dual language (two language groups) as a means of significantly raising student achievement of both groups while promoting full proficiency in two languages, not just one. This research followed students longitudinally and focused on gap closure, finding that only dual language education fully closes the achievement gap for both English learners and native English speakers of all ethnic and socioeconomic backgrounds participating in dual language classes. Interestingly, recent initiatives in 2017 and 2018 have now overturned the English-only voter referendums in California and Massachusetts, allowing dual language programs to be developed again, and similar changes are being considered in Arizona.

Cognitive benefits. A second body of research emergent in the past twenty years has also served to emphasize the educational and cognitive benefits of dual language (DL) education for all. We refer to the "bilingual brain research," in which many different researchers in varied contexts have identified specific cognitive attributes that are enhanced in proficient bilinguals when compared to monolinguals (National Institutes of Health, 2012; Thomas & Collier, 2017). This body of academic research actually predates the 21st century, but it has been greatly enhanced and extended in the past 20 years. It has also been widely summarized and popularized, activating the national imagination of parents wishing to give their children an educational advantage.

Dramatic expansion of dual language. Already, DL schooling is quite common throughout the U.S. with an estimated minimum of 2500 programs in place and operating, with many more appearing each year (Thomas & Collier, 2017). The vast majority of these are elementary programs for grades K-5 and PK-5. As detailed in this book, there are some challenges to be addressed when expanding to secondary DL classes. We and all the authors of this book strongly affirm that the first wave of PK-5 DL is now leading to an expanding second wave of grade 6-12 DL programs, building on the momentum and the successes of the first wave.

The Bilingual Seal and Statewide Dual Language Movements

Major state initiatives. Already, state by state, the U.S. is quickly recognizing the importance of at least one of the primary outcomes of DL education—greatly enhanced student proficiency in a second language. Between 2011 and 2013, starting with California, four states approved a bilingual seal for the high school diplomas of students who qualified. Only five years later, by mid-2018, there are now 33 states that have passed legislation for an official state bilingual seal to be awarded to graduates who can demonstrate academic proficiency in two languages, and 10 more states are in various stages of consideration for approval of a state bilingual seal. This represents a sea change during the present decade in the states' interest in promoting bilingualism as a powerful way of improving achievement and promoting superior proficiency in at least two languages!

A second indicator that the U.S. states are moving ahead with implementing DL instruction is the fact that three states (Delaware, North Carolina, and Utah) have declared or indicated serious interest in developing DL education statewide in all public school districts. In addition, several more states (e.g., California, Texas, Washington, and others) are currently considering this move after reviewing the substantial body of large-scale data-analytic research that supports DL program effectiveness and that documents its large effect sizes (a statistical measure of a program's impact). Thus, almost all of the tremendous increase in interest in DL education during the last decade has come from grassroots local and state action, with minimal support and encouragement from the United States' Department of Education.

Lack of federal funding. Education is not among the federal powers enumerated in the U.S. Constitution and thus is a power reserved to the states and to the people by the 10th Amendment of the Constitution. In the past, the federal government has aided education using its constitutional duty to promote the general welfare and to provide for the national defense. Since 2001, the federal legislation No Child Left Behind (NCLB) and Every Student Succeeds Act (ESSA) have provided some support for education in general—about 8% of total education expenditures in 2018. However, in the past 20 years there has been little targeted federal support for DL education, despite substantial amounts of federally funded research since 2000 that strongly supports the effectiveness of DL schooling in gap closure for English learners, as well as improved achievement for language minority students fluent in English and native English speakers. Since DL education is no less than a transformation of U.S. education, and since it promotes improved achievement and higher test scores that are also encouraged by NCLB and ESSA, the lack of federal interest in helping the states to develop DL education is difficult to explain.

Education for a Transformed World

Many states and localities have begun to be interested in developing DL education because their administrators and policy makers have realized the difficulty of educating today's students for the world they will live in by the years 2040-2050. New information and new fields of study are currently being developed and produced so rapidly that it is very difficult to predict what will be needed by today's 10-year-olds when they are in their 30s and 40s. And so educators have begun to support the contention that the best education we can provide now for mid-21st century adults should emphasize their "learning how to learn" new information, and should encourage accelerated cognitive development in today's students. This will enable them to meaningfully participate in the lifelong continuing education that they will need to be successful in a world of constant, unrelenting change and an employment environment influenced by massive automation and artificial intelligence developments.

Meeting these requirements with dual language education. Participation in well-implemented DL programs accelerates students' cognitive development, fosters much greater engagement with classroom instruction that leads to improved content learning, develops full proficiency in two languages, and offers cross-cultural experiences with diverse classmates and teachers who help students learn how to collaborate in preparation for diverse workplaces. In effect, DL programs offer a more efficient, more productive, and more comprehensively effective form of education that will enable today's students to better navigate the complex demands of life as global citizens in the mid-21st century.

Building on the Successes of PK-5 Dual Language Education

Research rationale for secondary dual language. In this book, we have focused on secondary DL programs that are designed to continue and increase the advantages of K-5 and PK-5 DL into the middle and high school years. In fact, the real "payoff" for PK-5 DL programs comes in the secondary years because research has shown that students who participate in secondary DL schooling (especially English learners) exhibit greatly increased rates of high school graduation and much lower dropout rates than students who do not attend DL classes. In addition, students in secondary DL programs receive opportunities to increase their second-language proficiency from high school levels to full adult and university levels that are appropriate for post-secondary education or employment. Third, our research has shown that English learners who were several years below grade-level in their first language early in their school years may not fully close their achievement gap with native English speakers until Grades 7-8. Thus, continuing the DL program past Grade 5 also increases the number of English learners who fully close their achievement gap over time. This also greatly reduces the number of students who can be labeled "long-term English learners" in middle school. The secondary DL program also importantly serves newly arriving immigrants, who, to graduate from high school, need to continue academic work in their primary language while acquiring English.

Opportunity costs for not providing secondary dual language. Fourth, research has shown that the long-term opportunity costs of not providing for English learners' full achievement gap closure are enormous. Not closing English learners' achievement gaps during their school years causes a lower high school graduation rate and higher dropout rate, but these are only part of the large opportunity costs to local and state jurisdictions. These long-term costs of not meeting English learners' needs in the schools include higher social services costs, such as expenses for institutional and economic support, and significantly lowered lifetime salaries as these students enter the adult world under prepared for work or further education.

Moreover, the long-term opportunity costs of not meeting student needs become truly large when groups other than English learners are included. Our research has shown that K-12 DL programs can also be powerful in closing the achievement gaps for historically low-scoring native English speakers, such as low-income students of all ethnic backgrounds and even special needs students (Thomas & Collier, 2014). Each of these groups scores significantly higher in DL programs than their comparable peers not in DL. Thus, we believe that a compelling case can be made for encouraging PK-12 DL programs, when all of the societal costs of not meeting students' needs over time are estimated and included in a cost-benefit study.

Improving NAEP test scores, state by state, with PK-12 dual language programs. Finally, we believe that a case for PK-12 DL programs can be made in terms of factors that influence differences among the U.S. states in the National Assessment of Educational Progress (NAEP) test scores. When we examine the scores of the various U.S. states as tested by the NAEP, we see that there is enormous variability among the states in their average reading and math test scores. Two factors, average state per pupil expenditures for education and percentage of English learners in the state's schools, appear to primarily account for the observed relative rankings in NAEP scores among the U.S. states (Thomas, 2018). The highest-spending five states in Fiscal Year (FY) 2016 spent $17,873-$22,366 per pupil while the lowest five states spent $6,953-$8,702 per pupil. The average state per pupil expenditure for FY2016 is $11,762 (U.S. Census, 2018). Thus, states in the upper NAEP rankings tend to spend more than the national average and to have smaller percentages of

English learners to educate. States with below average NAEP scores tend to spend less than the national average and to have higher percentages of English learners.

Neither per pupil expenditures nor percentage of English learners are factors easily changeable by those who would raise state test scores. However, there is ample research evidence of the large achievement gaps between English learners and native English speakers in all of the states, so it stands to reason that states with larger percentages of English learners with poorly met needs will also be states with lower overall NAEP scores. A focused effort to better educate English learners in any state would tend to raise that state's scores in proportion to its concentration of English learners. We submit that PK-12 dual language education is a powerful way of achieving this goal. In addition, increasing state per-pupil expenditures, especially for support of dual language education for all students, will add to the educational benefits and tend to increase state NAEP scores across the board for all states.

The Near Future: Transforming U.S. Education

We remind our readers of two important characteristics of PK-12 DL instruction. First, when well implemented, dual language is associated with very large effect sizes. In other words, dual language is a very powerful way to address current needs to raise student achievement and promote cognitive development. Dual language schooling in all grades, PK-12, is the most potent solution to education concerns that I, Wayne Thomas, have seen in my 45 years of professionally analyzing large-scale education data. Second, the strengths of dual language programs directly address the nation's greatest needs for improving education so that current students will be able to successfully navigate the quickly emerging and transformed world of the mid-21st century. Dual language instruction is a vehicle for education reform and a powerful method of helping students experience schooling in ways that will best equip them to most efficiently and productively "learn how to learn". This prepares students to navigate the new knowledge and accelerating changes that shape the world they will inherit. It is our role as dual language innovators to fully implement this transformative form of schooling for all of our students.

Finally, based on the points in this book, we respectfully invite our readers to join this national initiative as it continues to spread across the country and to contribute to the effort to significantly improve the effectiveness, efficiency, and productivity of U.S. education for all students, both English learners and English speakers, through dual language education for all. This is the most powerful way to bring about a truly transformed world for the benefit of all as we experience the great changes occurring in the next two decades, when our students become adults and begin to actively determine our quality of life as a nation. Thus, supporting well-implemented PK-12 dual language education truly represents an important and effective investment of time, energy, and resources in ourselves and our posterity.

References

Aldama, A., Sandoval, C., & García, P. (Eds.). (2012). *Performing the U.S. Latina and Latino Borderlands.* Bloomington, IN: Indiana University Press.

Alidou, H., Glanz, C., & Nikiema, N. (2011). Quality multilingual and multicultural education for lifelong learning. *International Review of Education, 57,* 529-539.

Allport, G. W. (1979). *The nature of prejudice.* Basic Books.

Arias, M. B. (2015). Parent and community involvement in bilingual and multilingual education. In W. Wright, S. Boun, & O. García (Eds.), *Handbook of bilingual and multilingual education* (pp. 282-298). Hoboken, NJ: Wiley-Blackwell.

Ascher, M. (1981). *Code of the quipu: A study in media, mathematics, and culture.* Ann Arbor, MI: University of Michigan Press.

Associated Press. (2008, September 13). States hire foreign teachers to ease shortages. *MSNBC News.* Available at: http://www.msnbc.msn.com/id/26691720/

Association for Middle Level Education. (2013). http://www.amle.org/portals/0/pdf/twb/TWB_colorchart_Oct2013.pdf

Association for Middle Level Education. (2017). https://www.amle.org/BrowsebyTopic/WhatsNew/WNDet/TabId/270/ArtMID/888/ArticleID/307/Setting-Higher-Expectations-Motivating-Middle-Graders-to-Succeed.aspx

Association for Supervision and Curriculum Development. (2013). http://www.ascd.org/news-media/Press-Room/News-Releases/ASCD-Authors-Headline-2013-Annual-Conference-Pre-Conference-Institutes.aspx

August, D., & Hakuta, K. (Eds.). (1997). *Improving schooling for language-minority children: A research agenda.* Washington, DC: National Academy Press.

Baker, C., & Wright, W. E. (2017). *Foundations of bilingual education and bilingualism* (6th ed.). Bristol, UK: Multilingual Matters.

Bazin, M., Tamez, M., & Exploratorium Teacher Institute (San Francisco). (2002). *Math and science across cultures: Activities and investigations from the Exploratorium.* New York: New Press.

Beach, R., Campano, G., Edmiston, B., & Borgmann, M. (2010). *Literacy tools in the classroom: Teaching through critical inquiry, Grades 5-12.* New York: Teachers College Press.

Bearse, C., & de Jong, E. J. (2008). Cultural and linguistic investment: Adolescents in a secondary two-way immersion program. *Equity & Excellence in Education, 41*(3), 325-340.

Beeman, K., & Urow, C. (2013). *Teaching for biliteracy: Strengthening bridges between languages.* Philadelphia: Caslon.

Bernal, D. D., Burciaga, R., & Carmona, J. F. (Eds.). (2016). *Chicana/latina testimonios as pedagogical, methodological, and activist approaches to social justice.* New York: Routledge.

Bhabha, H. K. (2004). *The location of culture*. London: Routledge.

Bialystok, E., & Craik, F. I. M. (2010). Cognitive and linguistic processing in the bilingual mind. *Current Directions in Psychological Science, 19*, 12–23. doi: 10.1177/0963721409358571

Bivins, E. (2014). Parent groups in one school. In V. P. Collier & W. P. Thomas (Eds.), *Creating dual language schools for a transformed world: Administrators speak* (pp. 120-125). Albuquerque: Dual Language Education of New Mexico-Fuente Press.

Bosma, L. M., Orozco, L., Barriga, C. C., Rosas-Lee, M., & Sieving, R. E. (2017). Promoting resilience during adolescence: Voices of Latino youth and parents. Youth & Society.

Boyle, A., August, D., Tabaku, L., Cole, S., & Simpson-Baird, A. (2015). *Dual language education programs: Current state policies and practices*. Washington, DC: American Institutes for Research. https://ncela.ed.gov/files/rcd/TO20_DualLanguageReport_508.pdf

Brecht, R., Abbott, M., Davidson, D., Rivers, W. P., Robinson, J., Slater, R., Weinberg, A., & Yoganathan, A. (2013). *Languages for all? The Anglophone challenge*. College Park, MD: University of Maryland.

Bunch, G.C., Walqui, A., & Pearson, P. D. (2014). Complex text and new common standards in the United States: Pedagogical implications for English learners. *TESOL Quarterly, 48*(3), 533-559.

Burkhauser, S., Steele, J. L., Li, J., Slater, R. O., Bacon, M., & Miller, T. (2016). Partner-Calderón, M. E. (2007). *Teaching reading to English language learners, Grades 6-12: A framework for improving achievement in the content areas*. Thousand Oaks, CA: Corwin.

Calderón M. E., Slavin R., & Sánchez, M. (2011). Effective instruction for English learners. *Future of Children, 21*(1), 103-127.

Cammarata, L., & Tedick, D. (2012). Balancing content and language in instruction: The experience of immersion teachers. *Modern Language Journal, 96*, 251-269.

Cely, A. (2017). Approximating learning experience to reality. Speech presented at the Communities of Learning Summit, California.

Cenoz, J., & Gorter, D. (2015). Minority languages, state languages, and English in european education. In W. Wright, S. Boun, & O. García (Eds.), *Handbook of bilingual and multilingual education* (pp. 473-483). Hoboken, NJ: Wiley-Blackwell.

Center for Applied Linguistics. (2012). *Directory of two-way bilingual immerson programs in the US*. Retrieved from http://www.cal.org/twi/directory

Center for Applied Linguistics. (2017). *National dual language forum: Dual language program directory*. Retrieved from http://www.cal.org/ndlf/directories/

Center for Applied Second Language Studies. (2013). What levels of proficiency do immersion students achieve? Eugene, OR: Center for Applied Second Language Studies, University of Oregon. Retrieved from https://casls.uoregon.edu/wp-content/uploads/pdfs/tenquestions/TBQImmersionStudent ProficiencyRevised.pdf

City, E. A., Elmore, R. E., Fiarman, S. E., Tietel, L. (2009). *Instructional rounds in education.* Cambridge, MA. Harvard Education Press.

Chenoweth, K., & Theokas, C. (2011). *Getting it done: Leading academic success in unexpected schools.* Cambridge, MA: Harvard Education Press.

Clarke, A., Triggs, V., & Nielsen, W. (2014). Cooperating teacher participation in teacher education: A review of the literature. *Review of Educational Research, 84*, 163-202.

Collier, V. P. (1995). Acquiring a second language for school. *Directions in Language Education, 1*(4). Retrieved from http://www.thomasandcollier.com

Collier, V. P., & Thomas, W. P. (2005). The beauty of dual language education. *TABE Journal, 8*(1), 1-6.

Collier, V. P., & Thomas, W. P. (2007). Predicting second language academic success in English using the Prism Model. In J. Cummins & C. Davison (Eds.), *International handbook of English language teaching, Part 1* (pp.333-348). New York: Springer.

Collier, V. P., & Thomas, W. P. (2009). *Educating English learners for a transformed world.* Albuquerque, NM: Dual Language Education of New Mexico-Fuente Press.

Collier, V. P., & Thomas, W. P. (2014). *Creating dual language schools for a transformed world: Administrators speak.* Albuquerque, NM: Dual Language Education of New Mexico-Fuente Press.

Cortina, R., Makar, C., & Mount-Cors, M. (2015). Dual language as a social movement: Putting languages on a level playing field. *Current Issues in Comparative Education, 17*(1), 5-16.

Coulter, C., & Jiménez-Silva, M. (Eds.). (2017). *Culturally sustaining and revitalizing pedagogies: Language, culture, and power.* Retrieved from https://ebookcentral.proquest.com

Council for the Accreditation of Educator Preparation. (2017). *What is accreditation.* Retrieved from: http://www.caepnet.org/accreditation/about-accreditation/what-is-accreditation

Creese, A., & Blackledge, A. (2010). Translanguaging in the bilingual classroom: A pedagogy for learning and teaching? *The Modern Language Journal, 94*(1), 103-115.

Cummins, J. (1979). Linguistic interdependence and the educational development of bilingual children. *Review of Educational Research, 49*(2), 222-251.

Cummins, J. (1991). Interdependence of first- and second-language proficiency in bilingual children. In E. Bialystok (Ed.), *Language processing in bilingual children* (pp. 70-89). Cambirdge: Cambridge University Press.

Cummins, J. (2000). *Language, power and pedagogy: Bilingual children in the crossfire.* Bristol, UK: Multilingual Matters.

Cummins, J. (2014). Beyond language: Academic communication and student success. *Linguistics and Education, 26*, 145-154.

Darling-Hammond, L. (2012). The right start: Creating a strong foundation for the teaching career. *Phi Delta Kappan, 94*, 8-13.

De Cat, C., Gusnanto, A., & Serratrice, L. (2017). Identifying a threshold for the executive function advantage in bilingual children. *Studies in Second Language Acquisition*, 1-33.

Dee, T. S. (2015). Social identity and achievement gaps: Evidence from an affirmation intervention. *Journal of Research on Educational Effectiveness, 8*(2), 149-168.

DeFour, M. (2012, September 23). Madison schools reaching overseas for bilingual teachers. *Wisconsin State Journal.* Retrieved from http://host.madison.com/news/local/education/local_schools/madison-schools-reaching-overseas-for-bilingual-teachers/article_39b8cae2-0586-11e2-b68b-0019bb2963f4.html

de Jong, E. J. (2011). *Foundations for multilingualism in education: From principles to practice*. Philadelphia: Caslon.

de Jong, E. J. (2016). Two-Way Immersion for the next generation: Models, policies, and principles. *International Multilingual Research Journal, 10*(1), 6-16. doi: 10.1080/19313152.2016.1118667

de Jong, E. J., & Bearse, C. I. (2011). The same outcomes for all? High school students reflect on their two-way immersion program experiences. In: D. Christian, D. Tedick, & T. Fortune (Eds.), *Immersion education: Practices, policies, possibilities*. (104-122). Bristol, UK: Multilingual Matters.

de Jong, E. J., & Bearse, C. I. (2014). Dual language programs as a strand within a s econdary school: Dilemmas of school organization and the TWI mission. *International Journal of Bilingual Education and Bilingualism, 17*(1), 15-31.

de Jong, E. J., & Howard, E. (2009). Integration in two-way immersion education: Equalising linguistic benefits for all students. *International Journal of Bilingual Education and Bilingualism, 12*(1), 81–99. http://doi.org/10.1080/13670050802149531

Doll, J. J., Eslami, Z., & Walters, L. (2013). Understanding why students drop out of high school, according to their own reports: Are they pushed or pulled, or do they fall out? A comparative analysis of seven nationally representative studies. *Sage Open, 3*(4). doi: http://dx.doi.org/10.1177/2158244013503834

Donaldson, G. (2006). *Cultivating leadership in schools: Connecting people, purpose and practice*. New York: Teachers College Press.

Dual Language Schools. (2018). National dual language school directory. http://www.duallanguageschools.org

Echevaría, J., Vogt, M. E., & Short, D. L. (2016). *Making content comprehensible for English learners: The SIOP model* (5th ed.). Boston: Pearson.

Emdin, C. (2015). *A STEM with no root bears no fruit.* Speech presented at 100kin10 Partner Summit, Chicago.

Emdin, C. (2017). *Progressive #HipHopEd education content.* Speech presented at the Learning Innovation ExCITe Center, Philadelphia.

England, T. W. (2009). Bilingual education: Lessons from abroad for America's pending crisis. *Washington University Law Review, 86,* 1211-1239.

Epstein, R. (2017). *Epstein parenting competencies inventory.* http://www.myparentingskills.com

Escamilla, K., Hopewell, S., Butvilofsky, S., Sparrow, W., Soltero-González, L., Ruiz-Figueroa, O., & Escamilla, M. (2013). *Biliteracy from the start.* Philadelphia: Caslon.

Faltis, C., & Ramírez-Marín, F. (2015). Secondary bilingual education: Cutting the Gordian knot. In W. Wright, S. Boun, & O. García (Eds.), *Handbook of bilingual and multilingual education* (pp. 336-353). Hoboken, NJ: Wiley-Blackwell.

Feinauer, E., & Howard, E. R. (2014). Attending to the third goal: Cross-cultural competence and identity development in two-way immersion programs. *Journal of Immersion and Content-Based Language Education, 2*(2), 257–272. doi:10.1075/jicb

Flores, B. B., Sheets, R. H., & Clark, E. R. (Eds.). (2011). *Teacher preparation for bilingual student populations: Educar para transformar.* New York: Routledge.

Forman, S. (2016). Interests and conflicts: exploring the context for early implementation of a dual language policy in one middle school. *Language Policy, 15*(4), 433-451.

Fortune, T. W., & Tedick, D. J. (2008). One-way, two-way and indigenous immersion: A call for cross fertilization. In T. W. Fortune & D. J. Tedick (Eds.), *Pathways to multilingualism: Evolving perspectives on immersion education* (pp. 3–21). Bristol, UK: Multilingual Matters.

Fortune, T. W., & Tedick, D. J. (2015). Oral proficiency assessment of English-proficient K–8 Spanish immersion students. *The Modern Language Journal, 99*(4), 637–655. http://doi.org/10.1111/modl.12275

Freeman, Y., Freeman, D. & Mercuri, S. (2005). *Dual language essentials for teachers and administrators.* Portsmouth, NH: Heinemann.

Fregoso, R. L. (1993). *The Bronx screen.* Minneapolis, MN: University of Minnesota Press.

Freire, P. (2014). *Pedagogy of hope: Reliving pedagogy of the oppressed.* New York: Bloomsbury Academic.

Fry, R. (2007). *How far behind in math and reading are English language learners?* Washington, DC: Pew Hispanic Center. Retrieved from www.pewhispanic.org/topics/?TopicID=4

Fry, R. (2008). *The role of schools in the English language learner achievement gap .* Washington, DC: Pew Hispanic Center. Retrieved from www.pewhispanic.org/topics/?TopicID=4

García, O. (2009). *Bilingual education in the 21ˢᵗ century: A global perspective.* West Sussex, United Kingdom: Wiley-Blackwell.

García, O., Johnson, S., & Seltzer, K. (2017). *The translanguaging classroom: Leveraging student bilingualism for learning.* Philadelphia: Caslon.

Geerlings, J., Verkuyten, M., & Thijs, J. (2015). Changes in ethnic self-identification and heritage language preference in adolescence: A cross-lagged panel study. *Journal of Language and Social Psychology, 34*(5), 501.

Gibbons, P. (2015). *Scaffolding language, scaffolding learning: Teaching second language learners in the mainstream classroom* (2nd ed.). Portsmouth, NH: Heinemann.

González Ornelas, I. & Ornelas, M.E. (2014). Expansion to intermediate grades (Grades 4-5) and middle school (Grades 6-8). In V. P. Collier & W. P. Thomas (Eds.), *Creating dual language schools for a transformed world: Administrators speak* (pp. 143-145). Albuquerque, NM: Dual Language Education of New Mexico-Fuente Press.

Gottlieb, M., & Ernst-Slavit, G. (2014). *Academic language in diverse classrooms: Definitions and contexts.* Thousand Oaks, CA: Corwin.

Grant, N. (2014). The middle school expansion of Collinswood Language Academy. In V. P. Collier & W. P. Thomas (Eds.), *Creating dual language schools for a transformed world: Administrators speak* (pp. 140-142). Albuquerque, NM: Dual Language Education of New Mexico-Fuente Press.

Guerrero, M. (1997). Spanish academic language proficiency: The case of bilingual education teachers in the U.S. *Bilingual Research Journal, 21*(1), 25-43.

Haley, M., & Ferro, M. (2011). Understanding the Perceptions of Arabic and Chinese Teachers Toward Transitioning into U.S. School. *Foreign Language Annals, 44*(2), 289-307.

Harmon-Martínez, L. & Jurado, M. L. (2014). Bilingualism/biliteracy seal legislation. In V. P. Collier & W. P. Thomas (Eds.), *Creating dual language schools for a transformed world: Administrators speak* (pp. 155-160). Albuquerque, NM: Dual Language Education of New Mexico-Fuente Press.

Herrera, S. G., Cabral, R. M., & Murry, K. G. (2013). *Assessment accommodations for classroom teachers of culturally and linguistically diverse students* (2ⁿᵈ ed.). Boston: Pearson.

Howard, E. R., Lindholm-Leary, K. J., Rogers, D., Olague, N., Medina, J., Kennedy, B., Sugarman, J. & Christian, D. (2018). *Guiding principles for dual language education* (3ʳᵈ ed.). Washington DC: Center for Applied Linguistics.

Hutchison, C. (2005). *Teaching in America: A cross-culutral guide for international teachers and their employers.* Dordrecht, The Netherlands: Springer.

Ikpeze, C. H. (2015). *Teaching across cultures: Building pedagogical relationships in diverse contexts.* Rotterdam: Sense Publishers.

Illinois State Board of Education. (2017). https://www.illinoisreportcard.com/

Joseph, N. (2010). Metacognition needed: Teaching middle school and high school students to develop strategic learning skills. *Preventing school failure, 54*(2), 99-103.

Kissau, S. & Algozzine, R. (2017). Effective foreign language teaching: Broadening the concept of content knowledge. *Foreign Language Annals, 50,* 114–134. doi:10.1111/flan.12250

Kissau, S., Yon, M., & Algozzine, R. (2011). The beliefs and behaviors of international and domestic foreign language teachers. *Journal of the National Council of Less Commonly Taught Languages, 10,* 21-56.

Knight, S. L., Lloyd, G. M., Arbaugh, F., Gamson, D., McDonald, S. P., Nolan, Jr., J., & Whitney, A. E. (2014). Performance assessment of teaching: Implications for teacher education. *Journal of Teacher Education, 65,* 372-374.

Kohl, H. (1994). *"I won't learn from you" and other thoughts on creative maladjustment.* New York: The New Press.

Lachance, J., (2017a May). *North Carolina teacher preparation: Transformations for dual language learning.* Paper presented at NCSU ESL Symposium, Raleigh, NC.

Lachance, J. (2017b). A case study of dual language program administrators: The teachers we need. *International Journal of Educational Leadership Preparation, (12)*1, 1-18.

Lachance, J. (2017c). Case studies of dual language teachers: Conceptualizations on the complexities of biliteracy for teacher preparation. *NYS TESOL Journal, 4*(2), 48-65.

Landes-Lee, J. (2015, January). USOE Dual Language Immersion Courses. *Utah Secondary Dual Language Immersion Newsletter,* 2-6. Retrieved July 26, 2017 from http://l2trec.utah.edu/utah-dual immersion/images/NewsletterFAQ/2015JanuaryNewsletter.pdf

Lapkin, S., Hart, D., & Swain, M. (1991). Early and middle French immersion programs: French language outcomes. *Canadian Modern Language Review, 48*(1), 11-40.

Leeman, J. (2015). Heritage language education and identity in the United States. *Annual Review of Applied Linguistics, 35,* 100-119.

Leikin, M. (2013). The effect of bilingualism on creativity: Developmental and educational perspectives. *International Journal of Bilingualism, 17*(4), 431-447.

Li, J., Steele, J., Slater, R., Bacon, M., & Miller, T. (2016). Teaching practices and language use in two-way dual language immersion programs in a large public school district. *International Multilingual Research Journal, 10*(1), 31-43.

Lindholm-Leary, K. J. (2001). *Dual language education.* Bristol, UK: Multilingual Matters.

Lindholm-Leary, K. J. (2012). Successes and challenges in dual language education. *Theory into Practice, 51*(4), 256-262.

Lindholm-Leary, K. J. (2016). Students' perceptions of bilingualism in Spanish and Mandarin dual language programs. *International Multilingual Research Journal, 10*(1), 59-70.

Lindholm-Leary, K. J., & Borsato, G. (2001). *Impact of two-way bilingual elementary programs on students' attitudes toward school and college.* Santa Cruz, CA: Center for Research on Education, Diversity & Excellence, University of California-Santa Cruz.

Lindholm-Leary, K. J., Hardman, L., & Meyer, P. (2007). Sharing success. *Language Magazine, 6(5)*, 20–23.

Malone, S., & Paraide, P. (2011). Mother tongue-based bilingual education in Papua New Guinea. *International Review of Education, 57*, 705-720.

Manning, M. L., & Bucher, K. T. (2012). *Teaching in middle school* (4th ed.). Boston: Pearson.

Marian, V., & Shook, A. (2012). The cognitive benefits of being bilingual. *Cerebrum: The Dana Forum on Brain Science, 2012*, 13.

Martí, J. (1939). Nuestra América. *Revista Ilustrada.*

Martin-Beltrán, M. (2014). "What do you want to say?" How adolescents use translanguaging to expand learning opportunities. *International Multilingual Research Journal, 8*(3), 208-230.

Modern Language Association of America. (2007). Foreign languages and higher education: New structures for a changed world. *Profession*, 234-245.

Molle, D., Sato, E., Boals, T., & Hedgspeth, C.A. (2015). *Multilingual learners and academic literacies: Sociocultural contexts of literacy development in adolescents.* New York, NY: Routledge.

Montessori, M. (1949). *To educate the human potential.* New York: Ravinio Books.

Montessori, M. (1967). *The absorbent mind.* New York: Holt, Rinehart and Winston.

Montone, C. L., & Loeb, M. I. (2000). *Implementing two-way immersion programs in secondary schools.* Santa Cruz, CA: Center for Research on Education, Diversity & Excellence, University of California-Santa Cruz.

Mu, G. M. (2015). A meta-analysis of the correlation between heritage language and ethnic identity. *Journal of Multilingual and Multicultural Development, 36*(3), 239-254. doi:http://dx.doi.org.mutex.gmu.edu/10.1080/01434632.2014.909446

New Mexico Public Education Department. (2016a). *Districts and charter schools with state bilingual multicultural education programs.* Retrieved from http://www.ped.state.nm.us/BilingualMulticultural/dl10/Bilingual%20Directory%2010-11.pdf

New Mexico Public Education Department. (2016b). *House Bill 543.* Retrieved from http:// http://ped.state.nm.us/ped/DDashDocs/BillAnalysis/HB0543.pdf

Nicolay, A. C., & Poncelet, M. (2015). Cognitive benefits in children enrolled in an early bilingual immersion school: A follow up study. *Bilingualism: Language and Cognition, 18*(4), 789-795.

North Carolina Department of Public Instruction. (2017). *Language diversity in North Carolina.* Retrieved March 17, 2017 from http://eldnces.ncdpi.wikispaces.net/file/view/Language%20Diversity%20Briefing%20February%202017.pdf/605680433/Language%20Diversity%20Briefing%20February%202017.pdf

North Carolina State Board of Education. (2013). *Preparing students for the world: Final report of the State Board of Education's task force on global education.* Retrieved from http://www.ncpublicschools.org/curriculum/globaled/

Omaha Public Schools. (2016). Dual language course information. Retrieved July 17, 2017, from http://south.ops.org/STUDENTS/DualLanguage/tabid/295/Default.aspx#5065123-course-information

Omaha Public Schools Research Department. (2016). Program Report Update 4/18/16 and 2016-17 Official Fall Membership Report 11/07/16.

Orange County Department of Education. (2018). NTC Project GLAD® http://www.ocde.us/NTCProjectGLAD/Pages/default.aspx

Oregon Association of Latino Administrators. (2005). *Nurturing the seeds of change for Oregon's educational leaders: Latino administrators for Oregon's changing schools: A school and district tool kit.* Portland, OR.

Oregon Department of Education. Oregon Equity Report. www.oregon.gov

O'Rourke, P., Zhou, Q., & Rottman, I. (2016). Prioritization of K–12 world language education in the United States: State requirements for high school graduation. *Foreign Language Annals, 49*(4), 789-800.

Ortega, R. (2014). Omaha Public Schools high school dual language program. In V. P. Collier & W. P. Thomas (Eds.), *Creating dual language schools for a transformed world: Administrators speak* (pp. 155-160). Albuquerque, NM: Dual Language Education of New Mexico-Fuente Press.

Paris, D. (2012). Culturally sustaining pedagogy: A needed change in stance, terminology, and practice. *Educational Researcher, 41*(3), 93-97.

Pascual y Cabo, D., Prada, J., & Lowther Pereira, K. (2017). Effects of community service learning on heritage language learners' attitudes toward their language and culture. *Foreign Language Annals, 50*(1), 71-83.

Perani, D., & Abutalebi, J. (2015). Bilingualism, dementia, cognitive and neural reserve. *Current Opinion in Neurology, 28*(6), 618-625.

Pérez Cañado, M. L. (2016). Teacher training needs for bilingual education: In-service teacher perceptions. *International Journal of Bilingual Education and Bilingualism, 19*(3), 266-295.

Pilotti, M., Gutierrez, A., Klein, E., & Mahamame, S. (2015). Young adults' perceptions and use of bilingualism as a function of an early immersion program. *International*

Journal of Bilingual Education and Bilingualism, 18(4), 383-394.

Purkarthofer, J., & Mossakowski, J. (2011). Bilingual teaching for multilingual students? Innovative dual-medium models in Slovene-German schools in Austria. *International Review of Education, 57*(5-6), 551-565.

Purkey, W. W. (1970). *Self-concept and school achievement.* Upper Saddle River, NJ: Merrill Prentice Hall.

Quality Teaching® for English Learners (QTEL). https://www.qtel.wested.org/

Rendón, L. I. (2009). *Sentipensante (Sensing/Thinking) pedagogy: Educating for wholeness, social justice and liberation.* Sterling, VA: Stylus.

Reyes, S. A., & Kleyn, (2010). *Teaching in two languages: A guide for K-12 bilingual educators.* Thousand Oaks, CA: Corwin.

Rhodes, N., & Pufahl, I. (2009). Foreign language teaching in U.S. schools: Results of a national survey. Retrieved from http://www.cal.org/projects/Exec%20SumRosanna_111009.pdf

Rivas-Drake, D., Seaton, E. K., Markstrom, C., Quintana, S., Syed, M., Lee, R. M., Schwartz, S. J., Umaña-Taylor, A. J., French, S., & Yip, T. (2014). Ethnic and racial identity in adolescence: Implications for psychosocial, academic, and health outcomes. *Child Development, 85*(1), 40-57. doi: 10.1111/cdev.12200

Rocque, R., Ferrin, S., Hite, J. M., & Randall, V. (2016). The unique skills and traits of principals in one-way and two-way dual immersion schools. *Foreign Language Annals, 49*(4), 801-818.

Rubinstein-Ávila, E., Sox, A. A., Kaplan, S., & McGraw, R. (2015). Does biliteracy + mathematical discourse = binumerate development? Language use in a middle school dual language mathematics classroom. *Urban Education, 50*(8), 899-937.

Ryan, A. M., & Shim, S. S. (2008). An exploration of young adolescents' social achievement goals and social adjustment in middle school. *Journal of Educational Psychology, 100*(3), 672-687.

Sandy-Sánchez, D. (2008). Secondary dual language guiding principles: A review of the process.
Soleado, 8. Retrieved July 28, 2017 from http://www.dlenm.org/index.php/resources/soleado-newsletters

Santos, C. E., & Collins, M. A. (2016). Ethnic identity, school connectedness, and achievement in standardized tests among mexican-origin youth. *Cultural Diversity & Ethnic Minority Psychology, 22*(3), 447-452. doi:http://dx.doi.org.mutex.gmu.edu/10.1037/cdp0000065

Schmoker, M. (2011). *Focus: Elevating the essentials to radically improve student learning.* Alexandria, VA: Association for Supervision and Curriculum Development Press.

Scott, J. C. (1990). *Domination and the arts of resistance: Hidden transcripts.* New Haven: Yale University Press.

Shaw, R. (2014, December 3). Leadership skills multiply with language skills. *Forbes.*

Short, D. J., & Boyson, B. A. (2004). *Creating access: Language and academic programs for secondary school newcomers.* Washington, DC: Center for Applied Linguistics.

Sizemore, C. (2014). Developing the secondary dual language program. In V. P. Collier & W. P. Thomas (Eds.), *Creating dual language schools for a transformed world: Administrators speak* (pp. 146-149). Albuquerque, NM: Dual Language Education of New Mexico-Fuente Press.

Sizemore, S. (2014). Student leadership. In V. P. Collier & W. P. Thomas (Eds.), *Creating dual language schools for a transformed world: Administrators speak* (p. 150). Albuquerque, NM: Dual Language Education of New Mexico-Fuente Press.

Spencer, S. J., Logel, C., & Davies, P. G. (2016). Stereotype threat. *Annual Review of Psychology, 67,* 415-437.

Steele, C. M., & Aronson, J. (1995). Stereotype threat and the intellectual test performance of African Americans. *Journal of Personality and Social Psychology, 69*(5), 797.

Steele, J. L., Slater, R. O., Zamarro, G., Miller, T., Li, J., Burkhauser, S., & Bacon, M. (2017). Effects of dual-language immersion programs on student achievement: Evidence from lottery data. *American Educational Research Journal, 54*(1_suppl), 2 82S-306S.

Tedick, D. J., & Wesely, P. M. (2015). A review of research on content-based foreign/second language education in US K-12 contexts. *Language, Culture and Curriculum, 28*(1), 25-40.

Thomas, W. P., & Collier, V. P. (2002). *A national study of school effectiveness for language minority students' long-term academic achievement.* Santa Cruz, CA: Center for Research on Education, Diversity and Excellence, University of California-Santa Cruz.

Thomas, W. P., & Collier, V. P. (2012). *Dual language education for a transformed world.* Albuquerque, NM: Dual Language Education of New Mexico-Fuente Press.

Thomas, W. P., & Collier, V. P. (2014). *English learners in North Carolina dual language programs: Year 3 of this study: School Year 2009-2010.* Fairfax, VA: George Mason University. A research report provided to the North Carolina Department of Public Instruction.

Thomas, W. P., & Collier, V. P. (2017). *Why dual language schooling.* Albuquerque, NM: Dual Language Education of New Mexico-Fuente Press.

Umansky, L., & Reardon, S. (2014). Reclassifying patterns among Latino English learner students in bilingual, dual immersion, and English immersion classrooms. *American Educational Research Journal, 51,* 871-912.

University of Washington Center for Educational Leadership. https://www.k-12leadership.org/

U.S. Department of Education. (2015). *Dual language education programs: Current state policies and practices.* Retrieved from http://www2.ed.gov/about/offices/list/oela/resources.html

U.S. Department of Education. (2017). *Office of Post-Secondary Education Accreditation.* https://ope.ed.gov/accreditation/Index.aspx

Valdez, L., (1990*). Early works: Actos, bernabe and pensamiento serpentino.* Puerto Rico: Arte Público Press.

Valentino, R. A., & Reardon, S. F. (2015). Effectiveness of four instructional programs designed to serve English learners: Variations by ethnicity and initial English proficiency. *Educational Evaluation and Policy Analysis, 37,* 612–637. doi:10.3102/0162373715573310

van Lier, L. (2004). *The ecology and semiotics of language learning: A sociocultural perspective.* Dordrecht, NL: Kluwer Academic.

Vygotsky, L. S. (1978). *Mind in society: The development of higher psychological processes.* Cambridge, MA: Harvard University Press.

Walqui, A., & van Lier, L. (2010). *Scaffolding the academic success of adolescent English language learners.* San Francisco, CA: WestEd.

Walton, J., Paradies, Y., Priest, N., Wertheim, E. H., & Freeman, E. (2015). Fostering intercultural understanding through secondary school experiences of cultural immersion. *International Journal of Qualitative Studies in Education, 28*(2), 216-237.

Westerberg, G., & Davison, L. (2016). *An educator's guide to dual language instruction: Increasing achievement and global competence, K–12.* Abingdon, UK: Routledge.

Wiggins, G., and McTighe, J. (2005). *Understanding by design.* Alexandria, VA: ASCD.

Wilson, D. M. (2011). Dual language programs on the rise, *Harvard Education Letter, 27*(2). Retrieved from http://hepg.org/hel-home/issues/27_2/helarticle/dual-language-programs-on-the-rise

Wong Fillmore, L. (2014). English language learners at the crossroads of education reform. *TESOL Quarterly, 48*(3), 624-632.

Wong Fillmore, L., & Fillmore, C. (2012, January). *What does text complexity mean for English learners and language minority students?* Paper presented at the Understanding Language Conference, Stanford, CA. Retrieved from http://ell.stanford.edu/papers/language

World-Class Instructional Design and Assessment. (2012). *The 2012 amplification of the English language development standards, kindergarten to Grade 12.* Madison, WI: Board of Regents of the University of Wisconsin on behalf of the WIDA Consortium.

Zadina, J. N. (2014). *Multiple pathways to the student brain.* San Francisco: Jossey-Bass.

Zarate, M. E., Bhimji, F. and Reese, L. (2005). Ethnic identity and academic achievement among Latino(a) adolescents. *Journal of Latinos and Education, 4*(2), 95–114.

Zied, K. M., Phillipe, A., Karine, P., Valerie, H. T., Ghislaine, A., & Arnaud, R. (2004). Bilingualism and adult differences in inhibitory mechanisms: Evidence from a bilingual Stroop task. *Brain and Cognition, 54*(3), 254-256.

Zwiers, J. & Crawford, M. (2011). *Academic conversations: Classroom talk that fosters critical thinking and content understandings.* Portland, ME: Stenhouse.

Index

A

Academic Achievement *37,40,52,55,56,57,75,78,59,62,68,69,88,94,95,96,100,120,144, 162,164,200*

Administrator(s) *ix, xiii, xv, 1,9,10, 15, 16, 31, 42, 45, 59, 60, 66, 68, 69, 81, 83, 97, 101, 106, 116, 121, 128, 129, 132, 157, 161, 167, 169, 170, 172, 183, 197, 198, 205, 209, 214, 216, 217, 218, 223, 224, 225, 230, 231, 234, 237*

Advocacy *viii, 19, 20, 28, 29, 35, 64, 74, 152, 157, 230*

Advanced Placement (AP) *6,33,40,65,79,174,201,207,230,261*

African American xiv, *13, 14, 53, 118, 144, 145, 175, 197, 205, 206, 251*

Afrocentric

B

Bilingual
    Sequential *85,87,155,257*
    Simultaneous *37, 59, 78, 85, 86, 133, 147,148,161, 182, 184, 203, 221, 225*

C

Center for Advanced Research on Language Acquisition (CARLA) *32*

Certification/Credential *83,135,136,138,143,233*

Classroom Libraries *105,112,113, 254*

Cognitive Demand *vii, 3, 172*

Collaboration *vii, xii, xvi, 2,10, 21, 40, 48, 61, 63, 67, 74, 102, 107, 118, 131, 135, 136, 138, 139, 140, 141, 143, 157, 162, 168, 199, 202, 203, 205, 224, 231, 266*

Common European Framework of Reference for Languages (CEFRL) *174*

Community *x, xi, xii, xvi, 7, 8, 12, 25, 26, 34, 39, 41, 42, 44-46, 51, 52, 58-62, 64, , 68, 71, 75-81, 88-90, 95, 99, 100, 101, 106, 114-116, 124, 125, 128-135, 138-141, 143, 145, 147, 148, 156-162, 168-171, 173, 174, 175, 177-182, 185-187, 190-195, 197-202, 205, 207, 208, 214, 215, 217, 219, 230, 241, 242, 265*

Course Offerings *33, 42, 43, 55, 56, 58, 102, 103, 122, 146, 157, 158, 169, 215*

D

Deficit Perspective *66,68-69, 74, 75*

Dual Language
    Immersion *xi, xiii, 8, 32, 36, 127, 128, 141, 163, 165, 168, 174, 186, 219, 241, 242, 244, 245, 247-252, 265, 266*
    Program Design *vii, 4, 22, 33, 36, 37, 64, 115, 128*
    Whole School *15, 132*

Dual Language Education of New Mexico (DLeNM) *v, 32*

Dual Language Schools Directory *1, 31, 233*

E

Electives *viii, xiii, xv, 6, 19, 21, 23, 24, 26, 29, 43, 102, 109, 111, 122, 130, 134, 135, 137, 139, 140, 141, 146, 159, 160, 219, 227, 255*

English as a Second Language (ESL, ESOL) *4,7,21, 23, 25, 54, 160, 266*

English Learners *vii, ix, 2, 4, 5, 6, 8, 9, 10, 11, 13-15, 23, 32, 34, 35, 45, 52, 54, 62, 64, 67, 68, 113, 114, 116, 119, 121, 122, 123, 130, 135, 157, 171, 182, 199, 204, 206, 208, 226, 231, 236, 237, 238, 239-, 242, 244, 250-252, 255, 262, 262, 263, 266, 269*

Equity *xii, cxiv, 2, 14, 17, 23, 77-79, 88, 95, 116, 125, 144, 145, 158, 197, 198, 204, 205, 207, 209, 249, 242, 262*

Expansion *xi, xvi, 10, 16, 17, 61, 64, 72, 117, 118, 122, 123, 125, 163, 198-203, 207, 227, 233, 236, 242, 246*

H

Heritage Language Speakers *255*

Hiring *vii, x, 6, 13, 44, 45, 66, 74, 80, 83, 84, 88, 124, 167, 172, 173, 202, 27, 224*

Honors *25, 40, 55-58, 78, 91, 151, 152, 157-159*

I

Identity *viii, xiv, 14, 19, 28, 34, 37, 38, 39, 42, 43, 44, 78, 87, 109, 125, 129, 133, 140, 144, 147,*

149, 151, 156, 158, 160, 185, 186, 204, 208, 209, 218, 230, 244, 245, 247, 248, 250, 253

Indigenous *xiii, 32, 100, 175, 177-180, 189, 194, 195, 245, 242, 265*

Instructional Strategies
    Project-Based Learning *xiii, 138, 139, 171, 178, 179, 182, 184, 232*
    Project GLAD® *7,84,139, 226, 242, 249*
    QTEL 84, 250
    SIOP 7, 84, 103, 113, 226, 244, 266
    The "Bridge" (bridging) *82*

International/Visiting/non-US Teachers *v, x, xv, 8, 10, 27, 39, 44, 46, 51, 54, 61, 83, 99-101, 107, 108, 114, 120, 131, 163, 168, 203, 218, 224, 241, 243, 244, 246, 250, 252, 259, 262, 265, 269*

L

La Cosecha *32, 92, 158, 168*

Language
    Partner *vii, xiv, xv, 2, 4-12, 19, 22-26, 32, 36, 40, 42-45, 104, 105, 124, 125, 130, 166, 168, 173, 199, 204, 206, 215, 219, 228, 229, 231, 234*
    Separation of *2, 8, 41*

Leadership *viii, xi, xiv, 2, ,9,12, 16, 19, 20, 22, 28, 29, 57, 61, 80, 82, 99, 100, 116, 117, 119, 120, 124, 125, 130, 135, 139, 158, 163, 166, 167, 171, 172, 198, 200, 203, 207, 244, 247, 251, 260, 261, 262, 263, 264, 265*

Learning Walks *10, 106*

Lesson Planning *17, 61, 74*

M

Materials *vii, x, xv, 2, 9, 26, 28, 34, 44, 45, 65, 66, 67, 70, 74, 99, 102, 104, 117, 121, 123, 136, 141, 156, 178, 223, 227, 228, 229, 232, 234, 263, 266*

Mission/Vision *x, 32, 69, 77, 81, 82, 106, 108, 116, 172, 220*

N

Newcomers *xi, 25, 68, 99, 114, 117, 121, 122, 123, 135, 251*

National Association for Bilingual Education (NABE) *32, 261*

Native English Speakers *vii, 2, 4, 5, 6, 8, 23, 36, 45, 52, 78, 88, 96, 101, 108, 122, 123, 171, 235-239, 257*

Native Spanish Speakers *58, 87, 95, 120*

O

Oracy *29*

Oregon Association of Latino Administrators (OALA) *116, 249*

P

Parents
    Advisory Council *77, 90*

Prism Model *175, 183, 184, 243*

Professional (Staff) Development *vii, x, xi, xv, 2, 10, 32, 44, 45, 46, 60, 74, 75, 77, 80, 84, 85, 87, 88, 100, 105, 110, 112, 113, 123, 125, 138, 139, 208, 216, 218, 219, 224, 232, 226, 229, 265, 266*

Primary Language *4, 7, 88, 101, 115, 238*

Program
    Evaluation *vii, xvi, 13, 34, 230*
    Expansion *118, 198, 201, 202, 224*

R

Research *v, ix, xvi, 1, 4, 8, 9, 10, 11, 13, 14, 16, 17, 23, 25, 31, 32, 34, 38, 39, 44, 45, 47, 52, 60, 72, 73, 78, 80, 84, 88, 90, 101, 104, 112, 118, 119, 120, 128, 131-134, 138, 139, 166, 168, 169, 171, 172, 190, 194, 198, 200, 206, 214, 218, 224, 225, 226, 233, 234, 237, 283, 242, 246, 248, 250, 251, 259, 262, 263, 266, 269*

S

Schedule
    Conflicts *43*
    Master *vii, xi, 27, 28, 45, 74, 117, 120, 121, 130, 145, 146, 157, 201*

Science, Technology, Engineering, and Mathematics (STEM) xiii, 175, 176

Seal (Bilingual, of Biliteracy, State) *x, xi, xii, xvi, 8, 16, 17, 41, 77, 80, 91, 92, 99, 108, 114, 143, 144, 145, 147-150, 151, 152, 154, 155, 158, 161, 162, 170, 204, 220, 225, 230, 236, 246, 263*

Sheltered
    Content Classes *25*
    Instruction *113, 115, 226*

Spanish for Spanish Speakers *54*

Staffing

Students
    Advisory Boards *74*
    Continuing from Elementary *viii, 23*
    English Dominant *45*
    Native English Speaking
    Native Spanish Speaking
    World Language *viii, 6, 8, 10, 20, 24, 25, 29, 33, 34, 36, 44, 61, 80, 82, 90, 92, 102, 103, 109, 104, 109, 11, 114, 120, 122, 163, 164, 201, 202, 205, 233, 248, 259, 260*

T

Translanguaging *viii, 8, 9, 41, 42, 45, 155, 246, 248*

W

World Language
    Classes/Courses *6, 8, 10, 22, 33, 82, 92, 102, 120, 122, 202*
    Department *82, 92*
    Materials *vii, x, xv, 2, 9, 26, 28, 34, 44, 45, 65, 66, 67, 70, 74, 99, 102, 104, 117, 121, 123, 136, 141, 156, 178, 223, 227, 228, 229, 232, 234, 263, 266*
    Textbooks *9, 67, 71, 74, 263*

Contributing Authors

Chapters One and Sixteen

Professors Wayne Thomas and Virginia Collier are internationally known for their research on long-term school effectiveness for linguistically and culturally diverse students. Dr. Thomas is a professor emeritus of evaluation and research methodology, and Dr. Collier is a professor emerita of bilingual/multicultural/ESL education, both of George Mason University.

Chapter Two

Cindy Sizemore is a long-time, staunch multilingual language advocate who began her career teaching German in an elementary school in Tucson, Arizona, where her passion for children and languages ignited. She moved to El Paso and the Ysleta Independent School District where she worked as a language coordinator at Alicia R Chacón International School and then at Del Valle High School. Together with her students she worked to build what became the model for dual language secondary programs at Del Valle High School. Cindy's passion for language education and for students resulted in the creation of the Dual Language Student Advisory Board which indelibly shaped and catapulted the dual language program and students to new heights. In her career, Cindy has served as a German and Russian teacher, campus and district dual language coordinator, and most importantly the mother of two dual language K-12 graduates. Currently Cindy continues to serve as a campus administrator and dual language consultant.

Chapter Three

Jeremy Aldrich is the Director of Testing, Career and Technical Education, and World Languages for Harrisonburg City (VA) Public Schools. Formerly an ESL and world language (French and Spanish) teacher, he now works to support the growing dual language programs in Harrisonburg which serve more than 800 students. He is the current President of the Virginia Dual Language Educators Network (VADLEN), a consortium of educators and school districts promoting dual language education in Virginia. He is also a doctoral student at George Mason University (Fairfax, VA), planning a dissertation focused on secondary dual language education.

Contributing Authors

Chapter Four

Katy Cattlett is the Supervisor of Dual Language and World Languages for the Omaha Public Schools. Her master's degree in educational leadership at Doane University was built on undergraduate studies in Spanish, ESL, and elementary education. Katy truly believes that dual language is the best education for all students. As an adjunct instructor at Concordia University and the University of Nebraska at Omaha, she shares that knowledge and passion with teachers as they pursue endorsements in those areas. Katy's most important role is being mom to her three children. Her two school-age daughters are currently enrolled in the Omaha K-12 dual language program, one in elementary and the other in high school. Katy has a front-row seat professionally and personally to the enriched education that dual language students experience.

Dr. Rony Ortega considers himself a lifelong learner and believes he works in the greatest profession that allows him both the possibility for continuous learning as well as the opportunity to influence and change lives through education. He has earned five college degrees and held numerous roles in urban and suburban middle and high schools. He served as the dual language administrator at Omaha South High School for 5 years before being promoted to principal of a distinguished middle school. Dr. Ortega was promoted in June 2017 to Executive Director of School Support and Supervision in the Omaha Public Schools, a leading urban school district with a comprehensive K-12 dual language program. In this role, Dr. Ortega supports and supervises a total of 16 elementary, middle, and high schools across the district, including four secondary dual language schools. Dr. Ortega and his wife, a career educator at the University of Nebraska at Omaha, have three daughters who are all dual language students in the Omaha Public Schools.

Contributing Authors

Chapter Five

Born in México, Dr. Mario Ferrón attended a PK-12 dual language school. He taught eighth grade U.S. history in Spanish for 8 years before becoming the Secondary Dual Language Coordinator at Pharr-San Juan-Alamo Independent School District in south Texas. There, he worked on expanding the dual language program districtwide, including serving 6,000 secondary students in eight middle and five high schools. He is currently the Dual Language Director for San Antonio (TX) ISD, in charge of expanding the program districtwide. Dr. Ferrón has a doctoral degree in Bilingual Studies from the University of Texas at Brownsville. In 2012, his dissertation on DL education won first place in the National Association for Bilingual Education's Outstanding Dissertation Award.

Mario Ferrón, Jr. is an experienced secondary dual language educator from the Río Grande Valley region of South Texas. His undergraduate, master's, and current doctoral studies at the University of Texas-Río Grande Valley (formerly the University of Texas-Pan American) focused on biology, chemistry, science education, Spanish, and educational leadership. Mr. Ferrón has served as a dual language teacher, adjunct college lecturer, testing coordinator, dean of instruction, assistant principal, and principal. As a teacher, he taught Advanced Placement and Dual Credit courses in both English and Spanish. His professional work with English learners has earned him statewide recognition by the governor in 2010, by the North Texas Dual Language Summit in 2014, and recognition by the National Association for Bilingual Education in 2013.

Contributing Authors

Chapter Six

Dr. Tom Koulentes has been working as a high school teacher and administrator for nearly 25 years. He began his career teaching social studies and ESL at Highland Park High School in Highland Park, Illinois. He was an early practitioner of content-based ESL and he designed an integrated, team-taught ESL American studies course that utilized thematic instruction to link concepts in U. S. history to American literature. After teaching for several years, Tom spent a year in Costa Rica where he taught English and created an adventure-based travel study course for high school students that integrated Latin American history and culture, environmental science, Spanish, and physical education. Upon returning to the U.S., Tom became Director of Bilingual Education and Assistant Principal at Highland Park High School. In 2014 Tom became the principal of Highland Park High School and led the design and implementation of the schools' dual language program which stands today as one of the few high school dual language programs in the state of Illinois. He is currently the principal of Libertyville High School in Libertyville, Illinois.

Chapter Seven

Dr. Victor Vergara is the director of bilingual education in Walla Walla, Washington. He completed his master's degree in education, policy, and administration and recently graduated with his doctoral degree in educational leadership from Portland State University. Dr. Vergara's research agenda includes K-12 bilingual education, retention and preparation of minority educational leaders, and all aspects of equity, diversity, and inclusion for all students.

His career in education began as an elementary bilingual teacher in Portland and Woodburn Public Schools, Oregon. After serving as an assistant principal, in 2007 he became the principal of Valor Middle School in Woodburn, one of the only secondary schools in the nation that offers academic content classes in Russian, Spanish and English. Valor Middle school was recognized by the state in 2010 and 2011 for "Closing the Achievement Gap" between minority and White students. In 2012 he became principal of the Academy of International Studies at Woodburn High School, and under his leadership this school was recognized by the state as the high school that best serves English learners. Dr. Vergara was recognized as 2012 Oregon Middle School Principal of the Year and 2016 Latino Principal of the Year for the State of Oregon. Dr. Vergara and his wife, a first grade bilingual teacher, have three bilingual/bicultural children, and their family loves to travel around the world, especially to their native countries of Chile and México.

Contributing Authors

Chapter Eight

Dr. Virginia Elizondo recently served as the Newcomer Multilingual Manager for the Houston Independent School District in Texas. She has experience as an ESL and bilingual teacher, assistant principal, and is certified as a superintendent. She has worked with various types of programming for English learners, including late-exit, transitional, pre-exit, newcomer, one-way, and two-way dual language education. Overall, her work has primarily focused on support and advocacy for English learners, and she has especially emphasized expanding dual language programming into secondary campuses. She is also an adjunct lecturer at the University of Houston-Downtown.

Chapter Nine

Erin Bostick Mason is an experienced dual language administrator, researcher, teacher trainer, teacher, and parent, with a master's degree in educational leadership. For more than 20 years, her professional work has emphasized systemic reform through multilingual education from pre-school through university levels. She enjoys teaching, creating instructional materials and textbooks, designing policy and programs, and developing public relations to support multilingual, multicultural school communities. Currently, she teaches at the Norton Science and Language Academy, a whole-school, TK-8 dual language public charter school in southern California. Her three bilingual children attend a dual language school.

Chapter Ten

Mishelle L. Jurado is a 15-year veteran teacher with Albuquerque Public Schools. A Spanish teacher, she currently works at Atrisco Heritage Academy where she teaches AP Spanish Literature and Culture and serves as the biliteracy coach. She has served on the board of Dual Language Education of New Mexico for the last 7 years. Mishelle and her husband have two children who have attended dual language schools. Her daughter Ali received her Bilingual Seal in 2016 and her son Aldo will receive his when he graduates in 2019. The Jurado family is dedicated to dual language education, and their lives revolve around crossing the many borders that bilingual U.S. citizens engage in on a daily basis. The support of her family motivates Mishelle to continuously advocate and demonstrate that dual language is the path that all students should take in their public education, especially bilingual Latino students. She is in the fourth year of her doctoral program at the University of New Mexico where she is working on biliteracy development within secondary education.

Contributing Authors

Chapter Ten

Lisa Harmon-Martínez is a native New Mexican. She earned her BA in English and American studies from the University of North Carolina at Chapel Hill before returning to New Mexico to teach and complete her MA in secondary education, and continuing doctoral studies at the University of New Mexico. She teaches AP English Literature at Albuquerque High School, chairs the English Language Arts Department, and co-coordinates the Bilingual Department. Her primary focus is to close the achievement gap for English learners by supporting students' English language development and aligning the English and Spanish language arts curriculum across grade levels within the dual language program. Lisa and her husband are awaiting their first child whom they plan to send to dual language schools.

Dr. Gabriel Antonio Gonzales is a native of Peñasco, New Mexico. His undergraduate, master's, and doctoral degrees at the University of New Mexico focused on secondary education and educational leadership. He began his career in Albuquerque Public Schools at Washington Middle School and then Albuquerque High School where he served as a bilingual teacher, activities director, and assistant principal. In 2012, he was appointed principal of Atrisco Heritage Academy High School. Currently, Dr. Gonzales serves as Associate Superintendent for Albuquerque Public Schools. He has three bilingual daughters who will attend dual language schools.

Chapter Eleven

Dr. David Samore hails from Sioux City, Iowa, fourth of five sons to immigrant parents. He is in his 18th year as the principal of Okeeheelee Middle School in Palm Beach County, Florida, and has been a teacher and administrator of elementary, middle, and high schools for over 30 years. He speaks five languages, was educated in Britain where he earned the International Baccalaureate diploma and has traveled widely in North and South America, India, and Europe, visiting many schools in these regions. Dr. Samore was recognized as 2015 Florida Principal of the Year by the National Association of Secondary School Principals, 2008 Florida Principal of the Year by the Florida Association of School Counselors, and was named to the 2017 Florida Commissioner's Leadership Academy. Okeeheelee Middle School was recognized as the first International Spanish Academy in the United States (of 134 in North America and 492 in the world), with formal ties to the Ministry of Education in Madrid, Spain, and in 2013 was named the International Spanish Academy Middle School of the Year for North America. Dr. Samore and his wife raised two bilingual sons in their dual language home.

Contributing Authors

Chapter Twelve

Mario Benabe is the founding STEM Educator at the South Bronx Community Charter High School in New York City. In 2016, The White House Initiative on Educational Excellence for Hispanics under the Obama Administration honored Mr. Benabe for his approach to teaching and learning in STEM. He is the initiator of Do the Right Thing Pedagogy, which frames the importance of examining the ways in which teaching and learning occur in Afrocentric and Indigenous populations and using that as Dialectical Opposites [Do] To Heal Education [The] that invites Reality, Immersion, Good-Hearted Teaching [Right] Through Historical Indigenous/Afrocentric and Native Grounds [Thing]. Mr. Benabe can be reached via email: mariobenabejr@gmail.com, or via twitter @ mrbenabe.

Chapter Thirteen

Dr. Michele Anberg-Espinosa is an assistant professor at Simpson University in Redding, CA. Her almost 30-year career in language education includes work in the U.S, México, and Japan in various teaching and administrative capacities. Prior to her current assignment, she worked in San Francisco (CA) Unified School District as an instructional facilitator. She also oversaw the district's multiple language programs for 3 years, including dual language immersion and world language programs, PK-12. She served as a state consultant at the California Department of Education, providing oversight and guidance to Two-Way Bilingual Immersion (TWBI) and Title III programs. She completed her master's and doctoral studies in applied linguistics, and international/multicultural education at the Instituto Tecnológico de Estudios Superiores de Monterrey, México, and the University of San Francisco. Her two Spanish-English bilingual daughters have attended a Cantonese dual language program.

Chapter Fourteen

Elizet Moret is currently the dual language coordinator in the English Learner Support team at the Texas Education Agency. Her experience in education includes roles as Director of Bilingual/ESL Programs, Coordinator of Multilingual Curriculum and Instruction, ELL Assessment Specialist, and dual language and ESL teacher. Additionally, she has worked as a consultant with the Center for Applied Linguistics, based out of Washington, DC, where she served PK-12 schools around the country by providing professional development, job-embedded support, and technical assistance regarding bilingual education programming and instructional best practices for multilingual education. Elizet holds bachelor's and master's degrees in education, Spanish, and bilingual/bicultural studies from Texas State University. She is currently working on her dissertation as part of the doctoral program in educational leadership at Lamar University. Elizet's daughter is currently a second grader in a dual language program.

Contributing Authors

Chapter Fourteen

Irán Tovar is a doctoral student at the University of Texas Río Grande Valley with a focus on curriculum and instruction in bilingual and dual language education. She is also a dual language and bilingual education consultant for the Center for Applied Linguistics and Edu Lengüa. Irán has created and facilitated dual language professional development focused on teacher development, curriculum, dual language fundamentals, data analysis, program models, balanced literacy, and parent information. In school districts, she has served as a dual language program coordinator, dual language instructional coach, and teacher serving emergent bilingual students. An English learner herself, she believes that a well-established dual language program should enhance overall district performance while meeting the needs of all students, regardless of language.

Chapter Fifteen

Dr. Joan Lachance is an assistant professor in Teaching English as a Second Language at the University of North Carolina (UNC) at Charlotte. She completed graduate coursework taught in Spanish, earning her master's degree in school counseling from Pontifical Catholic University in Ponce, Puerto Rico and her doctoral work in urban education, biliteracy, and TESL at UNC- Charlotte. Her research agenda encompasses dual language teacher preparation, academic literacy and biliteracy development with English learners, as well as authentic assessment with multilanguage learners. In addition to her faculty position, Dr. Lachance's service agenda supports the North Carolina Department of Public Instruction and the surrounding region, where she specializes in professional development for teachers, counselors, and administrators of schools. This work also involves NC state-led initiatives including Using the WIDA Standards, The North Carolina Guide to the SIOP Model, C-Teaching and Collaboration, The North Carolina Guide to ExC-ELL, LinguaFolio, and Dual Language/Immersion Program Support. The presentations and supporting materials she co-developed showcase best practices for multilingual learners' academic language development, culturally compatible pedagogies, comparative education, and dual language teacher preparation.

About the Authors

Professors Wayne Thomas and Virginia Collier are internationally known for their research on long-term school effectiveness for linguistically and culturally diverse students. Dr. Thomas is a professor emeritus of evaluation and research methodology, and Dr. Collier is a professor emerita of bilingual/multicultural/ESL education, both of George Mason University. This is their fifth title in a series published by DLeNM and Fuente Press, following *Educating English Learners for a Transformed World, Dual Language Education for a Transformed World, Creating Dual Language Schools for a Transformed World: Administrators Speak,* and *Why Dual Language Schooling.* For other publications by Dr. Thomas and Dr. Collier, please visit their website at *www.thomasandcollier.com.*